The Law and Economics of Antitrust and Intellectual Property

The Law and Economics of Antitrust and Intellectual Property

An Austrian Approach

Dina Kallay

Adjunct Professor of Law, Bar Ilan University, Israel
Associate, Naschitz Brandes, Tel Aviv, Israel

Edward Elgar
Cheltenham, UK • Northampton, MA, USA

Published by
Edward Elgar Publishing Limited
Glensanda House
Montpellier Parade
Cheltenham
Glos GL50 1UA
UK

Edward Elgar Publishing, Inc.
136 West Street
Suite 202
Northampton
Massachusetts 01060
USA

A catalogue record for this book
is available from the British Library

ISBN 1 84376 621 3

Printed and bound in Great Britain by MPG Books Ltd, Bodmin, Cornwall

Contents

Acknowledgments

A previous version of this book has been submitted to the University of Michigan Law School in fulfilment of the requirements for the S.J.D. degree.

Many people have contributed to the completion of this book, both directly and indirectly. I want to thank my advisors at the University of Michigan Law School: Professors Thomas Kauper, Ronald Mann and Brian Simpson. I am also greatly indebted to Assistant Dean Virginia Gordan, Isabelle Byrns of the Law School, and to Rachel Persico of the University of Michigan International Center, who kindly helped me with the many administrative issues that came up along the way. The University of Michigan's excellent libraries and reference librarians, and Barbara Garavaglia in particular, have provided me with outstanding research resources without which the completion of this book would not have been possible.

I also thank Dr Dudi Tadmor, Judge Boaz Okon, and Professors Dudi Schwartz and Amos Shapira (of Bar Ilan and Tel Aviv University) for their encouragement in different stages of the writing, and Dotan Baruch for his practical assistance, support and friendship. I also owe thanks to Professor Nina Zaltman of Tel Aviv University whose teachings taught me the basics of property law and academic thinking.

I am grateful to many dear friends in Ann Arbor whose friendship helped me get through this project, as well as overcome the uneasy health issues that I encountered along the way. These include Michelle Segar, Ruby and Benya Bin Nun, Steve, Yvonne and Daniel Kaplan, Anne Nacinovich, Mikiharu Shimizu, Vanessa Marquette, Larry Sager, Georg Umbricht, Matt Frank, Yaron Litwin, Valenta Hardiman-Kabo, Felix Kabo, Erik Jens and Martin Zimmermann (the last two also helped me tremendously with editing and proofing).

I am greatly indebted to many dear people that I have been fortunate to meet during my time in Brussels with the European Commission Directorate General for Competition, which set the basis for the application chapters in this book. Among these, I would especially like to thank Cecilio Madero-Villarejo, Christin Hartmann, Augustijn van Haasteren, Oliver Sitar, Magdalena Brenning, Hans Weber, Nelly Le Berre, Paul Van Houtte, Dirk Grewe, Gjisbert Hesselink, Burkhard Schmitt, Sejual Shah and Raul Nieto-Capon for their kind assistance, practical help, friendship and support.

I wish to thank Ehud Stein for his generous help, without which I would not have been able to handle the many difficult practical problems related to completing the book in absentia. Also, thanks to Anne Lustig-Picus for her wonderful editorial support.

Last, but not least, I give thanks to my family. My brothers Benjamin and Jonathan Kallay helped me with endless proofing. My husband, Asaf Cohen, and my parents, Ariella and Michael Kallay, have helped me in so many ways that I cannot even start to enumerate them. Their support has been invaluable indeed.

Dina Kallay
March 2003

1. A Framework for Analysis of the Antitrust–Intellectual Property Intersection

And the end of all our exploring
Will be to arrive where we started
And know the place for the first time

(T.S. Eliot, *Four Quartets*:
Little Gidding, V, 1940.)

1.1 INTRODUCTION

Since the emergence of modern antitrust law[1] over a century ago, scholars and courts have been repeatedly baffled by the appearance of a variety of tensions between intellectual property (IP) laws and nascent antitrust laws. Consequently, much consideration has been given to this troublesome realm. Different doctrinal analyses (many of them using economic methodology) have been offered to resolve it, alongside a growing amount of case law that has accumulated throughout the years. However, this case law, characterized by many scholars as inconsistent, confused or lacking in policy coherence,[2] has not produced a readily transparent workable solution for these tensions. This fuzzy characterization of the case law has contributed to the perplexing image of this realm, and explains the relatively large influx of analytical works written in an attempt to suggest coherent solutions for this troubled cusp. In recent years there has been a trend of growing interest in the intersection of antitrust and IP law. This interest is projected through the growing number of articles and court decisions on the matter, and through the important place it has taken on the agenda of the antitrust enforcement agencies and the legislative branch.[3]

In light of the growing interest in this debated field, this chapter goes back to the origins of the conflict, providing it with a fresh theoretical framework that reviews its roots and character and analyses existing approaches. Such a framework is useful both as a neutral introduction to this disputed conflict for readers who are new to this topic and as a theoretical perspective useful for evaluating existing literature on the subject.

1.2 THE FACTUAL SCOPE OF THE INTERFACE

Numerous court decisions have dealt with aspects of the antitrust–IP conflict, thus revealing its practical scope. IP–antitrust issues arise in many factual contexts. They occur on the vast surface created by the broad interface of two mature doctrines. On the one hand, the IP axis is expansive, since contemporary notions of intellectual property embrace an extensive bundle of rights that stem from patents, copyrights, trademarks and trade secrets. Each category of intellectual property grants a different bundle of rights that is typical of it. The different intellectual property rights (IPRs) and the rights and privileges they bestow upon their owners have developed into a broad legal doctrine over the past several centuries. On the other hand, the antitrust axis is expansive because modern antitrust doctrine has grown to implicate a wide variety of conduct that can generally be categorized into unilateral conduct and conjoint behavior patterns. Unilateral conduct is conduct carried out by one market participant, while conjoint conduct (as its name suggests) involves the coordinated action of more than one market participant.

In order to demonstrate how practical conflict scenarios come about, perhaps it is best to start with the following real-life example.[4] Suppose a corporation 'K', which possesses market power in the market for sales and services of high-volume photocopiers and micrographic equipment, and holds numerous patents and copyrights covering parts for its photocopiers and micrographic equipment. Let us assume that the market also contains 11 independent service organizations that service K's products. Now as competition in the service market grew, K decides to stop selling copier parts to the independent service organizations, and secures agreements from its original equipment manufacturers not to sell parts to these competing organizations. This move substantially restricts competition in the service market, since such competition requires that service providers have ready access to all parts of the equipment. K's conduct is suspect under §2 of the Sherman Act as monopolizing or an attempt to monopolize the sale of service for its machines. The question that arises is whether the rights conferred by K's patents and copyrights on some of the parts provide a legitimate justification for K's described refusal to sell, which will indeed shield it from potential antitrust liability. This is a classic example of an IP–antitrust clash – a case of unilateral refusal to sell internally developed IP. A variation of this scenario is a case of unilateral refusal to sell recently acquired IP (for example, IP that was not internally developed but rather was acquired for the purpose of its suppression).

IP licensing and sale practices constitute another category of IP–antitrust conflicts. This category includes a wide variety of behaviors; some are related to licensing, and others are standard antitrust-suspicious situations that contain an IP dimension that further complicates them. Clashing scenarios may include any of the following:

1. A condition of royalties that are based on total sales, under which licenses are granted upon the licensee's agreement to pay royalties based on total sales, regardless of the actual use made of the protected process.
2. Grantback clauses that require the licensee to grant back to the licensor any 'improvement patent' rights the licensee may obtain or acquire while using the licensed patent.
3. Announcements aimed at deterring competitors' innovation efforts (also known as 'vaporware').
4. Price discrimination by an IPR holder with respect to the protected product.
5. Tying arrangements: (a) tie-in of the protected component or product with a non-protected product or (b) block licensing, that is, licensing of a package of IP-protected products as the only option.
6. Price restrictive licensing (resale price maintenance of the protected product): licenses under which the IPR holder sets the price at which licensees must sell the patented item.
7. Territorial restrictions in the licensing of the protected product: sale or use confined to a particular area.
8. Functional division of use clause: a licensing clause requiring use of the licensed information for a particular purpose.

Finally, another category of these conflicts involves procedural aspects, namely antitrust issues that arise from enforcement of IPRs. Litigation to enforce IPRs is generally protected under the Noerr–Pennington doctrine, which protects conduct that is aimed at inducing government action.[5] However, there are a number of exceptions to this doctrine. Such exceptions include patents that are obtained by fraud, bad faith prosecution, the 'sham litigation' exception, and infringement actions that are part of an overall scheme to monopolize.[6] These exceptions are interesting from the aspect of exploring the cusp between the doctrines, because they represent an area in which conduct related to IPRs may raise antitrust liability. Another antitrust issue in this category is the enforcement of arbitration clauses contained in IP licenses in order to settle antitrust claims. This is a problem because it is not clear to what extent antitrust claims can be arbitrated.

Note that although antitrust policy embraces both unilateral and concerted behavior patterns, unilateral conduct antitrust concerns seem to prompt a greater risk of *direct* conflict with IP doctrine. There are a number of reasons behind this difference. First, the general notion of intellectual property deals with a personal-type property right. Such a right is granted to a *single* market participant (whether a single owner or joint owners) and allows its holder to exclude others from either using, making and selling[7] or reproducing and distributing[8] protected works during a statutorily specified period. Because these rights are typically granted to one market participant, IP statutes are generally not concerned with conjoint action in the context of a market of IPR holders. Consequently, a direct conflict that is created as a result of conduct claimed to be directly protected under an IPR is more likely to occur in a unilateral context. Second, for practical purposes, unilateral conduct of dominant position firms is linked with IP ownership. The nature of the research and development (R&D) that produces IPRs is usually secretive – it is in the best interest of every market participant to become the exclusive owner of a commercially useful IP and therefore collusion is less likely to occur with respect to IP.[9] Furthermore, monopolies (or firms with large market shares) are probably more likely than smaller players to invest more resources in R&D and harvest the resulting IP because they will be able to capture a large section of the resulting welfare gain, and because they are less likely to be compelled to team up with competitors in order to afford this activity

1.3 THE HISTORICAL CONTEXT OF THE ANTITRUST–IP CUSP

Although the antitrust–IP conflict itself could not have emerged until both doctrines were well on their feet, their conflict may be characterized as part of a wider and much earlier contradiction, namely, that between property and competition. It is easy to see why property and competition conflict. Property generally carries both a positive and a negative aspect. On the positive side, people's appropriation of things is recognized by awarding them a bundle of rights as property right owners. On the negative side, the recognition of individual property rights limits the availability of these owned assets to the rest of the community. Where the asset that is subject to a property right is essential for competing in the market, the negative aspect of the property right may kick in and curtail competition in that specific area of the market.[10] Furthermore, the property–competition conflict itself could be considered as a private case of an even broader centuries-old debate that forms the basic dilemma of liberal legal theory: the contradiction between security and freedom of action. This dilemma has continuously intrigued leading analytical jurists such as John Stuart Mill, John Austin, Jeremy Bentham, Oliver Wendell Holmes, Wesley Hohfeld and others.[11] This security-freedom conflict is central in any liberal legal system because such a system strives to reconcile the individual's security from harm with individual freedom to engage in the pursuit of happiness. The property versus competition equation fits closely into these variables of security and freedom of action, because property notions are closely linked with promoting stability through enhancing the security of owners[12] while free competition usually means a high standard of freedom of action (including freedom of entry) for market participants.

The IP–antitrust conflict seems, to some extent, like a contemporary private case of the described age-old broader conflict. This is so because on the practical level (as distinguished from the goal level) the two conflicts share many fundamental features. Intellectual property's declared goal is to provide security for inventors and authors by protecting and enforcing their property rights, while antitrust laws strive to preserve a certain standard of individual freedom, namely, the standard of a competitive market environment. Prima facie, the conflict seems a rather simple one. On the one hand, the free competition standard directly threatens the security and certainty that property rights seek to promote. On the other hand, IPRs confer exclusive rights and benefits upon their owners, which may provide them with significant advantages over their competitors. These exclusive rights contradict with the neoclassical model of perfect competition[13] whose presumptions include unobstructed market entry and equality between competitors in both the information they possess and their production capabilities.

However, it is important to note that there are two reasons that seem to render the IP–antitrust conflict a more complex one than the dichotomy of property versus freedom standard described above. First, IPRs and the antitrust doctrine themselves already function within complex market settings. Consequently, each of these doctrines independently copes with the same dilemma. IP scholars have long been aware that the property rights conferred by IPRs must be balanced against the degree of harm they may inflict upon competition, and similarly it has been suggested that antitrust doctrine itself faces a conflict between its commitments to fostering competition and its commitments to protecting property rights.[14] Therefore, it should be borne in mind that the intertwining doctrines that create the IP–antitrust cusp are multidimensional in their own way, in the sense that they already independently reflect a first-degree balance of the property–competition paradox. This makes the IP–antitrust conflict a second-degree derivative case of the conflict. The existence of the same tension within the doctrines themselves should not come as a surprise. In fact a credible generalization can be made of the security–freedom conflict to describe the legal system as a whole. Such a generalization portrays the legal system as a struggle between two models: the rule of law model (emphasizing security for life, liberty and property) versus the marketplace model (emphasizing the system as a process of competition and struggle).[15] Accordingly, almost any legal institution faces this struggle in one form or another, and antitrust and IP are no exception to this rule. Second, the antitrust–IP conflict differs from the more general property–freedom standard for the more obvious reason of the discrepancy in terms. IP is a unique property institution[16] that is distinct from tangible and abstract property notions. And although the antitrust mechanism is closely linked to the promotion of competition, freedom of action embraces far broader notions than a competitive marketplace, and the latter embraces some social and economic notions that are not to be found in the former. On the other hand, since IP protection extends to non-tangible goods it is seemingly more extensive than real property protection, which creates a broader confrontation surface for a competition doctrine to clash with. These discrepancies somewhat weaken the suggested categorization of the IP–antitrust conflict within the property–competition conflict.

Nevertheless, there seems to be a significant correlation between the IP–antitrust dilemma and the broader conflict of liberal legal theory. This correlation is useful because it helps to place the IP–antitrust conflict in its historical setting, thus allowing for a better understanding of its starting point. This is particularly useful in evaluating different solutions suggested for resolving this interface.

1.4 THEORETICAL ASPECTS OF THE INTERFACE

1.4.1 Policy Goals of the Two Institutions

A common approach to IP–antitrust conflict questions begins with assessing the substantive roots of the two doctrines. The debate regarding the theoretical foundation of the substantive (rather than procedural) interface ultimately draws upon the specific view taken on the question of the policies underlying these two doctrines. Alongside the underlying objectives level, another relevant aspect is the *method* by which each doctrine performs in order to achieve its objectives. This is because it is important to evaluate whether the troublesome cusp is created by the differing objectives of the two disciplines or rather by the different methods taken to achieve similar objectives. A third possibility is a descriptive one, namely, attributing the conflict to abusive behavior patterns that take advantage of the effective leeway contrived at the intersection of these two doctrines. According to such argument, the roots of the conflict lie in the area in which the doctrines are misused, and thus cannot be directly attributed to the fundamentals of the doctrines (although the feasibility of misuse can be characterized as a flaw in these institutions). Finally, a fourth possibility is of course a 'pluralist' solution, attributing the conflict to some combination of the elements mentioned above, which may also include cross-conflict between them, that is, goals of one doctrine colliding with the methods of another and vice versa.

This section will examine the interaction between the goals of IP and antitrust. Subsequent sections will review the interchanges between the methodology of the two institutions and between goals and methodologies. The possibility that abusive behavior patterns lie at the base of the conflict will not be considered in the context of this chapter, because its analysis requires an evaluation of specific conflict scenarios, while the discussion that follows will be mostly theoretical. Nevertheless, it is important to bear this possibility in mind.

Contemporary theory on the roots of the antitrust–IP conflict can generally be categorized into two main views. The first maintains that the two doctrines inherently conflict, while the second views the two doctrines as harmonious. It will therefore be easier to begin the discussion with a review of these two categorical views.

The inherent conflict school

Some scholars have held that the IP and antitrust doctrines inherently conflict with each other. In general, this notion has taken on a number of forms.

The traditional view The traditional (and perhaps rather simplistic) analysis identified the following dichotomy between the two doctrines: IPRs were thought to confer a legal monopoly power upon their owner, which was identified with the concentrated 'monopoly power' that antitrust laws strive to dispel.[17] Accordingly, it was presumed that both copyright and patent were accurate predictors of 'market power' in the antitrust meaning of the term.[18] In other words, the argument was that the IP institution leads to the very same market conditions that antitrust was created to eliminate, or at least to control.

Nowadays, this approach has been rightly abandoned by scholars and courts[19] as well as by the federal antitrust enforcement agencies[20] and legislative voices,[21] all of which make it inconsistent with modern antitrust doctrine. Today, intellectual property rights are no longer viewed as necessarily conferring market power upon their owner. This is because it became clear that in many cases the IPR owner is still subject to significant competitive pressures. Even a protected idea or expression may have excellent substitutes, and therefore consumers may well be indifferent between a product that is based on the protected technology and a competing product that is not protected. Such consumer behavior could take place if the consumer does not find the new technology significantly better, if he/she is unwilling to pay the price difference for the new technology, or during the time when the consumer is not yet aware of the new technology and its benefits. Either way, under such a scenario in which close substitutes are available, the cross-elasticity of demand between the competing products in this market is high, and hence the protected technology does not confer 'market power' upon its owner, let alone 'monopoly power'. Another aspect worth noting is the transitory nature of IPRs that confer only temporary powers. This feature not only carries direct implications for the duration of the right, but also may affect the behavior of a commercial IPR owner, who, towards the end of the legal protection period may tend to behave more competitively in order to gain customer loyalty and identify the post-expiration market that is about to be created.

The 'conflict of purposes' view Another variation of the 'inherent conflict' argument is based on the proposition that the purposes of the two doctrines contradict each other. The argument is that antitrust laws seek to preserve free competition while the IP laws may act to curtail competition by granting legal monopolies as a reward to inventors.[22] This argument may suffer from both inaccuracy and incompleteness. First, note that it is not clear whether this proposition indeed addresses the *purpose* of IP laws. While it may well be that under certain conditions IP laws act to curtail competition, it seems rather unlikely that curtailing competition is a *purpose* of IP laws. None of the vast literature on the purposes of the IP institution suggests that reducing competition is one of the ends of the IP institution. Curtailing competition seems to be a possible byproduct of IP laws, rather than a purposeful IP goal.[23] Second, there is no consensus on whether maintaining competition is indeed a *goal* of antitrust laws. There is no doubt that antitrust and competition are closely linked. However, while some case law presumes competition as a goal,[24] most modern scholars view competition as a means (rather than an end) for obtaining whatever they view as the goal of antitrust laws[25] (on which there is no unanimous consensus). Therefore this 'inherent conflict' proposition lacks any real treatment of the 'means versus ends' distinction that is referred to here.[26]

Intellectual property as an exemption to antitrust laws A different variation of the inherent conflict suggests that the grant of an IPR creates an exemption from the antitrust laws.[27] Although this notion may seem, prima facie, to deny the existence of a conflict, this is probably not the case. Defining the IP zone as an exempted zone reflects a basic axiom under which IP and antitrust are fundamentally at odds, so that the exemption was created to resolve this conflict (otherwise there would not have been any need for an exemption in the first place). The IP misuse doctrine is commonly cited as evidence of this exemption argument. The misuse doctrine is an equitable doctrine that renders a patent or a copyright[28] unenforceable when the owner attempts to extend the statutory monopoly beyond its lawful scope or otherwise engages in conduct contrary to the 'public policy' inherent in the patent or copyright statute. Such conduct results in 'unclean hands' that disqualify the owner from obtaining enforcement of his/her IPR. By definition, misuse occurs only where the IPR owner 'extends' the use of his/her patent or copyright beyond the scope granted by law. Hence, it is presumed that within the boundaries of the IPR, there is no antitrust problem, and conflict exists only on the outside of the exclusivity realm that is created by the IP protection.

Note that while on the theoretical level a finding of misuse does not annul the IPR but merely hinders its enforcement under the given circumstances, the unique nature of intellectual property renders these two notions practically identical. This is so because unlike tangible property, the possession and use of intellectual property is largely 'non-rivalrous'. Its non-rival nature means that IP can be used simultaneously by an infinite number of users. Information, as opposed to tangible goods that can be physically fenced, cannot be reduced to exclusive possession by the acts of its owner. Thus, the fact that the owner is already making use of the intellectual property does not exclude others from using it (unlike the way possession works in tangible property) and vice versa: even when the rights to information's exclusive use are transferred by agreement, the information is actually still retained by the original owner. Furthermore, not only does the prior owner's use of the IP not hinder use by others, but in many cases such prior use actually assists them in making use of the protected technology. That is the case where the IP owner's prior use demonstrated how to commercialise the technology or expression, created a market for it and so on. This unique nature of IPRs underlies the practical conclusion that protection of IP must be viewed as a matter of positive law, rather than a matter of natural rights. Accordingly, an IPR that is found to be misused, and hence unworthy of positive law protection, for all practical purposes no longer exists as a protected form of property.

Additional support for the argument that the core of IPRs is exempted from the reach of the antitrust doctrine can be inferred from Judge Learned Hand's opinion in the seminal case of Alcoa.[29] Alcoa involved a charge of monopolization under Section 2 of the Sherman Act. In his opinion, Judge Hand observed that market dominance resulting from 'skill, foresight and industry' and monopolistic power that was thrust upon its owner, or was gained from 'force of accident' will not be condemned.[30] It seems feasible that IP-protected innovative market technology or other protected original expressions that are commercially useful and provide their creator with market dominance will easily fit into Judge Hand's definition of legitimate conduct since they clearly reflect 'skill and foresight', and will thus be exempt from antitrust liability.

Of course, a solution that views IP as an exemption from antitrust does not solve the practical conflict problem, but merely sets a zone in which IP is sweepingly triumphant in its conflict with antitrust. Hence it presumes that there is no conflict within this zone. This approach means that the problem simply transforms into a need to accurately depict the boundaries of the exemption. This can be done by determining the core of the IP doctrine, setting the radius of protection extending from this core, and then evaluating where different factual instances fall – within the exemption radius or outside it. As it seems unlikely that such analysis will yield a black-or-white result in all cases, it will probably be more accurate to depict a number of circles around the IP core, with diminishing antitrust exemption the further the circumstances of the case are from the IP core.

The illusory conflict school

Harmony in the two doctrines' goals The illusory conflict school, which seems to have gained favor in recent years, maintains that on the goal level, there is no contradiction between IP and antitrust since both doctrines share mutual goals and complement each other.[31] Scholars and courts have articulated the common goal in two similar ways: the goal of maximizing wealth and economic efficiency by producing what consumers want at the lowest price,[32] and that of encouraging innovation, industry and competition and enhancing consumer welfare.[33] The illusory conflict notions are mostly embedded in a Chicago school of economics world-view, in which both antitrust and IP (and in fact any other legal doctrine) are designed to serve the sacred purpose of maximizing market efficiency, and thus by definition cannot contest one another. One clear criticism of such a view is that the different focuses of the IP and antitrust doctrines, and the different methods they employ, may still result in a practical conflict even if theoretically they share the same end goals. Moreover, the plethora of economic analysis literature reflects no clear consensus on a particular economic model within antitrust and economics which explains why even end results of economic analysis of these doctrines may not be harmonious. A third notion is that the 'common goals' cited above are overly sweeping and thus imprecise. It seems clear the IP's primary goal is not 'producing what consumers want *at the lowest price*'. IP focuses on solving free-riding problems with respect to intangible property, and naturally results, at least in the short run, in higher prices charged for the protected products. Similarly, antitrust is *not* directly aimed at 'encouraging innovation' (although this may be a byproduct or one aspect of competition). Common sense also renders it highly questionable whether IP is aimed at 'encouraging competition', at least where price competition is concerned (here too, competitive effects such as a wider variety of offered products may be the byproduct, rather than the goal, of a prosperous IP regime). Finally, the illusory conflict argument is difficult to reconcile with the empirical data. In an era where economic efficiency analysis reigns supreme both in courts and administrative antitrust agencies, such an argument would have been expected to result in a substantial decrease of antitrust–IP conflict court cases. However, this does not seem to be the case as courts today still deal with a substantial number of such conflicts.[34]

Are the doctrines' goals indeed in immediate conflict?

The goals of antitrust The question of the goals of antitrust law is at the center of an historic academic dispute over the goals of the antitrust legislation,[35] which has somewhat subsided in recent years. The multitude of approaches to the question of the goals of antitrust stresses different social, political, and normative ends. These ends can generally be divided into two categories. On the one hand there is a category focusing on economic ends, namely the maximization of economic efficiency;[36] on the other, there is the category that emphasizes non-economical social and legal ends, which is also known as the modern populist school.[37] The latter's goals include protecting small independent businesses;[38] eliminating bigness on the grounds that it is intrinsically evil;[39] protecting the democratic state and process from enormous economic powers;[40] protecting individual freedom and opportunity for entrepreneurs from 'great aggregations of capital';[41] neutral treatment of minorities;[42] and the promotion of certain market morals such as *laissez faire* capitalism[43] and 'fair competition'.[44] Accordingly, arguments that assert that the goals of the two doctrines conflict are highly dependent upon the specific view held with respect to antitrust goals. It should be noted that European Union competition law embraces a different formal justification for regulating competition, namely, the integration of the European economic market through assuring the free flow of goods across member state lines.[45] However, it is this declared justification that may be a necessary formal instrument for establishing the authority for enacting antitrust legislation.[46]

As mentioned, in recent years the battle over the different goals of antitrust seems to have diminished somewhat. Economic efficiency proponents have gained near-monopoly status in American antitrust case law and much of the academic environment – perhaps an ironic phenomenon in a doctrine which strives to dispel monopolies. Nevertheless, the para-economic antitrust goals are still relevant (although neglected) because economic efficiency analyses shed insufficient light on the difficult questions lying at the base of antitrust law, such as the proper coordination between private right and public domain and where to draw the line between a legitimate and an excessive exercise of power. The questions presented by antitrust cannot be resolved within the secluded province of economic theory, because they raise fundamental normative and political questions that cannot be solved on purely economic grounds.[47] Consequently, the non-economic antitrust analysis arguments are still, and will always be, ostensibly significant in shaping antitrust policy.

The goals of IP The IP justification theories seem less diversified and less controversial than the theories on the roots of antitrust laws. There are three commonly cited arguments for justifying intellectual property. It is arguable that unlike some of the different antitrust goals, the different IP justifications are not necessarily opposed but rather complement one another, although two of them are embedded in a natural rights tradition and the third is a social utility argument.[48] The fundamental justifications for IP include:

1. Desert-for-labor arguments These arguments are linked to the natural rights theory of property developed in the writings of the philosopher John Locke.[49] The Lockean labor theory makes a connection between labor and property by virtue of divine command or natural law. The core of the argument is that whenever a person mixes his/her labor with something in the commons he/she thereby makes it his/her property.[50] This argument takes place within a set of assumptions about the world: that God has given the world to people in common; that every person has a property in his/her own person; and that a person's labor belongs to him/her. Locke assigns the task of defending the property of citizens to the state. The property rights created by this argument are limited by Locke's normative structure of community. Thus, the property right is conditional upon a person leaving enough, and as good, for the others in the community, and a person cannot take out of the commons more than he/she can use to his/her advantage.

The desert-for-labor argument seems part of a somewhat instrumental tradition, since it views work as an investment that justifies ownership. However it probably originally stemmed from a religious view of the world.

2. Personhood arguments These arguments are closely linked to the writings of the philosopher Georg Hegel.[51] According to Hegel a person's mind is free and its personality begins when it has self-knowledge unhindered by any restriction. This freedom is not enough because a personality has to achieve some more concrete form of existence in the world to become a real self. This more concrete form is obtained by the appropriation of things.[52] According to Hegel, intellectual property, like other forms of property, plays an essential role in the development of the individual person through attainment of subjective freedom. Consequently, his teachings speak of a close link between the author's personality and his/her creation.[53]

It should also be noted that alongside the personhood approach there is a second, similar argument for the moral right recognized in copyright. The IP moral right rationale is based on the personality sentiment of an author's entitlement in his/her creation simply because he/she is the author and thus associated with his/her intellectual work in an intimate way.[54]

3. Innovation-Promoting Utilitarian Arguments Many of the contemporary innovation-promoting arguments are closely linked to the neoclassical economic price theory (which will be discussed below).[55] They share a utilitarian perspective that views IP as an institution that was consciously created (or is at least desirable) for the purpose of serving the social good.[56] A portrayal of these arguments requires some introductory remarks about information goods which are characterized by a non-rival nature, that is, a single person's use of the information does not diminish its availability to others. This non-rival characteristic is responsible for the 'public good' qualities of intangible property since a public good is a good the consumption of which does not detract from the possibility of consumption of the same good by others.[57] Free-riders are market participants who want to obtain the benefits of a good without contributing to its cost of production, and under contemporary neoclassical price theory free-riding is the best market strategy. As a result of the free-riding phenomenon and the public good nature of intellectual property, a system in which IP is not regulated is predicted to experience diminished incentives for producing intangible property, because producers of information will only be able to collect revenues from few (if any) of the consumers of their product. This is predicted to result in underinvestment in development of intellectual property in light of the producers' difficulty in recouping their investment, let alone making profits. The argument is that IP laws solve this specific market failure by granting IP producers an exclusive right to distribute their goods, and thus allowing them to recoup the investment they made and make profits.

Promoting innovation (through preventing underinvestment in it) is held to be important because innovation encourages economic progress. This argument is laid out as follows. It is apparent that providing legal security and protection for persons who have invested in innovation promotes intellectual creativity and innovation. Productivity (output per units of input) is commonly used as a measure of economic progress (both for a country and for individual enterprises). Improved productivity is closely linked to advancement in economic growth since under an improved technology fewer inputs are required to produce the same amount of output, thus allowing for an overall expansion of output and economic growth.[58]

Although productivity depends upon a wide variety of economic and social factors, technological innovation is widely held to be the most important contributor to improvements in productivity. Accordingly, it is assumed that innovation directly contributes to technological progress.[59] The idea is that economic progress requires a constant stream of new ideas and products in order to improve life conditions and production efficiency.

IP protection fosters such a stream of ideas in a number of ways. Where patents are concerned, they seem to solve the problem of the very high costs of R&D by allowing the patent holder to recoup his/her initial expenses later on during the life term of the patent. Second, patents help create the conditions under which the necessary capital is risked for creating a commercially useful product or process. Finally, a patent contributes to the dissemination of new knowledge because the details of the invention are disclosed and thus become available to the public.

Copyright protection differs from patent protection since copyright protects artistic *expression* rather than an idea or a process. Accordingly, it is arguable that copyrights may not be as closely related to economic progress as patents are, because they do not protect improved production processes as such. On an abstract level, such an argument may not be as powerful as it initially seems. First, copyright protection is used nowadays to protect expressions such as computer software, which are closely linked with production processes and technological progress. Second, the copyright allows diffusion of ideas and facilitates a rich and robust intellectual environment, which promote further technological innovation due to a wide cross-pollination effect in the market of ideas. Consequently, copyright protection, like patent protection, enriches the stream of ideas, which then may well result in economic progress. The argument is parallel to the one made above with respect to patents – the high cost of creation is mitigated by allowing the copyright holder to recoup the costs by commercializing the creation. This provides the required conditions under which necessary capital and mental energy are risked in order to develop an artistic creation. Finally, the public benefits from the release of an original creation – which fosters intellectual creativity.

A comparative review of the goals On a theoretical level, it may seem as if the above review of the goals of antitrust and intellectual property reveals no direct policy conflicts between the two doctrines. The arguments propounded to justify legal protection of intellectual property, namely desert-for-labor, personhood and utilitarian arguments, do not seem to be in any inherent conflict with any of the different goals attributed to antitrust. The antitrust ends list included maximization of economic efficiency, protection of small businesses, elimination of bigness, protection of the democratic process, protection of individual freedom and opportunity for entrepreneurs, neutral treatment of minorities or promotion of certain capitalistic market morals.

None of the goals that are fundamental to an IP regime appears to be in direct ideological conflict with these ends. IP goals are generally not concerned with bigness of market participants or market concentration. In fact, there may even seem to be some positive correlation between the goals of the two doctrines. First, as the aforementioned unified-goal school suggests, it seems that the goal of maximizing economic efficiency is indeed shared by the two doctrines to the extent that one adopts the utilitarian economic approach. Furthermore, it seems that the antitrust goal of protection of individual freedom and opportunity for entrepreneurs is closely related to the rationale of the IP personhood arguments. According to Hegel, recognition of property is essential for the development of individual personality and freedom – concepts that are credibly close to 'individual freedom and opportunity for entrepreneurs'. This argument is limited by the fact that antitrust laws admittedly restrict the freedom and personality of certain market participants, namely monopolizing actors and parties to cartels. Finally, note the empirical correlation between the innovation promoted by IP and competition protected by antitrust. While it is not clear whether innovation and the technological progress it delivers are independent antitrust goals,[60] the Antitrust Division and Federal Trade Commission's modern documents stress the close positive correlation between antitrust enforcement and innovation.[61] More importantly, further to the 'mutual goal' aspect there seems to be an empirical correlation between the two that works in both directions – the importance of competition as promoting innovation[62] and the value of an innovative market environment as a remedy for anticompetitive behavior since new ideas can transform the marketplace overnight.[63]

In light of the above, the impression is that on a purely theoretical level the goals of IP and antitrust do not directly conflict. This conclusion is further supported by recognition of the fact that the two doctrines originally purport to act out in two different fields. Antitrust laws were enacted to deal with competition failure patterns in tangible goods markets such as collusion among players, competition-curtailing behavior by actors with market power and mergers. IP laws deal with the problem of the 'public good' nature of intangible property that would have resulted in a lower-than-optimal activity in the market of ideas without such intervention. Clearly, the two doctrines are aimed at solving problems in different territories. To be sure, this interim conclusion that antitrust and IP do not conflict on the rudimentary goal level does not imply a lack of significant conflicts between them. This conclusion is limited to the abstract level in alleging that theoretically the goals of the two doctrines do not seem to conflict. However, it may well be, as discussed below, that the practical consequences of these doctrines are at odds because of their nature (for example, the nature of IP rights), or the way market participants harness these doctrines to their needs. Thus, for example, there is little doubt that under certain circumstances an IP right can be used for the purpose of creating a national monopoly that may serve as fertile ground for various behavior patterns that conflict with the antitrust goals (including the EC system goal).[64] Nevertheless such conflicts do not seem to arise from the fundamental goals of the two doctrines.

1.4.2 The Methodologies of the Two Institutions

The relationship between IP and antitrust seems complex indeed and is yet to be agreed upon. One reason for this lack of consensus is that although the 'efficiency maximization' goal has reigned supreme in recent years, there are still a number of alternative views on the goals of antitrust. Therefore, analysis of the problem remains dependent upon the individual scholar's antitrust-goal mantra. Another reason for the perplexity is the complexity of the interface at hand, which requires resolving elaborate issues from the economic, public policy, private property, market innovation and constitutional arenas. Accordingly, any solution that works through a narrowing abstraction of the issues into one of these realms is bound to be criticized as incomplete and oversimplified.

The search for a more generally accepted IP–antitrust interface analysis may lead us to seek help nearby by setting aside the goal level, and focusing on the methodology level. There seems to be a general consensus that antitrust policy and competition are closely linked. Antitrust laws are committed to competition, and strive to promote and protect a competitive marketplace[65] with laws that render certain anticompetitive practices criminal, that allow for civil suits against such conduct, and that monitor the market by administrative agencies that seek to prevent such behavior patterns. The preservation-of-competition tenet of antitrust policy is shared by the legal systems around the globe that acknowledge antitrust policy, and is also reflected in the EC terminology for antitrust laws, which is 'competition law'.

Consequently, an analysis of the IP–competition interface can prove useful for exploring the IP–antitrust interface, bearing in mind at the outset that although competition and antitrust are closely linked, competition seems to be a means rather than an antitrust goal,[66] and that competition and antitrust are not always synonymous from ground zero, especially as the definitions for 'competition' vary. The following section assumes the task of such IP method–competition account analysis.

Antitrust's methodology (competition) defined

Although it may seem that the concept of competition is an objective scientific axiom on which there is little dispute, reality begs to differ. There are many different schools of economics that offer different economic models of competition.[67] Moreover, there is a legal competition model developed in antitrust literature and case law. The following is a brief review of the three most relevant mainstream competition models.

The neoclassical economics theory of competition The neoclassical school of economics is clearly the dominant school in the Western world.[68] Neoclassical microeconomics theory makes use of the term 'perfect competition' as a theoretical construct. A perfectly competitive market is one that adheres to the following conditions:[69]

- There are many buyers and sellers such that the action of no one individual buyer or seller can have a perceptible influence upon the market price of a good.
- Producers and consumers have perfect knowledge of events in the market and act on this knowledge.
- The product in every market is homogeneous so that consumers are indifferent between the produce of alternative suppliers.
- Firms act independently of one another in such a way as to maximize their individual profits and each consumer acts similarly so as to maximize his/her utility from consumption.
- There are no barriers to the movement of goods or factors of production. Firms are therefore free to enter or leave the production of a product and are able to supply to the market whatever quantity it so requires.

As a result of these market conditions, each producer faces a perfectly elastic demand curve for its product and hence is a 'price taker' who is unable to influence the market price for its product. The market price is set by the market at a level equal to the marginal cost of producing the last unit of the product.

The neoclassical economic model has evolved into two distinct schools of thought: the Chicago and the Harvard school.

The *Chicago school of economics*,[70] which dominates much of modern antitrust thought,[71] emphasizes the efficiency gains to society from large size. Consequently it does not view highly concentrated market power as necessarily evil. Rather, it stresses the benefits of economies of scale and superior efficiency accruing to large firms. The Chicago school points to competition as a means of achieving the sole objective of allocative efficiency. It is generally averse to government regulation of the market, which it claims establishes market entry barriers that interfere with the free market's tendency to achieve the most efficient equilibrium by itself through free competition. Consequently, it may seem surprising that in a predominantly Chicago-school oriented legal world, antitrust policy and the market-intervening discipline it exerts came to prosper as they do today. Indeed, Judge Robert Bork noted this inner contradiction in his seminal book.[72]

Nevertheless, it should be borne in mind that antitrust policy represents an alternative to a classic regulatory solution.[73] Antitrust rules involve less market intervention than a regulatory solution because they usually leave the outcomes to the market processes rather than enforce a regime directly on all the market participants. Perhaps this is exactly the reason for their popularity even in a Chicago–school biased world, as the least restrictive form of a necessary evil intervention[74] (most economics agree on the need for a policy on horizontal mergers and collusion). These notions will be further developed in Chapter 3.[75]

The *Harvard 'Oligopoly' School*[76] regards market power, resulting from a few large firms operating in a market, as harmful *per se* to society. Market concentration, according to the Harvard school, is an indicator of collusion and therefore such concentrated power should be made illegal. Consequently, the Harvard school is not as hostile as the Chicago school is to governmental intervention in private industry. Furthermore, it is concerned not only with objective allocative efficiency, but also with more liberal ideals such as equitable income distribution, technological progress, and the reduction of concentrated power in the hands of a few large organizations. The modern offspring of the Harvard school is called the *structuralist school.*[77] As its name suggests, the structuralist school is less concerned with firm conduct and more concerned with market structure. It believes that market structure is the ultimate source of market power, and that therefore a competitive industry *structure* is determinative of competitive behavior.[78] According to structuralist doctrine, large oligolopolistic firms operating in highly concentrated markets can maintain prices well above the competitive level through the use of so-called 'exclusionary' practices. The structuralist approach to this problem emphasizes barriers to entry, market share, and industry concentration.

The monopolistic competition model The model of monopolistic competition was developed simultaneously by Edward Chamberlin[79] and Joan Robinson,[80] and had its greatest influence on antitrust policy during the New Deal era of the 1930s.[81] This model takes a competition approach that differs from the neoclassical one.[82] The basic assumptions of this model are:

- A large number of independent firms are selling products in the market.
- The products are slightly differentiated in composition or brand image. This means that products in the same market are close but not perfect

substitutes for one another. Buyers in the market do not view similar products as perfect substitutes, but rather develop individual preferences between different similar products.
• Firms are free to enter or leave the production of the product – there are no barriers to market entry or exit.

Note that the monopolistic competition model is essentially identical to the perfect competition described above, only with a product differentiation assumption that replaces the product homogeneity assumption. Under the monopolistic competition model, competition applies not only to the price charged, but also to the quality of the product, its labeling, and its advertising. This makes non-price competition an important component of this model. The product-differentiation character affects the demand curve that producers face, which is not perfectly elastic like the demand curve in the perfect competition model, but sloping downward. This means that a firm can charge a higher price for a product than its rivals without losing all its customers thanks to either to brand loyalty, or to consumer preference for a feature that is unique to the firm's product.[83] The equilibrium in a competitive monopoly model is set at a point where the price is higher than the marginal cost of the last unit produced and in which firm size is inefficiently small. Criticism of the 'monopolistic competition' model includes its inability to predict how a firm would respond to a change in the demand or cost conditions facing it; the unlikelihood of the free entry and exit assumption in reality; and the difficulty in accurately defining the industry being used in this theory (that is, defining 'similar products'). Neoclassical economic jargon often describes this as an imperfect competition model.[84]

The 'Austrian' economics model of competition The Austrian school of economics, which has drawn increasing interest in recent years,[85] takes its name from a group of Austrian scholars who established it, such as Carl Menger,[86] Ludwig von Mises,[87] Joseph Schumpeter,[88] Friedrich Hayek[89] and others.[90] As the Austrian school's development has been evolving for nearly 130 years[91] there are different perspectives among 'Austrian' economists. Nevertheless, there seem to be some common ground among them including:

• A belief that society can only be understood in terms of the motives and attitudes of the rational individuals comprising it. The profit motive of individuals is thought to drive the market process.
• An emphasis on the inevitable incompleteness of knowledge and information in the real world. The Austrian school places great emphasis on the role of the entrepreneur. This concept describes a businessperson who is alert to new profitable opportunities previously ignored by others.[92] The

concept of the 'entrepreneur' replaces the neoclassical model's assumption of complete and equal information to all market players. Accordingly, in the Austrian model knowledge is not taken for granted but rather it assumes lack of knowledge whereby any information has to be discovered by someone.

- An emphasis on product differentiation. Under the Austrian model, competition is all about product differentiation. Thus, for example, if a certain firm dominates the pretzel market, entrepreneurs are on a constant search for new kinds of pretzels to gain a share of the market, rather than blatantly copy those of the dominant firm. This can be done by manufacturing pretzels with new shapes, new exotic flavors and so on, which leads to the widening of consumer choice. This outlook explains why traditional Austrian economists were not overly concerned about monopolies, as they believed that new ideas and entrepreneurs are continually threatening the dominance of existing producers (even monopolies). Furthermore, some Austrian scholars have proposed that large firms with monopoly power are desirable because they tend to speed up technical innovation.[93]
- A distrust of collectivism and its implication that governments know better than the private sector.

The most critical respect in which the Austrian paradigm differs from the mainstream neoclassical approach seems to be its approach toward the competitive model.[94] The 'Austrian' competition model rejects the neoclassical mechanism of a competitive industry structure with a stagnant equilibrium quality,[95] replacing it instead with an entrepreneurial competitive dynamic process. Austrians speak about a broad concept of 'dynamic competition'[96] in which producers find themselves in a 'perennial gale of creative destruction'[97] where any stagnation is continually being defeated by market innovation.

Because of this dynamic outlook, Austrians pay little attention to entry barriers – they assume nothing can get in the way of the dynamic competition. The dynamic approach is quite compelling, as the first association that comes to mind with respect to 'competition' is indeed one of a dynamic environment where actors are constantly moving around while actively competing with one another. The dynamic competition notion is linked to innovation. Austrian economists are great believers in the patent system, since patent law protects the profits of innovators, thus increasing the incentives for discovery and development (despite the costs in terms of higher prices to consumers). For example, one 'Austrian' view presented by Schumpeter[98] asserts that the general level of material well-being depends upon a dynamic market course of technological innovation.

The legal competition model Since antitrust procedures are employed to restore or protect competition, antitrust theory is concerned mainly with identifying conditions of competition failure in which it can spring into action, and is less interested in delineating the competition process itself. Therefore the legal competition model needs to be derived negatively from legal definitions of competition-failure situations. A useful approach to understanding the legal competition model starts with the legal definition of *market power*, which seems to be a term used to denote failure of the perfect competition model.

The U.S. Department of Justice and Federal Trade Commission have defined market power as follows: 'Market power to a seller is the ability to profitably maintain prices above competition levels for a significant period of time'.[99] In order to prove market power, plaintiffs must define a relevant market; show that the defendant owns a dominant share of that market; and demonstrate the existence of significant barriers to entry and that existing competitors lack the capacity to increase their output in the short run.[100] *Monopoly power*, in contrast, has been defined as the power to control prices or exclude competition in a relevant market or the power to force a purchaser to do something that he/she would not do in a competitive market.[101] These notions seem close to the neoclassical competition model described above: a competitive model where the producers (or sellers) are price-takers who cannot influence the market price which is determined by the 'hidden hand' mechanism of the competitive market. In addition to the inability to set prices above a competitive range, the legal model assumes lack of barriers to entry, so that competitors may enter at any time, even in the short run. As in the neoclassical model, price is the only competition indicator employed, revealing the above assumption that the product is homogeneous so that customers are indifferent between products of alternative suppliers.

One major criticism of the employment of price as the sole competition indicator is that this is probably an oversimplifying assumption. In today's market consumers evidently do distinguish between apparently identical products, as brand loyalty and images created by advertising set in and play a growing role in consumers' buying decisions.[102] Consequently, considering price as the only competition indicator may be imprudent, as in the case of a seller who is able to obtain the market price for goods which are clearly inferior in quality to other goods in that market category. It seems that such a market condition reflects market power no less than the more obvious case of successful sales in higher-than-competitive prices.[103] It should be noted that although the current legal competition model is largely synonymous with the neoclassical Chicago school world-view, certain legal notions still seem to embrace other rationales, such as that of the 'Austrian' competition model. Such is the argument that IP rights are pro-competitive because they promote the dynamic efficiency of an economy by encouraging innovation.[104] This argument is essentially an 'Austrian' one since it assumes competition as a dynamic and innovative process.

Intellectual property's methodology defined

Intellectual property rights work in a rather straightforward manner, protecting applications of ideas and information that are of commercial value. The protection, like other forms of property protection, is of a negative character: the right to stop others from doing certain things. Patents confer the right to exclude others from making, using, selling, offering for sale, or importing the invention for a specific term of years. The boundaries of this exclusionary right are defined by the claims of the patent, which form the legal definition of the invention. A copyright provides the owners of literary, artistic and musical creations with exclusive rights to make and authorize reproductions of the work. Additional exclusive rights are the rights to prepare derivative works based on the protected work, to distribute copies of the work and to perform the work publicly or to display it publicly.

The relationship between competition and the IP mechanism

In order to evaluate the IP–competition methodological cusp, let us now assess the implications of a practical IP regime on the different competition models described above.

IP and the neoclassical and legal competition models It is easy to see how the IP institution interferes with the basic assumptions of the perfect competition model, when we look at the different elements of this model.

- *Entry barriers* The first and most obvious conflict is IP's conflict with the assumption of a market without entry barriers. The exclusionary rights conferred by patents and copyrights allow the IPR owner to exclude others from making use of his/her protected idea or expression. This means that to the extent that the protected idea or expression in fact defines a specific market, the owner has an enforceable barricade (for the duration of the protection term) against any other producer attempting to enter the same market. The breadth of the conflict (or whether it exists at all) depends upon additional variable factors. First, the market definition: the IPR can serve as an impermeable entry barrier only if the protected technology creates an arguably separate market. Second, the scope of the IP protection determines the extent of the entry obstacle. Narrow interpretation of the patent claims, or narrow application of the copyright 'substantial similarity' test, will lower the barrier and vice versa: the broader the patent claims or the copyright, the more difficult it becomes to enter that market for the product carrying the protected technology. Similarly, the duration of the granted IP protection dictates the length dimensions of the entry barrier. Third, the level of practical enforcement of the IP protection will be directly proportional to the scope of the entry barrier. In sum, whichever way the above variable factors take form, the potential conflict of IP with the lack-of-market-barriers assumption seems evident.

- *Homogeneity of products* IP protection also seems to create a reality that contradicts the neoclassical assumption of product homogeneity. This is because the protected features themselves may not be copied into the competitors' products, which creates a uniqueness in certain products that may, in turn, foster consumer preference towards them. In other words, under neoclassical theory, competition theory is all about producers (or traders) imitating one another's product or service. In contrast, IPRs are concerned mainly with the prevention of copying and imitation,[105] which generally creates a more heterogeneous marketplace. Note that the product differentiation feature created by an IP regime may also function as a market entry barrier since some consumers may develop loyalty to unique protected products, and become reluctant to switch to similar-but-differentiated competing goods.[106]
- *Perfect knowledge* Intellectual property laws are also likely to interfere with the neoclassical model's perfect knowledge assumption. Although this notion is probably particularly strong with respect to trade secrets, in which the protected information is wrapped with secrecy, it is also true with respect to copyrights and patents. This is because producers who are about to come out with a new technology have the advantage of planning in advance their future steps and market behavior with respect to that new technology. And even after the patent is granted, or after the expression is published, the original rights-owner will often retain a knowledge-based edge on competitors. This could be because the owner is aware of important technical details discovered during the R&D process; or because the patent specification typically reveals as little information as possible about the invention, so the information revealed may be insufficient for competitors. A similar consideration is created by the time lag it takes competitors to catch up on important commercialization information that, although available, still requires time to internalize.
- *Government Regulation* As mentioned earlier, the Chicago school neoclassical competition model tends to be averse to all forms of governmental market intervention. In that sense, an IP regime that confers exclusionary rights upon IP owners and is accompanied by an administrative network (such as the Patent Office) may be rejected by this competition model because it would be deemed to employ excessive governmental intervention in the market.[107]

IP and the monopolistic competition model

- *Entry barriers* Since the monopolistic competition model shares the assumption of lack of entry barriers with the neoclassical competition model, IP protection interferes with this assumption in the same way as described in the previous section.
- *Differentiated products* The differentiation in products assumed by this model makes it less at odds with IP protection that tends to create a more heterogeneous product environment since exact copying is prevented or at least impeded. Nevertheless, here too, where the protected substance is highly innovative and the scope of the protection is broadly construed, it could be the case in which the innovative product will create a market of its own, which leaves no leeway for legitimate non-infringing 'similar but differentiated' products to compete with it.

IP and the Austrian economics competition model The basic premises of the Austrian competition model seem to accord with the mechanism of an IP regime. First, an IP regime is consistent with the Austrian assumption that individuals' profit motives drive the market because it explains why such a regime will be successful, namely, because the right to exclude others ensures maximization of profits from the protected idea and hence will motivate inventors and authors to invest in activities that will gain them IPRs. Second, IP protection is also closely linked to the Austrian notion of market entrepreneurs, since it refers to the type of market activity that is largely responsible for innovative ideas that need IP legal protection in order to thrive. Third, the Austrian school's view on product differentiation as an element that forms the essence competition fits well into a market which contains various protected ideas and products that cannot be exactly copied by competitors. Finally, the information gaps associated with IP do not seem to conflict with the Austrian competition model since this model does not assume either complete or equal information for all market participants, but rather acknowledges the fact that information is not distributed equally among all market participants.

It should be noted, however, that an extensive application of an IP regime may somewhat collide with the Austrian model. This will be the case, for example, where the scope of protection conferred by the patent or copyright is construed very broadly. In such a case it may be very difficult to compete by offering a similar but differentiated product, because the IP protection (that is, right to exclude) will extend over any peripheral products that could potentially compete with the protected product. Also note that the Austrian model's rejection of the notion that governments know better than the private sector may also be deemed to contrast with IP (as described above under the

IP versus neoclassical model caption). It is useful to note that this notion may be weakened by two arguments. First, an IP regime is based on detailed statutory acts. Hence, IP does not involve the same level of governmental intervention as other regulated regimes whose nature and perhaps vague statutory structure involve ongoing governmental regulation. Second, this notion is at odds with the Austrian model's belief in the essentiality of a patent system to support a dynamic market course of technological innovation and entrepreneurship. The centrality of innovation as part of the Austrian competitive market course calls for a forgiving approach towards a mechanism that is aimed at promoting innovation.

The above analysis shows how an IP protection regime is in significant conflict with the assumptions of the prevalent neoclassical competition model, and thus with the current legal competition model that adopts it. It also shows that an IP policy seems to conflict, although to a lesser extent, with the monopolistic competition and Austrian competition models, respectively. Since the majority of economic analysis of law literature to date has been based upon neoclassical economic models, the above conclusion highlights the usefulness of alternative economic models, such as the Austrian models, in reconciling antitrust and IP differences. It is suggested that it is time for economic analysis legal scholars to think outside the neoclassical mainstream economic framework,[108] as such 'out of the box' thinking may prove highly beneficial for resolving IP and antitrust tensions.

1.4.3 Some Thoughts about Colliding Goals and Methods

Sections 1.4.1 and 1.4.2 examined the interchange between the goals and methods of both the antitrust and IP doctrines. However, since in practice the goals and methods are not isolated from each other there is some dialogue between them. There are three interesting remarks to note in this respect. First, the personhood element of IP is somewhat incongruent with the neoclassical and monopolistic competition models. This is because these competition models portray a world in which personal aspects play little role if any, while these same aspects lie at the core of the personhood argument. While this notion reflects a very different doctrinaire world-view, it does not necessarily suggest the existence of a direct conflict, but rather it may imply some theoretical inconsistency between the two doctrines. It is quite plausible to argue that in many commercial scenarios (that is, scenarios in which antitrust has an interest) personhood aspects are played down nowadays, since a majority of the cases involve IP rights employed by large corporations, which display few personhood characteristics.

A second notion is that IP's method of granting exclusionary rights may seem at odds, to a certain extent, with the antitrust goals of protecting individual freedom and opportunity for entrepreneurs. This is because the fence erected by these exclusionary rights may hamper individual freedom and entrepreneurial opportunity in cases where these strive to act in a protected zone.

Finally, a third noteworthy comment in this context, that is important because antitrust policy affects market structure and IP is designed for promoting innovation, is to make reference to the economic field that examines the links between market structure and innovation.[109] This often-debated realm has been developed in two aspects. One is the relationship between market concentration and innovation. This notion developed following Joseph Schumpeter's findings that the possession of monopoly power is conducive to innovation, or in other words, that innovation thrives better in monopolistic market structures.[110] Another aspect that has been investigated is the correlation between firm size and technological progress.[111] Much theoretical and empirical research ensued over these issues,[112] which resulted in a variety of contradictory conclusions. On the first aspect, results have ranged from findings supporting Schumpeter's argument, through findings supporting the existence of an 'inverted-U' relationship between the two (medium concentration structure as most encouraging for innovation while highly concentrated or atomistic structures yield less innovation) and finally to findings opposing Schumpeter's argument. On the second aspect, market-dominant firms' tendency to develop new products varied according to a number of different circumstances. The link between competition and innovation has also been the disputed subject of some recent legal discourse which has taken notice of it.[113] Without going into this separate debate in depth, it should be noted that since market structure and innovative activity seem to be somewhat interdependent, antitrust policy which directly affects market structure may affect innovative activity, and thus either frustrate or support the IP goal of promoting innovation. The course of this relationship is still empirically unclear.

1.5 CONCLUSION

This chapter delineated a framework for explaining the roots of the vast and much-explored conflict between antitrust and intellectual property, and provided some perspectives on its nature. It concludes that the goals of antitrust and IP law do not seem to be in direct conflict with each other and therefore are not the likely sources of the conflict. However, there seem to be a number of other possible culprits. First, antitrust policy's strict adherence to the Chicago school of economics may account for much of the conflict. In following the Chicago school model, antitrust scholarship may have erroneously focused on a narrow static model of competition, while overlooking important dynamic aspects of competition such as entrepreneurship and innovation. Antitrust analysis' failure to take innovation aspects into account leaves one of IP's main goals outside the scope of the antitrust policy equation, and thus could be responsible for much of antitrust's conflict with intellectual property. Consequently, it is suggested that a shift in current economic analysis of antitrust policy from Chicago to Austrian school thinking may alleviate some of the antitrust–IP tensions. Recent antitrust discourse that has begun to take notice of innovation considerations seems to be a right step in this direction.[114] Additionally, it is suggested that certain interactions between the goals and methodologies of antitrust and intellectual property create tensions that could contribute to the doctrines' conflict. These include the dissonance between competition and the personhood aspects of intellectual property and the discord between the exclusionary powers granted by intellectual property rights and the individual freedom and free market conduct that antitrust is said to promote. Finally, it is suggested that some of the conflict may possibly arise from human nature itself, which drives business players to misuse these doctrines in a manner that is inconsistent with their original premises. This proposition will be further developed in the following chapters.

NOTES

[1] The author regards the 1890 enactment of the U.S. Sherman Act (15 U.S.C. §1–4 & §7–8) as the genesis of the modern antitrust law era. It is important to note that modern antitrust law builds upon preceding common law notions of antitrust that acknowledged the right of free competition and voided restraint of free trade as against public policy. See generally: William L. Letwin, *Law and Economic Policy in America – The Evolution of the Sherman Act* 18–52 (New York: Random House 1965); William L. Letwin, *The English Common Law Concerning Monopolies*, 21 U. Chi. L. Rev. 355 (1954); and *Oregon Steam Navigation Co. v. Windsor*, 87 U.S. 74 (1873). Similar notions were expressed by liberal jurisprudence scholars; see, for example: Edward P. Weeks, *The Doctrine of Damnum Absque Injuria Considered in its Relation to the Law of Torts* 16 (San Francisco, CA: S. Whitney 1879); and John W. Salmond, *First Principles of Jurisprudence* 161 (London: Stevens & Haynes 1893).

[2] See, for example: Louis Kaplow, *The Patent–Antitrust Intersection: A Reappraisal*, 97 Harv. L. Rev. 1813, 1815 & 1848 (1984). More generally, see: Lawrence A. Sullivan, *Handbook of the Law of Antitrust* 542 (St. Paul, MN: West Publishing 1977); and Robert H. Bork, *The Antitrust Paradox: A Policy at War with Itself* 405 (New York: Free Press 1993 – a reprint of the 1978 edition with a new introduction and epilogue).

[3] See generally: Ilene Knable Gotts and Howard W. Fogt Jr., *Clinton Administration Expresses More Than Intellectual Curiosity in Antitrust Issues Raised by Intellectual Property Licensing*, 22 AIPLA Q. J. 1 (1994). The growing interest is also reflected by the U.S. Department of Justice and Federal Trade Commission's *Antitrust Guidelines for the Licensing of Intellectual Property* (April 6, 1995) [hereinafter: (1995 IP Guidelines) available at http://www.usdoj.gov/atr/public/guidelines/ ipguide.htm (January 10, 2003). The importance of

the realm is also commonly acknowledged by Antitrust Division officials; see, for example: Joel I. Klein, former head of the Antitrust Division in: *A. Cross-Licensing and Antitrust Law B.* U.S. v. G.E. *in the U.S. District of Montana*, 483 PLI/Pat 339, at 341 (1997). The subject has received special attention at the Joint DOJ–FTC Hearings on Competition and Intellectual Property Law and Policy in the Knowledge-based Economy, which were held in 2002 and are available at: http://www.ftc.gov/ (August 2, 2002). See also the U.S. Senate Judiciary Committee's Hearings: S. Hrg. 105–790, Serial No. J-105-66 on 'Competition, Innovation, and Public Policy in the Digital Age' (November 4, 1997, March 3, 1998 and July 23, 1998).

4 The following example describes the fact pattern of the Eastman Kodak case: *Image Technical Services, Inc. v. Eastman Kodak Co.*, 125 F. 3rd 1195 (9th Cir. 1997), *cert. denied* 523 U.S. 1094 (1998).

5 See *Eastern Railroad President's Conference v. Noerr Motor Freight, Inc.*, 365 U.S. 127 (1961).

6 See the 1995 IP Guidelines, supra note 3, §6.

7 This wording is taken from the Patent Act, 35 U.S.C. §154 (*a*) (1994).

8 This wording is taken from the Copyright Act, 17 U.S.C.A. §106 (1976).

9 See 'Should Antitrust Enforcers Rely on Potential Competition Analysis or the Concept of Innovation Markets?', Testimony of Sumanth Addanki, Vice President, National Economic Research Associates, Inc., Federal Trade Commission Hearings on Global and Innovation-based Competition (October 25, 1995), pp. 2–3 of the testimony which express similar notions – that illegal collusive conduct in R&D is unlikely. The testimony is available at the Federal Trade Commission's web site, supra note 3. Note that there are exceptions to this argument: scenarios in which firms cooperate in the original R&D in order to save resources (or be able to afford the technology development altogether). Another exception is demonstrated in situations where firms are compelled to cross-license because of the similarity of the later to the earlier patent.

10 A good example of such a scenario is an 'essential facilities' case where the exercise of control as part of a real property right in a facility is recognized as curtailing competition. See, for example: *Aspen Skiing Co. v. Aspen Highlands Skiing Company*, 472 U.S. 585 (1985) (ownership right); *Hecht v. Pro-Football, Inc.*, 570 F. 2d 982 (D.C. Cir. 1977), cert. denied, 436 U.S. 956 (1978) (rental right); and *U.S. v. Terminal Railroad Ass'n*, 224 U.S. 383 (1912) (ownership right).

11 See generally: John Stuart Mill, *On Liberty* (Elizabeth Rapaport ed., Indianapolis, IN: Hacket Pub. Co. 1978) (1859); John Austin, *Lectures on Jurisprudence* (Robert Campbell ed., London: J. Murray 1911); Jeremy Bentham, *Of Laws in General* (H. Hart ed., London: Athlone Press 1970); Oliver W. Holmes, *Privilege, Malice, and Intent*, 8 Harv. L. Rev. 1, 6 (1894); and Wesley N. Hohfeld, *Some Fundamental Legal Conceptions as Applied in Judicial Reasoning,* 23 Yale L.J. 16 (1913) also available as a book: Wesley Newcomb Hohfeld, *Fundamental Legal Conceptions as Applied in Judicial Reasoning and Other Essays* (New Haven, CT: Yale University Press 1920).

12 See, for example, Dudley Knowles, *Hegel on Property and Personality,* 33 Philosophical Q. 33, 45–62 (1983).

13 The neoclassical competition model will be discussed in greater detail below, see p. 17.

14 See a development of this notion in Rudolph J. Peritz, *The 'Rule of Reason' in Antitrust Law: Property Logic in Restraint of Competition*, 40 Hastings L. J. 285 (1989).

15 For the original articulation of this argument, see Joseph W. Singer, *The Legal Rights Debate in Analytical Jurisprudence from Bentham to Hohfeld*, 1982 Wis. L. Rev. 975, 982–3 (1982).

16 Scholars cannot even agree on whether intellectual property is property at all, that is, whether it fits within the common definitions of property. See, for example: Frank H. Easterbrook, *Intellectual Property is Still Property*, 13 Harv. J.L. & Pub. Pol'y 108 (1990); Timothy J. Brennan, *Copyright, Property, and the Right to Deny*, 68 Chi.-Kent L. Rev. 675 (1993); and Edmund W. Kitch, *The Nature and Function of the Patent System*, 20 J. L. & Econ. 265 (1977).

[17] See, for example: Ward S. Bowman Jr., *Patent and Antitrust Law: A Legal and Economic Appraisal* 3 (Chicago: University of Chicago Press, 1973); *Jefferson Parish Hospital Dist. No. 2 v. Hyde*, 466 U.S. 2, 16 (1984), (Dicta); *Digidyne Corp. v. Data General Corp.*, 734 F.2d 1336, 1341–2 (9th Cir. 1984) & 473 U.S. 908 (1985); *Zenith Radio Corp. v. Hazeltine Research, Inc.*, 395 U.S. 100, 135 (1969); *U.S. v. Loew's Inc.*, 371 U.S. 38, 45–6 (1962); and *Hartford-Empire Co. v. U.S.*, 323 U.S. 386, 452 (1944).

[18] It is important to note the legal definition of the term 'market power' as distinguished from 'monopoly power'. *Market power* of a seller is commonly defined as the 'seller's ability to profitably maintain prices above competition levels for a significant period of time' (see U.S. Department of Justice and Federal Trade Commission, *Horizontal Merger Guidelines* § 0.1 (April 2, 1992, Revised April 8, 1997) reprinted in 4 Trade Reg. Rep. (CCH) pp. 13,104, also available at http://www.usdoj.gov/atr (January 10, 2003). See also William M. Landes and Richard A. Posner, *Market Power in Antitrust Cases*, 94 Harv. L. Rev. 937 (1981). In order to prove market power, plaintiffs must define a relevant market; show that the defendant owns a dominant share of that market; and show the existence of significant barriers to entry and that existing competitors lack the capacity to increase their output in the short run (see the Eastman Kodak case, supra note 4 at 1202–3). *Monopoly power* has been defined as the power to control prices or exclude competition in a relevant market or the power to force a purchaser to do something that he/she would not do in a competitive market (see *U.S. v. E.I. du Pont* 351 U.S. 377, 391–5 (1956); *Jefferson Parish Hospital Dist. v. Hyde*, id. at 13–14 (1984). Accordingly, market power in itself is not determinative of monopoly power. However, the two terms are closely linked, because whoever has market power (that is, owns a dominant share of a market to which competitors cannot enter in the short term), obviously has the power to control the product's price in that market as well as some edge on the competition and consumers in that market. In other words, monopoly power can be understood as a significant degree of market power (see Phillip Areeda and Louis Kaplow, *Antitrust Analysis – Problems, Text, Cases* 448 (New York: Aspen Law & Business, 5th edn 1997).

[19] See, for example: Allan S. Gutterman, *Innovation and Competition Policy* 429–31 (London: Kluwer Law International 1997); Russell Lombardy, *The Myth of Market Power: Why Market Power Should Not Be Presumed When Applying Antitrust Principles to the Analysis of Tying Agreements Involving Intellectual Property*, 8 St. Thomas L. Rev. 449 (1996); Dieter Laudien, 'Patents and Competition', in *Intellectual Property Rights and Global Competition* 255–6 (Berlin: Edition Sigma Horst Alback and Stephanie Rosenkranz eds 1995) Easterbrook, supra note 16; Edmund W. Kitch, *Patents: Monopolies or Property Rights?*, 8 Res. in L. & Econ. 31 (1986) (economic price theory analysis); and William Montgomery, *The Presumption of Economic Power for Patented and Copyrighted Products in Tying Arrangements*, 85 Colum. L. Rev. 1140 (1985).

[20] See the 1995 IP Guidelines, supra note 3 §2.2 ('The Agencies will not presume that a patent, copyright, or trade secret necessarily confers market power upon its owner').

[21] See: Intellectual Property Antitrust Protection Act of 1995, H.R. 2674, 104th Cong. (1996); Intellectual Property Antitrust Protection Act of 1989, H.R. 469, 101st Cong. (1989); and Intellectual Property Antitrust Protection Act of 1988, S. 438, 100th Cong. (1988) (earlier titled 'A Bill to Modify the Application of the Antitrust Laws and to Encourage the Licensing and Other Use of Certain Intellectual Property', S. 438, 100th Cong. (1987)). All these bills sought to eliminate the presumption of market power from the existence of a patent or copyright.

[22] See Paul S. Grunzweig, *Prohibiting the Presumption of Market Power for Intellectual Property Rights: The Intellectual Property Antitrust Protection Act of 1989*, 16 J. Corp. L. 103, 104 (1990).

[23] Note that curtailing competition is a possible but not a necessary effect of IP. Another conceivable possibility is the case of a protected idea or expression that is never commercialized, and thus bears no effect on the market whatsoever because it does not enter the market or create a new market niche. In such a case the IPR has no actual effect on the market. Also note that there are some indirect aspects in which a prosperous IP regime may actually

promote competitive aspects of the market. A good example of that is the way innovative advances in communications and computer technologies that are spurred by IP incentives are changing business environments and allowing individual entrepreneurs to compete successfully with large corporations in today's market – for a development of these notions, see Tom Petzinger, *The New Pioneers* (New York: Simon & Schuster 1999).

[24] See, for example, *Standard Oil Co. v. FTC*, 340 U.S. 231, 248–9 (1951).

[25] See, for example, Richard A. Posner, *Antitrust Law: An Economic Perspective* 22 (Chicago: Chicago University Press 1976). Posner's view reflects the bedrock of the Chicago school antitrust theory that he represents.

[26] It has been generally acknowledged that the relationship between means and ends of doctrines is far from simple as ends are commonly modified by means and vice versa. See, for example, Lon L. Fuller, 'Means and Ends', in *The Principles of Social Order: Selected Essays of Lon L. Fuller* 48 (Kenneth I. Winston ed., Durham, NC: Duke University Press 1981).

[27] See, for example, Gerald Sobel, *The Antitrust Interface with Patents and Innovation: Acquisition of Patents, Improvement Patents and Grant-Backs, Non-Use, Fraud on the Patent Office, Development of the New Products and Joint Research*, 53 Antitrust L. J. 681, 682–3 (1985).

[28] The misuse doctrine has its roots in patent law, but was subsequently extended to apply to copyright infringement suits as well, see, for example, *Lasercomb America Inc. v. Reynolds*, 911 F.2d 970 (4th Cir. 1990); and *Union Carbide Corp. v. Ever-Ready*, 531 F.2d 366 (7th Cir. 1976). For a broad review of the doctrine's development see Brett Frischmann and Dan Moylan, *The Evolving Common Law Doctrine of Copyright Misuse: A Unified Theory and Its Application to Software*, 15 Berkeley Tech. L. J. 865 (2000).

[29] *U.S. v. Aluminum Co. of America et al.*, 148 F.2d 416 (2d Cir. 1945).

[30] Id. at 429–30. For a similar view that a monopoly acquired through superior skill will be 'tolerated but not cherished' see *Berkey Photo, Inc. v. Eastman Kodak Co.*, 603 F. 2d 263, 273 (2nd Cir. 1979), cert. denied, 444 U.S. 1093 (1980).

[31] For an extensive articulation of this notion and its practical implications see: Willard K. Tom and Joshua A. Newberg, *Antitrust and Intellectual Property: From Separate Spheres to Unified Field*, 66 Antitrust L. J. 167 (1997). See also Ronald S. Katz, Janet Arnold Hart and Adam J. Safer, '*Intellectual Property v. Antitrust: A False Dilemma*', in *Antitrust/Intellectual Property Claims in High Technology Markets: Litigating and Advising* (ALI-ABA Course, April 22–23, 1999).

[32] See: Bowman, supra note 17 at 1; and *Northern Pacific Railway v. U.S.*, 356 U.S. 1, 4–5 (1958).

[33] *Atari Games Corp. v. Nintendo of America, Inc.*, 897 F. 2d 1572, 1576 (Fed. Cir. 1990). See also 1995 IP Guidelines, supra note 3, §1.0.

[34] Advocates of the 'illusory conflict' view could potentially take this argument one step further, in arguing that the courts and the 'conflict' view scholars have erred all along and therefore depicted a false conflict. While there may be a grain of truth in this argument, it should be borne in mind that law as a practical philosophy should not exist in splendid isolation from the legal reality.

[35] See, for example, *Symposium, Antitrust Jurisprudence: The Economic, Political and Social Goals of Antitrust Policy*, 125 U. Pa. L. Rev. 1182 (1977). The parlance of the differing scholars reflects how far apart they view their approaches to be. See, for example: Terry Calvani, *Rectangles and Triangles: A Response to Mr. Lande*, 58 Antitrust L. J. 657–9 (1989), where Calvani describes the debate among the different approaches as a battle and refers to advocates of the extra-economic approach as 'the modern day Luddites of antitrust'; Richard A. Posner, *The Chicago School of Antitrust Analysis*, 127 U. Pa. L. Rev. 925, 928–9 (1979) where he describes non-economical antitrust approaches as 'untheoretical, descriptive...and even metaphorical' and characterizes them as a 'casual observation' and 'colorful characterization'; and Robert H. Bork in E. William Barnett et al., *Panel Discussion: Merger Enforcement and*

Practice 50 Antitrust L. J. 233, 238 (1981) where he referred to the extra-economic approach as an 'intellectual mush'.

[36] See, for example: Charles F. Rule and David L. Meyer, *An Antitrust Enforcement Policy to Maximize the Economic Wealth of all Consumers,* 33 Antitrust Bull. 677 (1988); Robert H. Bork, Judicial Precedent and the New Economics, in *Antitrust Policy in Transition: The Convergence of Law and Economics* 16 et seq. (Chicago: American Bar Association 1984); Bork, supra note 2; Posner, supra note 25; Oliver E. Williamson, *Economics as an Antitrust Defense: The Welfare Tradeoffs,* 58 American Econ. Rev. 18 (1968); and Robert H. Bork, *Legislative Intent and the Policy of the Sherman Act*, 9 J.L. & Econ. 7 (1966). The traditional economic models are concerned with allocative efficiency. Economists generally distinguish between allocative efficiency, Pareto optimality, Pareto superiority and Kaldor–Hicks efficiency, see Jules L. Coleman, *Markets, Morals and the Law* (Cambridge: Cambridge University Press 1988).

[37] See Barbara A. White, *Countervailing Power – Different Rules for Different Markets? Conduct and Context in Antitrust Law and Economics*, 41 Duke L. J. 1045, 1055 (1992).

[38] See, for example: *U.S. v. Von's Grocery Store Co.*, 384 U.S. 270 (1966); *Brown Shoe Co. v. U.S.*, 370 U.S. 294, 344 (1962); *U.S. v. Aluminum Co. of America*, supra note 29 at 427; and *U.S. v. Trans-Missouri Freight Association*, 166 U.S. 290, 323–4 (1897). See also: *Mr. Justice Brandeis, Competition and Smallness: A Dilemma Re-examined (Note)*, 66 Yale L. J. 69, 74–5 (1956); and Harlan M. Blake and William K. Jones, '*Toward a Three-Dimensional Antitrust Policy*', 65 Colum. L. Rev., 422, 429, 431 (1965). For a recent articulation of the Federal Trade Commission staff's view on small businesses see, Federal Trade Commission Staff, *Anticipating the 21st Century: Competition Policy in the New High-tech Global Marketplace*, Vol. I, ch. 5: 'Small Businesses and Competition Issues' (May 1996).

[39] See, for example: Rudolph J.R. Peritz, *Some Realism About Economic Power in a Time of Sectorial Change*, 66 Antitrust L. J. 247 (1997); Walter Adams and James Brock, *The Bigness Complex* (New York: Pantheon Books 1986); Victor H. Kramer, *The Supreme Court and Tying Arrangements: Antitrust as History*, 69 Minn. L. Rev. 1013 (1985); and Louis D. Brandeis, *Other People's Money* 109 et seq. (Washington, DC: National Home Library Foundation 1933).

[40] See, for example: Milton Friedman, *Capitalism and Freedom* (Chicago: University of Chicago Press 1962); Friedrich A. Hayek, *Individualism and Economic Order* (Chicago: Chicago University Press 1948); Henry C. Simons, *Economic Policy for a Free Society* (Chicago: Chicago University Press 1948); and Friedrich A. Hayek, *The Road to Serfdom* (Chicago: Chicago University Press 1944, 50th Anniversary Edition, 1994). See also Justice Douglas in a dissenting opinion in *Standard Oil of California v. U.S.*, 337 U.S. 293, 318–19 (1949) where he quotes from a book by Justice Brandeis.

[41] *U.S. v. Aluminum Co. of America*, supra note 29 at 428–9. See also: *Paramount Famous Lasky Corp. v. U.S.*, 282 U.S. 30 (1930); *Fashion Originators' Guild of America v. FTC*, 312 U.S. 457 (1941); *Klor's, Inc. v. Broadway-Hale Stores, Inc.*, 359 U.S. 207 (1959); Robert Pitofsky, *The Political Content of Antitrust*, 127 U. Pa. L. Rev. 1051, 1053–4 (1979); and Senator Reed's comments in 1914: 'We construed "liberty" to mean ... liberty ... to engage in commerce, to solve for one's self the problem of one's own happiness and success. So we began enacting legislation calculated to ... leave open for all men, big and little, the opportunity to engage in the affairs of life', in *Congressional Record* 51 (1914): 15867.

[42] See: Thomas Sowell, *Race and Economics* (New York: Longman 1977); William G. Shepherd, *Market Power and Racial Discrimination in White-collar Employment*, 14 Antitrust Bull. 141 (1969); Armen A. Alchian and Reuben A. Kessel, 'Competition, Monopoly, and the Pursuit of Money', in *Aspects of Labor Economics* 157 (Princeton, NJ: Princeton University Press 1962); and Gary S. Becker, *The Economics of Discrimination* (Chicago: Chicago University Press 1957).

[43] See: Paul R. Dixon and Charles E. Mueller, *Competition: The Moral Justification for Capitalism*, 27 Antitrust L. & Econ. Rev. 11, 20–21 (1996); and Paul R. Dixon and Charles E.

Mueller, *Antitrust Law: The Magna Carta of the Free Enterprise System*, 27 Antitrust L. & Econ. Rev. 25 (1996).

[44] See: Robert H. Lande, *Wealth Transfers as the Original and Primary Concern of Antitrust: The Efficiency Interpretation Challenged,* 34 Hastings L. J. 65, 95, 101, 115 (1982); and Donald Dewey, *The Economic Theory of Antitrust: Science or Religion*, 50 Va. L. Rev. 413, 429–30 (1964).

[45] See the Preamble and Art. 2 of the Treaty establishing the European Economic Community. See also *Consten & Grundig v. Commission*, Cases 56, 58/64 [1966] ECR 299.

[46] In the same way that early American antitrust law relied upon the Interstate Commerce Clause as authority to legislate the Sherman Act: see §1 of the Sherman Act ('Every contract … in restraint of trade or commerce among the several States'); and Hans B. Thorelli, *The Federal Antitrust Policy – Origination of an American Tradition* 96–107 (Baltimore, MD: Johns Hopkins University Press 1955).

[47] For similar notions, see Michael S. Jacobs, *An Essay on the Normative Foundations of Antitrust Economics*, 74 N. C. L. Rev. 219 (1995). Note that this notion was admitted by some mainstream economists, see, for example, Joel B. Dirlam and Alfred E. Kahn, *Fair Competition – The Law and Economics of Antitrust Policy* 14 (Ithaca, NY: Cornell University Press 1954).

[48] See James Madison, *The Federalist* No. 43, in *The Federalist Papers* 279 (Isaac Kramnick ed., Harmonsdworth: Penguin 1987) where he speaks of the public good utilitarian IP justification coinciding with the natural rights argument. But compare with Friedrich A. Hayek, *Law, Legislation and Liberty*, 71–72 (Chicago: University of Chicago Press 1978) where he argues that utilitarian market rewards arguments have nothing to do with desert-for-labor considerations.

[49] John Locke, *Two Treatises of Government*, Book II, ch. V (Peter Laslett ed., Cambridge: Cambridge University Press 1988) (1690). The notion was adopted by early court decisions that mark the emergence of modern IP law. See, for example: *Millar v. Taylor,* 4 Burrows 2303, 98 Eng. Rep. 201 (1769) in England; and *Wheaton v. Peters*, 33 U.S. (8 Pet.) 591, 669–70 (1834) in the U.S.

[50] There are many interpretations for Locke's writings on property. See, for example: James Tully, *A Discourse on Property* (Cambridge: Cambridge University Press 1980); Crawford B. Macpherson, *The Political Theory of Possessive Individualism* (Oxford: Clarendon 1969); and Frank I. Michelman, *Property, Utility and Fairness: Comments on the Ethical Foundations of 'Just Compensation' Law*, 80 Harv. L. Rev. 1165 (1967). For an application of Lockean themes to intellectual property, see Peter Drahos, *A Philosophy of Intellectual Property*, Ch. 3 (Aldershot, UK: Dartmouth 1996); Lawrence C. Becker, *Deserving to Own Intellectual Property*, 68 Chi.-Kent L. Rev. 609 (1993); and Wendy J. Gordon, *A Property Right in Self Expression: Equality and Individualism in the Natural Law of Intellectual Property*, 102 Yale L. J. 1533 (1993).

[51] Georg Wilhelm Friedrich Hegel, *Philosophy of Right* (T.M. Knox trans., Oxford: Clarendon 1952 1st edn 1967 reprint) (1821). For a contemporary interpretation of Hegel's works see, for example: Margaret J. Radin, *Property and Personhood,* 34 Stan. L. Rev. 957 (1982); Charles Taylor, *Hegel and Modern Society* (Cambridge: Cambridge University Press 1979); and Z.A. Pelczynski, *Hegel's Political Philosophy: Problems and Perspectives* (Z.A. Pelczynski ed., Cambridge: Cambridge University Press 1971).

[52] See Hegel, id. at 35–44.

[53] See also *Bleistein v. Donaldson Lithographing Co.*, 188 U.S. 239, 250 (1903), which expands on the issue of the author's personality right in his/her creation.

[54] See, for example, Lloyd Weinreb, *Copyright for Functional Expression*, 111 Harv. L. Rev. 1149, 1217–20 (1998).

[55] For a utilitarian framework for intellectual property, see, for example, Patrick Croskery, *Institutional Utilitarianism and Intellectual Property*, 68 Chi.-Kent L. Rev. 631 (1993). For a

utilitarian economic perspective overview, see Erich Kaufer, *The Economics of the Patent System* (Chur, Switzerland: Harwood Academic 1988).

[56] Note that this notion is also embedded in the U.S. Constitution. See U.S. Const. Art. I §8[8] which provides that 'the Congress shall have the Power ... to promote the Progress of science and useful Arts, by securing for limited Times to Authors and Inventors the exclusive Right to their respective writings and Discoveries'.

[57] For a broad treatment of public goods see, for example, Anthony De Jasay, *Social Contract, Free Ride: A Study of the Public Goods Problem*, (Oxford: Clarendon 1989).

[58] For empirical articulation of technical advance as a source of growth, see: Robert M. Solow, *Technical Change and the Aggregate Production Function*, 39 Rev. of Econ. and Stat. 312 (1957); Edward F. Denison, *Accounting for U.S. Economic Growth: 1929–69* 131–7 (Washington DC: Brookings Institution 1974) (both focus only on process innovation, omitting product innovation which is also the other element of technological progress). On the causal association between innovation and growth, see Kenneth W. Dam, *The Economic Underpinnings of Patent Law*, 23 J. Legal Stud. 247 (1994).

[59] This line of argument is very common. See, for example, World Intellectual Property Organization (WIPO), *Introduction to Intellectual Property – Theory and Practice* (Boston, MA: Kluwer Law International 1997) ch. 4.

[60] See Bork, supra note 2 at 132.

[61] See 1995 IP Guidelines, supra, note 3, §1.0 ('The intellectual property laws and the antitrust laws share the common purpose of promoting innovation').

[62] See, for example, *Opening Markets and Protecting Competition for America's Business and Consumers* (April 7, 1995) Part V available at http://www.usdoj.gov/atr (August 2, 2002).

[63] John M. Nannes, Deputy Assistant Attorney General, Antitrust Division, U.S. Dept. of Justice, '*Antitrust in an Era of High-tech Innovation*' (October 22, 1998), available at http://www.usdoj.gov/atr (January 10, 2003).

[64] See, for example, the 'Magill' case: Cases C-241/91P and C-242/91P *Radio Telefis Eireann (RTE) et al. v. Commission of European Communities*, 1 CEC (CCH) ¶400 (1995).

[65] See, for example: *Standard Oil Co. v. U.S.*, 221 U.S. 1, 58 (1911); *SCM Corp. v. Xerox Corp.*, 645 F.2d 1195, 1203 (2nd Cir. 1981); the Federal Trade Commission's declaration that 'economic efficiency and any other social benefit [is] pertinent only insofar as it may tend to promote or retard the vigor of competition' quoted by Bork, supra note 2 at 254; the Department of Justice Antitrust Division's policy statement *Antitrust Enforcement and the Consumer* available on its web site, supra note 62; and Eleanor M. Fox and Lawrence A. Sullivan, *Antitrust Retrospective and Prospective: Where Are We Coming From? Where Are We Going?*, 62 N.Y.U. L. Rev. 936, 936 (1987).

[66] See, for example, Bork, supra note 2, where he claims that the neoclassical competition model 'is an enormously useful model for economic theory, but ... is utterly useless as a goal of law'.

[67] For a broad review on the various economic schools of thought see, for example: *A Modern Guide to Economic Thought* (Douglas Mair and Anne G. Miller eds, Cheltenham, UK and Northampton, MA, USA: Edward Elgar 1999); and Terry Burke, Angela Genn-Bash and Brian Haines, *Competition in Theory and Practice* (Kent: Croom Helm 1988).

[68] The neoclassical economic literature is vast. Seminal texts by 'founders' of the school include: Alfred Marshall, *Principles of Economics* (London: Macmillan, 8th edn 1920) (1890); Francis Y. Edgeworth, *Papers Relating to Political Economy* (London: Macmillan 1925); John R. Hicks, *Value and Capital* (Oxford: Clarendon Press 1939); and Paul A. Samuelson, *Foundations of Economic Analysis* (Cambridge, MA.: Harvard University Press 1947). For an excellent summary of neoclassical economics see Tony Aspromourgos, '*Neoclassical*' and Antonietta Campus '*Marginalist Economics*' in *The New Palgrave – A Dictionary of Economics* (John Eatwell, Murray Milgate and Peter Newman eds, London: Macmillan Press 1987). For a good summary of this school's competition model, see Jean Tirole, *The Theory of Industrial Organization* 6–12 (Cambridge, MA: MIT Press 1988).

[69] If all of the above conditions except for 'perfect knowledge' are met, then the term 'pure competition' as opposed to 'perfect competition' is used. This distinction in terms between 'pure' and 'perfect' competition was coined by Chamberlin, see Edward H. Chamberlin, *The Theory of Monopolistic Competition: A Reorientation of the Theory of Value*, ch. 1 (Cambridge, MA: Harvard University Press 1933).

[70] The Chicago school of economics describes a thinking incorporated in the writings and teachings of a group of scholars associated with the University of Chicago. Leading scholars associated with the school include Milton Friedman and George J. Stigler. The Chicago school of *law* and economics is closely related to the Chicago school of economics, and was developed in Chicago University's Law School. This school describes a thinking incorporated in the writings and teachings of a group of scholars associated with the university's Law School from 1939 to about 1975. The book most commonly associated with the Chicago school is Richard A. Posner, *Economic Analysis of Law* (New York: Aspen Law & Business, 5th edn 1998). Other significant contributors include Ronald Coase, Henry C. Simons and Aaron Director. Much of the work of the school can be found in various volumes of the *Journal of Law and Economics*. For an excellent summary of these schools, see Edmund W. Kitch, 'Chicago School of Law and Economics', in *The New Palgrave Dictionary of Economics and the Law* (Peter Newman ed., New York: Stockton Press 1998). For a more detailed account, see *The Chicago School of Political Economy* (Warren J. Samuels ed., East Lansing, MI: Michigan State University 1976).

[71] For a review of how the 'Chicago school' economic analysis has profoundly influenced U.S. antitrust enforcement, see Lawrence T. Festa III, Comment, *Eastman Kodak Co. v. Image Technical Services, Inc.: The Decline and Fall of the Chicago Empire?*, 68 Notre Dame L. Rev. 619, 619–23 (1993).

[72] Bork, supra note 2.

[73] This is reflected through the fact that regulated industries are typically immune from antitrust policy.

[74] For a similar notion, see Gerald P. O'Driscoll and Mario J. Rizzo, *The Economics of Time and Ignorance* 142–3 (Oxford: Blackwell 1985).

[75] See Chapter 3, p. 107.

[76] Leading Harvard School economists include Edward S. Mason, John M. Clark, Joe S. Bain and Michael H. Mann. For a comparative survey on the antitrust concepts of the Chicago and Harvard schools see: Ingo L.O. Schmidt and Jan B. Rittaler, *A Critical Evaluation of the Chicago School of Antitrust Analysis* 117 (Dordrecht: Kluwer Academic 1989).

[77] For an overview of the structuralist school and its comparison with the Chicago school, see James W. Meehan, Jr. and Robert J. Larner, 'The Structural School, Its Critics, and Its Progeny: An Assessment', in *Economics and Antitrust Policy* 179–208 (Robert J. Larner and James W. Meehan eds, Westport CT: Quorum Books 1989).

[78] The leading writer in this structure–conduct–performance paradigm is probably Joseph Bain. See: Joe S. Bain, *Barriers to New Competition* (Cambridge MA: Harvard University Press 1956); and Joe S. Bain, *Industrial Organization* (New York: John Wiley 1959, 2nd edn 1968). See also George J. Stigler, *The Case Against Big Business*, 47 Fortune May 1952, 123, 167 ('an industry which does not have a competitive structure will not have competitive behavior').

[79] Chamberlin, supra note 69.

[80] Joan Robinson, *The Economics of Imperfect Competition*, (London: Macmillan 1933).

[81] See Frederick M. Rowe, *The Decline of Antitrust and the Delusions of Models: The Faustian Pact of Law and Economics*, 72 Geo. L. J. 1511, 1541–7 (1984). For an interesting retrospective critical review of this school, see George J. Stigler, '*Monopolistic Competition in Retrospect*', in George J. Stigler, *The Organization of Industry* 309 (Chicago: University of Chicago Press 1968).

[82] The founding neoclassicists were highly critical of this model, see, for example, Hicks, supra note 68. Perhaps the harsh criticism to this model originated because it threatened the heart of

the neoclassical model ('pure competition'), and this could also explain why the monopolistic competition model is much neglected today.

[83] For a depiction of the product-differentiation feature in the market, see William S. Comanor, *Vertical Territorial and Customer Restrictions: White Motor and Its Aftermath*, 81 Harv. L. Rev. 1419, 1423–5 (1968) (the context of the article is a Chicago school analysis, and therefore the differentiation is portrayed as anticompetitive).

[84] See, for example, Stanley Fischer, Rudiger Dornbusch and Richard Schmalensee, *Introduction to Microeconomics* 196 et seq. (New York: McGraw-Hill, 2nd edn 1988).

[85] See: Alan Oakley, *The Revival of Modern Austrian Economics* (Cheltenham, UK and Northampton MA: Edward Elgar 1999); and Karen I. Vaughn, *Austrian Economics in America – The Migration of a Tradition* 1, 103–11 (New York: Cambridge University Press 1994).

[86] See: Carl Menger, *Principles of Economics* (James Dingwall and Bert F. Hoselitz trans.) (New York: New York University Press 1981) (1871); and Carl Menger, *Investigations Into the Method of the Social Sciences with Special Reference to Economics* (Francis J. Nock trans., Lawrence White ed., New York: New York University Press 1985) (1883). See also *Carl Menger and the Austrian School of Economics* (John R. Hicks and Wilhelm Weber eds, Oxford: Clarendon 1973).

[87] See: Ludwig von Mises, *Human Action: A Treatise on Economics* (New Haven, CT: Yale University Press 1949, reprinted 1963); and Ludwig von Mises, *The Ultimate Foundations of Economic Science: An Essay on Method* (Kansas City, KS: Sheed, Andrews & McMeel, 1962 reprinted 1978). For an excellent summary of von Mises' scholarship, see Israel M. Kirzner, *Ludwig von Mises: The Man and his Economics* (Wilmington, DE: ISI Books 2001).

[88] Joseph A. Schumpeter, *Capitalism, Socialism and Democracy* (New York: Harper & Row, 1st edn, 1942 reprinted 1965, London: Unwin University Books).

[89] See, for example, Friedrich A. Hayek, 'The Meaning of Competition', in *Individualism and Economic Order* (Chicago: University of Chicago Press 1948); Friedrich A. Hayek, *Individualism and Economic Order* (Chicago: Chicago University Press 1948); and Friedrich A. Hayek, 'Competition as a Discovery Procedure', in *New Studies in Philosophy, Politics, Economics, and the History of Ideas* (London: Routledge 1978). Friedrich Hayek's contributions to Austrian economic theory are extensive. He was awarded a Nobel Prize in economics in 1974.

[90] Other important contributors to the development of the Austrian school of economics include: Eugen von Böhm-Bawerk and Friedrich von Weiser. Contemporary Austrian school academics include Murray Rothbard, Israel Kirzner, Peter Boettke and Ludwig M. Lachmann.

[91] Dating from Carl Menger's seminal 1871 work *Principles of Economics*, supra note 86. For a good review of Austrian scholarship, see: *The Elgar Companion to Austrian Economics* (Peter J. Boettke ed., Cheltenham, UK and Brookfield, USA: Edward Elgar 1994); and *Time, Uncertainty, and Disequilibrium: Exploration of Austrian Themes* (Mario J. Rizzo ed. Lexington, MA: D.C. Heath & Co. 1979).

[92] See Israel M. Kirzner, *Competition and Entrepreneurship* (Chicago: University of Chicago Press 1973).

[93] See Schumpeter, supra note 88.

[94] See Israel M. Kirzner, 'The Driving Force of the Market: The Idea of "Competition" in Contemporary Economic Theory and in the Austrian Theory of the Market Process', in *Why Economists Disagree* 37 (David L. Prychitko ed., Albany, NY: State University of New York Press 1998). Kirzner is considered one of the leading Austrian economists of our time.

[95] See D.J. Harris, *On the Classical Theory of Competition*, 12 Cambridge J. of Econ. 139–67 (1988).

[96] See: O'Driscoll and Rizzo, supra note 74 at 100–109, 130–31; Israel M. Kirzner, *The Meaning of the Market Process: Essays in the Development of Modern Austrian Economics* 85 (London: Routledge 1992); Hayek, *The Meaning of Competition*, supra note 89 at 92–106; and Hayek, *Competition as a Discovery Procedure*, supra note 89, at 179–90.

[97] This phrase was coined by the Austrian economist Joseph A. Schumpeter in *Capitalism, Socialism, and Democracy,* supra note 88 at 87; see ch. VII: 'The Process of Creative Destruction'.

[98] Schumpeter, supra note 88 at 106 (and ch. VIII in general).

[99] See supra note 18.

[100] Id.

[101] See: *U.S. v. E.I. du Pont*, supra note 18; and the Jefferson Parish case, supra note 17, at 13–14.

[102] See, generally, John Phillip Jones, *When Ads Work: New Proof That Advertising Triggers Sales* (New York: Lexington Books 1994). For a formal economic elaboration of the subject, see Robert B. Ekelund, Jr. and David S. Saurman, *Advertising and the Market Process: A Modern Economic View* (Foreword by Israel M. Kirzner, San Francisco, CA: Pacific Research Institute for Public Policy 1988).

[103] For an argument that monopoly effects go beyond price–cost divergence, see, for example, O'Driscoll and Rizzo, supra note 74 at 146–8. For an articulation of the importance of non-price competition, see 'Innovation, Rivalry and Competitive Advantage', Interview with Professor Michael E. Porter, *Antitrust* 5 (Spring 1991). It should be noted that the relevance of non-price competition notions is not new, but rather it dates back to the 1933 monopolistic competition model that was discussed earlier.

[104] Organization for Economic Cooperation and Development (OECD), *Competition Policy and Intellectual Property Rights* (Paris: OECD 1989), 11–12. See also 1995 IP Guidelines, supra note 3, §1.0.

[105] For a similar idea, see Drahos, supra note 50 at 135.

[106] For development of the notion that product differentiation acts as a market barrier, see Bain, *Barriers to New Competition*, supra note 78 at 114–43 (and in general ch. 4: 'Product Differentiation Advantages').

[107] See Steve P. Calandrillo, *An Economic Analysis of Property Rights in Information: Justifications and Problems of Exclusive Rights, Incentives to Generate Information, and the Alternative of a Government-run Reward System*, 9 Fordham Intell. Prop. Media and Ent. L. J. 301 (1998). (A Chicago school analysis advocating the benefits of a reward system, and concluding it should replace the current IP regime); Frederic M. Scherer and David Ross, *Industrial Market Structure and Economic Performance* 626–30 (Boston, MA: Houghton Mifflin, 3rd edn 1990) (questioning the benefits of a patent system and suggesting alternative mechanisms).

[108] For a similar view, see Gregory Scott Crespi, *Exploring the Complicationist Gambit: An Austrian Approach to the Economic Analysis of Law*, 73 Notre Dame L. Rev. 315 (1998). There have already been some attempts to apply Austrian concepts to legal questions by scholars, see, for example: Crespi id. at 334–64 which reviews the existing literature; Mario Rizzo, *A Theory of Economic Loss in the Law of Torts*, 11 J. Legal Stud. 281 (1982); Mario Rizzo, *Foreword: Fundamentals of Causation*, 63 Chi.-Kent L. Rev. 397 (1987); Gerald O'Driscoll, *Justice, Efficiency, and the Economic Analysis of Law: A Comment on Fried*, 9 J. Legal Stud. 355 (1980); Christopher T. Wonnel, *Contract Law and the Austrian School of Economics*, 54 Fordham L. Rev. 507 (1986); Roy Cordato, *Subjective Value, Time Passage, and the Economics of Harmful Effects*, 12 Hamline L. Rev. 229 (1989); Michael E. DeBow, *Markets, Government Intervention, and the Role of Information: An 'Austrian School' Perspective, with an Application to Merger Regulation*, 14 Geo. Mason U.L. Rev. 31 (1991); Thomas C. Arthur, *The Costly Quest for Perfect Competition: Kodak and Nonstructural Market Power*, 69 N.Y.U. L. Rev. 1 (1994); Linda A. Schwartzstein, *An Austrian Economic View of Legal Process*, 55 Ohio St. L. J. 1049 (1994); Linda A. Schwartzstein, *Austrian Economics and the Current Debate Between Critical Legal Studies and Law and Economics*, 20 Hofstra L. Rev. 1105 (1992); and John M. Czarnetzky, *Time, Uncertainty, and the Law of Corporate Reorganization*, 67 Fordham L. Rev. 2939 (1999) which develops an application of Austrian

economics for analysis of corporate bankruptcy. See especially at 3003–4, where the author expresses the view that 'the Austrian economic approach … holds tremendous potential for the profitable study of legal institutions, particularly in fields such as antitrust, intellectual property and corporate law'.

[109] For an excellent summary of this field, see Frederic M. Scherer, 'Market Structure' and Morton I. Kamien 'Market Structure and Innovation', in *The New Palgrave – A Dictionary of Economics* (John Eatwell, Murray Milgate and Peter Newman eds, London: Macmillan 1987).

[110] Schumpeter, supra note 88, ch. VIII. For more on this aspect of Schumpeterian theory see generally William L. Baldwin and John T. Scott, Market Structure and Technological Change (Chur, Switzerland: Harwood Academic 1987).

[111] See, for example, Morton I. Kamien and Nancy L. Schwartz, *Market Structure and Innovation: A Survey*, 13 J. of Econ. Literature 16 (1975).

[112] For reviews of developments in the field, see: Baldwin and Scott supra note 110; Scherer and Ross, supra note 107, ch. 17: 'Market Structure, Patents, and Technological Innovation'; *Evolving Technology and Market Structure – Studies in Schumpeterian Economics* (Arnold Heertje and Mark Perlman eds., Ann Arbor, MI: University of Michigan Press 1990); and Jennifer F. Reinganum, 'The Timing of Innovation', in *Handbook of Industrial Organization* (Richard Schmalensee and Robert D. Willig eds, New York: Elsevier Science 1989).

[113] See: Thomas M. Jorde and David J. Teece, 'Innovation, Cooperation, and Antitrust', in *Antitrust, Innovation, and Competitiveness* 47–63 (Jorde and Teece eds, New York: Oxford University Press 1992); Gutterman, supra note 19; Jonathan B. Baker, *Promoting Innovation Competition Through the Aspen/Kodak Rule*, 7 Geo. Mason U. L. Rev. 495, 508–18 (1999); Richard T. Rapp, *The Misapplication of the Innovation Market Approach to Merger Analysis*, 64 Antitrust L. J. 19 (1995); William J. Baumol and Janusz A. Ordover, 'Antitrust: Source of Dynamic and Static Inefficiencies?', in *Antitrust Innovation and Competitiveness* id. at 85; Sean P. Gates, *Standards, Innovation, and Antitrust: Integrating Innovation Concerns into the Analysis of Collaborative Standard Setting*, 47 Emory L. J. 583, 588 (1998); and *Anticipating the 21st Century: Competition Policy in the New High-tech, Global Marketplace*, supra note 38, ch. 6 at 11–12.

[114] Id.

2. The Austrian Economics Solution and the Property Narrative

2.1 INTRODUCTION

This chapter will further develop the framework for analysis of antitrust-intellectual property clashes.[1] Section 2.2 fleshes out the general methodology of the Austrian school of economics and focuses attention on this school's treatment of the concept of competition while outlining the key differences between Austrian and conventional neoclassical competition theory. Section 2.3 will demonstrate theoretically how an application of the engaging principles of Austrian economics to cases of interaction between competition and innovation will provide some relief for their conflict by narrowing its recognized scope. Section 2.4 will look into a proposed property characterization of the conflict. The property narrative is explained through the different utilitarian justifications for antitrust and intellectual property, and the manner in which they drive such property notions. These notions bear some general implications with respect to solving the conflict and with respect to the previously developed Austrian economics notions.

2.2 THE AUSTRIAN ECONOMICS VIEW OF COMPETITION

Austrian economics is a school of economic theory that originated in the writings of Carl Menger in the second half of the nineteenth century[2] and was further developed by a growing number of subsequent economists who are identified as Austrian or neo-Austrian economists.[3] This section will present some of the compelling features of Austrian economics in general and its treatment of competition in particular.

2.2.1 Austrian Economics: a Pragmatic Doctrine

An important character of Austrian economics, which differentiates it from neoclassical economics, is its descriptive sociological nature. It begins from individual behavior and how it responds to changes in economic circumstances, as opposed to neoclassical economics, which designs a general theoretical model of alleged general applicability (within the boundaries of a specific narrow and often unrealistic set of basic assumptions).[4] Carl Menger described this Austrian notion as 'subjective value theory'. Unlike neoclassical models, Austrians do not offer neat formal models based on a set of strict assumptions which may have little in common with reality. Rather, they start by observing the state of social market behavior, and use these observations as the basis of their scholarship. Austrian economics differs from a behavioral approach in the sense that it does not purport to provide a psychological explanation for the observed patterns,[5] but rather regards them as given.

The realistic aspect of the Austrian approach is well captured in the words of Friedrich Hayek, who noted that 'The economic problem is a problem of making the best use of what resources we have, and not one of what we should do if the situation were different from what it actually is'.[6] This quote reveals the analysis method that underlies Austrian thought, namely, one that adheres to pragmatic market conditions, rather than adopts an imaginary set of unrealistic model conditions. This pragmatic nature is of special importance in a legal setting such as the one in this book. This is because law, as opposed to pure economic theory, is a practical philosophy. Therefore the practical attributes of any legal market model lie in direct relation to its value. This is not to say that legal market models should be strictly constrained to realistic market conditions or valued only according to their adherence to them. However, for many years, antitrust analysis has utilized market models based on assumptions that have little to do with reality. The widespread use of such imaginary models as the norm is puzzling, and should no longer be carried out routinely without questions being asked.[7]

It should be noted that the vexatious nature of much of the current neoclassical economic treatment of antitrust law should not be blamed solely on the contemporary economic theory. Economic theory has come a long way since it focused on the static, rational limited models that will be criticized below. In fact, alternative economic models have been around for well over a hundred years,[8] alongside scholarship that portrayed some of the irreparable fallacies of the Chicago school of economics. However, for many years the economic scholarship tools applied by antitrust commentators have been limited predominantly to the narrow walls of the Chicago school of economics. Therefore, much of the criticism that follows stems from antitrust theory's choice to follow the narrow path attached to one specific school from the wide and robust sphere of economic doctrines.

While Austrian economics doctrine encompasses the treatment of a broad spectrum of market phenomena, this section will focus on a specific realm of Austrian economics, namely its analysis of competition. The Austrian competition doctrine elements will be reviewed below in comparison with its neoclassical counterparts. This will demonstrate how the Austrian economics treatment of competition seems more coherent, convincing and reality consistent in the antitrust arena than the Chicago school of economics. It is therefore concluded that Austrian competition analysis provides a promising alternative to the Chicago school market assumptions.

2.2.2 The Inherent Dynamic Nature of 'Austrian' Competition

The term 'dynamic competition' has come to form the shibboleth of Austrian economists' scholarship.[9] The meaning of this term, which considers competition as a 'succession of events',[10] extends to a number of levels. On the first level, Austrian economics recognizes that economic life goes on in a social and natural environment which constantly changes, and this change alters the date of economic action.[11] The changes are numerous: wars and revolutions are extreme examples; others include increase in population, changes in capital and social trends. Although acknowledging these changes, the Austrians claim they are secondary, as the real engine that keeps the free market in motion comes from the 'new consumers' goods, the new methods of production or transportation, the new markets, the new forms of industrial organization that capitalist enterprise creates.[12]

Thus, competition is treated as an inherently vigorous process in which production methods and markets are ever changing as part of an ongoing struggle between market participants who strive to better their positions. This rivalrous struggle benefits consumers as competing producers come up with innovative products and lower prices in order to gain new customers, maintain the loyalty of existing customers, and maximize sales from their inventories. Prices serve as instrumental signals in this process. Producers set prices and utilize the resulting sales patterns to extract particular facts about the characteristics of the market for their product. This information serves them in the competitive struggle strategy they use in order to try and gain advantage over their competitors.[13]

A useful metaphor that demonstrates the Austrian competition notion is to say that competitive market data regulate market activity and expectations in a manner similar to that in which traffic lights regulate vehicles' interactions through a four-way intersection.[14] Drivers approaching the intersection form expectations on the basis of the traffic light and stop or drive through accordingly. Thus, traffic lights carry information about anticipating which traffic lane will drive into the intersection at a given time, and drivers utilize this information to form expectations and reduce collisions. The obvious analogy to a market context is that market prices summarize the true underlying story of supply and demand conditions. They create some order for market transactions to take place, and assist buyers and sellers in forming standard expectations that are necessary to ensure a sufficiently smooth marketplace.

It is important, however, to note the more abstract level of competition as a discovery process, which is that the game of competition itself changes from day to day, and the information collected by it is used for the purpose of constantly redefining the game arena. To use the traffic lights metaphor again, this will mean that the lights have a built-in electronic eye which records the car flow from the four intersection directions throughout the day and then readjusts the allocation of the right-of-way traffic orders each according to the traffic patterns recorded the day before. This process is beneficial for the drivers since it spares them from time-wasting delays of having to wait for the light to change while the intersection is empty. Another way to look at it is that it renders road usage more efficient as cars arrive at their destination faster.

The Austrian characterizing of 'competition as a discovery process'[15] works in a similar manner. The notion is that the market itself changes over time as part of competitors' efforts to accommodate themselves to the market's desires. This self-adjustment process is far more profound than in the traffic lights example. It includes a variety of phenomena: new products spring up; the production of unsuccessful products is discontinued; advertisement plays a vital role in promoting consumption of less popular products and in building up brand loyalty; new technologies are invented for cheaper production of existing products or for production of new-concept products; commercial enterprises wear different shapes as companies merge, or create subsidiaries as part of their competitive strategies. Prices also play a part in these corrective action dynamics: they are reduced as a reaction to numerous market conditions such as falling demand, an attempt to penetrate a saturated market niche, the need to clear up storage space, when production costs become cheaper and so on; and they are raised for many other reasons such as increasing demand, an effort to alter the image of a product to cater for a more discerning clientele and so on. However, pricing is a secondary mechanism in a wider process that is more active in nature. Competition is then the combined process of these two levels of correction along with the 'noise' created by the exogenous changes mentioned earlier such as wars, social trends, changes in population and so on.

The notion of dynamic competition includes two facets. First, that competition is a general term for a *process* rather than a market structure. Second, that the nature of this competitive process is that firms survive the competitive market struggle not only by manipulating prices and trade practices within set product and technological parameters, but mostly by resorting to original ways of competing. These new ways of competing include technological innovation (resulting in new products, cheaper ways of making existing products and so on), original advertising campaigns, product differentiation, setting new consumer trends, appealing to new markets (geographical or different domestic consumer markets). The last notion creates an association between competition and innovation, because if competition is all about change, it is new ideas and production methods which facilitate change. Indeed, even some non-Austrian scholars have already noted that it is important for law in general to provide incentives to innovate. Recent antitrust discourse has stressed this notion in two ways. The first focuses on the fact that antitrust law should recognize the importance of leaving sufficient incentives to innovate. The second stresses a causal association between the two, namely that competition promotes innovation.[16] However, adopting the Austrian economic approach yields a slightly different argument. The argument promoted here is rather that innovation forms part of the definition of competition. It is not that 'competition promotes innovation' or vice versa, but rather that competition *is* innovation, or put more precisely: that innovation is a crucial element of competition.

It should be reiterated that in speaking of 'dynamic' competition we do not refer solely to innovation, let alone to legally protected innovation such as intellectual property. The term 'dynamic' rather refers to a variety of dynamic competitive activities such as advertising, undercutting and improving (differentiating) the goods produced, in addition to exogenous market changes (such as social trends, wars, and recessions). These activities are obviously somewhat consistent with the dictionary definition of innovation, which is 'the introduction of something new'.[17] Thus while innovation is one common way to improve or distinguish a produced good, this is not necessarily the only way (for example, a common competition strategy is to offer the very same product in a higher quality version; many advertising campaigns contain no new concepts). Furthermore, many obviously novel products or ideas do not succeed in obtaining IP protection. This is because in order to gain such protection, innovative ideas (in the case of patents) or works (in the case of copyrights) must fulfil certain formal criteria as required by the IP laws. These requirements may refer to the degree of novelty compared with the prior art, the subject matter of the invention, the originality of the work and so on.

One reason why the dynamic notion of competition is so attractive, is probably that it is close to the natural language (as opposed to economic science) use of the word competition. Any layperson or dealer would probably agree that competition is the 'action of endeavoring to gain what another endeavors to gain at the same time'.[18] Such a notion is indeed inherently dynamic.

In addition to its tidal nature, the result of such a struggle is usually unpredictable. Consider the term 'competition' in a sports or poetry competition.[19] In these competition scenarios we do not know in advance what the end results will be; this is in fact what characterizes the scenario as a competition. These notions are far more intuitive than the neoclassical competition notions that depict a static competition equilibrium at a specific point where the demand and supply curves intersect and the price equals the marginal cost of the last unit produced. Under this competition model there are no winners. Ultimately, everyone will sell the same product at the same price and will not be able to influence price levels that are set at marginal cost level. This competition notion deals only with a snapshot of a hypothetical finishing line, and pays little attention to the process that brought about the end result. In other words, it strips competition from the whole dimension of time.

A significant affirmation for the strength of the Austrian dynamic competition notion can be found in recent texts written by the U.S. antitrust authorities. Some 60 years after Schumpeter wrote about 'The Process of Creative Destruction', the Department of Justice Antitrust Division is expressing similar beliefs in embracing innovation as an inseparable part of competition.[20] In fact today, even outside the domestic antitrust institutions, there seems to be growing consensus that globalization, new markets, and technological developments are indeed the engines of economic growth.[21] It should also be noted that some recent antitrust literature has begun to proclaim the importance of dynamic (rather than static) notions of competition as a more accurate tool for addressing antitrust.[22] Some market practitioners (non-lawyers) have expressed similar opinions in hearings held by the Federal Trade Commission.[23] However, these notions have not been presented in conjunction with the formal Austrian economic theory, which provides them with an orderly theoretical framework. Furthermore, they have not been directly applied in the antitrust–IP conflict realm.

The Austrian treatment of competition is remarkably different from its neoclassical counterpart. Neoclassical economic analysis of competitive market focuses on the notion of a determinable static equilibrium ('Walrasian equilibrium'), in which all the equilibrium variables can be (and are) simultaneously computed, and there is a minimal number of known exogenous variables.[24] This market equilibrium lies at the heart of neoclassical microeconomic theory. Conversely, the Austrian competition market theory, as Hayek has put it, 'is by its nature a dynamic process whose essential characteristics are assumed away by the assumptions underlying static analysis'.[25] Austrian economics does not purport to compute any 'equilibrium' market variables because the essence of competition is taken to be the dynamic pattern in which it comes about, rather than equilibrium.

2.2.3 The Role of Entrepreneurship in Austrian Competition

Entrepreneurship is the central element of Austrian competition analysis, which stresses its importance as the prime engine of the economic process.[26] Entrepreneurs play a very important function in the competitive market: they react to and create the dynamic change in the market; they are the role models of individual leadership; and they provide the new opportunities, ideas, and new blood that refresh the 'bourgeois stratum'.[27] The basic notion is that the market keeps changing as new opportunities, production methods and ideas are discovered or invented by entrepreneurs who introduce them to the market in an effort to gain a competitive edge and make profits. Therefore the argument is that entrepreneurial activity is always competitive and that competitive activity is always entrepreneurial, namely that entrepreneurship and competitiveness are two sides of the same coin.[28]

The Austrian treatment of entrepreneurship as an engine of competition distinguishes it from neoclassical economic analysis. One of the three fundamental principles of mainstream economic analysis of law is that 'resources tend to gravitate toward their most valuable uses' as markets drive out any unexploited profit opportunities.[29] Neoclassical price theory's competitive equilibrium thus assumes no unexploited profit opportunities. As a result, the concept of entrepreneurship is practically expunged from neoclassical economics competition analysis.[30]

It should be noted that some scholars have been arguing along these lines for quite a while now – that competition is an unlimited sequence of moves and responses in which profits can be seen as a motive for initiation and imitation of economic efforts. Thus, they argue, competition is the means for ensuring that entrepreneurial forces are mobilized, which enhances both economic efficiency and consumer welfare.[31] Here too (as in the competition-innovation association argument) the adoption of an Austrian world-view hones the argument in another direction. The basic argument promoted here is that entrepreneurship is an element of competition. The process itself is inherently one of entrepreneurial conduct. It is a descriptive notion, namely, that competition by definition comprises a strong entrepreneurial element. It is not a means for encouraging entrepreneurial activity, but rather it is the latter that makes it what it is.

The entrepreneurial notion of competition, as a developed private case of the previously mentioned general dynamic notions, is likewise linked to innovation notions, much more tightly. Entrepreneurs are innovative by definition because they occupy a previously undiscovered market niche, which means they are acting in a territory that is new in some sense. Here too, the innovative nature of their activity will not automatically award them legal IP protection, as the latter is subject to more exacting legal requirements.

2.2.4 On the Fallacies of the Neoclassical Competition Model

The value of Austrian economics as a compelling and useful theoretical tool in an antitrust context becomes clearer when we review the practical fallacies of the neoclassical theory, many of which were observed by Austrian scholars. In addition to the fallacy of the static model mentioned above, there are a number of other senses in which the neoclassical competition model is far removed from reality. The first is the *differentiation of products*. The neoclassical model assumes no product differentiation.[32] The assumption is that all producers make the same widget (for example, the same bread), and consumers are indifferent between the bread made by different manufacturers. However, in reality products are differentiated. Products of two producers are never exactly alike. Consumers will almost always prefer a certain product over its counterpart, either because of its brand, because they like the colors of its packaging better, because they are already familiar with one of the two and so on. In fact, the mere fact that products by different producers leave the plant at different places[33] renders them different, as it implies, for example, different shipping costs to the same store locations. Furthermore, even the same product has a different subjective value in different contexts. Thus for example, people will probably prefer a yoghurt container with a more distant expiry date to one of the same brand but with a closer expiry date. Or to take another example, no two 1994 Toyota Corolla vehicles are exactly the same since their mileage and maintenance history distinguish them. Even in the case of two brand new cars, consumers will prefer to buy from a friendly dealer rather than from one notorious for his/her discourteousness. These examples prove that no matter how narrowly a 'market' will be defined, consumers will almost always differentiate in some way between similar products.

A second demonstration of the impractical nature of the neoclassical model is reflected in the *separation of markets* assumption. In reality, markets are hardly ever clearly separated.[34] Hence, the conception of the economic system as divisible into distinct markets for separate commodities seems to be more present in the imagination of the economists than in real life.[35] In real life, markets appear to move in mysterious ways that are not well defined. There is always a possibility, one that often materializes, of the existence of some interdependence between products belonging to so-called separate markets. Examples are numerous: many products serve as components in the production of other products; many are economic complements (meaning that a fall in their price causes the quantity demanded of other products to rise, for example, vehicles and vehicle insurance policies or cameras and processing film); some innovative products affect traditional products from a market that is thought to be 'separate' (for example, it can be said that personal computers are replacing transistor radios as a means of receiving radio broadcasts); growing demand for Kentucky Fried Chicken may affect the demand for a whole variety of other products or services such as paper buckets, weight loss services, cardiologists or acne skin products to name a few. In short, there is always some interdependence between products. And as if domestic products' interdependence is not complex enough, today's global trade opens the door for an array of interdependence effects between national markets.[36] Note, however, that the latter is recognized by antitrust policy, which extends antitrust standards' enforcement to conduct by international enterprises whose activities affect the domestic U.S. market.

A third sense in which neoclassical theory appears to be removed from reality is its *assumption of a given consumer demand curve*, that is, a given demand for a product at different price levels. This leads to the traditional neoclassical monopoly characterization according to which if in a certain time point T_1 a producer charged a certain price P_1 for his/her product, then once he/she becomes a monopolist at another point in time T_2 he/she would restrict production and would charge a higher monopoly price P_2 since the monopolist presumably knows the demand function for its product.[37] But this presumes that the demand curve is given and constant, which is never the case in reality.[38] Demand curves are hypothetical academic instruments that assume that everything else remains equal except for the commodity price. This is in direct contrast to the more realistic view of a competitive system that keeps changing, both due to exogenous reasons such as trends or seasonal changes and also due to endogenous reasons such as the existence of substitutive alternative products. In other words, it is never the case in real life that 'everything else remains equal'. As Hayek put it 'Indeed, all those aggregate demand and supply curves with which we like to operate are not really objectively given facts, but results of the process of competition going on all the time'.[39] Therefore those hypothetical supply and demand functions are constantly changing due to the dynamic nature of competition. So it is not possible to determine which portion of the price or quantity change is really attributable to the so-called 'monopolistic' effect, and what part of it is attributable to other changes. A further complicating cause is, of course, the empirically unsupported assumption that the monopolist is familiar with the details that make up this hypothetical demand curve.[40]

A fourth weakness of neoclassical price theory is, as its name suggests, its disproportionate focus on price mechanisms as signals of competition. While the Chicago school parlance speaks of 'producing what the consumer wants, *at the price he wants*', the analysis itself focuses on price and output, shying away from any serious treatment of how closely the consumer's wishes are met.[41] The focus on price mechanisms derives mainly from the fact that prices are far easier to quantify numerically than consumer preferences, which are probably quite hopeless in this regard. Nevertheless, a failure to treat the non-price competition mechanisms is inexcusable[42] because, as argued earlier, the preponderance of competition elements are non-price ones (for example, advertisements or differentiation of products). Furthermore, even though some of these elements are reflected through price (for example, advertisement or development costs may well boost a product's price), neoclassical price theory does not acknowledge this pricing detail.

The focus on price competition alone seems to have especially erratic consequences in an IP context. The granting of an IP right on an element of a commercially produced good which consumers find significantly useful, will almost inevitably raise the price demanded for the good above its reasonable price.[43] Beyond the formal justifying reason for such a price rise, namely that IPR holders seek to recoup their R & D costs for the innovative element, lies a far more practical reason. A patentee producer of an innovative product that consumers clearly prefer will simply raise the price as much as he/she can. Where consumers are excited about the protected element, it might indeed mean a significant price rise that goes well beyond recouping the development costs.

It is, however, important to note that there is a trade-off here. Consumers are getting a product they are happier with and are willing to pay the extra price to enjoy it (else they would still be consuming the traditional cheaper alternative products they were using before). It is this trade-off that is totally overlooked by a price-only competition analysis, and that may unrightfully render the IP price-raising mechanism iniquitous under such an analysis. Indeed, in some cases IPRs might lead to results that may be characterized as unfavorable, for example, where adequate substitutes for the innovative product are not available and producers utilize IPRs for colossal price rises over long periods of time, pocketing enormous revenues. However, it is important to bear in mind the trade-off nature of the price increase.

These notions reveal certain profound practical shortcomings of the neoclassical competition model,[44] which have led Austrian scholars to criticize this model, some going as far as describing it as 'entirely remote from all that is relevant to an understanding of the process of competition' and similar characterizations.[45] The strength of the Austrian economics competition model that is promoted is that it describes the market process for what it is, rather than analyses an unrealistic model of academic assumptions made for the purpose of allowing a formal mathematical solution. It seems that the value of such a mathematical solution and its implications is questionable since it has little to do with reality. This conclusion is even more important in a legal context because law is a practical philosophy, and therefore it is suggested that only so much weight should be given to non-practical models.

2.3 NOTIONS NARROWING THE IP–ANTITRUST CONFLICT

2.3.1 Austrian Economics Drawing Competition and Innovation Together

As mentioned before, Austrian economics regards innovation as an important element of competition; namely, it is the engine of the competitive market. It considers innovation as a phenomenon that constantly introduces new things and thus forms the core of a dynamic competitive process, and creates a mechanism that reduces the long-term scope of any traditional monopoly.[46] This association between competition and innovation seems to go beyond a synonymous nature in their meanings. Competition and innovation are self-fertilizing in the sense that not only does innovation drive competition but also a vigorous process of competition stimulates even further innovation. These notions have been supported by empirical work. Thus, for example, such work has suggested that competition in product markets as well as in R&D activities is likely to promote innovation and growth[47] in domestic and international markets.[48] Convincing observations have also been made to the effect that major antitrust statutes (the Sherman Act of 1890 and the Clayton and Federal Trade Commission Acts of 1914) inadvertently enhanced the incentives for large firms to invest in new technologies that promoted innovation.[49] Furthermore, empirical evidence also supports the existence of such a symbiotic relationship from the negative point of view. It has been suggested that the linkage between innovation and IPR protection may play a weaker role in less-competitive markets, namely that the innovation-boosting effect of IPRs becomes greater the more competitive the market process is.[50] In short, Austrian analyses as well as empirical observations both imply a symbiotic association between innovation and competition in two ways: a synonymous way and a causal way.

Since, as mentioned in the previous chapter,[51] one of intellectual property's major justifications is the promotion of innovation, it follows that IP doctrine and competition (taken in the Austrian sense) share innovation as a common basic premise. This is because if competition and innovation are synonymous and mutually advancing, and IP's main goal is the promotion of innovation, then theoretically, it follows in a second-order manner that intellectual property should encourage competition. This view is not purely theoretical – similar notions can be found in views expressed by the Department of Justice Antitrust Division and the Federal Trade Commission, although they do not make explicit reference to Austrian economics.[52] However, the next section will show why this theoretical notion encounters some difficulties in real-life scenarios.

2.3.2 The Faults of the IP Mechanism

The shortcomings of IP as an innovation-promoting mechanism

The promotion of innovation is often mentioned as a major justification for the IP institution. This reveals an underlying assumption that IP protection enhances incentives to innovate because of the greater rewards awaiting innovators who would be able to secure legal protection for their innovations and thus exclude others from making use of them throughout the term of the legal protection. However, this argument is problematic because the correlation between intellectual property and incentive for innovation does not necessarily endure unchanged under different degrees of IP protection. In other words, it is one thing to argue that the initial establishment of an IP institution generally encourages innovation, as opposed to a legal scenario that lacks any IP institutions. It is yet another to argue that the greater the defined scope of IP protection, the greater are the incentives for innovation. The latter argument may in fact be inconsistent with some empirical findings.[53] It may well be that from some degree of IP protection, any increase in the breadth of such protection will be counterproductive; that is, it will deter further innovation rather than promote it. This is because the innovation process is sequential in its nature; namely, it works so that one innovation builds on another.[54] Therefore an overly broad interpretation of patent rights[55] can have adverse effects on innovation in the long run, because a whole bundle of follow-up innovations are held at bay, prevented from further development until the legal protection expires. Furthermore, the longer the duration of the set legal protection, the longer will the delay in innovation subsist. The conclusion of this argument is that there is a need to strike a balance within IP protection itself to make sure that the scope of protection does not deter innovation.[56]

Note that the argument made here is not against the IP institution root and branch. Feasibly, some deterrence of innovation should still be acceptable if the overall benefit of IP still outweighs this aspect of hindrance of third-party innovation. Note also that it is practically impossible to pinpoint the optimal protection scope, namely one that maximizes individual innovation incentives without discouraging third-party innovation incentives. Furthermore, it is even complex to define this optimal point theoretically. First, note that for determining the optimal protection scope we must normatively weigh the benefit from increased individual incentive to innovate against any loss resulting from disincentives for third-party innovative activity as it is possible that at some levels, increasing protection further will increase individual incentives to innovate but stifle third-party incentives to do the same. The question of how to balance these two conflicting notions is a difficult one. Second, bear in mind that promotion of innovation is only one of the justifications for the IP institute, the others being desert-for-labor and personhood arguments.[57] These two additional aspects relate to individual inventors. They focus around the individual innovator – his/her reward (desert-for-labor) and his/her self-definition through his/her non-tangible work (personhood) – and pay no direct attention to third parties. Therefore the aforementioned optimal balance between individual and third-party innovation is much dependent upon which IP justification is considered to be the dominant one. On the one hand, a focus on the innovation justification will yield an optimal protection point which is more concerned with third-party innovation than with individual incentives, namely a generally lesser IP protection. On the other hand, a focus on the two individual-oriented justifications will yield an optimal protection point that is more concerned with individual incentives, namely a generally greater IP protection. The argument here is basically that although an IP mechanism surely promotes innovation to a certain extent, it may yield some undesirable byproducts in this very same respect, namely, a suppression of certain innovation aspects that are unwanted by policy makers (although not necessarily by certain market participants).

While it is practically impossible to determine empirically whether current IP protection levels are higher or lower than optimal,[58] there are two rationales that suggest rather that the former scenario is the prevailing one, namely that current IP protection levels are higher than optimal. The first is the existence of a substantial number of antitrust–IP conflict litigations. Since, as suggested earlier, innovation and competition are closely associated, this reality suggests that current IP protection does impair innovation and competition to some degree.[59] A second rationale suggesting that current IP protection is excessive stems from the fact that certain interest groups seek to gain from an overly broad IP protection; that is, established rich enterprises which have large IPR portfolios and make frequent use of their IPRs are more politically powerful than the interest groups that sustain most of the damage from such overprotection, namely private consumers and new enterprises seeking to enter a market niche. This imbalance is likely to bias IP legislation towards an overprotection error, rather than an underprotection one, in light of the more powerful lobbying efforts of the more financially secure group. This argument includes a generalization, as indeed some IP owners are not financially powerful to begin with or they offer inventions that are commercially useful for a very brief period if at all, and vice versa some established corporations stand to lose out from hindrance of follow-up innovation. Nevertheless it is suggested here that the aggregate lobbying power of those in favor of broader IP protection is likely to be superior to that of those who are opposed to it.

Another dent in the argument that intellectual property is a major instrument for successfully promoting innovation lies in empirical arguments that have been made that patents are not the strongest incentive for innovation.[60] These arguments are especially convincing since they have been made by private market participants who are already somewhat predisposed to favor overprotection of IP due to the huge profits it promises. These empirical arguments may seem surprising to scholars who are familiar with the long-time predominance of innovation promotion as a major justification for IP protection. However, they should not come as such a surprise. The innovation-promoting justification is a powerful self-serving claim for any market actors who see to gain from stronger IP protection, and this is probably a major reason for its continuing predominance.

In conclusion, this section has raised doubts as to how well IP mechanisms indeed promote innovation. Furthermore, it is argued that IP protection that is too broad may impair innovation, and that the protection levels in the current legal climate are probably excessive. These arguments open the door to a process of fine-tuning IP protection in order to bring it closer to a point of maximizing market innovation. This process will be developed further in section 2.4.

The problem of unintended consequences of human action in an IP context

Austrian economics pays special attention to the phenomenon that is often referred to as 'the unintended consequences of human actions' as part of the 'surprise' or uncertainty feature of competition.[61] This phenomenon can be described on two levels – the level of individual human action and the governmental interventionist coordination level. On the individual level, the argument is that in a dynamic competition scenario, there will always be unintended byproducts from the individual actions of market participants. In application to the IP context the argument asserts that the utilization of intellectual property in a market-restricting manner is an inevitable byproduct of producers' cognitive goal of maximizing profits. IP owners do not specifically aim to restrict competition. Their only cognitive goal is to maximize their revenues so as to render their businesses more profitable, but the conjunction of this goal with the structure of the IP mechanism invokes detrimental consequences. On the governmental level, this argument will be adapted to claim that governmental effort to coordinate the market activity problem, namely market failure in information products, through the institution of intellectual property will have some unintended consequences, because as a rule, centralized attempts to coordinate a market problem by an exact solution tend to invoke unintended social consequences.[62] This is because of the dynamic nature of a market. A clear-cut static coordination mechanism such as IP is inherently incompatible with an ever-changing dynamic market environment, as the former is static and the latter is dynamic. This is a matter of definition, because in a changing market, a perfect solution for one point in time may become decreasingly appropriate later on in time as crucial circumstances change. This argument therefore suggests that a *pattern* solution is probably better than an exact solution, since a pattern solution is a dynamic one that fits the dynamic market reality.

2.4 THE PROPERTY NARRATIVE OF THE ANTITRUST–IP CONFLICT

2.4.1 The Property Account of Antitrust

Competition as a public good

An economic public good (as distinguished from a private good) is a good that benefits society as a whole and cannot be fully accounted for by the natural market processes.[63] Competition can be characterized as what economists call a 'public good' because without an antitrust mechanism in place competitors tend towards collusive and monopolizing conducts which yield a sub-optimal level of competition in the market. Furthermore, competition is also consistent with the intuitive linguistic meaning of the term 'public good'[64] in the sense that competition is commonly thought of as an environment that is beneficial to all members of society as a whole because it maximizes the economy's output and gives consumers what they want. The public good nature of competition has been mentioned briefly in some of the contemporary antitrust literature,[65] and we shall now develop this further for the purpose of the present discussion.

Public goods form a specific type of economic goods that differ from private goods in the unique characteristics of the benefits that they confer. More specifically, there are three aspects that are typically used to describe the benefits of public goods. The first one commonly cited as typical of public goods benefits is *non-rivalry of consumption* (interchangeably called indivisibility of benefits in some sources).[66] A good is non-rival or indivisible when its consumption does not diminish the possibility of its simultaneous consumption by another. In other words, everyone in the market can enjoy a non-rival good at the same time without detracting from the consumption opportunities still available to others. Typical examples of non-rival goods include benefits derived from pollution control devices, weather monitoring stations, and daylight (when a view is unobstructed). A second commonly accepted aspect of public goods is *non-excludability* of their benefits. The non-excludability character means that once the good is provided, it is not possible economically to exclude others from utilizing it. In other words, nobody has exclusive control over a non-excludable good once it has been provided. Typical examples of non-excludable goods include firework displays, street lighting and pollution control devices. Finally, *absence of free disposal* is the third distinctive feature mentioned in conjunction with the benefits of public goods,[67] although less often than the previous two characteristics. This feature means that when a public good is provided, agents may not have the freedom not to consume the good. The common example of this feature is national defense.

Traditionally, economic analysis regards public goods as a source of a social dilemma because their unique benefit characteristics give rise to the so-called 'free-rider' problem, namely the reliance of market agents on the provision of public goods by others.[68] This reliance is made possible by the non-rivalry and non-excludability nature of these goods, which make it possible for agents to extract benefits from public goods provided by others. In other words, public goods confer benefits on people other than those who provided them, and this feature evokes people who consciously benefit from such goods to rely on others to bear the costs of providing them. The result of such reliance is a sub-optimal provision of the public good by the market forces, as most market agents expect people to enjoy the good provided by others at no cost, and thus have little incentive to produce it for this reason, and also because they will not be able to recoup their costs if they choose to provide the good themselves.

Competition can feasibly be portrayed as a public good because its benefits display all the characteristics of a public good outlined above.

Competition is non-rivalrous in the sense that everybody can enjoy the benefits of a competitive environment at the same time – different consumers and different market entrants profit simultaneously from a competitive environment. Competition is non-exclusive because once a market is dynamically competitive, it is inherently non-exclusive, as new participants are free to try to enter the market and all goods are sold in such an environment. Competition is also non-disposable since its benefits are impelled upon all market participants and consumers who live in a competitive environment. It should also be noted that existing public goods analysis has not been limited to tangible goods. Economic contributions include a public good analysis of abstract goods such as income distribution[69] and a system of law.[70] Therefore a portrayal of competition as a public good is probably not as avant-garde as it may initially seem.

Anticompetitive conduct patterns as externalities

Externalities are economic phenomena whose exact definition is controversial and that are closely related to public goods. Externalities can generally be defined as scenarios in which the action of one economic agent influences the utility or production function of another and no compensation mechanism exists, which therefore calls for government intervention.[71] Where an externality is present, the cost of a certain activity is external to its decision-making process[72] and this results in a market failure. In effect, the notion of an externality is somewhat diametrical to that of a public good because an externality is more like a public bad – it describes an activity that exerts harm on others, although it is not necessarily harmful to the public as a whole.[73] While producers of a public good face difficulty in recouping the full costs of supplying it, the 'producers'[74] of an externality do not bear the full costs sustained by others (in other words, society has a problem in making the externality creators realize the social costs of their behavior). A classic example of an externality is the case of pollution, where a producer's production lines cause pollution as a byproduct. Unless there are effective legal rules preventing pollution, the producer will fail to take into consideration the pollution harm sustained by residents in the vicinity of the factory. This will result in market failure because the producer will produce too much pollution, which will inflict a negative cost on society that nobody will be accountable for. An effective pollution controlling legal rule can solve this problem.

Anticompetitive conduct which violates antitrust laws can be portrayed as an externality, because the monopolizing or collusive conduct inflicts damage on consumers who were not consenting parties in reaching the decisions to collude or monopolize that led to the damage. The culprits arguably do not take into account the damage to consumers in reaching the decision to engage in unlawful anticompetitive conduct. This state of affairs forms the justification for the legal system's intervention by way of antitrust laws, just as the legal system intervenes in pollution scenarios through nuisance, torts and environmental laws. Metaphorically, monopolizers and market conspirators pollute the 'clean' competitive market atmosphere with conduct that inflicts harm on other market participants, namely consumers, and antitrust laws intervene to prevent such conduct by making them realize the costs of such injurious behavior. The metaphor can be taken even further: environmentalists often argue that land is abused because it is treated as personal property instead of being understood as part of a community to which we belong.[75] Antitrust laws induce market actors to realize that the market, just like land, is a community to which we all belong, and therefore the conduct patterns allowed within it will be limited to prevent excessive damage to the market community.

Before proceeding any further, it is important to acknowledge a number of valid critiques that have been made with regard to the public goods theory. The first criticism is the lack of a clear-cut dichotomy between public and private goods.[76] The argument is that there is a whole continuum between public and private goods, rather than definite categorization of all goods' benefits as either public or private. Thus, the public–private good spectrum hosts a variety of so-called 'impure' public goods, which are goods whose benefits are to a varying extent partially rival and/or partially excludable.[77]

A second criticism focuses on whether an allegedly public good indeed has positive consequences for everyone. This critique questions whether a public good is in fact, as its name suggests, good for everyone and suggests that such a case is an unrealistic hypothetical scenario. Traces of similar doubts in specific application to competition can be found in legal declarations such as the one that observed that the 'antitrust goal is to protect competition, not competitors'.[78] Such quotes reflect a reality in which some market participants, namely competitors, do in fact realize certain negative consequences from competition and antitrust as its guardian. It should therefore be noted that even competition which may seem a widely accepted public good is not necessarily a pure public good, because perhaps not everyone benefits from it – some producers would rather monopolize than face competition if that was a legal option.

A third critique which is an extension of the second one and is consistent with the dynamic notions promoted so far, argues that all goods, whether more or less private or public in nature (since pure public or pure private cases seem rare), constantly change with respect to their degree of 'privateness or publicness' since people's values and evaluations change.[79] This critique is highly convincing because indeed social values do change, and the change in social climate leads to changes in the law, as democratically elected legislators strive to please their electorate. It is these value changes that probably account for much of the swings of the pendulum in antitrust enforcement (and in antitrust–IP decision cases). Thus, for example, during the Great Depression, competition was considered less desirable, which explains notions like the one expressed in the Appalachian Coal case that under certain dire social circumstances the preservation of competition becomes less important.[80]

Finally, a fourth criticism emphasizes the hidden normative element within public good theory, namely that this theory inevitably contains a *normative* element.[81] The argument that everyone will be better off with a larger supply of a certain so-called public good (for example, competition, innovation, or highways) is inherently a normative rather than an economic argument. From an economic point of view, market processes produce a good in a certain quantity. The argument that this market-set yield of a good is suboptimal, namely the basic argument of public goods theory, is a normative one which must be accounted for rather than be assumed as a given. Along these lines it may be questionable whether indeed competition was under-supplied prior to the initiation of antitrust laws (or whether the current degree of competition is suboptimal in countries that are yet to introduce antitrust laws). The answer to these questions will, again, be normative, because the optimal level of dynamic competition may be subject to different normative interpretations. The extreme libertarian view takes this fourth critique even further to argue that even to the extent that public goods (as previously defined) do exist, production in the public sector is neither necessary nor sufficient for the efficient production of public goods. This view emphasizes the fact that empirically many public goods are successfully produced in the private sector (for example, private radio stations), and many of the goods the government actually does produce do not correspond to the economic definition of public goods.[82] This criticism can be used to support the argument that public goods theory is both inadequate and inappropriate as an explanation of public expenditure on so-called 'public goods'.[83] Note, however, that this criticism loses some of its power in the germane examples of antitrust and innovative or original works as public goods because in these cases it is not the government who supplies these public goods, but rather the market processes themselves. The governmental intervention merely takes the form of establishing general conduct-regulating rules that create private property rules (as will be discussed further in the next section), and therefore it is subject to this libertarian critique to a lesser degree.

The property solution paradigm

The narrative of competition as a public good and of anticompetitive conduct patterns as externalities sets the pretext for delineating antitrust laws as a property solution for the problems of suboptimal competition levels implied by this narrative. The causal association between both public goods and externalities on the one hand and property rights on the other has been acknowledged in the past. Political theory scholarship on the origins of property rights has argued that the problem of public goods provides governments with an incentive to grant and enforce property rights because the establishment of a well-defined property rights regime expropriates so-called 'public goods' from the public sphere and transforms them into private goods.[84] This shift from a public to a private good takes place once governments decide to protect the property rights of right-holders over these goods.[85] The emergence of property rights was thus explained as a collective instrument for transforming public goods into private goods in an effort to solve problems of underprovision of public goods.[86] A similar correlation has been argued between externalities and property rights, namely that externalities and property rights are instrumentally related. The argument is that the main allocative function of property rights is the internalization of beneficial and harmful effects of individual conduct on third parties, effects that by definition are not fully internalized in an externality scenario.[87]

Buying into this taking notion of property rights as a remedy for public good and externality scenarios and the problems they entail requires a credible framework of antitrust laws as a scheme that creates a property regime, a task which will now be assumed. The meaning of the term 'property right' is obscure. Indeed some skeptics have suggested that the category of property rights as such is no longer an important category in legal theory.[88] However, I believe that property rights as a state of affairs do exist wherever two requirements are met: an object of ownership can be identified (abstract or tangible) and there are conditions that identify who own it.[89] Since antitrust laws meet these two requirements, they clearly protect competition through a property mechanism: they bestow an identified property right, namely, the right to a competitive environment, upon an identifiable group, which is the market participants. The characterization of antitrust laws as conferring property rights is not entirely new. It has been acknowledged that antitrust laws grant consumers the right to buy at competitive prices.[90] However, the notion advocated here is wider, namely that antitrust laws grant all market participants[91] a private property right to a competitive environment in the wide dynamic competition sense of the term that is not limited to price elements. A primary indicator for the accuracy of the property paradigm suggested here is revealed, as in most property stories, through the remedies' side of the story, namely the prevalence of injunctive relief and ordering decree remedies in antitrust cases.[92] Courts issue injunctions quite readily in successful antitrust suits[93] while they do not necessarily enforce contractual provisions stipulating specific performance or other injunctive remedies in other commercial or contractual contexts.[94] It is well established that pecuniary remedies are the primary remedial form in contract or commercial contexts,[95] while injunctions or specific performance remedies are the classic instance of a property rule.

The notion that antitrust laws create a property right in an abstract good (competitive environment) should not form an obstacle to their property portrayal. Legal systems have long recognized property rights in abstract goods, for example in the case of patent rights, where the law recognizes property rights in ideas.[96] A helpful analogy is to think of antitrust laws as entitling people to a competitive environment clean of monopolizing or collusive pollutants in the same manner that certain environmental laws grant people rights to the enjoyment of a reasonably quiet and clean environment. In both cases, the right-holders are entitled to protection of their rights by injunctions, which serve as indicators for the property nature of the right.

The fact that antitrust laws wear a communal cloak in the sense that they are granted to everyone at the same time is not inconsistent with their private property characterization. Although traditionally communal property might not have been the favorable form of property in America,[97] notions of communal private property rights are by no means a new concept,[98] and the private nature of the right conferred by antitrust is maintained because under U.S. law any injured individual can bring an antitrust suit (there is no need to join other injured individuals to the suit). The duality in the methods of initiating antitrust suits highlights another aspect of the property rights created by antitrust laws – their dual nature. On the one hand, antitrust suits can be brought by the Department of Justice and the Federal Trade Commission. In this case, the property right created by antitrust can be characterized as a trust where the beneficiaries are market participants injured by anticompetitive conduct, and the trustee protecting their interests is the Department of Justice or the Federal Trade Commission. On the other hand, U.S. law allows for the option of private antitrust suits. In this case the property right to a competitive environment is exercised directly by individuals rather than through a trust mechanism of the type mentioned above.

The property rights conferred by competition are clearly inalienable.[99] Corporations cannot negotiate these rights with consumers – they cannot offer them financial benefits in return for a waiver of their right to bring antitrust suits against them. Similarly, the beneficiaries of antitrust rights cannot willingly sell or waive them, even for a consideration, because the administrative agencies can always step in themselves and prosecute which voids the sale or waiver by the beneficiaries. Therefore these rights are practically non-transferable and non-saleable. Furthermore, the right to certain competitive market standards is non-relinquishable and cannot be lost because they are set by law. The inalienable nature of the rights created by antitrust may seem to raise another conceptual obstacle to their perception as property-creating, however this is probably not the case since a plausible rationale may be offered for their inalienable feature.

While legal scholars are often hooked on the traditional common law notion that property law always proscribes restraints on property rights alienability, modern treatment of the inalienability issue recognizes a variety of less common cases of inalienable property rights.[100] Existing literature has nowhere argued that an inalienable character denies the rights of their property nature;[101] instead it provided explanations for the less common inalienability scenario. Inalienability was treated within one of two approaches. The first is a market methodology, which views the market as theoretically all-encompassing. The market methodology offers two justifications for inalienability that are interesting for our case: as a means for resolving externality problems and the market failure they entail,[102] which produces an inefficient equilibrium;[103] and a paternalistic justification[104] where the person furthers his/her long-run welfare goals by forbidding short-term transactions ('self paternalism') or where everyone is better off by forbidding transactions ('true paternalism'). The second approach is the 'personhood' or 'human flourishing' approach,[105] which views inalienability as justified where it better serves human flourishing to decommodify certain goods by rendering them inalienable.[106]

Antitrust laws seem to be consistent with all three of these inalienability justifications. Antitrust laws answer an externality problem presented by anticompetitive conduct.[107] They are inherently tinted with paternalism because they presuppose their action as rendering consumers better-off,[108] and because their mechanism is paternalistic: the question of whether antitrust rights have been violated is ultimately determined by public institutions, the administrative branches that decide whether to prosecute and the judicial branch which ascertains the case. The state has a direct interest in monitoring antitrust, as reflected in the criminal nature of antitrust laws, in that administrative agencies can bring a suit, and in the fact that antitrust cases are not arbitrable and thus must be heard in public courts. And finally, antitrust discourse contains narratives that view antitrust laws as promoting human flourishing through their protection of individual freedom and entrepreneurship and economic opportunity for all.[109] In short, the inalienable nature of the rights conferred by antitrust does not contradict their property nature, and can be justified on the same grounds for inalienability suggested in other property contexts.

The property story of antitrust laws may seem inconsistent with a Blackstonian absolutist view of property rights[110] because it eats away at the more traditional property rights of the individuals subject to it, namely their rights to use their tangible property in any manner they choose to satisfy their own preferences through market exchange. However, the suggested antitrust property paradigm is consistent with welfare liberalism property notions, namely notions that suggest that the interests protected by private property include personal independence, individual autonomy and personal flourishing.[111] It depicts a private property right that accounts for our responsibility for community interests in the modern environment, namely the market environment, which bestows certain responsibilities on traditional property owners to handle their property in a manner that is not too detrimental to the market community.[112]

Under the suggested paradigm, antitrust laws do not interfere with the traditional private property rights of the transgressors to use their property in any manner they choose (including a collusive or monopolizing manner) because certain conduct is inherently wrongful. Thus, it is argued that antitrust laws do not limit the exercise of property rights by corporations but rather correct the injustice caused when a certain corporation erroneously interprets its traditional property rights to be broader than they actually are.[113] Such notions are also consistent with philosophical arguments that link the market process to individual autonomy.[114]

Note also that the property paradigm of antitrust is not inconsistent with the quintessential criminal nature of antitrust laws. On the contrary – the property paradigm provides a formal justification for the criminal sanctions imposed by antitrust. Legal systems generally contain a whole category of punishable crimes against property. The same rationale lies behind crimes against property[115] that can explicate the punitive nature of antitrust, namely, antitrust sanctions for offenses against the communal property right to a competitive environment. Or, in other words, it is the property nature of the right to a competitive environment that justifies the sanctioning of anticompetitive conduct.

2.4.2 The Property Account of Intellectual Property

Innovation as a public good

The promotion of innovation is one of the widely accepted justifications for the establishment of an IP regime.[116] Innovation itself, displayed as innovative knowledge, can be characterized as what economists call a 'public good' because the utilitarian IP justification assumes that without an IP mechanism individuals would have little incentive to innovate, which would yield a suboptimal level of innovation in the market. Similarly to the argument about competition, the benefits of innovation seem to display all the classical characteristics of a public good.[117] The consumption of an abstract innovative idea is non-rival because one person's use of an informational good will not deplete the ability of anyone else to use the good,[118] therefore many people can make use of the idea at the same time. Innovation is inherently non-exclusive because owners of an idea or original expression have no physical way of fencing their abstract creation from use by others.[119] Innovation is also an inherently indisposable good because its benefits reward all members of society, including those who do not make individual use of it. Thus, for example, a person who develops an idea whose application greatly reduces the cost of production of a good benefits society as a whole rather than merely the consumers of that good.

Piracy as an externality

Piracy, which will here be defined as the use of intellectual property created by others without obtaining the consent of the original creator, is a clear case of an externality, because the pirate inflicts damage on the original IP owner without his/her consent. In fact the pirate does not consider the damage to the original owner at all in reaching his/her decision to use the invention. The unauthorized use causes damage in the form of lost profits to the creator who would naturally want to be compensated for every use of his/her invention. The environmental metaphor is again helpful in this context. Piracy forms the justification for the legal system's intervention by way of IP laws; in a similar manner to the way pollution causes the legal system to intervene by way of introducing environmental laws. Metaphorically, pirates pollute the orderly market because their conduct yields a suboptimal level of innovation that harms the market as a whole, just as high levels of carbon monoxide harm all living creatures.

It is important to admit again in this context to some existing critiques of public good and externality theories. The portrayal of innovation as a public good and of piracy as an externality presupposes that everyone will be better off with more innovation. This assumption is commonly supported by the argument that innovation advances technology, which in turn induces economic growth.[120] However, the assumption that innovation holds only good for everyone and that an increase in innovation is beneficial for all can be questioned. Thus, for example, it can be argued that promoting innovation is not always beneficial. For example, innovation might arguably take its toll on the environment, or it arguably involves costs as consumers and producers must constantly readjust, a process that may render whole lines of production and incompatible products obsolete as soon as innovation changes the standards in an industry. Therefore the argument that in the absence of IP rules the innovation level provisioned by the market will be suboptimal should be accounted for, as it embraces the normative assumption that everyone is better of if innovation levels are increased.

The individual elements of the story

Intellectual property laws may seem very different from antitrust laws in the sense that the former's recognized underlying elements include certain elements that are not strictly economic, namely personhood and desert-for-labor notions.[121] As a result, it may be argued that the public good narrative does not fit as neatly in the IP story as it did in the antitrust story. However, this argument is probably not very strong because personhood and desert-for-labor notions arise wherever humans and human labor, respectively, are involved and therefore antitrust is not excluded from such notions. To be sure, desert-for-labor and personhood notions are not common in contemporary antitrust literature since the kind of economic theory that has seemed to take over antitrust theory in recent decades is blind to such inefficiency considerations. Desert-for-labor arguments are non-existent under Chicago school economic analysis because, for example, once an invention is made, the costs of its development are regarded as 'sunk costs', which means that in economic terms they are zero. Hence any price that includes a royalty to the inventor will be considered economically wrong because it exceeds the opportunity cost of the product in which the invention is embodied.[122] Therefore, the rationale of a desert-for-labor IP justification seems to be in direct conflict with neoclassical economic analysis (economic analysis does not bother to criticize desert-for-labor notions in an antitrust context because it does not even consider them at all).

Personhood notions are perhaps even further removed from economic analysis than desert-for-labor, as economic analysis is about as far from human flourishing and individual autonomy goals as a theory can get. Nevertheless, personhood and desert-for-labor rationales surely play a role in antitrust theory as well as in IP theory. The property antitrust narrative developed above is an example of one personhood rationale within antitrust law. Earlier antitrust case law and texts also reveal judicial thinking that views antitrust as associated with personal human flourishing and desert-for-labor.[123] This is not the place to develop these notions in detail. All that is suggested here is that personhood and desert-for-labor rationales play roles both in intellectual property and antitrust. Accordingly, one should be made aware that a competition (antitrust) versus innovation (IP) portrayal of the antitrust–IP conflict is oversimplified. With that said, the analysis offered here focuses on the elements of promotion of innovation and competition rationales by IP and antitrust accordingly as the main story.

The property solution

The IP regime is a property mechanism for solving the assumed subprovision of innovation resulting from the public good nature of innovation (and the 'public bad' or externality nature of piracy).[124] The argument is that potential innovators would shy away from investing in innovation if they cannot appropriate returns for their costly development efforts.[125] The establishment of IPRs solves this dilemma by attempting to transform the nature of innovation from an economic public good into a private one. Note, however, that this effort seems successful only in part. While an enforceable IP regime solves the non-excludability feature as it grants innovators and authors a fencing mechanism that excludes others from non-permitted use of their protected inventions or creations for the duration of the right, it does not solve the inherently non-rivalry nature of intellectual property.[126] Intellectual property appears to deserve the 'property' title it bears because the claims of a patent or the registered copyrighted expression identify the specific object of ownership, and there are conditions that identify who owns it, namely the inventor or author.[127]

The property perception of intellectual property seems more broadly accepted and intuitive than the property notion of antitrust suggested above. A number of reasons may account for this difference. One is probably that although both property rights are in relation to an abstract subject matter, information goods are regarded as more productive than a competitive environment standard. This common contemplation of innovation as more productive is not necessarily true because overall it is entirely feasible that in some instances a competitive environment enriches society more than certain trivial inventions. Nevertheless, it is easier for people to think of inventions as profitable, and this renders them conceptually closer to traditional tangible property subject matters. A second reason why IPRs are more easily understood as property rights stems from the fact that unlike antitrust laws, IP statutes spell out the incidents of IP ownership, namely the ways in which IP owners are legally permitted to use and benefit from the object.[128] The description of the incidents of ownership of IP cognitively materializes the property nature of the rights because it amplifies the definition of the rights. A third reason that seems to render innovation more readily perceivable as a property subject matter is probably its stronger private characteristics, which are more compatible with traditional private property contexts. Intangible goods are created by specific identifiable individuals, and IPRs allocate the revenues to these people. In contrast to innovation goods, competition as a good is aggregately produced by the market mechanism and antitrust laws allocate its revenues communally to everyone. Hence, intellectual property is closer to traditional private property notions because the conditions that identify who own it point to specific individuals, the same individuals who labored to create it.[129] Finally, a fourth reason why intellectual property is deemed more readily identifiable as property is because it is mostly alienable in all meanings of the term, it can be sold, transferred, waived or lost.[130] The alienability feature renders IP compatible with the traditional common law alienable character of property, and with the lay notion of property, namely, an asset that can be traded for money. In short, intellectual property is broadly accepted as conferring property rights upon its owners.[131]

2.4.3 Implications of the Property Narrative

The foregoing property narratives of antitrust and intellectual property offer a new way of reviewing the antitrust–IP conflict, namely as a conflict between two competing *property* right regimes, the property rights of authors and inventors in their intangible work against the property rights of citizens to a competitive market environment. This property versus property positioning is closely connected to the foregoing rationales underlying these property rights – the problems of underprovision of innovation and competition. However, as mentioned before, in addition to the underlying economic rationales, the story displays certain personal aspects.[132]

Unfortunately, the property characterization does not offer a magic solution to the antitrust–IP conflict because property in general is not a self-defining institution[133] in the sense that it is not created with a complete description of the exact boundaries of the incidents of the ownership. To demonstrate this point we can look at the example of nuisance. Nuisance involves a case where the incidents of ownership from two traditional property rights (in land) compete with each other. The plethora of literature on this question proves that there are no clear-cut answers even in the nuisance cases where two identical traditional property rights compete. If that is the case with respect to traditional property rights, it is easy to see why the property characterization in and of itself does not resolve the antitrust–IP conflict where the two property rights involved are different, and both involve an abstract (and hence non-traditional) subject matter. However, although the property paradigm is not a magic solution, there are still a number of interesting implications that can be drawn from it.

The first notion arising out of the property structure is that it accounts for much of the difficult and ambiguous nature of the antitrust–IP conflict. Scholars have long noted the inconsistent and confused nature of the law surrounding the conflict between antitrust and intellectual property.[134] The property narrative of the conflict suggests one reason why it is so problematic. The conflict of property rights is never an easy case, and where the two property rights involved are abstract, the case becomes even more complicated because even the boundaries of the rights themselves (let alone their incidents of ownership) are not visibly recognizable. Therefore the delineation of the rights themselves is highly dependent upon legal doctrine construed by the antitrust enforcing authorities, the patent and trademark office and the courts. This adds an additional level of complication to the already difficult problem of the incidents of ownership that is inherent in any property conflict scenario.

A second implication of the property narrative is that it significantly endorses antitrust theory in three ways. First, it reconciles antitrust theory with the Austrian economics critique of it as a non-justified market-intervention mechanism. Austrian economics is an inherently anti-interventionist school of thought that treats any governmental market intervention with suspicion.[135] According to Austrian economists the premise underlying *laissez faire* capitalism is that the only actions that should be illegal are those involving an act of aggression against another person or his/her property.[136] Taking this point further supports the argument that antitrust law is a violation of this principle, because it prohibits business practices that are not alleged to constitute such depredations.[137] Once the property narrative is adopted, it recognizes people's rights to a competitive standard market environment as property rights. The property seal characterizes certain anti-competitive conduct as an act of aggression against other people's property and thus serves as a theoretical instrument that supports the existence of an antitrust policy, root and branch. In other words, the story of antitrust as the guardian of people's property right to a competitive market gains it the support of Austrian analysis, which stresses private initiative, free enterprise and the property in which they are reflected as the core engine of competition.

A skeptical reply to this point might of course be that antitrust laws themselves created that same property right which is argued to justify them. The answer to such critique would probably be that the rationale of protecting people's right to a competitive environment was not created by the antitrust laws, but rather existed eons before them, a fact that is reflected in the old common law rules forbidding monopolization and contracts in restraint on trade.[138] In other words, antitrust laws, like all other laws, did not originate in a vacuum, but rather reflect a certain social reality preceding them that recognized an enforceable right to a competitive market.

A second way in which the property narrative of antitrust can be used to support antitrust theory is by reconciling it with some of the Chicago school antitrust critique. The Chicago school, just like its Austrian counterpart, treats antitrust as a necessarily evil interventionist policy that creates a distortion because it interferes with the invisible hand of the market.[139] The magic word that largely redresses any Chicago school complaint is not 'property', but rather 'allocative efficiency'. It is, however, the property story of antitrust that opens the door to at least one justifying efficiency argument. This argument relates to neoclassical economics rule regarding the decreasing marginal utility of money. According to this argument, the first dollar a person receives gives him/her far more utility than the tenth dollar or the millionth dollar, the argument being that with the first few dollars he/she buys life-saving necessities while the millionth dollar simply goes into his/her savings account.[140] In light of this rule, the property narrative of antitrust seems efficient because in effect it ensures inherently lower competitive price levels which de facto puts more dollars in the pocket of consumers who are on average poorer than large corporations.[141]

A third sense in which the property structure supports antitrust is found specifically in the antitrust–IP context. The term 'property' is commonly used to imply the strength of the right, namely that it is the right that should win a legal battle. Since, as detailed earlier, the property nature of intellectual property is widely accepted and intuitive, it might be argued that when balancing intellectual property against antitrust, deference should be made to IP, which is the property right between the two and therefore arguably should dominate in a clash scenario. A property antitrust story works against any such argument and puts antitrust on a par with intellectual property as a property-conferring mechanism. Furthermore, it can even be argued that antitrust confers a more beneficial property right than IP because everyone benefits directly from it, while an IP right confers direct benefits only upon the individual author or inventor. This point is of course debatable, as it is impossible to measure the extent to which the innovation promoted by IP indirectly benefits society, as opposed to the indirect benefits from the competition protected by antitrust, let alone the aggregate value of the direct and indirect benefits. The importance of this notion is that the property nature of IP does not provide it with any preliminary advantage over antitrust doctrine because the latter creates property rights too.

Finally, the last implication of the property narrative is that it reaffirms our conclusion from the previous chapter, namely, that antitrust and competition do not inherently conflict, but rather that their methodologies conflict. While there is no theoretical conflict between competition and innovation (the dynamic competition notion practically views them as one), the utilization of neighboring property rights does seem to inherently conflict (think, for example, of the case of land ownership versus a neighbor who creates a nuisance). The antitrust–IP conflict cases indeed demonstrate how the property right of IP owners clashes with the communal property right to a competitive environment. The clash stems from the property mechanism used. It is the peripheries of the property bundles of rights conferred by the two doctrines that interfere with each other, while the underlying rationales of innovation and competition are virtually harmonious.

2.4.4 Some Thoughts Arising From the Property Narratives Conflict

On the growing association between property and public interests

As argued above, it seems that both IP laws and more so antitrust laws confer a modern non-traditional type of property rights. Intellectual property protects an abstract right whose boundaries are set only by legal rules since they are not visually determinable. Antitrust laws stretch the traditional private property notion even further, as not only do they protect an abstract subject matter but also the abstract subject matter they protect is also non-marketable and conferred upon everyone at the same time. There is one common thread running through both the intellectual property and antitrust institutions, and that is that both property doctrines are heavily reliant upon a public interest rationale. IP legislation is supported by the U.S. Constitution as a means of serving the public good[142] and antitrust laws are similarly justified as an instrument to promote the public interest.[143] This notion differs from traditional Blackstonian-type private property rights that focused on the sole interests of the property right owner, which were thought to overcome any competing community interests.[144] It seems that the common feature of antitrust and intellectual property is characteristic of all of the more recently created property rights. As our planet becomes more densely populated, people are becoming more interdependent. Legal systems are sensitive to this pattern, and thus are in the process of moving towards creating rights that take the public interest into consideration.[145] This process is gradually rendering the model of self-focused private property obsolete.

Rationales that explain the complexity of the conflict

It is common knowledge that property rights are not absolute but are rather always limited by competing rights.[146] One example of such a limitation is that property law is full of limits on free use and disposition. Any two property rights that share an actual interface may conflict. For example, a house owner will be restricted in his/her enjoyment of the house by nuisance laws that represent the property rights of the neighbors. Furthermore, his/her property rights will also be limited by public policy rules such as zoning laws or a possible eminent domain taking. For example, a car owner is still bound by traffic laws; there are also rights that are inferior to ownership – for renters there are many proscribed activities, and land users who are licensees may have to vacate at the owner's request. The conflict between an IP right and antitrust demonstrates a case where the opposing antitrust-created right is a unique hybrid between these two types of opposing rights. On the one hand, like the nuisance scenario, the competing right is a property right,[147] but on the other, like the zoning or eminent domain taking scenario, the competing right is vested in the public as a whole and not in specific individuals. It should be noted that this state of affairs is perhaps not altogether novel, as it is comparable to a scenario of certain environmental laws that confer similar rights, and environmental laws also tend to be rather controversial.[148]

Nevertheless, there are a number of reasons that render the antitrust–IP conflict particularly ill-natured and vociferous. One explanation derives directly from the structure mentioned above. Unlike more traditional property rights, IP rights themselves were created to solve a public good problem, namely the public good of innovation, and are therefore sensitive to public policy considerations.[149] Traditional ownership in real property whose benefits are rivalrous and excludable lacks a similar rationale. Therefore IP displays an additional dimension of *raison d'être* that is not common in traditional forms of property. This complicates the traditional property conflict scenario because public good notions are pertinent on both sides of the conflict.

A second reason for the perplexing nature of the antitrust–IP conflict involves a realist argument. IP owners are often large rich corporations, whose short-sighted self-serving interests naturally involve maximum IP protection and minimum antitrust enforcement if any. In pursuing these interests, rich corporations are efficient in utilizing the legal system for their purposes and in raising a significant outcry over these issues. This trend is reflected through the large interest in the antitrust–IP field, which is substantively quite narrow.

A third reason behind the difficult nature of the conflict lies in the fact that antitrust laws, as opposed to environmental or nuisance laws, protect an abstract interest and therefore are less intuitively related to issues of quality of life. As detailed above,[150] antitrust laws are closely related to quality of life issues because of the personal freedom aspects they protect. However, these aspects are not readily understandable, and therefore the fact that antitrust laws challenge IP rights in certain scenarios may seem confusing because of the lack of easily identifiable life issues protected by them.

A fourth explanation for the fierceness of the antitrust–IP conflict stems from the rooted libertarian myth of the free market as an arena of freedom, that is, as free from any coercion or governmental control.[151] Adoption of such a myth makes it difficult to account for interference in the use of IP laws.

Finally, a fifth possible rationale behind the intensity of the conflict has to do with a reliance interest. IP laws existed for over two hundred years before modern antitrust statutes were introduced.[152] Therefore antitrust's interference with IPRs may seem rather flagrant because of a reliance rationale developed by IP owners with respect to the extent of their right.[153] This rationale is of course rather limited since, to the extent that such a reliance rationale was present, it has probably evaporated in the climate of the past century which included antitrust laws; in addition note that antitrust notions had roots based in earlier common law rules, which further weakens the reliance argument.

NOTES

[1] As mentioned earlier, the antitrust context will be limited to unilateral monopolizing conducts and the intellectual property aspect will focus on patents and copyrights.

[2] Carl Menger, *Principles of Economics* (1871) (James Dingwall and Bert F. Hoselitz trans., New York: New York University Press 1981); Carl Menger, *Investigations Into the Method of the Social Sciences with Special Reference to Economics* (1883) (Francis J. Nock trans., Lawrence White ed., New York: New York University Press 1985). See also *Carl Menger and the Austrian School of Economics* (John R. Hicks and Wilhelm Weber eds, Oxford: Clarendon Press 1973).

[3] These include scholars such as Friedrich A. Hayek, Ludwig von Mises, Joseph A. Schumpeter, Israel M. Kirzner, Murray N. Rothbard and Fritz Machlup. It should be cautioned that not all that is promoted as Austrian economics today is consistent with Carl Menger's subjective theory of value foundations, and therefore there can be some controversy as to the boundaries of Austrian Economics' scholarship. For a collection of Austrian economics literature, see, for example: *Austrian Economics* (Schools of Thought in Economics Series, Stephen Littlechild ed., Vols I, II, and III, Aldershot, UK and Brookfield, US: Edward Elgar 1990). See also Sandye Gloria-Palermo, *The Evolution of Austrian Economics: From Menger to Lachmann* (New York: Routledge 1999). The Ludwig von Mises Institute online at http://mises.org (August 2, 2002) offers a catalog of Austrian journals and publications. For more references, see also Chapter 1, notes 85–98.

[4] See, for example, Lawrence R. Klein, a Nobel laureate economist in *The Keynesian Revolution* 107 (New York: Macmillan, 1947 2nd ed. 1966). Klein dismissed serious empirical studies that challenged Keynes' empirical observations by remarking, 'Our main concern ... is not with the empirical problem, but with the theoretical'. This quote reflects the gist of much of the neoclassical economics approach, which can be characterized in short along the lines of 'Don't bother us with market data, we are scientific economic theorists striving to formulate purely theoretical economic models. As long as our models are theoretically flawless, our goal is achieved'. For this and additional examples of neoclassical economics dismissive attitudes towards empirical data, see, for example: Lowell Gallaway, *Some Austrian Perspectives on Unintended Consequences*, 10 (2) Rev. of Austrian Econ. 91 (1997) (the notion occurs repeatedly throughout the article, which is why I cannot refer to a specific page. The Klein example is at 99). The journal is available online through the Ludwig von Mises Institute, supra note 3.

[5] For a review of behavioral economic analysis, see Christine Jolls, Cass R. Sunstein and Richard H. Thaler, 'A Behavioral Approach to Law and Economics', in *Behavioral Law and Economics* 13 (Cass R. Sunstein ed., Cambridge: Cambridge University Press 2000).

[6] Friedrich A. Hayek, '*The Meaning of Competition*' (Stafford Little Lecture Princeton 1946). Reprinted in *Individualism and Economic Order* 104 (Chicago: University of Chicago Press 1948).

[7] A more extensive discussion of the unrealistic features of neoclassical competition theory follows below in Section 2.2.4.

[8] For example, Carl Menger's 1871 seminal book, supra note 2. In this context one should also mention modern game theory, which although having its roots set in the neoclassical school,

drops the assumption of 'complete information' and thus refers to models with a multiplicity of equilibria. See, for example, Jean Tirole, *The Theory of Industrial Organization* 6–12, 373 (Cambridge, MA: MIT Press 1988). This book does not deal with the field of game theory because it is not relevant to the topic that forms the heart of this book, namely, Austrian economics.

[9] See, for example: Joseph A. Schumpeter, 'The Process of Creative Destruction', in *Capitalism, Socialism, and Democracy* 81–6 (London: Unwin University Books 1942, 10th Impression 1965); and Israel M. Kirzner, 'The Driving Force of the Market: The Idea of "Competition" in Contemporary Economic Theory and in the Austrian Theory of the Market Process', in *Why Economists Disagree – An Introduction to the Alternative Schools of Thought* 37 (David L. Prychitko ed., Albany, NY: State University of New York Press 1998).

[10] Hayek, supra note 6 at 102.

[11] Schumpeter, supra note 9 at 82–3.

[12] Id. at 83.

[13] See Friedrich A. Hayek, 'Competition as a Discovery Procedure', in *New Studies in Philosophy, Politics, Economics and the History of Ideas* 181 (Chicago: University of Chicago Press 1978). This article is also available in *Austrian Economics* 185 (Schools of Thought in Economics Series, Stephen Littlechild ed., Vol. III, Aldershot, UK and Brookfield, US: Edward Elgar 1990).

[14] See Israel M. Kirzner, 'Prices, the Communication of Knowledge, and the Discovery Process', in *The Political Economy of Freedom: Essays in Honour of F.A. Hayek* 193, 194–5 (Kurt R. Leube and Albert H. Zlabinger eds, Munich: Philosophia Verlag 1985). This article is also available in *Austrian Economics* 197, 198–9 (Schools of Thought in Economics Series, Stephen Littlechild ed., Vol. III, Aldershot, UK and Brookfield, US: Edward Elgar, 1990).

[15] Kirzner, id. at 193–206.

[16] These notions are associated with the work of the Nobel Laureate Kenneth J. Arrow, 'Economic Welfare and the Allocation of Resources for Innovation', in *Essays in the Theory of Risk-bearing* 144 (NY: North-Holland, 3rd edn 1976). See also Richard Gilbert and Steven Sunshine, *Incorporating Dynamic Efficiency Concerns in Merger Analysis: The Use of Innovation Markets*, 63 Antitrust L. J. 569, 574–6 (1995).

[17] See the Merriam-Webster dictionary online at http://www.m-w.com.

[18] Hayek, supra note 6 at 92 and 96.

[19] See Hayek, *New Studies in Philosophy, Politics, Economics, and the History of Ideas*, supra note 13 at 179.

[20] See, for example, the notion that competition policy recognizes that licensing restrictions may be welfare increasing because they often encourage the efficient diffusion of intellectual property in §2.3 of the U.S. Department of Justice and Federal Trade Commission's *Antitrust Guidelines for the Licensing of Intellectual Property* (April 6, 1995) (hereinafter: 1995 IP Guidelines) available at: http://www.usdoj.gov/atr/public/guidelines/ipguide.htm (August 2, 2002). See also decisions that challenge high-technology mergers on the grounds that future innovation will be curtailed, for example: *Roche Holdings,* 113 F.T.C. 1086 (1990); *Sensormatic Electronics Corp.*, F.T.C. File No. 941-0126 (January 4, 1995); and *Boston Scientific Corp.*, F.T.C. File No. 951-0002 (February 24, 1995).

[21] See, for example: David D. Li and Changqi Wu, *Economic Growth and Productivity Around GATT/WTO Accessions: Evidence from The World, 1960-89*, 13th NBER East-Asian Seminar on Economics (Melbourne, Australia, June 20–22, 2002) available at http://www.nber.org/books/ease13/li-wu8-26-02.pdf (January 10, 2003); and Robert J. Gordon, 'Technology and Economic Performance in the American Economy', NBER Working Paper No. w8771 (February 2002) available at http://papers.nber.org/papers/w8771 (January 10, 2003).

[22] See, for example: David J. Teece and Mary Coleman, *The Meaning of Monopoly: Antitrust Analysis in High-technology Industries,* 43 Antitrust Bull. 801 (1998); Daniel L. Rubinfeld, *Antitrust Enforcement in Dynamic Network Industries*, 43 Antitrust Bull. 859 (1998); Peter

Howitt, 'On Some Problems in Measuring Knowledge-Based Growth', in *The Implications of Knowledge-Based Growth for Micro-economic Policies* 9 (Peter Howitt ed., Calgary: University of Calgary Press 1996); Gilbert and Sunshine, supra note 16; and *Antitrust Innovation and Competitiveness* (Thomas M. Jorde and David J. Teece eds, New York: Oxford University Press 1992).

[23] See Federal Trade Commission Staff, *Anticipating the 21st Century: Competition Policy in the New High-tech Global Marketplace*, ch. 6, pp.10 ff, 42 which refer to the hearings of the testimony of Joseph E. Stiglitz, Professor F.M. Scherer, Robert H. Kohn, Professor John Barton and Edward J. Black. The text of the hearings is available at http://www.ftc.gov (August 2, 2002).

[24] See Andreu Mas-Colell, Michael D. Whinston and Jerry R. Green, *Microeconomic Theory*, Part IV p. 511 et seq., especially pp. 511, 578–630 (New York: Oxford University Press 1995).

[25] Hayek, supra note 6, ch. V: 'The Meaning of Competition', at 94.

[26] See, for example: Israel M. Kirzner, *Competition and Entrepreneurship* (Chicago: University of Chicago Press 1973); Schumpeter, supra note 9 at 132; Ludwig von Mises, *Human Action: A Treatise on Economics* 246 (Chicago: Gateway/Regnery, 3rd edn 1966); and Israel M. Kirzner, 'Uncertainty, Discovery, and Human Action: A Study of the Entrepreneurial Profile in the Misesian System', in *Method, Process and Austrian Economics: Essays in Honor of Ludwig von Mises* (Kirzner ed., Lexington, MA.: Lexington Books) ch. 12, p. 139 – can also be found in *Austrian Economics* (Schools of Thought in Economics Series, Stephen Littlechild ed., Vols I, II, and III, Aldershot, UK and Brookfield, US: Edward Elgar, 1990).

[27] Schumpeter, supra note 9 at 133–4.

[28] See Kirzner, *Competition and Entrepreneurship*, supra note 26 at 94.

[29] See, for example, Richard A. Posner, *Economic Analysis of Law* 11 (New York: Aspen Law & Business, 5th edn 1998).

[30] See William J. Baumol, *Entrepreneurship in Economic Theory,* 58 Am. Econ. Rev. 66 (1968) (noting the absence of the entrepreneur notion from much of neoclassical economics discourse).

[31] See Ingo L.O. Schmidt and Jan B. Rittaler, *A Critical Evaluation of the Chicago School of Antitrust Analysis* xiv–xv, and footnote 11 (Dordrecht: Kluwer Academic 1989). See also Tirole, supra note 8 at 243–5 for criticism of the static neo-classical model from a game theory perspective.

[32] See also the work of the economist Donald Dewey, *The Antitrust Experiment in America* 72–3 (New York: Columbia University Press 1990) who observed that static economic analysis has no contribution to make to the study of differentiation of products.

[33] See Hayek, supra note 6 at 97–9.

[34] On the problematic nature of defining separate markets, see: *U.S. Healthcare, Inc. v. Healthsource, Inc.*, 986 F.2d 589, 598 (1st Cir. 1993); and James A. Keyte, *Market Definition and Differentiated Products: The Need For a Workable Standard,* 63 Antitrust L. J. 697, 702–3 (1995).

[35] See Hayek, supra note 6 at 98.

[36] See John H. Jackson, *The Jurisprudence of GATT and the WTO* 3–4 (Cambridge: Cambridge University Press 2000).

[37] See Mas-Colell, Whinston and Green, supra note 24 at 384–6. Note the nonchalance with which the huge assumption of the monopolist's knowledge of the demand function is addressed. It is presented in one short sentence: 'Throughout, we suppose that the monopolist knows the demand function for its product and can produce output level q at a cost of $c(q)$', id. at 384.

[38] For a similar argument, see Murray N. Rothbard, *Man, Economy and State* 604–14 (Los Angeles, CA: Nash 1972).

[39] Hayek, supra note 13 at 187.

[40] See supra note 37.

---

[41] See, for example: Robert H. Bork, *The Antitrust Paradox: A Policy at War with Itself* 117 (New York: Basic Books 1978); and Richard A. Posner, *Antitrust Law – An Economic Perspective* 8–18 (Chicago: University of Chicago Press 1976).

[42] On the importance of non-price competition and its neglect by economists, see Paul J. McNulty, *Economic Theory and the Meaning of Competition*, 82 Q. J. of Econ. 639, 645–8 (1968).

[43] It is questionable whether goods indeed have a reasonable or fair price. The Court of Justice of the European Communities seems to assume the plausibility of a determinable fair price, see: Case 226/84 *British Leyland v. Commission of the European Communities* in Court of Justice of the European Communities: Reports of Cases Before the Court 1986, 3297, 3304–5; Case 27/76 *United Brands Company and United Brands Continental B.V. v. Commission of the European Communities* ('Chiquita Bananas') in Court of Justice of the European Communities: Reports of Cases Before the Court 1978, 207, 299–302; and Case 26/75 *General Motors Continental NV v. Commission of the European Communities* in the Court of Justice of the European Communities: Reports of Cases Before the Court 1975, 1367, 1378–9. Note, however, that U.S. courts usually refrain from referring to a price as unfair or excessive. Under an Austrian economics view there will be no fair price because whatever a producer is able to get is fair, and it will probably continue to change as the market changes. For the purpose of the argument here, the 'reasonable price' will be defined as the cost of production (variable cost and a fraction of the fixed cost) plus the average profit margin in that specific industry.

[44] For a different take on the shortcomings of economics as a coherent key for portraying antitrust, see: Donald Dewey, *What Price Theory Can – and Cannot – Do for Antitrust*, 3 Contemp. Pol'y Issues 3 (1984–85); and Donald Dewey, *Antitrust and Economic Theory: An Uneasy Friendship* (Book Review), 87 Yale L. J. 1516 (1978) (Dewey, a professor of economics, is pessimistic as to the ability of both neoclassical and dynamic economic theories to account for antitrust).

[45] See Hayek's *Individualism and Economic Order,* supra note 6 at 102. See also: Schumpeter in *Capitalism, Socialism, and Democracy,* supra note 9 at 106, where he noted that 'perfect competition is not only impossible but inferior, and has no title to being set up as a model of ideal efficiency'; and Dominick T. Armentano, *Antitrust and Monopoly: Anatomy of a Policy Failure* 32 (San Francisco, CA: The Independent Institute, 2nd edn 1990), where he declares that 'Perfect competition theory is both illogical and irrelevant'. For a review of Austrian economists' criticism of the neoclassical model, see Israel M. Kirzner, *Entrepreneurial Discovery and the Competitive Market Process: An Austrian Approach*, 35 J. of Econ. Literature 60, 63–6 (1997). For a more general critique of neoclassical economics, see Peter J. Boettke, 'What is Wrong with Neoclassical Economics (and What is Still Wrong with Austrian Economics?)', in *Beyond Neoclassical Economics: Heterodox Approaches to Economic Theory* 22 (Fred E. Foldvary ed., Cheltenham, UK and Brookfield, USA: Edward Elgar 1996) where the author summarizes what is wrong with neoclassical economics in just a few words: 'It is precisely irrelevant'. See also the work of Harold Demsetz, who coined the phrase 'Nirvana Fallacy' to describe the tendency of economists to draw conclusions from a comparison of the real world with some idealized version of reality which exists only in mathematical models, for example, Harold Demsetz, *Information and Efficiency: Another Viewpoint*, 12 J. of L. & Econ. 1 (1969). For a different critique of a neoclassical model from a legal antitrust perspective, see Thomas C. Arthur, *The Costly Quest for Perfect Competition: Kodak and Nonstructural Market Power*, 69 N.Y.U. L. Rev. 1, 7–20 (1994).

[46] Schumpeter, *Capitalism, Socialism, and Democracy*, supra note 9 at 87.

[47] Philippe Aghion and Peter Howitt, 'A Schumpeterian Perspective on Growth and Innovation', in *Advances in Economics and Econometrics: Theory and Applications* (David Kreps and Ken Wallis eds, Cambridge: Cambridge University Press 1997).

[48] See the Federal Trade Commission Staff Report, supra note 23, Vol. I, ch. 6 at 12–14, 16 ('Business participants ... were emphatic that competition is a primary incentive for innovation and that continuous innovation is critical for success in increasingly global markets').

[49] David C. Mowery, *The U.S. National Innovation System: Origins and Prospects for Change*, 21 Res. Pol'y 125 (1992).

[50] David M. Gould and William C. Gruben, *The Role of Intellectual Property Rights in Economic Growth*, 48 J. of Dev. Econ. 323, 345–6 (1996).

[51] See Chapter 1, pp. 10.

[52] See IP Guidelines, supra note 20 last par. of §1.0.

[53] See, for example, Mariko Sakakibara and Lee Branstetter, 'Do Stronger Patents Induce More Innovation?' Evidence from the 1998 Japanese Patent Law Reforms (1999), Working Paper No. 7066, National Bureau of Economic Research, available at http://www.nber.org/papers/w7066.pdf (February 24, 2002) (questioning whether the expansion of patent scope in Japan indeed results in more innovation efforts by firms).

[54] See, for example: Pamela Samuelson, Randall Davis, Michell D. Kapor and J.H. Reichman, *A Manifesto Concerning the Legal Protection of Computer Programs*, 94 Colum. L. Rev. 2308, 2330–32 (1994) (on how innovation in computer programs is largely incremental and cumulative in character); William M. Landes and Richard A. Posner, *An Economic Analysis of Copyright Law*, 18 J. Legal Stud. 325, 332 (1989) (on the cumulative nature of new works); and Chris Freeman and Luc Soete, *The Economics of Industrial Innovation* 103 (3rd edn Cambridge, MA: MIT Press, 1997) (on the importance of minor improvements to existing processes).

[55] The term ''broad' refers here to substantive scope of protection, as opposed to its duration.

[56] For a similar notion, see Joseph E. Stiglitz, Chairman of the Council of Economic Advisers, speech at the Federal Trade Commission hearings held in fall 1995 (October 12, 1995) at 24–5; Esther Dyson, President of EDventure Holdings, speech at the Federal Trade Commission hearings held in fall 1995 (November 29, 1995) at 3332, both available at http://www.ftc.gov (January 10, 2003).

[57] For more on these, see Chapter 1, p. 12.

[58] The difficulty of such a task is evident from the many disputes between courts as to the proper degree of IP protection in different scenarios, which stem from a lack of a widely accepted measure for optimal protection. See, for example, the dispute regarding the proper degree of copyright protection for computer programs as reviewed in David M. Maiorana, *Privileged Use: Has Judge Boudin Suggested a Viable Means of Copyright Protection for the Non-literal Aspects of Computer Software in* Lotus Development Corp. v. Borland International?, 46 Am. U. L. Rev. 149, 157–62 (1996).

[59] Although the Chicago school of economics, which has dominated antitrust analysis for many years now, does not appear to see eye to eye with this conjoint innovation–competition notion which forms the core of Austrian competition, the common sense employed by the courts seems to embrace these notions, although without mentioning the Austrian school of economics. Practically all the antitrust–IP conflict cases address the fact that excessive IP protection hinders competition; see, for example, *International Wood Processors v. Power Dry, Inc.*, 792 F.2d 417, 426–7 (1986).

[60] See: Federal Trade Commission Staff Report, supra note 23, Vol. I, ch. 6 at 6–7 and the footnotes there; Wesley M. Cohen, Richard R. Nelson and John Walsh, 'Protecting Their Intellectual Assets: Appropriability Conditions and Why U.S. Manufacturing Firms Patent (or Not)', NBER Working Paper No. w7552 (February 2000) available at http://papersdev.nber.org/papers/W7552 (January 10, 2003); Richard C. Levin, Alvin K. Klevorick, Richard R. Nelson and Sidney G. Winter, *Appropriating the Returns from Industrial Research and Development,* 3 Brookings Papers on Economic Activity 783 (M. Baily and C. Winston eds, Washington DC: Brookings Institution 1987); and C.T. Taylor and Z.A. Silberston, *The Economic Impact of the Patent System* (Cambridge: Cambridge University Press 1973). But compare with Robert P. Merges, 'Antitrust Review of Patent Acquisitions: Property Rights, Firm Boundaries, and Organization', in *Competition Policy and Intellectual Property Rights in the Knowledge-based Economy* 111, 125–6 (Robert D. Anderson and Nancy T.

Gallini eds, Calgary: University of Calgary Press 1998) (emphasizing the importance of patents as effective incentives for R & D).

[61] See, for example, Gerald P. O'Driscoll Jr. and Mario J. Rizzo, *The Economics of Time and Ignorance* 107–18 (London and New York: Routledge 1996 reissue of the 1985 1st edn).

[62] Id. at 115–18. For a critique of a centralized solution in the context of the antitrust–IP conflict, see David M. Hart, *Antitrust and Technological Innovation*, Issues in Science and Technology 9, Winter 1998 available at http://www.nap.edu/issues/15.2/hart.htm (January 10, 2003).

[63] Literature on public goods is vast. Seminal works include: Paul A. Samuelson, *The Pure Theory of Public Expenditure*, 36 Rev. of Econ. and Stat. 387 (1954); Paul A. Samuelson, *A Diagrammatic Exposition of a Theory of Public Expenditure*, 37 Rev. of Econ. and Stat. 350 (1955); and Mancur Olson Jr., *Logic of Collective Action* (Cambridge, MA: Harvard University Press 1965, 2nd ed 1971). For an excellent economic evaluation of the theoretical contributions of the literature on public goods and externalities, see Richard Cornes and Todd Sandler, *The Theory of Externalities, Public Good, and Club Goods* (New York: Cambridge University Press, 2nd ed, 1996).

[64] In the lay sense of the phrase, namely, something that is beneficial for the public as a whole.

[65] See: Steven C. Salop and R. Craig Romaine, *Preserving Monopoly: Economic Analysis, Legal Standards, and Microsoft*, 7 Geo. Mason U. L. Rev. 617, 628 (1999); Thomas G. Krattenmaker and Steven C. Salop, *Anticompetitive Exclusion: Raising Rivals' Costs to Achieve Power Over Price*, 96 Yale L. J. 209, 270 (1986); Louis Kaplow, *Extension of Monopoly Power Through Leverage*, 85 Colum. L. Rev. 515, 531–6 (1985) (free-riding problem of buyers unwilling to bear the costs of preventing further concentration of the market); and Kenneth G. Elzinga and William Breit, *The Antitrust Penalties: A Study in Law and Economics* 3–4 (New Haven, CT: Yale University Press 1976).

[66] See: Cornes and Sandler, supra note 63 at 8; Elzinga and Breit, id. at 3; and Hans-Hermann Hoppe, *The Economics and Ethics of Private Property* 12 ff, 17 (Boston/Dordrecht/London: Kluwer Academic 1993).

[67] Mas-Colell, Whinston and Green supra note 24 at 359 (where this feature is referred to as the nondepletable nature of public goods); Itai Sened, *The Political Institution of Private Property* 80 (Cambridge: Cambridge University Press 1997).

[68] These notions are drawn from the economic Nash equilibrium. For a brief yet concise review of it, see Cornes and Sandler, supra note 63 at 26–30.

[69] Harold M. Hochman and James D. Rodgers, *Pareto Optimal Redistribution*, 59 Am. Econ. Rev. 542 (1969).

[70] Tyler Cowen, *Law as a Public Good*, 8 Econ. & Phil. 249 (1992).

[71] The first introduction to the externalities concept is found in Arthur C. Pigou, *The Economics of Welfare* (London: Macmillan, 4th edn 1946). Follow-up literature is vast – see, for example, Cornes and Sandler, supra note 63; James E. Meade, *The Theory of Economic Externalities – The Control of Environmental Pollution and Similar Social Costs* (Geneva: Sijthoff-Leiden 1973); and Ronald H. Coase, *The Problem of Social Cost*, 3 J. of Law and Econ. 1 (1960).

[72] See Posner, supra note 29 at 81.

[73] For a depiction of the example of pollution as a public bad, see Cornes and Sandler, supra note 63 at 243.

[74] Quotation marks are used here because externalities are not produced purposefully, but rather are typically a byproduct of other activities. This is because generally people have little rational incentive to engage in an economic activity for the sole purpose of harming others.

[75] See, for example, Aldo Leopold, *A Sand County Almanac* xviii–xix (New York: Oxford University Press 1966). On the environment as common property see Zev Trachtenberg, *The Environment: Private or Common Property?*, 50 Okla. L. Rev. 399 (1997).

[76] Hoppe, supra note 66 at 3–25, especially p. 7 (on the fallacies of the public goods theory). Hoppe is an Austrian economist. Some of the chapters of this book are copyrighted by the Ludwig von Mises Institute. See also Rothbard, supra note 38 at 883–90 for a criticism on public goods.

[77] This critique is admitted by economists, see, for example, Cornes and Sandler, supra note 63.

[78] See. *Brooke Group Ltd. v. Brown & Williamson Tobacco Corp.*, 509 U.S. 209, 224 (1993); *Brunswick Corp. v. Pueblo Bowl-O-Mat, Inc.* 429 U.S. 477, 488 (1977); and *Brown Shoe Co., Inc. v. United States*, 370 U.S. 294, 320 (1962).

[79] Hoppe, supra note 66 at 7.

[80] See: *Appalachian Coals Inc. v. U.S.*, 288 U.S. 344, 372 (1932) ('When industry is grievously hurt, when producing concerns fail, when unemployment mounts and communities dependent upon profitable production are prostrated, the wells of commerce go dry.'); and Justice Benjamin Cardozo in *Baldwin v. G.A.F. Seelig, Inc.*, 294 U.S. 511, 523 (1935) ('all that a state will have to do in times of stress and strain is to say that its farmers and merchants and workmen must be protected against competition … lest they go upon the poor relief lists or perish altogether').

[81] Hoppe, supra note 66 at 9–11.

[82] See Randall G. Holocombe, *A Theory of the Theory of Public Goods*, 10 (1) Rev. of Austrian Econ. 1, 7–12 (1997).

[83] See Holocombe id. at 21.

[84] See, for example: Sened, supra note 67 at 80–86; Itai Sened and William H. Riker, *Common Property and Private Property: The Case of Air Slots,* 8 J. of Theoretical Politics, 527 (1996); Robert W. Hahn and Gordon L. Hester, *Marketable Permits: Lessons for Theory and Practice,* 16 Ecology L. Q. (1989); and Harold Demsetz, *Toward a Theory of Property Rights*, 57 Am. Econ. Rev. Pap. & Proc. 347 (1967).

[85] See, for example, Sened supra note 67 at 81.

[86] See also: Boudewijn Bouckaert, *What is Law?,* 13 Harv. J. of L. & Pub. Pol'y 775, 797 (1990) (on how property rules solve problems of distributive scarcity); and Carl Menger's earlier similar observation that: 'Human economy and property have a joint economic origin since both have, as the ultimate reason for their existence, the fact that goods exist whose available quantities are smaller than the requirements of man', in *Principles of Economics*, supra note 2, ch. II at 97.

[87] See: Demsetz, supra note 84 at 347–58; and Cornes and Sandler, supra note 63 at 43 (on how the lack of well-defined property rights is an important ingredient of many externality situations).

[88] See, for example: John Christman, *The Myth of Property*, 47–139 (New York: Oxford University Press 1994); Thomas C. Grey, 'The Disintegration of Property', in NOMOS XXII: *Property* 69, 81 (J. Roland Pennock and John W. Chapman eds, 1987); Joseph L. Sax, *Some Thoughts on the Decline of Private Property*, 58 Wash. L. Rev. 481, 481–3 (1983).

[89] For the original detailed articulation of this view, see Emily Sherwin, *Two- and Three-dimensional Property Rights*, 29 Ariz. St. L. J. 1075, 1076 (1997).

[90] See: *Reiter v. Sonotone Corp.*, 442 U.S. 330 (1979); Robert H. Lande, *Chicago's False Foundation: Wealth Transfers (Not Just Efficiency) Should Guide Antitrust*, 58 Antitrust L. J. 631 (1989); Robert H. Lande, *The Rise and (Coming) Fall of Efficiency as the Ruler of Antitrust*, 33 Antitrust Bull. 429 (1988); and Robert H. Lande, *Wealth Transfers as the Original and Primary Concern of Antitrust: The Efficiency Interpretation Challenged*, 34 Hastings L. J. 65, 93–6, 112–14, 135–6, 151 (1982).

[91] Antitrust literature and administrative agencies commonly refer to 'consumers' as the beneficiaries of antitrust laws. However, this phrase seems of little value (other than its marketing appeal). All market participants are consumers in some capacities, either as private

individuals (the more intuitive case), or as commercial entities who consume raw materials, labor services, office or production space and so on.

[92] See Phillip Areeda and Louis Kaplow, *Antitrust Analysis – Problems, Text, Cases* 60–62 (New York: Aspen Law & Business, 5th edn 1997). Areeda and Kaplow detail the wide variety of equitable remedies available to federal courts in enforcing antitrust laws.

[93] The seminal case that laid down the interpretation of the Sherman Act as conferring equitable remedies such as corporate divestitures and injunctions is *Northern Securities Co. v. U.S.*, 193 U.S. 197, 354–8 (1904). The formal justification for the decision was a phrase in §4 of the Sherman Act that authorizes the Attorney General to seek enforcement though proceedings in equity (see at 360).

[94] See: Alan Schwartz, *The Myth that Promisees Prefer Supracompensatory Remedies: An Analysis of Contracting for Damage Measures*, 100 Yale L. J. 99, 369 (1990); and Scot E. Masten, 'A Legal Basis for the Firm', in *The Nature of the Firm: Origins, Evolution, and Development* 195, 205 (Oliver E. Williamson and Sidney G. Winter eds, New York: Oxford University Press 1993) ('specific performance is infrequently applied in commercial settings').

[95] See: E. Allan Farnsworth, *Contracts* (Boston, MA: Little, Brown & Company, 2nd edn 1990) 852–4; and John D. Calamari and Joseph M. Perillo, *The Law of Contracts* 611 (St. Paul, MN: Hornbook Series, 4th edn 1998).

[96] A discussion of intellectual property rights as property rights follows in Section 2.4.2: 'The Property Solution'.

[97] See, for example, Benjamin Franklin's famous 1756 quote in '*Poor Richard's Almanac*': 'mine is better than ours.' in *The Sayings of Poor Richard: The prefaces, proverbs, and poems of Benjamin* (Paul Leicester Ford ed., New York: Burt Franklin Reprints 1975, reprint of the 1890 ed.).

[98] They have been around for centuries in the form of common property. On the distinction between common property and public goods, see Glenn G. Stevenson, *Common Property Economics: A General Theory and Land Use Applications* 53–6 (Cambridge: Cambridge University Press 1991). Note also that environmental laws operate in a similar manner to antitrust laws: they grant everyone the right to certain environmental standards at the same time.

[99] Note that the term 'inalienable' is subject to a number of possible meanings, for example: non-transferable, non-saleable, non-relinquishable by a right-holder, or a right that cannot be lost at all. See discussion in Margaret Jane Radin, *Market-Inalienability*, 100 Harv. L. Rev. 1849, 1849–50, 1852–9 (1987). The property rights conferred by antitrust laws are probably inalienable in all of these senses.

[100] See: Radin id.; Susan Rose Ackerman, *Inalienability and the Theory of Property Rights*, 85 Colum. L. Rev. 931 (1985); Richard A. Epstein, *Why Restrain Alienation?*, 85 Colum L. Rev. 970 (1985); and Guido Calabresi and A. Douglas Melamed, *Property Rules, Liability Rules, and Inalienability: One View of the Cathedral,* 85 Harv. L. Rev. 1089, 1111–15 (1972).

[101] See Radin, supra note 99 at 1888–9 where she goes even further to argue that John Stuart Mill's scholarship can be interpreted as asserting that alienability is inherent in the concept of private property. See also Ackerman, supra note 100 at 949–50 (1985) where she refers to inalienable property rules simply as modified property rules.

[102] See: Calabresi and Melamed supra note 100 at 1111; and Epstein, supra note 100 at 988–90.

[103] See the discussion on externalities earlier in this chapter, pp. 53–4.

[104] Calabresi and Melamed, supra note 100 at 1113–15. See also Anthony Kronman, *Paternalism and the Law of Contracts*, 92 Yale L. J. 763 (1983) which treats restraints on alienation as a form of paternalism.

[105] See Radin, supra note 99 at 1888–9.

[106] Radin, supra note 99 at 1909–14 and 1936–7.

[107] See previous discussion of externalities in this chapter, pp. 53–4.

[108] See *Antitrust Enforcement and the Consumer*, a Department of Justice pamphlet available at http://www.usdoj/atr/public/div_stats/1638.htm (January 10, 2003) at §1 titled 'What Do The Antitrust Laws Do For The Consumer'.

[109] See, for example: Areeda and Kaplow, supra note 92 at 25–6; *Paramount Famous Lasky Corp. v. U.S.*, 282 U.S. 30 (1930); *Fashion Originators' Guild of America v. FTC*, 312 U.S. 457 (1941); and *Klor's, Inc. v. Broadway-Hale Stores, Inc.*, 359 U.S. 207 (1959).

[110] See Sir William Blackstone, *Commentaries on the Laws of England*, vol. I: *Of the Rights of Persons* 134–5 (1765, Chicago: University of Chicago Press, with an Introduction by Stanley N. Katz 1979) where he speaks of the absolute right of property ('so great moreover is the regard of the law for private property that it will not authorize the least violation of it; not even for the good of the whole community').

[111] See: John Rawls, *Political Liberalism* 289 (New York: Columbia University Press 1993) (personal property as essential for personal independence and self respect); Margaret Jane Radin, *Reinterpreting Property* (Chicago: University of Chicago Press 1993) at 53ff. (property regime as promoting personal flourishing); Friedrich A. Hayek, *Law, Legislation and Liberty* 106–10 (Chicago: University of Chicago Press 1973) (property as the foundation of liberty); Georg Wilhelm Friedrich Hegel, *Philosophy of Right* 40–57 (T.M. Knox trans., Oxford: Clarendon 1967) (1821) (property as essential for developing personal freedom and individuality); and Jeremy Waldron, *The Right to Private Property* 343–89 (Oxford and NY: Oxford University Press 1988).

[112] Compare with Gregory Alexander's ideas of property as propriety, which describe the notion of property as a trusteeship that permeated the idea of property as propriety, which results in the view that property not only endows with rights, but also with responsibilities. See Gregory Alexander, *Commodity and Propriety: Competing Visions of Property* in *American Legal Thought 1776–1970* 26–42 (Chicago: University of Chicago Press 1997).

[113] For the development of a similar theoretical argument, see Radin, supra note 111 at 146–65. For a practical flavor of this argument, namely the notion that giant corporations are arguably robbing consumers of what is rightfully theirs, see Hans B. Thorelli, *The Federal Antitrust Policy – Origination of an American Tradition* 98, 134ff. 144ff., 146, 227 (Baltimore, MD: Johns Hopkins University Press 1955).

[114] For a philosophical development of the association between the market concept and personal autonomy, see John O'Neill, *The Market: Ethics, Knowledge and Politics* 73–83 (London: Routledge 1998).

[115] This is not the place to open up the broad jurisprudential question of justifications for criminal sanctions. However, note one interesting rationale for criminal sanctioning of crimes against property, namely deterring future attempts to convert property rules into liability rules. See Calabresi and Melamed, supra note 100 at 1126.

[116] See Chapter 1, pp. 13–14.

[117] For a fuller development of treating knowledge as a public good, see Partha S. Dasgupta and Paul A. David, *Resource Allocation and the Institutions of Science* (Stanford, CA: Stanford University 1991).

[118] See Kenneth J. Arrow, 'Economic Welfare and the Allocation of Resources for Invention', in *The Rate and Direction of Inventive Activity: Economic and Social Factors* (Princeton: NBER, Princeton University Press 609, 614–15 (1962)).

[119] For an opposite view portraying information goods as excludable, see Patrick Croskery, *Institutional Utilitarianism and Intellectual Property*, 68 Chi.-Kent L. Rev. 631, 632–3 (1993). Note that Croskery refers to a somewhat differently defined term, namely 'excludability'.

[120] For empirical articulation of technical advance as a source of growth, see: Robert M. Solow, *Technical Change and the Aggregate Production Function*, 39, Rev. of Econ. and Stat. 312–13 (August 1957); and Edward F. Denison, *Accounting for U.S. Economic Growth: 1929–69* 131–7 (Washington, DC: Brookings Institution 1974) (both focus only on process innovation omitting product innovation which is also the other element of technologic progress). On the

causal association between innovation and growth, see Kenneth W. Dam, *The Economic Underpinnings of Patent Law,* 23 J. Legal Stud. 247 (1994).

[121] These issues were treated in more detail in Chapter 1, pp. 12–13.

[122] See Posner, supra note 29 at 45.

[123] See: *U.S. v. Aluminum Co. of America et al.*, 148 F.2d 416, 428–9 (2d Cir. 1945); *Klor's, Inc. v. Broadway-Hale Stores*, supra note 109 at 213; and Thorelli, supra note 113 at 180 et seq.

[124] For a fuller outline of the association between public goods and externalities on the one hand and property on the other, see previous Section 2.4.1 above: 'The property solution paradigm'. The same principles apply in this context.

[125] See, for example: Stanley M. Besen and Leo J. Raskind, *An Introduction to the Law and Economics of Intellectual Property,* 5 (1) J. Econ. Persp. 3 (1991); and C. Owen Paepke, *An Economic Interpretation of the Misappropriation Doctrine: Common Law Protection of Investments in Innovation*, 2 High Tech. L. J. 55, 61 (1987).

[126] Note that there are some technical solutions to this non-rivalry problem. Thus, for example, certain software products are made so that they can only be installed once or twice. This mechanism renders their consumption more rivalrous as fewer people are able to make use of the good.

[127] See Sherwin, supra note 89 and accompanying text.

[128] In §261 and §271 of the Patent Act; §106 of the Copyright Act.

[129] On the traditional scholarship's focus on private rather than communal property notions, see, for example, Duncan Kennedy, *A Symposium of Critical Legal Study: The Role of Law in Economic Thought: Essays on the Fetishism of Commodities,* 34 Am. U. L. Rev. 939 (1985).

[130] Note that not all of the rights conferred by intellectual property are alienable. The moral right in copyright is probably inalienable in all senses, namely it is market inalienable, that is, non-saleable and non-transferable and also cannot be lost or waived – this is the reality in Europe where the moral right notion was developed; see Jeremy Phillips, *Introduction to Intellectual Property Law* 8 (London: Butterworths 1986). The moral rights notions are relatively new to the U.S. and therefore we have little comments yet as to their alienability; see generally, Michael A. Epstein, *Epstein on Intellectual Property* (New York: Aspen Law & Business, 4th edn 1994) 4.51–4.52, 12.24. Moral rights are commonly taken to be inalienable because they protect personal aspects of artists that are presumed to possess meager financial bargaining power. Trade secrets rights can easily be waived or lost because their protection fades away as soon as the information they contain is no longer secret.

[131] Note that the author is not making a judgment here on whether a property mechanism is indeed the best way of solving this problem, but rather merely describes the IP mechanism as a property one. For more on IP as property, see: Frank H. Easterbrook, *Intellectual Property is Still Property,* 13 Harv. J. L. & Pub. Pol'y 108 (1990); and Stephen L. Carter, *Does It Matter Whether Intellectual Property is Property,* 68 Chi.-Kent L. Rev. 715 (1993). See also J.H. Reichman, *Legal Hybrids Between the Patent and Copyright Paradigms,* 94 Colum. L. Rev. 2432 (1994) (calling for an IP liability rule to replace the property paradigm).

[132] See this chapter, pp. 50, 60 and 62.

[133] See Stephen R. Munzer, *A Theory of Property* 22–4 (Cambridge: Cambridge University Press 1990).

[134] See, for example, Louis Kaplow, *The Patent–Antitrust Intersection: A Reappraisal,* 97 Harv. L. Rev. 1813 at 1815, 1848 (1984). More generally, see: Lawrence A. Sullivan, *Handbook of the Law of Antitrust* 542 (St. Paul, MN: West Publishing 1977); and Bork, supra note 41 at 405.

[135] For a clear exposition of Austrian economics hostility towards governmental market intervention, see Ludwig von Mises, *Interventionism: An Economic Analysis* (Bettina Bien Greaves ed., Irvington-on-Hudson, NY: Foundation for Economic Education, Inc. 1998. The text was written by von Mises in 1940 but was first published in 1998).

---

[136] See, for example, Walter Block, *Total Repeal of Antitrust Legislation: A Critique of Bork, Brozen, and Posner,* 8 (1) Rev. of Austrian Econ. 35 (1994). See also Hayek, *Competition as a Discovery Procedure*, supra note 13 at 190 ('governmental power should be confined to protecting individuals against the pressures of society. The protection for private initiatives and enterprise can only be achieved through the institution of private property and the whole aggregate of libertarian institutions of law.').

[137] Block, id. at 35.

[138] See review in William Letwin, *The English Common Law Concerning Monopolies,* 21 U. Chi. L. Rev. 355 (1954). See also cases such as *Mitchel v. Reynolds,* 24 Eng. Rep. 347 (K.B.) 1711.

[139] See, for example, Bork supra note 41 at 418–22.

[140] This is a phenomenon that is commonly accepted in economic theory, and is referred to as 'the decreasing marginal utility of wealth'. See, for example, Mas-Colell, Whinston and Green, supra note 24 at 54–5.

[141] See Lande, *Wealth Transfers as the Original and Primary Concern of Antitrust*, supra note 90.

[142] See U.S. Const. Art. I §8[8] which provides that 'the Congress shall have the Power ... to promote the Progress of science and useful Arts, by securing for limited Times to Authors and Inventors the exclusive Right to their respective writings and Discoveries.'

[143] See supra note 108.

[144] See Blackstone, supra note 110 at 134–5.

[145] Interestingly, a similar parallel process is taking place on the national level, as the globalization of markets and the resulting interdependence between nations are increasingly recognized – which gives rise to a global outlook on legislation, for example, the TRIPs agreement. See Jackson, supra note 36 at 3–6.

[146] See, for example, Kenneth Vandevelde, *The New Property of the Nineteenth Century: The Development of the Modern Concept of Property,* 29 Buffalo L. Rev. 325, 357–67 (1980).

[147] See the analysis earlier in Section 2.4.1: 'The property solution paradigm'.

[148] Richard A. Epstein, *Takings: Private Property and the Power of Eminent Domain* 57 et seq. (Cambridge, MA: Harvard University Press 1985).

[149] See, for example, *Lear v. Adkins,* 395 U.S. 653, 670; 89 S. Ct. 1902, 1911 (1969) (intellectual property as limited by the demands of the public interest). But compare with *Studiengesellschaft Kohle M.B.H. v. Shell Oil Co.*, 112 F.3d 1561, 1567 (Fed. Cir. 1997) (where the U.S. Court of Appeals Federal Circuit characterized Lear as echoing from a 'past era of skepticism over intellectual property principles').

[150] See section 2.4.1: 'The property solution paradigm'.

[151] See Joseph William Singer, *The Reliance Interest in Property*, 40 Stan. L. Rev. 611, 644–8 (1988).

[152] For a review of the common law notions which lay the foundations to modern antitrust laws, see, for example, William Letwin, *Law and Economic Policy in America - The Evolution of the Sherman Act* 18–52 (New York: Random House 1965); and Donald Dewey, *Monopoly in Economics and Law* 109–38 (Chicago: Rand McNally 1959).

[153] See generally Singer, supra note 151.

3. The Dynamic Antitrust Analysis Model

'*Eppur si mouve.*' [But it does move.]

(Attributed to the Italian astronomer and physicist Galileo Galilei, 1564–1642 after his recantation that the earth moves around the sun)

3.1 INTRODUCTION

Human life in general, and market phenomena in particular, form an ongoing dynamic process. This observation is even truer when made with respect to our modern age marketplace, which often experiences high innovation rates and a rapidly changing product scene. It is the recognition of this vigorous state of affairs that renders the dynamic competition (also known as the Austrian) market model so attractive, as was noted in detail in the second section of Chapter 2.

This chapter will take the enthusiasm with the Austrian dynamic competition model one stage further, in utilizing it as a basis for a suggested set of standards for evaluating and deciding antitrust–intellectual property conflict scenarios. The task is not an easy one. Edward S. Mason once wrote that 'it is difficult to the point of impossibility to derive from Schumpeter's process of 'creative destruction' an analytical framework on which applicable and effective antitrust standards might be built'.[1] From a complex task to begin with, matters become even more complex once we amplify it by an additional consideration, namely intellectual property. Nevertheless, even Mason duly admitted[2] that the task of employing the dynamic competition model as an analytical antitrust instrument is a worthy and meaningful one and, as this chapter will show, the task is practicable, even within an IP context. Furthermore, the task is probably easier than Mason had imagined, thanks to further developments that have taken place within Austrian scholarship since Schumpeter's work, such as the writings of Israel Kirzner, Peter Boettke, Murray Rothbard, Fritz Machlup, Gerald O'Driscoll, Mario Rizzo and many others.

The dynamic competition notions, whose relationship to the property notions developed in Chapter 2 will be reviewed in this chapter, suggest an original line of analysis and invoke considerations that play a constructive role in formulating the antitrust public policy area in general, and the antitrust–IP niche in particular. In addition to its theoretical merits, there is a utilitarian rationale behind the employment of dynamic competition standards for evaluating antitrust–IP clashes, namely, its alleviating effect on such matters which was discussed in the earlier chapters.[3] The foundations of the dynamic competition model lay down common grounds that are sensitive both to competition and IP considerations. Accordingly, it is suggested that putting these implied dynamic competition standards into use as guidelines for evaluating clashes would ensure a sensible solution that takes into account the considerations of both doctrines.

This chapter proceeds as follows. Section 3.2 will reveal the untold basic empirical assumptions that lie behind the principles of the dynamic competition model. Although dynamic competition, unlike its neoclassical counterpart, 'perfect competition', does not depend on a set of formal empirical assumptions, there seem to be a number of objective empirical circumstances that are required in order for it to hold water, and the lack of which may directly affect the relevance of the theory. This section will review these circumstances. Section 3.3 will begin by outlining the differences between the nearly identical neoclassical and legal monopoly concepts on the one hand, and the dynamic monopoly concept on the other. It will then go on to suggest a general formula for utilizing dynamic competition theory for creating a general antitrust analysis standard that is particularly useful for evaluating challenging antitrust–IP factual scenarios. Section 3.4 will revisit the property narratives developed in the previous chapter and place them with respect to the dynamic competition model suggested here. A final section concludes.

3.2 THE UNTOLD AUSTRIAN ASSUMPTIONS

Austrian economists often define their economics as a praxeological science.[4] Praxeology refers to the set of sciences that stem by logical inference from the axiom of human action,[5] and exclusively from it, without the adoption of any empirical assumptions. Therefore by characterizing their models as praxeological, Austrian scholars convey the notion that their methodology does not call for any empirical assumptions as a starting point for their models except for assumptions on the nature of human action (which are theoretical in nature). However, the fact that Austrian scholarship claims not to require any formal empirical assumptions and the fact that it does not adopt them do not mean that there are absolutely no necessary assumptions that are required in order for Austrian theories to hold water. To better explicate this point, it is perhaps best to start with some general observations.

Any market theory can be divided into three categorical areas: the first involves the empirical circumstances that define the genesis upon which the model emerges; the second is the process described by the model ('process category'); and finally the third is the market situation resulting from that process. Different market theories develop and focus on particular categorical areas. The neoclassical competition model, which was discussed at length in Chapter 1, focuses on the third category, namely on the presumably static end result market structure (described as an equilibrium) that is yielded by a competitive market process, and it uses formal mathematical expressions to define this structural end result. This compels the neoclassical model to adopt a strict set of empirical prerequisite assumptions, for two reasons: first, because the mathematical methodology used by the neoclassical competition model requires a set of formal basic empirical assumptions that are necessary for supporting the mathematical formulations that follow;[6] and second, a set of basic empirical assumptions fills in the first market theory category, namely the original empirical environment, which is especially important because the neoclassical model offers a very simplistic treatment of the competitive process itself (thus the second category is very narrow). Therefore in order to reach a solid static model of the end market result of competition, neoclassical theory needs a concrete base of formal assumptions to anchor it.

Austrian economics on the other hand focuses on the second market theory category, namely on the competitive process itself that it regards as a process of dynamic coordination of independently-acting market participants, which promotes discovery by market participants of the availability of and need for exchangeable goods and services.[7] Its process-oriented analysis makes no use of formal mathematical tools. Austrian scholarship's general disregard of underlying empirical assumptions seems to stem from this very focus on the second category (competition as a process) which accounts for competition through a reasoned process, namely the process of human action, rather than through a static end result relying on certain empirical assumptions. Furthermore, since Austrian methodology makes no use of mathematical formulations, it requires no assumptions to support such formulations.

While the notion that a process whose nature is known requires no empirical assumptions may seem initially convincing from a theoretical point of view, as a practical matter it is not entirely plausible. In practice, processes do not take place in a vacuum. On the contrary, the nature of every process, let alone a process of market coordination, is highly dependent on the environment in which it takes place, which is why even a market theory that focuses on the process category must pay at least some attention to the first category of underlying empirical data. Therefore, even if we wholly agree with the human action model suggested by the Austrians, which is indeed attractive, the practical manner in which the model comes about is highly dependent upon the initial environment in which it takes place.

For a demonstration of this argument look, for example, at the extreme case of a highly centralized, concentrated, and planned socialist market economy. Although the people in such an economy are obviously identical to those in an open capitalistic regime and therefore their human action is presumably the same, nevertheless the human action of people in a socialist regime plays little role if any in coordinating the socialist market process. In practice their human action comes about in a totally different manner because the lack of private property diminishes their motivation for profits and because governmental regulation of the market interferes with individuals' roles as market engines. As a result, the human action of individuals under a socialist market regime is rendered practically irrelevant due to the market's empirical circumstances in which all entrepreneurial and competitive activity are by definition absent.[8]

The truth behind an extreme example such as the socialist market one is also applicable to less extreme cases. The circumstantial context forms an inseparable part of any economic model that focuses on human action. Even in less extreme cases, the empirical context will inevitably determine both the relevance of such theory (that is, the extent to which it comes into play) and the correlated end-market picture (which the process-oriented Austrian theory deems less important, because it views it as subject to constant change). The more restrictive the initial circumstances are, the less relevant the human action theory becomes, as the ability of entrepreneurs and competitors to bring about the perennial change and coordination that form the core of the model's competition concept is curtailed. As a matter of fact, Austrians themselves were probably aware of this axiom. Their awareness of the importance of the empirical context can be inferred from their solid anti-interventionist agenda, in which they stressed the importance of restricting any governmental intervention to a bare minimum, because such intervention hampers the competitive process.[9] In other words, Austrians oppose governmental intervention because its existence interferes with the human action process that lies at the heart of their market model. However, the anti-interventionist principle does not tell the whole story. There are other empirical assumptions that are necessary in order to maintain the Austrian competition concept as a meaningful and relevant one. This section will spell out these assumptions.

It should be noted at the outset that while the practical Austrian assumptions, which will be explored below, go well beyond the anti-intervention theme formally expressed in Austrian discourse, these are nevertheless practically feasible workable assumptions, in other words, they are still a far cry from the neoclassical model's empirical assumptions whose imaginary nature and questionable touch with reality was commented upon earlier.[10] Indeed, a set of strictly defined empirical standards would not be very workable, simply because reality in itself is not strictly defined but rather materializes in many different shades of gray. Therefore in order to stay true to the practical nature of the legal doctrine embraced in this study (and to the practical nature of Austrian economics), the assumptions will be formulated in an open substantive manner that strives to explain the likely implications of certain circumstances while bearing in mind that specific mitigating or complicating fact patterns may change the picture. Therefore the list that follows is not a closed one. For demonstration purposes, the review of the assumptions will be accompanied by a review of typical antithetical factual scenarios in which the assumptions are not met. Here too, the list of scenarios in which the assumptions are not met is not closed, but rather takes the form of a set of examples.

Austrian economics is often referred to as the economics of time and ignorance.[11] A review of these two concepts indeed seems to be the key for discovering and reviewing the circumstances necessary for maintaining the relevance of its models, and particularly its competition model which is at the center of attention here.

3.2.1 Dynamic (Time) Notions

The Austrian concept of dynamic competition, as its name suggests, encompasses a dynamic multilevel process. This process is manifested primarily through the product scene: producers continually modify products in order to gain and increase their market shares over those of their competitors. Accordingly, the product picture is constantly changing, both in terms of price and of the features that products display. Prices keep changing as entrepreneurs discover previously overlooked opportunities that allow them to offer an existing product at a lower price.[12] Another dimension of entrepreneurship is the innovative dimension that Schumpeter focused on. Entrepreneurs invent new products either as part of new market niches or as competing products in existing market niches.[13] The entrepreneurial advantage[14] stems from the entrepreneurs' innovative ideas or astuteness, which help them explore new market niches that were previously unknown or invent better ways of exploiting existing niches. The essence of the dynamic competition model can be captured in the term 'change'; the competitive market is defined as an ever-moving concept. Nothing is ever static – and therefore any static observations are rendered worthless because they become obsolete soon after they are made. The market changes constantly because producers and entrepreneurs try to accommodate consumer demands, and the better they adjust or guess, the greater commercial success this ensures them, because consumers will opt for their products.

In order for the dynamic character of the competition process to come about and therefore bear practical relevance, the market environment must comply with certain implicit empirical assumptions without which a market is incapable of such constant change because of obstacles to the process. The required empirical circumstances include the following two assumptions.

Lack of governmental market intervention

The first of these empirical assumptions, and the only one the Austrians explicitly mention, is the exogenous element of lack of governmental market intervention. Clearly where the government steps in and regulates prices or production quotas (as in the example of a socialist regime) the market's natural endogenous dynamic process is curtailed, and the utility of the competitive process as a dynamic discovery process loses much of its relevance since the market reflects governmental proclamations rather than consumers' preferences.

However, in addition to governmental refrain from regulating the market, there are a number of endogenous elements that must be present in order for a dynamic process of discovery to take place.[15] These elements ensure that there are no insurmountable empirical obstacles that will prevent the competition process from evolving.

Availability of entrepreneurial opportunities

Entrepreneurs cannot bring about the competitive change (which includes both legally protected innovation as well as non-protected innovation) if the empirical circumstances pose obstacles that diminish their available entrepreneurial opportunities significantly. Therefore the extent to which the initial market circumstances facilitate entrepreneurial opportunities is crucial. There are two general types of possible obstacles for entrepreneurial activity: first, there are circumstances in which entrepreneurs are less motivated to enter the market; and second, there are circumstances in which they are motivated to join the market and add their fresh outlook to it, but nevertheless face practical objective obstacles in their way. The following is an open-ended list of possible circumstances that may create obstacles to the presumed natural competitive process, and hence may in practice interfere to some extent with the dynamic competition model.

First, circumstances that may diminish entrepreneurial motives to join markets:

• Circumstances where joining the market entails an exceedingly large initial investment. This is the case, for example, in markets where there is a huge amount of R&D required before entering the market. A common example is pharmaceuticals, in which governmental health regulations impose significant R&D activities before allowing entry into the product market.
• Market areas[16] where profit margins are notably small provide smaller incentives for joining them, and therefore may display a sluggish competitive process due to the unattractive profit margins they offer.
• Where market areas are in the process of dying out, as for example may be the case of the market for typewriters or other market areas involving products that are becoming obsolete, the competition process will naturally die out as demand diminishes. This is perhaps a private case of the previous category (low profit margin), which is additionally characterized by a shrinking of the market. In these cases, new technology is introduced that pushes out the old one (for example, word processors replace typewriters). Therefore those who for some reason prefer the older technology (for example, old-fashioned authors who prefer to use a typewriter) may be facing a market area where the competitive process is significantly reduced because overall demand is dwindling.
• Market areas where entrepreneurs have little opportunity to offer distinct or innovative products may display a less vigorous competitive process. For example, markets for certain agricultural products where the production processes and products may be quite straightforward, and where genetically modified foods are not allowed.

Second, circumstances where entrepreneurial motives exist but entrepreneurial opportunities are blocked:

• Objective circumstances where the nature of the industry entails barriers or great difficulties for entry of new entrepreneurs into the market area obstructs the process of dynamic competition.[17] Freedom of entry into activity in the market area is therefore crucial for sustaining dynamic competition. This assumption is similar to that of the neoclassical model. A common example of obstruction to entry is an organic state of affairs in which competitors lack access to a vital production element. This category involves cases that come under the legal antitrust doctrine of 'essential facility', namely, cases where a competitor's absolute control over a facility essential for competing effectively hinders competition.[18]

There is a distinction to be made between cases where the controlled essential facility belongs to a third party who is not directly involved in the market area and cases where the essential facility belongs to a market player. The term 'objective' is used here to denote the fact that the entry barrier stems directly from given facts of the industry. For example, the lack of access to a resource derives directly from simple property notions rather than from some intentional active conduct, or a conduct that claims to be derived from the property notion.[19] In the antitrust–IP context this category involves cases where control over information that is vital in order to compete is preventing market entry (for example, very high-tech industries that make extensive use of patents).

- New market areas where the circumstances are such that it takes a significant amount of time for competitors to catch on and introduce competing products (again, especially in technological contexts, but also, for example, where it takes time to build a production line or a plant that will offer the competing product). In many such cases the fact that a market area is new will mean that the first to introduce and to essentially create the new market area will enjoy both a substantial advantage over its competitors and reduced competition, for a limited period of time until the competition catches on.

3.2.2 Uncertainty (Ignorance) Notions

The second basic premise upon which the dynamic competition notion is dependent is its assumption regarding information in the market. Unlike the neoclassical model, Austrian competition does not assume perfect information by everyone, but rather assumes that information is not freely available to everyone and that therefore market participants do not hold perfect information about the market. Hence, the assumption is one of imperfect knowledge or 'market ignorance'.[20] It should be noted that the term 'uncertainty' can mean two things. First, it could relate to the present, and mean that market actors (whether consumers or sellers) lack full information about the current market (for example, they do not know for sure what is the lowest price for which a certain commodity or raw material can be obtained, or where the lowest price for that commodity is offered). Second, it could be prospective and mean that market participants do not know what will happen in the market in the future. The Austrian literature seems to focus on the former notion, namely, on uncertainty with respect to current market circumstances.

It should be re-emphasized that the uncertainty relates to both the producer and the consumer. On the one hand, producers do not know exactly what consumer preferences are (or how these will form on introduction of a new product), or how much consumers are willing to pay for a certain product. On the other hand, consumers do not have full information about the different features of competing products – they base their individual purchasing decisions on what limited subjective information they have. For example, it seems that most individual consumers who purchase a new personal computer are not fully aware of how a PC works or its full manufacturing specifications. Therefore they lack full information on the product (or comprehensive ability to evaluate it), and base their product selection on the limited information that they do possess.

The uncertainty feature is one of the generators of the competitive process for three reasons. First, the imperfect knowledge or uncertainty makes the whole notion of entrepreneurial gain possible. It turns the competitive process into a kind of a 'guessing game' in which successful entrepreneurial market participants are the ones who will best read the clues that the market supplies and thus create a product that consumers prefer. In other words, since no market players possess perfect information about the present market, let alone the future one, the successful market players will be entrepreneurs who will make the closest guesses as to consumers' demand patterns. Second, as the result of uncertainty and imperfect market information, wily entrepreneurs can make arbitrage profits on this information gap, for example, by discovering hidden resources for obtaining raw materials at a cheaper price.[21] If you will, this theory has much in common with Darwin's evolution theory because it can be closely related to concepts like 'survival of the fittest' and 'dominance of those who are competent enough to adjust themselves (or in this case – adjust their products and services) to the *changing* circumstances of the market environment'.[22] Finally, innovation theory has suggested that innovation proceeds faster under uncertain circumstances created when a large number of participants are trying multiple approaches simultaneously, because this leads to a more rapid trial-and-error learning process.[23] According to this premise, uncertainty promotes innovation. Since Austrian economics views innovation and competition as all but synonymous, this notion therefore proves that uncertainty promotes competition.

In an IP context, these imperfect information (uncertainty) notions may wear a slightly different form. It is not that something is being sold at different prices in different areas of the market, but rather that there are different ways to make functionally similar products, and entrepreneurs can figure out previously unrecognized ways to make a better product, and can gain legal protection for their invention. Although the IP itself is disclosed when it is registered, the practical reality remains as if it were undisclosed because competitors are barred from utilizing the information.

In light of the above, it becomes clear that the relevance of the Austrian competition notion, namely that of competition as a discovery process, is dependent not only on the assumed dynamic notions developed earlier (which are necessary for ensuring the flow of the *process*) but also on the assumption of uncertainty (which ensures that a process of *discovery* indeed takes place).

Similarly to the dynamic notions discussed earlier, the initial extent of information available to market participants (or its correlating uncertainty) is much dependent upon the complex empirical circumstances. Again, there are no strict assumptions here – but the following considerations may be relevant.

The mere possession of a legally protected IPR, which as a working assumption throughout this study is presumed legitimate, may often affect the amount of uncertainty in the market. For example, where an IP protected widget becomes essential in the production of other products, there will be only one commonly known source for buying that widget, namely, the IP owners. Also, possession of IP may bestow a huge information advantage upon its owner (for example, he/she will decide independently what price to charge for protected widgets, or when, if at all, to release protected widgets to the market) – but that in itself does not interfere with any Austrian assumptions, which merely state that the information is not free and is not readily available to everyone. The practical extent and significance of IP possession's effect on the uncertainty assumptions will of course depend upon a plethora of factors, such as the absolute demand for the product that includes the protected segment, the elasticity of demand between that product and non-protected products and so on.

3.2.3 Prerequisite Circumstantial Assumptions Distinguished from End Results of the Competitive Process

Note that the elements mentioned above are all objective market circumstances, in the sense that at certain times they may be organically created in the market as a natural part of the market's dynamics, without any suspicious or foul play by market participants. This may seem confusing in the sense that the same elements may appear to be playing a dual role: on the one hand they are claimed to be empirical prerequisites required in order for the dynamic competition process to take place; on the other, similar elements arguably serve both as earmarks for the end results of the human competitive action process and also as indicators of the fact that dynamic competition is indeed taking place. This is because the elements required for dynamic competition to occur in the first place are similar to the empirical circumstances that reflect an ongoing pattern of dynamic competition. This should not come as a surprise, because if we assume a natural tendency towards a competitive process, then the initial circumstances that allow it are the same ones that we encounter again at the end of the process. Furthermore, the picture may become even more complex, due to the fact that some of the elements mentioned seem mostly consistent with the assumptions of the neoclassical perfect competition model, which include initial assumptions of lack of any entry barriers (equal access to the market) and perfect and equal manufacturing information, assumptions that continue to exist throughout the end-result characteristics of competition.[24]

It is therefore time to clarify the nature and usage of the elements identified above. The heart of the Austrian competition concept that is utilized later in this chapter for the construction of an antitrust analysis is the competitive process itself. However, the initial market circumstances play a vital role in the manner in which this process comes about. Therefore this section proposed an open-ended list of empirical circumstances that may in practice interfere with the theoretical process model. Section 3.3 will employ these empirical circumstances as part of an antitrust analysis that focuses on the manner in which human action generates a competitive market process and interacts with these empirical circumstances. This choice of focus stems from two factors: first, it is derived from the view that the process itself, rather than structural end results, is the more interesting market phenomenon to explore (and it is also the aspect that influences people's lives the most); and second, it is compatible with the recognition of the importance of the time factor that renders the market to be an ever-changing concept. Accordingly, the dynamic nature regards a focus on the end results of competition as unworkable because the collection of end results constantly changes over time.

3.3 THE DYNAMIC ANALYSIS

3.3.1 Different Monopoly Concepts

As a direct result of the differences between the dynamic and the neoclassical competition concepts, the monopoly concepts of the two models are similarly different. Noting the distinction between these two concepts is essential before proceeding to the analysis that follows.

The neoclassical economic concept of monopoly, which is less interesting for our purposes, simply refers to a situation where there is only a single seller of a given good.[25] Since such factual situations are rare, the more interesting concept for the purposes of this study is that of *monopoly power* or *market power*.[26] The neoclassical economics definition of market power focuses on price, describing market power as a situation where a producer is able to control or influence the market price of a good.[27] In other words, a seller possessing monopoly power is independent of any effects of price changes on behalf of other sellers.[28] This definition is antithetical to the neoclassical perfect competition scenario, which assumes that no producer is able to have a perceptible influence upon the market price.[29] The contemporary legal definition of monopoly closely follows the neoclassical economics paradigm.[30] U.S. courts have defined *monopoly power* as the state of affairs in which a market player has the power to control prices or exclude competition in a relevant market or the power to force a purchaser to do something that he/she would not do in a competitive market.[31] *Market power* has been legally defined as a 'seller's ability to profitably maintain prices above competition levels for a significant period of time'.[32] To avoid confusion, the congruent neoclassical and legal monopoly power scenarios will be addressed hereinafter as 'traditional monopoly' (a term that will be used interchangeably with 'static monopoly' or 'structural monopoly').

Dynamic competition, on the other hand, defines a monopolist as a market player who is immune from the competitive threats of other entrepreneurs who might, in other circumstances, enter his or her field of activity.[33] Metaphorically speaking, it is a situation where a market player feels 'insulated from the cold winds of potential competition'.[34] In this sense the definition complements the dynamic competition notion – if dynamic competition is the process of struggle between entrepreneurs, dynamic monopoly is its negative scenario, namely a situation in which this core struggle comes to a halt in a certain market area, where a market player is effectively shielded from the struggle. The common scenario creating a dynamic monopoly is a resource monopoly, specifically, where control over the supply of certain resources that serve as inputs is the virtue that gains the monopolist his/her sought-after status,[35] and in an antitrust–IP scenario such problematic control is gained through ownership of an IP resource. It should be emphasized that, except in a case of exclusive control over production resources by governmental intervention, a case where a producer happens to be the only producer of a particular product is *not* likely to constitute a 'monopoly' under the definition discussed here, because that producer is still assumed to be subject to the competitive market threats from entrepreneurs who may try to compete with him/her.[36] The monopoly concept discussed in this section will hereinafter be addressed as 'process monopoly' (a term interchangeable with the terms 'dynamic monopoly' or 'Austrian monopoly concept').[37]

The analysis that follows will harness the dynamic monopoly and competition notions as a basis for a legal analysis. In other words, it will suggest a legal analysis that is congruent with the dynamic monopoly and competition concepts, and thus differs from much of the current antitrust theory, which is mostly associated with the neoclassical economic concepts.

3.3.2 Dynamic Antitrust Analysis

The dynamic-oriented antitrust analysis paradigm for assessing conduct suspected to be anticompetitive applies a substantive twofold test as follows: an assessment of the level of robustness of the competitive process in the specific market area; and an empirical evaluation of the initial circumstances.

Assessment of the level of robustness of the competitive process in a specific market area

The first part of the analysis will determine whether and to what degree the particular market area displays a picture of process monopoly (that is, a state of affairs where a market player is shielded from competition to a substantial degree). Perhaps it is useful to use a metaphor in this context, to better explain the nature of the notion put forward here. If the competition process were a robust river, this stage evaluates the vigor of the river's flow. This vigor can be measured by two factors: the speed of flow (analogous to the speed in which the market area changes, for example, product changes, entry of new market players and so on); and the volume of the river (the number of competitors in the large sense of the term, bearing in mind that competition may come from adjacent market areas).[38] The main element examined in this stage is the extent to which the suspected market players are exposed to or insulated from competitive threats.

The key question is of course the practical one, namely, how to identify a process monopoly and measure its extent. We need to develop screening mechanisms and indicators that can serve as red flags for identifying the existence of a process monopoly. Furthermore, these mechanisms must be of a pragmatic and workable nature so that courts will be able to apply them within a reasonable framework of time and resources. In other words, we cannot prescribe an in-depth industry study that will be conducted by economists over a period of time since it may prove too costly and lengthy for the court system to handle, and furthermore because by the time such a study is carried out some of the early observations might have become outdated. The task is clearly not an easy one. It is perhaps even more challenging because the legal test must use photo-finish indicators to evaluate an ongoing dynamic pattern (in this sense, developing a legal measure for static monopoly seems easier, if only because it is defined as a static phenomenon). Furthermore, it is certainly disheartening to observe that the parallel question of identifying and measuring traditional monopoly power, which has been around for decades now, is still at the center of the debate.[39] Nevertheless, we should not let this difficulty deter us: it has been said that the difficult is simply what takes a little time,[40] and therefore the following paragraphs lay out the suggested elements for measuring a process monopoly.

The factors used to evaluate the dynamics and pattern of the market process in order to determine its vigor and detect any traces of dynamic monopoly should include the following:

- *The observed rate of innovation* in the examined market area, both by way of IP-protected innovation and by 'simple' non-protected market innovation – introduction of novel products, adding new features to existing products, new product imaging and so on. The rationale behind this factor is quite simple. In a robust competitive struggle environment competitors are constantly trying to innovate their products and market techniques in an effort to gain an edge over existing and potential competition. A process monopolist who is insulated from competitive threats is under no similar pressure to innovate. As one economist has put it: 'the best of all monopoly profits is a quiet life'.[41] Therefore a dynamic monopoly is likely to slow down the relevant market area's innovation rate. Conversely, a market area where a healthy competitive process takes place is likely to display a trend of innovation demonstrated both through a trend of newly-formed IP, and through differentiation in the features of products competing in the same market area (for example, product features, product marketing notions, consumers targeted by the product and so on).[42]
- *The observed sensitivity of the suspected firm's behavior to consumer trends and behavior of the other market area players.* This point may seem somewhat close to the legal and static market power definitions mentioned earlier, as it refers, inter alia, to the suspect's control over its product's price. The notable difference is that the evaluation goes beyond price sensitivity (although this is admittedly an important factor) to observe other features such as customer-care policies, quality of products, embarking on advertising campaigns and so on. The rationale is that a firm exposed to competitive threats will try to match or top its competitors' efforts with regard to attracting consumers.
- *The volatility of the market area population over time.* Common sense dictates that within a competitive process significant consumer demand attracts a large number of entrepreneurs hoping to cash in on this demand. Therefore little volatility in the market composition over time may raise suspicions of dynamic monopoly. Note that a continuous scenario of a small number of stable sellers (known in price theory as oligopoly), or even a single seller (static monopoly), is not necessarily of interest in a process analysis context. The competitive process and competitive threats it entails can be very fierce even where there are only a few sellers or one long-term one; an example is the case of Coca Cola and Pepsi Cola. Furthermore, evident short-lived entrepreneurial efforts to compete with the long-term players,

even if unsuccessful, may indicate that the dynamic process and its competitive threats are still in place.

- *The fluctuating volatility of the suspect firm's static market shares over time,* namely market data that reflect both upward and downward changes of its static market share. This factor should be considered positively as an indication that a dynamic competition process is in place and there is no process monopoly. However, the lack of such market share volatility should not be considered as a conclusive indication of a process monopoly. A vigorous competition process will often be accompanied by swinging trends of the players' static market shares, as different players gain the upper hand in the competitive struggle, and in a process-monopoly situation, the suspect's static market share is likely to remain unchanged over time as he/she faces no competitive threats. However, a healthy dynamic environment can still display stable market shares, for example, where everyone is constantly maximizing their competitive efforts – introducing new products, improving their service and so on, and expanding at the same rate – so that the relative market shares picture remains stagnant. Furthermore, a vigorous competitive process may also display a consistent increase in the suspect's market share, for example, where the suspect legitimately gains the upper hand in the competitive struggle as his/her entrepreneurial and market skills simply surpass those of the competing player, in which case the competitive threats are still very much in place. Therefore, a fluctuating volatility of the suspect's market share should primarily serve as a defense for a process-monopoly allegation, namely for substantiating dynamic competition in the market area. Having said that, the observation that a company has held a solid dominant position for several years or more may also be utilized as a prima facie indicator for a shuffling of the competitive process rather than a clear indication of a process monopoly.[43]
- *The degree of price volatility in the market area* both in products' real prices (excluding inflation of course) and in the relative prices of different players' products. As observed earlier in this study, in a dynamic market discovery process prices serve as signals for consumer preferences; sellers carefully read these signals and try to adjust their production accordingly. Consumer preferences are likely to change over time as seasons and consumer trends evolve. Furthermore, consumers' relative preferences are likely to change to reflect the preference adjustments as new products and entrepreneurs enter the market area. Therefore a high degree of price volatility is likely to reflect a healthy dynamic competition process. Similarly, a lack of such price volatility is likely to reflect a sluggishness of the competitive discovery process, perhaps to a level of dynamic monopoly.
- *The availability of alternatives to the suspect firm's products.*[44] Dynamic thinking implies that consumer demand will always be met as entrepreneurs

are constantly trying to discover what it is that consumers want. Therefore a robust competitive market area is likely to offer consumers a number of alternative products in response to a certain demand, reflecting competing entrepreneurial efforts to cater to consumer tastes. Furthermore, the consumers' function as engines of such a discovery process is somewhat curtailed when they are unable to express their preferences (for lack of alternatives). Therefore the availability of alternatives for the suspected firm's product (and their number) may be indicative of the vigor of the competitive process. Note that the dynamic notion of alternatives is broader than the static concept of product substitutes, because under the dynamic model products in adjacent markets may also be considered as alternatives.[45] Therefore to be considered as alternatives, products need not be 100 percent substitutable.

The conclusiveness of a lack of alternatives for a product as an indication for a process monopoly should be addressed carefully. For example, such a lack may be due to the fact that a market area is a new one.[46] Furthermore, a more vigorous entrepreneurial process is likely to yield a large number of new market niches (in which alternatives may require time to develop). Nevertheless, in the long run where the untold assumptions are met, a healthy market area should display a number of alternatives for a product. Therefore a conspicuous lack thereof should create a presumption for process monopoly and shift the burden of proof to the defendant to rebut the presumption by evidence that the situation does not stem from process monopoly (that is, from lack of competitive threats). Note that since antitrust laws entail criminal liability, this burden of proof will be moderate, as the defendant merely has to establish reasonable doubt that the lack of alternatives is not due to a dynamic monopoly.[47]

- *The degree of uncertainty in the market area.* As noted above, the dynamic competition notion entails a certain degree of uncertainty because information is neither perfect nor free and because market players cannot predict the next competitive moves taken by existing competitors or potential new entrants (in fact they do not even know the latter's identity). Therefore the degree to which a suspect market player is able to insulate him/herself from the problem of uncertainty is relevant for identifying a process monopoly. This study will focus on the use of IP as an instrument for beating the market's uncertainty disadvantage. For example, where a market player owns a commercially useful patent that is crucial in the production of all products in the market area, licensing his/her patent under a grantback-licensing clause might be considered as excessively defeating the market process. This is because a grantback clause assures the patentee that all future innovations by other entrepreneurs will have to be granted back to him/her, which makes the patentee immune to the bulk of competitive innovative threats in that market area. Note that the basic working assumption throughout the study will assume intellectual property as a desirable legal institution. Therefore the mere existence (namely grant and possession) of an IPR will be regarded as an inherently legitimate fact as it will be assumed that any relevant market-stifling considerations have already been taken into account by the IP statutes or the Patent and Trademark Office which granted the IPR in accordance with IP statutes. However, such immunity will not be extended for IP derivative conduct, namely for application of the IPR rather than its existence.[48]

- *The existence of barriers to entry into the market area that obstruct the course of the competitive process.* In this sense the dynamic analysis is similar to the neoclassical and legal analyses in that it recognizes freedom of entry as essential for sustaining a vigorous competitive process. The rationale here is clear: the competitive process depends upon free entrepreneurial entry into the market area as part of the competitive struggle. As soon as entry obstacles are erected they shield the current market players from the competitive threats of potential competitors and may create a process monopoly. The factor described here differs from the entry barriers factor mentioned earlier in the untold assumptions section because here the focus is not on objective entry barriers that are inherent to the industry, but rather on barriers that have been erected as a result of specific behavior carried out by the suspect. To give a concrete example, we are not talking here about cases like the market for oil, where prospective market sellers must obtain control over a fuel pump in order to enter the market, because they cannot produce oil from other substances. Rather, this factor involves cases where specific behavior of the market player is the direct cause of the entry barrier. As we shall see in the next chapters, in an IP context such barriers to entry may arise where IPR owners utilize IP as a sword, rather than as a shield, in conduct that effectively impedes other entrepreneurs from joining their market area and therefore obstructs the natural flow of the dynamic competition process.

It should be noted that the static market share datum, namely whether the suspect firm possesses a lion's share of the market area, is intentionally omitted from this list. Static market share is in itself irrelevant from a dynamic competition point of view. The single relevant issue is the market *pattern*, namely whether a vigorous competition process is in place, one that naturally exposes all the market players to the 'cold winds of competition'. Unlike the neoclassical model, whose assumptions include a large number of sellers each holding a small market share, a scenario of a lion's market share split between only a couple of competitors is not inconsistent with any of the Austrian competition assumptions.[49] Indeed the assumption is that as long as a healthy competitive process is in place, even large market players are exposed to its threats. It is true that because a process monopolist is shielded from competition, then in practice, a producer that becomes a dynamic monopolist is likely to gain the lion market share of that market area soon thereafter. Nevertheless, a static lion's share in itself is an inconclusive indicator of the vigor of the competitive process, because unless proven otherwise, there is no reason to believe that it was not gained as the result of legitimate successful entrepreneurial behavior (the basic premise being that obtaining a lion's share of the market in itself does not affect the competitive *process* as smaller market players will keep struggling to earn part of the share). Similarly, a smaller market share is not conclusive proof that the suspect is not a process monopolist, as he/she could still enjoy an illegal degree of insulation from competition, although it may still be an insufficient degree for him/her to acquire a lion's share.[50] There is another practical reason why market share is not useful for dynamic antitrust analysis. Determining static market share is an inherently imprecise task. Static market share depends on the relevant market definition, which, as noted earlier, is an arbitrary and inaccurate concept. Therefore the large margin of error surrounding the market share finding renders it less attractive as a guidance consideration.

Empirical evaluation of the initial circumstances

The second part of the analysis calls for an empirical evaluation of the initial circumstances, namely, to what extent the market area circumstances correspond with the untold assumptions of the dynamic model that were laid out earlier in Section 3.2. Since the untold assumptions are essential for the organic growth of a competitive process, such evaluation is useful because it assesses the relevant market area background upon which the market process emerges, namely to what extent the objective empirical characteristics serve as fertile ground for the growth of a competitive process. Note that the empirical characteristics of a market area may vary over time, and therefore this evaluation will have to be made anew for each case (for example, a market niche remains new only for so long). This examination of the objective market area circumstances is useful in order to determine whether or not a causal connection can be established between the suspicious conduct and the process monopoly observed above.

Application of the dynamic model

The two-part analysis should be applied as follows. The first part is applied as a first stage in order to determine whether a significant degree of process monopoly is in place. If the competitive process in the market area is found to be sufficiently healthy, namely the suspect is not found to enjoy a process-monopoly scenario, then the analysis stops right there, since the suspect has not carried out the 'monopolizing' *actus reus* that is required by §2 of the Sherman Act.[51] On the other hand, where the first part of the analysis yields a finding of a substantial degree of process monopoly, then the second part of the test evaluating the initial characteristics of the industry must be applied in order to assess what part of the competitive process failure may be attributed to the objective initial industry characteristics (which may include patents), and what part may be attributed to the suspect conduct. The test is sensitive to the specific circumstances of the industry at hand, because it takes into consideration the extent to which the initial characteristics of the industry provide fertile ground for organic growth of a vigorous competition process. The usefulness of the analysis for determining antitrust liability stems from the fact that it identifies the extent to which a process monopoly is in place and the causal connection between the suspect's conduct and the dynamic monopoly. In other words, the analysis determines whether the suspect has 'monopolized'.

Note that the dynamic model's praxeological assumption on human nature renders redundant an evaluation of the suspect's subjective intent element. The dynamic model relies on the axiom that a competitive market process is a naturally occurring phenomenon derived from universal human action characteristics. In other words, a vigorous competitive process is the presumed default. Therefore, where an evaluation finds that the process has been curtailed, as a process monopolist has surfaced, there must be some specific reason behind it, as there can be no smoke without fire. There are two possible culprits: objective market circumstances (as detailed above in Section 3.2), or the subjective suspect conduct at hand. Therefore after evaluating the degree to which the process failure may be attributed to the objective market characteristics, any remaining blame may and should be attributed to the suspected conduct (bearing in mind the presumption that any competitive behavior, no matter how fierce, will never result in restriction of competitive process. On the contrary, bold competitive moves will invigorate the competitors' efforts to offer original market moves of their own). The defendant should of course be free to try to raise reasonable doubt as to this assumption by directing the blame towards the conduct of another market player.

A number of caveats

It is important to note that the results of an evaluation based on the factors listed above will be neither accurate nor conclusive. The factors are simply an open-ended list of guidelines for assessing the potency of the competitive process in a market area, and whether a suspect market player has become a process monopolist. The suggested analysis does not purport to produce magical observations that will simplify reality into legitimate–competitive versus illegitimate–process–monopoly market situations. Real-life scenarios are complicated and ambiguous; they do not come in black and white. Therefore real-life legal solutions, let alone their application, are mere approximations. Accordingly, the application of the suggested standard, whose guidelines cannot be numerically measured, will be an approximation of the vigor of the competitive process in a market area, and the causal connection between the suspected conduct and the resulting circumstances. In this sense, the results of the suggested test are no different from any existing applications of legal and traditional economic notions to complex factual scenarios. The difference lies in the fresh outlook that is suggested here. Rather than focusing on static market share and the mental element behind the conduct, this model focuses on evaluating the vigor of the dynamic process through a combined analysis of the original market characteristics and the state of the competitive process.

A comparison of the dynamic analysis with the current legal analysis

A practical comparison Current law appears to adopt the structural monopoly power concept. Therefore the first element in its analysis is a finding of static monopoly power.[52] However, being a static monopoly in itself is not held to constitute the offense according to §2 of the Sherman Act. Thus for example, a traditional monopoly that stems from supreme skill or innovation is held as legitimate.[53] The offense of monopolization under §2 requires a second element, namely a finding of a subjective element that will establish 'the wilful acquisition or maintenance of [monopoly] power as distinguished from growth or development that come as a consequence of a superior product, business acumen, or historical accident'.[54] Accordingly, a firm that actively seeks to gain or maintain power by 'purely competitive means' is not seen as violating Sherman Act §2.[55] This second element complicates the test, because it calls for a definition of such 'wilful acquisition or maintenance' as well as for a determination of the burden of proof required for establishing it (namely, the legal way of measuring it). Indeed, courts have struggled with developing a definition of the required subjective element,[56] and with the type and level of evidence that is required for proving it.[57] The task is further complicated by the need to balance between 'considerations of fairness and the need to preserve proper economic incentives'[58] so as to ensure that condemning the defendant's conduct will not unduly deter desirable business behavior.[59]

In short, current legal analysis of a Sherman Act §2 'monopolizing' case entails two difficult tasks. First, identifying static monopoly power. This is usually done by using the market structure as evidence for such power, namely by identifying the suspect as possessing the lion's share in the market (which involves the notoriously complicated question of defining the relevant 'market'). Other indicators for traditional monopoly power include persistent excess profits[60] and 'monopoly conduct', for example, conduct that reflects the ability to raise prices without losing market share.[61] The second difficult task requires courts to examine the subjective element behind the suspicious conduct in order to discern whether this element is a purely competitive one and hence legitimate or whether it amounts to illegitimate anticompetitive 'exclusionary conduct' because of the subjective element behind it.

The dynamic analysis suggested in this study is different. It focuses attention solely on the condition of the *competitive process* in a market area, which is, not accidentally, also the methodological core of antitrust policy and performs a subjective evaluation of this process (taking into account the objective characteristics of the market area). In metaphoric terms, the traditional analysis is built on an analysis of: the size of the pond and the size of the fish compared to the pond, and whether the suspicious fish is able to maintain or enlarge a private domain in the common pond. The dynamic analysis does not concern itself with the size of the pond, but rather focuses on the relationship between the suspect fish and the rest of the fish in that pond, and more specifically on the observed daily behavior of the suspect fish. It utilizes different phenomena from the pond's daily life as clues for evaluating whether the suspected fish is able to successfully ignore the rules of the pond to an extent that is detrimental to the public good. This shift in focus renders the dynamic analysis easier than the current one in two ways. First, it precludes the court from the need to evaluate whether the suspect possesses static monopoly power, an evaluation that requires the determination of static market share (which is a highly complex and debated evaluation, one that is arguably subject to a large margin of error).[62] As noted earlier, the suspect's static market share is irrelevant in the context of the suggested dynamic analysis (even if he/she is the only seller in the market!). Similarly, the question of traditional monopoly power is deemed irrelevant in a context that focuses on process monopoly rather than on structural monopoly. Second, as explained earlier, the dynamic analysis precludes the court from the duty of evaluating the subjective purpose behind the suspected conduct for the purpose of determining whether it is competitive or anticompetitive. Such a task is not only extremely difficult in a pragmatic sense, but it is also open to serious doubt as to whether it is even theoretically feasible. As a natural part of a vigorous competitive struggle, market players constantly wish that their competition would vanish (for example, for their competitors to retire or go out of business). In this sense all market players are inherently guilty of anticompetitive intentions. Therefore it is hard to imagine a scenario in which the true subjective purpose behind a suspicious market conduct is not anticompetitive. The goals will always be anticompetitive; therefore the only relevant question is the means. The dynamic analysis suggests that an objective test is sufficient for deducing these means.[63]

A theoretical comparison The current legal analysis and the suggested dynamic analysis are very different, as discussed above in the review of the traditional and the dynamic monopoly concepts. This is where the heart of the difference lies. The current legal analysis relies on neoclassical economic concepts, and therefore proscribes activities that create a structural monopoly. Its ensuing focus of concern is on precluding market players from being able to control prices, to maintain prices above a certain 'competition level', to exclude competition in a relevant market or to force a purchaser to do something that he/she would not do in a competitive market.[64] The suggested dynamic analysis on the other hand, relies on the Austrian competition concept. Therefore it seeks to eliminate conduct that leads to a process-monopoly scenario. Its ensuing focus of concern is on ensuring a healthy competitive market process by preventing market players from curtailing the process by insulating themselves from the competitive threats.

The two analyses are neither antithetical nor mutually exclusive. As has been noted earlier, they share certain points of view, such as viewing barriers to entry as a dangerous cause for monopoly, and observing that a seller's insensitivity to competitors' prices may be indicative of a monopoly. In fact, dynamic notions are not entirely foreign to the current legal analysis. Certain dynamic notions can be traced in some traditional legal cases, see for example Judge Hand's statement in the Alcoa case: 'possession of *unchallenged* economic power deadens initiative, discourages thrift and depresses energy; ... *immunity from competition is a narcotic,* and *rivalry is a stimulant, to industrial progress*' (italics added).[65] The theoretical difference between the two analyses is twofold. First and foremost, it lies in the *shift of focus.* Look again at the above Alcoa quote. The traditional analysis focuses on detecting economic power as an instrument for identifying a market failure. In other words, it focuses on the 'economic power' part of the phrase.[66] The suggested dynamic analysis focuses on ensuring a healthy competitive process and the competitive threats it poses. In other words, it focuses on the 'unchallenged' portion of the phrase. The dynamic notions are not entirely new. They have been around all the time, and their traces can be detected in both case law and the antitrust agencies' guidelines. It is a shift of focus that defines the theoretical difference between the two approaches. The second difference is a methodological one. The current legal approach relies on neoclassical price theory which, as its name suggests, focuses on prices as the main indication for the market's condition. The dynamic analysis relies on the Austrian competition concept. It is broader, and utilizes additional instruments beyond price for evaluating the health of the market process (such as quality of products, innovation, customer service, differentiation levels and so on).

The antitrust–IP theoretical context This context enables us to compare the suggested analysis with the existing traditional antitrust–IP theoretical analysis. The leading work in the field is probably Louis Kaplow's seminal article, which relies on traditional economics.[67] Kaplow's conceptual solution to the antitrust–IP interface calls for a ratio test that compares the patentee's reward from the patent with the monopoly loss imposed on society by the practice. Accordingly, Kaplow suggests that practices with higher ratios are the ones that should be allowed. In other words, the solution measures the amount of reward to the patentee against the monopoly loss to society.[68] The dynamic analysis focuses on the problem from a very different angle. It begins with a working assumption that IP in itself is a desirable institution that does not result in a process monopoly (as its grant is carefully monitored by the IP statutes and the Patent and Trademark Office). It goes on to regard the dynamic economic analysis as the optimal approach for harmonizing antitrust and intellectual property because its premises are sensitive to the rationales of both institutions.[69] Therefore it regards an antitrust analysis that is based on dynamic competition notions as the best instrument for resolving antitrust–IP conflict scenarios. Chapter 2 has touched upon the question of identifying the optimal trade-off between antitrust and IP.[70] The utilitarian IP justification hails IP as an incentive for promoting innovation, which in turn results in economic growth. Antitrust, on the other hand, is said to focus on eliminating the harms of monopoly. The question is how to identify the point past which allowing the pertinent practice would be undesirable because its detrimental cost to the market exceeds its respective benefits. It is suggested that an application of the dynamic solution effectively mitigates this problem. Since the dynamic model is regarded as reasonable both by IP and antitrust, then if the dynamic considerations imply that the competitive process is being curtailed, this will signal that the IP–antitrust trade-off is negative, and therefore that the practice should not be allowed. In other words, it is suggested that the application of a dynamic solution should serve as a guideline for resolving the antitrust–IP interface.

General policy implications

The dynamic model's assumed principles of human action suppose that without a specific intentional anticompetitive conduct the nature of human action will create a competitive environment (in other words, it assumes a self-sustained, and perhaps even self-correcting natural market process). This notion along with the model's dedicated anti-interventionist agenda may cause this analysis to prefer a generally less activist antitrust policy that will give market players more of a benefit of the doubt. Furthermore, the dynamic analysis will probably favor the more cautious rule of reason approach for all cases, perhaps even in straight price-fixing cartelizing cases.

It is interesting to review this from a historical perspective. In 1890, there were two models of common law analyses that competed for the approval of U.S. courts.[71] The first model assessed both naked and ancillary restraints in the same manner using a rule of reason approach, and focused on whether the challenged conduct could create a monopoly by precluding other merchants from entering the market and competing. This view assumed that without coercive limits on new entry, the market's self-correcting tendencies would protect consumers from exploitation. The second model divided trade restrictions into two categories, evaluating ancillary restrictions with a rule of reason and treating cartels as inherently unreasonable and illegal, regardless of market circumstances. In the seminal Addyston Pipe case,[72] Judge William H. Taft examined these two models, and embraced the latter notion. However, judicial decisions in the decades that followed seem to have marked a trail of movement towards the first model, as more and more factual scenarios have been considered under a rule of reason analysis (or its corollary, the truncated 'quick look' rule of reason analysis) rather than under the '*per se*' rule. The dynamic competition model is probably theoretically closer to the first approach mentioned here, because it assumes that without proven objective or subjective limitations on the competitive process, the market's self-correcting tendencies would generate a vigorous competitive process in which consumers are well off since entrepreneurs are competing for their business. In this sense, the dynamic approach is compatible with the contemporary pendulum swing towards a rule of reason analysis.

3.4 PLACING THE PROPERTY NARRATIVES WITHIN THE DYNAMIC ANTITRUST PARADIGM

After fleshing out the dynamic solution paradigm we shall now briefly revisit the property narratives that were developed in Chapter 2 in order to see where these fit into the dynamic solution picture. In Chapter 2, we established that there are two property rights here: the IP right, which is more traditional, and the property right to a competitive environment that is bestowed upon consumers by the antitrust laws. These two rights are far removed from each other; they are very different in nature and therefore should be addressed separately.

3.4.1 Intellectual Property Rights

Austrian economics admits that the naturally robust and untamed competitive market process it envisages requires a certain minimal degree of governmental intervention, in the form of recognized property rights. Accordingly, Austrian methodology asserts that the government should not interfere with the natural market process, *except* for the protection of private property and such libertarian institutions as are required for ensuring an effective competitive order.[73] In other words, it allows for market intervention that is necessary for protection of private property, which is considered a vital cornerstone of any market society – similar to an axiomatic 'rule of the game' that is necessary in order for the game (market process) to take place. Furthermore, traditional private property (ownership) is also cherished because of its key role in motivating entrepreneurs to display efficient consumer-pleasing economic behavior that enables the competitive market process to evolve.[74]

While this portrayal seems rather simple and straightforward, complications begin to arise where in practice the recognition of a legitimate property right may interfere with the vital assumptions of the dynamic competition model. This is central to the antitrust–IP problem when viewed from the dynamic competition point of view, that is: at what point does the IP protection which started off as the cornerstone of the market process, namely private property, cross the line to create a situation where market actors can use it to erect socially undesirable obstacles to the competitive process, obstacles that conflict with the untold initial assumptions (circumstances) of the dynamic competition model.[75] Semantically, this can be portrayed in two ways: first, by asking at what point does IP protection allow competitors to use it as a competition-stifling instrument; second, as used above, by asking at what point does IP protection create (or result in) obstacles to the competitive process. However, the two different ways of defining the question are probably substantively identical – because the human action is presumed to be whatever people do for profit.[76] Lack of or significant reduction in competitive threats ensures higher profits, and therefore whenever market actors are presented with an opportunity to reduce competition, we can safely assume that they will indeed choose to do so, and thereby erect obstacles to competition (perhaps to a level of a process monopoly).

3.4.2 The Antitrust Rights

The interpretation of antitrust laws as creating a consumers' property right, as developed in Chapter 2, depicts a type of property right that is slightly different from the traditional forms of private property. The most notable difference is that the property right created by antitrust laws is of a communal type, namely it is bestowed equally on all members of society. Prima facie it may seem that antitrust rights are far less interesting than IP rights from the dynamic competition point of view, for two reasons. First, the dynamic competition world-view involves an ongoing market process that is characterized by competitive struggle. In a process of struggle, market participants are constantly looking to gain a competitive advantage over their competitors, and therefore rights that are bestowed equally on all members of society are of little interest since they generally do not shift the relative power balance between specific market actors. Second, antitrust rights might seem less significant in a dynamic competition paradigm because antitrust rights focus on consumers, rather than on entrepreneurial producers, while dynamic competition seemingly focuses on the change generated by the latter.

However, the prima facie impression described above may be somewhat misleading, since there are at least two noteworthy and relevant links between antitrust rights and the dynamic competition paradigm. The first one comes from the fact that there is another, perhaps more important explicit link between the dynamic model and property rights. The dynamic model historically recognized the legitimacy of governmental intervention in the form of property rights, since these were considered as the cornerstones of any functional market society, and therefore as institutional prerequisites for the existence of a competitive market.[77] In this sense, antitrust rights fit into that niche as snugly as more traditional property rights. The argument here is that antitrust rights, similarly to other property rights although from another angle, are essential instruments in a market society order; they are part of a basic line of 'rules of the game' that allow the dynamic competitive process to take place and guard it from empirical situations that stifle it. The second link between antitrust rights and the dynamic model stems from the fact that entrepreneurs make up only half of the dynamic story. The notion of competition as a discovery process involves the consumers' crucial function as the ones pushing the whole process forward. The market players are constantly trying to guess the preferences, wishes and other features of the consumers' demand curve in order to maximize their profits. Since there is no perfect information assumption in place, competitors have to buy or collect information for themselves and the best source for gathering information is of course the consumers themselves.[78] The primary way in which consumers convey the information that producers are eager to obtain[79] is through the market process. The demand, choice between alternative products, and the price consumers are willing to pay are all ways in which consumers express information and send signals to which producers and entrepreneurs listen carefully, because the more accurately the latter interpret what consumers tell them, the more profitable their businesses are likely to be. Antitrust rights safeguard this process. They safeguard the consumers' role in the competitive discovery process that competition is. It prevents stalling of the process (that is, process-monopoly conditions) in which consumers might not be able to reward the entrepreneurs who best meet their needs because of lack of alternatives or price diversity, and in which producers will not pay attention to consumers' signals because in the absence of competitive threats they are unlikely to gain additional profits by listening to consumers.

Embracing the antitrust property notion (and antitrust in general), although perhaps not directly inconsistent with the dynamic model, may seem to be outside its theoretical realm. This is because the model's formal core rejects centralized market intervention as part of its anti-interventionist agenda,[80] and its assumptions on the naturally robust nature of the competitive process, infinite number of market possibilities, and ingenuity of the human entrepreneurial brain are sufficient to ensure an ongoing energetic market process that will overcome any apparent obstacles (such as extended IPR practices). Indeed, the extreme Austrian argument interprets this as calling for the abandonment of the market-interventionist antitrust policy, root and branch.[81]

The view supported here is that the antitrust laws are a relatively recent property right addition to the codebooks, an addition that was added as a social instrument whose purpose is to overcome certain practical shortcomings of the Austrian dynamic model. Indeed, the Austrian model is probably the best competition model available; it describes the real process that takes place in markets more effectively than competing competition models. It is because of this appeal that it was chosen as a basis for the model developed earlier in this chapter. Nevertheless, in practice, reality teaches us that in certain borderline scenarios the market does not perform according to the dynamic model. It is only in these relatively rare practical cases in which the dynamic competitive process begins to falter that we should recognize and enforce the consumers' antitrust property rights.

For the sake of accuracy, it should therefore be acknowledged that enforcing antitrust property rights might render the paradigm suggested here as part of a 'softened' dynamic competition model, one that partially waived its original anti-interventionist notions to embrace antitrust policy in a manner that may not be accepted by all Austrian scholars.[82] Nevertheless, there are a number of reasons why this compromise is very small, and why it is unavoidable.

First, some of the inconsistency is rooted within Austrian economics doctrine itself. Austrian economists argue that governmental intervention should be confined to protecting private initiatives and enterprise through the institution of private property and libertarian institutions of law.[83] Therefore they justify private property as a fundamental prerequisite for any market economy.[84] However, it is unclear how we can identify a clear-cut borderline between a legitimate intervention, one that merely protects private initiatives, and an excessive illegitimate intervention which goes beyond that. A reasonable antitrust policy can feasibly be categorized as the former, namely a legitimate intervention that is necessary for ensuring the competitive market order.

Second, the analysis suggested in this study is still very close to the original Austrian economics competition model in all other aspects both theoretically and methodologically (with no use being made of mathematical formulations).

Third, the theoretical concession made here is justified by rationales that are embraced by the Austrian model, namely, by characterizing antitrust as private property, which as such is legitimately protected by the government as a cornerstone of the social and therefore market order, without which the market process cannot take place (which takes us back to the implicit Austrian market assumptions that opened this chapter).

Fourth, it is argued that Austrian scholarship would probably be less critical of antitrust policy if it were assured that such a policy would be based on dynamic competition premises, as in the analysis developed in this chapter.

Fifth, the following important distinction is in order: antitrust policy does not entail a classic centralized regulatory process. Antitrust, even when viewed as a property regime, is not a form of ongoing governmental regulation of trade, but rather involves episodic one-off intervention, while allowing the market process as a whole to evolve organically.[85] The centralized market intervention that Austrians were so vehemently opposed to was clearly in the form of an ongoing trade regulation, which they rightfully viewed as destructive for the organic flow of the competitive process. Antitrust does not represent such a form of intervention, and therefore the argument promoted here is that antitrust should not be considered extremely problematic in an Austrian competition context.[86]

Finally, we should bear in mind that law is a practical philosophy, while economics is not necessarily bound by similar practical requirements.[87] The praxeological nature of Austrian economics (and its ensuing resemblance to real-life market processes) is what rendered it so attractive for this study in the first place. As economic models go, the Austrian competition model is relatively law-friendly because it closely resembles the way markets work in real life. However, allowing for antitrust notions is the one last necessary step that is needed in order to utilize the dynamic competition model within a legal setting. Law, as a practical science, simply cannot allow empirical borderline cases, where the dynamic competition process falters, to go unnoticed or unresolved. A similar argument is mentioned in the writings of Hayek himself,[88] and is also demonstrated in one other legal application of Austrian economics.[89]

3.5 CONCLUSION

The analysis suggested in this chapter harnessed the dynamic competition and dynamic monopoly models as the foundations for an original dynamic antitrust analysis. It is suggested that an antitrust approach based on the process-monopoly and competition concepts offers a number of invaluable advantages over an antitrust approach that relies on their neoclassical counterparts, both as a general antitrust model and particularly with respect to antitrust–IP clashes. First, the dynamic competition model more closely resembles real markets and therefore is more suitable for resolving real-life market situations. Furthermore, its realistic nature renders it more compatible with antitrust that as a legal doctrine is practical rather than purely theoretical. A second advantage stems from the fact that both the dynamic model and antitrust policy focus on the same practical phenomenon, namely a flowing competitive process. The dynamic model focuses on the features of the process and the antitrust policy is dedicated to safeguarding the competitive process. Finally, as noted in the previous chapters,[90] the dynamic model appears to be particularly beneficial for resolving antitrust–IP clash scenarios because of the theoretical threads that render it sensible to the rationales of the IP institution. Therefore an analysis that is based upon the dynamic competition concept reduces the tensions between antitrust and IP.

The suggested analysis would be useful in a number of contexts. First, it can help to explicate some of the legal practice displayed by courts in antitrust–IP cases. Legal cases reflect judicial thinking that embraces much of the dynamic model's assumptions and rationales. This study will trace these Austrian notions and relate them to the formal analytical model suggested here. This will show that the courts' thinking in monopolizing cases is probably not as confused or incoherent as many Chicago school antitrust analysts have portrayed it to be. Rather, much of the courts' thinking is simply embedded in an alternative more intuitive and arguably superior economic model, namely the dynamic model. Second, since the dynamic model accounts for much of the way courts think, its application may serve as a predictive tool for future cases. Finally, and perhaps most importantly, the formal dynamic apparatus could be put to concrete use in resolving hypothetical antitrust–IP fact patterns that may arise in future cases.

Certainly, the suggested analysis does not provide a magic panacea for all of the practical challenges that antitrust policy in general and the antitrust–IP cases in particular, entail. It does not even cover all Sherman Act §2 cases, since it does not apply to attempt-to-monopolize cases. Furthermore, its application will surely not be a simple task. Nevertheless, it provides a promising and original alternative to the current legal analysis that relies on the Chicago school, and offers some profound advantages for the antitrust–IP interface. Note also that on a practical level, this alternative dynamic analysis comes at a time when antitrust courts are receptive to new ideas; Recent Supreme Court decisions have downplayed the Chicago school principles and displayed receptivity to what is known as the post-Chicago economic analysis.[91] Therefore it seems that the current legal trend is interested in and open to theoretical alternatives to the Chicago school of antitrust analysis.

The following chapters will demonstrate pragmatic applications of the suggested formal analysis to real-life antitrust–IP issues and cases. The review will include a comparative outlook that will compare the application to existing case law, in terms of thinking, methodology and the end results. Special attention will be paid to tracing dynamic competition and antitrust property notions in the existing cases (which as we shall see may not be as entirely captivated by neoclassical theory as we would expect them to be).

NOTES

1 Edward S. Mason, *Schumpeter on Monopoly and the Large Firm*, 33 Rev. Econ. & Stat. 139, 144 (1951).

2 Id. (Mason referred to antitrust doctrine in general, not specifically to the antitrust–IP cusp).

3 Chapter 1, p. 12; Chapter 2, pp. 48–9.

4 For a review of Austrian economics as a praxeological science, see: Hans-Hermann Hoppe, *The Economics and Ethics of Private Property* 141–64 (Boston/Dordrecht/London: Kluwer Academic 1993); Murray N. Rothbard, 'Praxeology: The Methodology of Austrian Economics', in *The Foundations of Modern Austrian Economics* 19 (Edwin Dolan ed., Kansas City, KS: Sheed & Ward 1976); Murray N. Rothbard, 'Praxeology, Value Judgments, and Public Policy', in *The Foundations of Modern Austrian Economics* 89 (Edwin Dolan ed., Kansas City, KS: Sheed & Ward 1976); and Ludwig von Mises, *Human Action: A Treatise on Economics* 1–3 (Chicago: Henry Regnery Company, 3rd edn 1966).

5 Praxeology is linguistically defined as the study of human action and conduct, see Webster's *Third New International Dictionary* 1782 (Philip B. Gove ed., Springfield, MA: G. & C. Merriam 1966).

6 Ernst Nagel, *Assumptions in Economic Theory*, 53 Am. Econ. Rev. 211 (1963); and Milton Friedman, 'The Methodology of Positive Economics', in *Essays in Positive Economics* 3–43 (Chicago: University of Chicago Press 1953).

7 On the coordinating function of the competitive market process, see: Israel M. Kirzner, *Competition and Entrepreneurship* 215–22 (Chicago: University of Chicago Press 1973); and Gerald P. O'Driscoll Jr., *Economics as a Coordination Problem: The Contributions of Friedrich A. Hayek* (Kansas City, KS: Sheed, Andrews & McMeel 1977). On its particular aspect as a discovery process, see: Friedrich A. Hayek, 'Competition as a Discovery Procedure', in *New Studies in Philosophy, Politics, Economics and the History of Ideas* (Chicago: University of Chicago Press 1978), a text which is also available in *Austrian Economics* 185

(Schools of Thought in Economics Series, Stephen Littlechild ed., Vol. III, Aldershot, UK and Brookfield, US: Edward Elgar 1990); Israel M. Kirzner, *Discovery and the Capitalist Process* (Chicago: University of Chicago Press 1985); Israel M. Kirzner, *Discovery, Capitalism and Distributive Justice* (Oxford: Basil Blackwell 1989); and Israel M. Kirzner, *Entrepreneurial Discovery and the Competitive Market Process: An Austrian Approach*, 35 J. of Econ. Literature 60 (1997).

[8] For a fuller depiction of the reason why a fully socialist economy lacks entrepreneurial and competitive activity, see Israel M. Kirzner, *Competition and Entrepreneurship*, id. at 107.

[9] See Ludwig von Mises, *Interventionism: An Economic Analysis* (Bettina Bien Greaves ed., Irvington-on-Hudson, NY: Foundation for Economic Education, Inc. 1998). (The text was written by von Mises in 1940 but was first published only in 1998.) The entire text is dedicated to revealing the fallacies of governmental intervention, see, for example, at 91. See also Hayek, 'Competition as a Discovery Procedure', supra note 7 at 190. This article is also available in *Austrian Economics*, supra note 7 at 196; Dominick T. Armentano, *Antitrust and Monopoly: Anatomy of a Policy Failure* (San Francisco, CA: The Independent Institute, 2nd edn 1990).

[10] See Chapter 2, Section 2.2.4.

[11] See, for example, Gerald P. O'Driscoll Jr. and Mario J. Rizzo, *The Economics of Time and Ignorance* (London and New York: Routledge 1996, reissue of the 1985 1st edn).

[12] This is the type of pure entrepreneurship that Kirzner develops, see Kirzner, *Competition and Entrepreneurship*, supra note 7 at 48–9 and also 85–6 on (on an 'arbitrage' theory of profit). See also Israel M. Kirzner, 'Roundaboutness, Opportunity and Austrian Economics', in *The Unfinished Agenda: Essays on the Political Economy of Government Policy in Honour of Arthur Seldon* 93, 98–100 (Martin J. Anderson ed., London: Institute of Economic Affairs 1986).

[13] The question of what constitutes a new market niche as opposed to an existing one is both complex and murky. This essentially goes back to the issue of definition of separate markets (see Chapter 2, pp. 44–5). The task of clearly defining separate independent markets seems almost impossible. Nevertheless, all new products can be categorized somewhere along a continuum that starts with a mere replica of an existing product and ends with a new concept product that performs a function no other product has done before. Even the last are probably interdependent with other products, but it can be said that they establish a new market niche.

[14] See: Kirzner, *Competition and Entrepreneurship*, supra note 7 at 48–9; and Kirzner, 'Roundaboutness, Opportunity and Austrian Economics', supra note 12 id.

[15] Note that we are speaking here of these elements as necessary for dynamic competition to take place or to be relevant. The two phrases are interchangeable. For example, in the case of a regulated socialist market regime there is probably little activity of the type described by the dynamic competition model, or alternatively, to the extent that such activity is taking place, it cannot play the relevant role of revealing market preferences because prices, products and output are governmentally regulated.

[16] The term 'market area' will be preferred hereinafter over the narrower 'market' term, for the following reason. As noted in the previous chapter (at pp. 44–5), it is difficult to define totally separate markets that are known to be absolutely independent of one another because markets are interdependent, and some competition may comes from producers of goods that are not perfect substitutes but are rather partial substitutes to the goods at hand. To take an example, for certain wealthy consumers patronizing a tanning salon would reduce their demand for Caribbean vacations – but it is unlikely that under neoclassical analysis the two services would ever be categorized as being in the same market. Therefore the specific market to be chosen for evaluation purposes will be an admitted approximation of the germane market area, while bearing in mind that under dynamic analysis competition may always arise from neighboring market areas as part of an unavoidable cross-influence between markets phenomenon (see Kirzner, *Competition and Entrepreneurship*, supra note 7 at 105–7). For support of the notion that drawing hard market boundaries is questionable, see: Franklin M. Fisher, John J. McGowan and Joen E. Greenwood, *Folded, Spindled and Mutilated: Economic Analysis and U.S. v. I.B.M.*

31–3 (Boston, MA: Charles River Associates 1983); and Richard Schmalensee, *Another Look at Market Power*, 95 Harv. L. Rev. 1789, 1798–1804 (1982).

[17] This assumption is directly acknowledged by some Austrian scholars: see, for example, Kirzner, *Competition and Entrepreneurship*, supra note 7 at 96–9.

[18] The elements of the 'essential facility' doctrine were set out in *Hecht v. Pro-Football, Inc.*, 570 F.2d 982 (D.C. Cir. 1977), cert. denied, 436 U.S. 956 (1978) as follows: cases where the plaintiff proves that access to the facility in question is essential to the plaintiff's competitive survival; and the facility cannot practically be duplicated; and the plaintiff can use the facility without interfering with the defendant's use. On the essential facility doctrine, see also: *U.S. v. Terminal Railroad Association*, 224 U.S. 383 (1912); and *Aspen Skiing Co. v. Aspen Highlands Skiing Corp.*, 738 F2d 1509 (10th Cir. 1984), aff'd 472 U.S. 585 (1985)

[19] This point will be noted upon and further explained in the next section.

[20] This term was coined by Kirzner, see Kirzner, *Competition and Entrepreneurship*, supra note 7 at 73; see also Kirzner, *Entrepreneurial Discovery and the Competitive Market Process*, supra note 7 at 62 where he speaks of a concept of 'sheer ignorance'. More generally on the Austrian school's notion of uncertainty see: von Mises, supra note 4, at 105–18; and Israel M. Kirzner, 'Subjectivism, Freedom and Economic Law', in Kirzner, *The Driving Force of the Market – Essays in Austrian Economics* 60–61 (Routledge: London and New York 2000).

[21] See Kirzner, *Competition and Entrepreneurship*, supra note 7 at 48, 85.

[22] For a comparison of Austrian competition and Darwin's model, see Sandye Gloria-Palermo, *The Evolution of Austrian Economics: From Menger to Lachmann* 150–53, 160 (New York: Routledge 1999). See also von Mises, supra note 4 at 174–6 (his views on Darwinism). For a broader development of Austrian economics as an evolutionary approach (that is, an approach in which the system under consideration transforms itself over time), see Ulrich Witt, 'Turning Austrian Economics into an Evolutionary Theory', in *Austrian Economics: Tensions and New Directions* 215 (Bruce J. Caldwell and Stephan Boehm eds, Boston/Dordrecht/London: Kluwer Academic 1992).

[23] See Richard R. Nelson and Sidney G. Winter, *In Search of a More Useful Theory of Innovation*, 5 Res. Pol'y 36 (1977).

[24] In fact, perhaps this duality in nature, which renders the prerequisites and end-result elements similar, is what assisted the neoclassical competition model in successfully getting away for so many years with a model that all but ignores the heart of competition, namely the competitive process. The notion implied by the neoclassical model is that since certain circumstances are imperative in order for competition to take place, and the end result of competition yields another set of arguably determinable circumstances, then there is no need to fully develop the whole interim process that takes place in between these two sets of rudimentary and consequential circumstances, because the leap from the first to the third category does not significantly diminish the coherency of the model.

[25] See Andreu Mas-Colell, Michael D. Whinston and Jerry R. Green, *Microeconomic Theory* 383 (New York: Oxford University Press 1995). This definition is of course embedded in the neoclassical economic assumptions (some of which were critically reviewed in Chapter 2, Section 2.2.4). These include the separation of markets assumption, which ensures that the monopolist will not face competition from sellers in markets defined as separate.

[26] The text that follows uses the two terms interchangeably in an economic context since economists themselves seem to do so; see, for example, Frederic M. Scherer and David Ross, *Industrial Market Structure and Economic Performance* 17 (Boston, MA: Houghton Mifflin, 3rd edn 1990). Furthermore, as we shall see below, also in a legal context the two concepts seem to be substantively identical, differing only in degree.

[27] See: Scherer and Ross id.; and William M. Landes and Richard A. Posner, *Market Power in Antitrust Cases*, 94 Harv. L. Rev. 937, 839–943 (1981).

[28] See Mancur Olson and David McFarland, *The Restoration of Pure Monopoly and the Concept of the Industry,* 76 Q. J. of Econ. 613 (1962).

---

[29] See Chapter I, Section 1.4.2: 'Antitrust's methodology (competition) defined'.

[30] For a full review of the congruence between the neoclassical economics and legal approach to market power and monopoly power, see Landes and Posner, supra note 27 at 976–82.

[31] *U.S. v. E.I. du Pont de Nemours & Co.*, 351 U.S. 377, 391–5 (1956); cited in *Dimmit Agri Industries, Inc. v. CPC International, Inc.*, 679 F.2d 516, 525 (5th Cir. 1982), cert. denied, 460 U.S. 1082 (1983); and *Jefferson Parish Hospital Dist. No. 2 v. Hyde*, 466 U.S. 2, 13–14 (1984).

[32] See U.S. Department of Justice and Federal Trade Commission Horizontal Merger Guidelines (April 2, 1992, Revised April 8, 1997) §0.1 available at http://www.usdoj.gov/atr (January 10, 2003) (note that the Guidelines do not reflect the agencies' policy concerning §2 of the Sherman Act. Nevertheless, the definition is useful for our purposes because it reflects their general view on this concept). See also Landes and Posner, supra note 27 at 937. Clearly, market power in itself is not determinative of monopoly power, and does not entail antitrust concerns. However, the two terms are closely linked, because whoever has market power (that is, owns a dominant share of a market to which competitors cannot enter in the short term), obviously has the power to control the product's price in that market as well as some edge on the competition and consumers in that market. In other words, monopoly power can be understood as a significant degree of market power which may give rise to antitrust concerns (see: Landes and Posner, id. at 939; and Phillip Areeda and Louis Kaplow, *Antitrust Analysis – Problems, Text, Cases*, 448 (New York: Aspen Law & Business, 5th edn 1997).). Since the monopoly power and market power legal notions are substantively identical they will be used somewhat interchangeably in the text that follows.

[33] See Kirzner, *Competition and Entrepreneurship*, supra note 7 at 105–7.

[34] This phrase is taken from Israel M. Kirnzer, 'The Driving Force of the Market: The Idea of "Competition" in Contemporary Economic Theory and in the Austrian Theory of the Market Process', in *Why Economists Disagree – An Introduction to the Alternative Schools of Thought* 37, 44 (David L. Prychitko ed., Albany, NY: State University of New York Press 1998).

[35] See: Kirzner, *Competition and Entrepreneurship*, supra note 7 at 103, 105–7; and von Mises, supra note 4 at 360. It should be noted that this notion is an exception to the general respect that Austrian economists pay to the private property institution as the cornerstone of any competitive market process. It is a scenario in which the institution of private property over the resources does not spell a harmony of interests between the resource owners and the consumers (see von Mises, supra note 4 at 271–2 where he recognizes a resource monopoly scenario as an exception to the general rule).

[36] See Kirzner, *Competition and Entrepreneurship*, supra note 7 at 103, 132–3.

[37] Perhaps the term 'process monopoly' is, to a certain extent, a misnomer since it uses the term 'process' to describe a scenario wherein the competitive process is actually stifled.

[38] See supra note 16.

[39] For a review of the contending economic approaches for measuring static monopoly power, see: Garry K. Ottosen, *Monopoly Power: How It Is Measured and How it Has Changed* 3–70 (Salt Lake City, UT: Crossroads Research Institute 1990); and Kenneth G. Elzinga, 'Unmasking Monopoly: Four Types of Economic Evidence', in *Economics and Antitrust Policy* 11 (Robert J. Larner and James W. Meehan Jr. eds, Westport, CT: Quorum Books 1989). In the legal context, this reality is evident from the lack of unanimous clear-cut definition for a legal monopoly.

[40] See the famous quote of Fridjtof Nansen, the Norwegian polar explorer (1861–1930): 'The difficult is what takes a little time; the impossible is what takes a little longer' (*Listener* 14 December 1939, at 1153), which is probably the basis for the known US Armed Forces slogan: 'The difficult we do immediately; the impossible takes a little longer'.

[41] The Nobel laureate Sir John R. Hicks in *The Theory of Monopoly,* 3 Econometrica 1, 8 (1935).

[42] Arguably, the very simple nature of certain products leaves relatively little room for IP-protected innovation or for differentiating their features. However, this notion has already been discussed earlier, in the section on the assumed market circumstances as part of the discussion

of circumstances where entrepreneurial motives to join markets are diminished. See pp. 85–7 of this chapter (and especially p. 86).

43 For a similar notion, see Carl Shapiro, *Competition Policy in the Information Economy* (August 1999), Section II.F, available at http://haas.berkeley.edu/~shapiro (January 10, 2003).

44 The use of the term 'alternatives' is preferred here over the use of the more formal neoclassical term 'substitutes'. The reason is that the term 'substitutes' assumes a well-defined market by which all the available substitutes can be readily recognized. However, reality is not as simple, since substitutive products can in fact originate in adjacent markets – see supra note 16.

45 See supra note 16.

46 See the discussion of untold assumptions earlier in this chapter, p. 85.

47 It should be noted that despite the clear criminal nature of the Sherman Act, courts have consistently played down its criminal nature in their interpretation and application of the act (see review in Areeda and Kaplow, supra note 32 at 57–9). Nevertheless, the criminal burdens of proof are best suited for this context because they minimize the margin of error.

48 This, of course, brings up the central question of distinguishing between the existence of an IPR and its exercise. This issue will be addressed in Chapters 4 and 5, which develop practical applications of the model.

49 This notion was well captured by von Mises in *Human Action*, supra note 4 at 362, where he noted as follows: 'The concept of competition does not include the requirement that there should be a multitude of competing units. Competing is always the competition of one man or firm against another man or firm, mo matter how many others are striving after the same prize. Competition among the few is not a kind of competition praxeologically different from competition among the many. ...The number of competitors plays a role in the analysis of monopoly prices only as far as it is one of the factors upon which the success of the endeavors to unite competitors into a cartel depends'.

50 Furthermore, in any monopoly case the suspect will try to present his/her market share as minuscule, which may in practice bias the court and result on average in an underestimate of this figure.

51 The analysis in this study will be restricted to the complete offense of 'monopolizing' and thus will not address the less common derivative offenses covered by the Sherman Act §2, namely, attempt-to-monopolize and conspiracy-to-monopolize (the latter is clearly beyond the scope of this study, which focuses on unilateral conduct).

52 Again, note that the derivative offenses of attempt-to-monopolize and conspiracy-to-monopolize are excluded from the discussion here.

53 See *U.S. v. Aluminum Co. of America et al.*, 148 F.2d 416, 429–30 (2d Cir. 1945) (hereinafter: Alcoa) (a monopoly gained by force of accident, or merely by virtue of superior skill, foresight and industry does not entail §2 liability). See also *Berkey Photo, Inc. v. Eastman Kodak Co.*, 603 F.2d 263, 281 (2d Cir. 1979), cert. denied, 444 U.S. 1093 (1980) 'Because ... a monopolist is permitted, and indeed encouraged by §2 to compete aggressively on the merits, any success that it may achieve through "the process of invention and innovation" is clearly tolerated by the antitrust laws' (citing *U.S. v. United Shoe Machinery Corp.*, 110 F. Supp 295, 344 (D. Mass 1953), aff'd per curiam, 347 U.S. 521 (1954)).

54 *U.S. v. Grinnell Corp.* 384 U.S. 563, 570–71 (1966); see also *Aspen Skiing Co. v. Aspen Highlands Skiing Corp.* 472 U.S. 585, 602 (stating that subjective intent is relevant for determining whether the conduct may properly be characterized as exclusionary).

55 See *Berkey Photo,* supra note 53 at 274.

56 See, for example: the Alcoa case, supra note 53 at 432 ('In order to fall within §2, the monopolist must have both the power to monopolize, and the intent to monopolize'). The court did not define the standard beyond this vague statement; *Union Leader Corp. v. Newspapers of New England, Inc.*, 180 F. Supp. 125, 140 (D. Mass. 1959), modified, 284 F.2d 582 (1st Cir. 1960), cert. denied, 365 U.S. 833 (1961) ('a person does not necessarily have an exclusionary

intent merely because he foresees that a market is only large enough to permit one successful enterprise. Instead, §2 comes into play only when 'the person who foresees a fight to the death intends to use or actually does use unfair weapons'); *Great Western Directories, Inc. v. Southwestern Bell Telephone Company*, 63 F.3d 1378, 1385 (5th Cir. 1995) (courts must 'distinguish between those exclusionary effects that are inherent in the forces of free competition and those that are substantially enhanced or made possible by the possession and exploitation of monopoly power'); *Trans Sport, Inc. v. Starter Sportswear, Inc.*, 964 F.2d 186, 188–9 (2nd Cir. 1992). (The requirement is that the defendant 'willfully acquired or maintained its power, thereby causing unreasonable "exclusionary" ... effects'); *Sargent-Welch Scientific Co. v. Ventron Corp.*, 567 F.2d 701, 712 (1977) *cert. denied* 439 U.S. 822 (1978) ('a persistent determination to maintain a monopoly by anticipating and forestalling all competition'); and *Blue Cross & Blue Shield United of Wisconsin v. Marshfield Clinic,* 883 F. Supp. 1247, 1257 (D. Wis. 1995) (see the court's struggle there with a complex and lengthy definition).

[57] See for example Union Leader id. at 140 where the court held that there is no sharp distinction between the existence of intent to exclude and the use of unfair means, and therefore the same evidence which shows the use of unfair means is taken to show the existence of an exclusionary intent; *Andrew Byars v. Bluff City News Company,* 609 F.2d 843, 862 (6th Cir. 1979) (on utilizing a lack of any valid business justification to infer monopolistic intent); and *Sargent-Welch* id. at 712 (noting the fact that the line is a difficult one to draw).

[58] *Berkey Photo*, supra note 53 at 274.

[59] Id.

[60] However, note that this indicator works only for positively finding monopoly power, that is, low profits were not deemed useful as a defense that excludes the possibility of market power, see Judge Learned Hand in the Alcoa case, supra note 53 at 427.

[61] See, for example, *U.S. v. E.I. du Pont de Nemours & Co.*, 96 F.T.C 653, where du Pont's practical ability to raise prices without losing all its business to rivals was taken as an indication to its monopoly power (which of course implicitly includes the rather difficult neoclassical assumption of uniformity of products, namely the assumption that du Pont's rivals were selling the exact same products).

[62] See, for example, Areeda and Kaplow, supra note 32 at §343, 571–2 (noting that 'market power is intrinsically a matter of degree, which is often lost sight of by a process of market definition ... But even if such problems are overcome, the power implications of any particular market share remain obscure. The courts have not stated how much power they believe to be associated with given market shares'. The current market power analysis is therefore described as a 'crude approximation'); Stephen F. Ross, *Principles of Antitrust Law* 55 (Westbury, NY: Foundation Press 1993) ('there is no clear formula for market definition. It is all too easy for antitrust lawyers and economists to get lost in the morass of demand curves and price elasticities'). The troublesome nature of determining market share and market power is also reflected through the scholarly debate on the matter, and the long judicial struggle with the task. See, for example: Louis Kaplow, *The Accuracy of Traditional Market Power Analysis and a Direct Adjustment Alternative* (Landes and Posner on Market Power: Four Responses), 95 Harv. L. Rev. 1817 (1982); Richard Schmalensee, *Another Look at Market Power* (Landes and Posner on Market Power: Four Responses), 95 Harv. L. Rev. 1789 (1982); and Timothy J. Brennan, *Mistaken Elasticities and Misleading Rules* (Landes and Posner on Market Power: Four Responses), 95 Harv. L. Rev. 1849 (1982). For a review of the court's struggle with this issue, see Mark R. Patterson, *The Market Power Requirement in Antitrust Rule of Reason Cases: A Rhetorical History*, 37 San Diego L. Rev. 1 (2000).

[63] In light of the criminal nature entailed by the Sherman Act it could be argued that an analysis excluding the subjective purpose requirement for establishing §2 liability is offensive to constitutional sensitivities, because it may be overly restrictive of defendants' First Amendment rights of freedom of commercial speech, to the extent that their conduct constitutes such speech (see: *Virginia State Board of Pharmacy v. Virginia Citizens Consumer Council, Inc.*, 425 U.S. 748, 765 (1976); *Central Hudson Gas & Elec. Corp. v. Public Service Communication*, 447

U.S. 557, 566 (1980); and E. Thomas Sullivan, *First Amendment Defenses in Antitrust Litigation*, 46 Mo. L. Rev. 517 (1981)). Furthermore, it could be argued that such analysis goes beyond the narrow construction that should be applied to criminal statutes. There are a number of arguments that allay these fears. First, the analysis suggested here is believed to be a solid one, entailing a minimal margin of error, and therefore its application should not infringe on the commercial speech rights of defendants. This argument becomes even more convincing when considering the current legal criminal intent requirement, whose nature is so murky and unworkable that it surely offers no better protection of the commercial speech rights of defendants. Perhaps it offers even less protection, because of the uncertainty it entails. Second, as noted earlier, despite the Sherman Act's criminal nature, courts have consistently interpreted and applied it as a civil statute (see supra note 47). Therefore such argument of an overly broad interpretation is likely to be rejected. Finally, the general required intent for criminal liability in §2 cases (of the completed monopolizing offense) has always been very broad. The requirement is simply 'an intent to bring about the forbidden act' (see Alcoa, supra note 53 at 432). Such general intent is pretty much automatically inferred, since it is argued that in practice 'no monopolist monopolizes unconscious of what he is doing' (Alcoa id.). In this sense of the required mental element for criminal antitrust liability, the suggested analysis that renders redundant an examination of the subjective element behind the conduct is no different from the current legal situation.

[64] All these definitions have been mentioned earlier in this chapter; see p. 90.

[65] Alcoa case, supra note 53 at 427.

[66] It should be noted that current law theoretically regards market power as a mere starting point for evaluating the competitive impact of a practice (see, for example: the U.S. Department of Justice and Federal Trade Commission Horizontal Merger Guidelines, supra note 32, §2.0; and Areeda and Kaplow supra note 32 at 571–2 ('It cannot be emphasized too strongly that market definition and the defendant's market share give, at best, only a suggestion of defendant's market power'). Nevertheless, in practice, the static market power factor is at the center of attention of current antitrust analysis.

[67] Louis Kaplow, *The Patent–Antitrust Intersection: A Reappraisal*, 97 Harv. L. Rev. 1813 (1984).

[68] See id. at 1821–42, especially p. 1842 which summarizes the article's suggested solution. This is, of course, an extreme simplification of the model suggested there. A broader discussion would be superfluous to the point here. For a critical review of the use of the efficiency concept as a balancing instrument between competition and intellectual property, see Harold Demsetz, *Information and Efficiency: Another Viewpoint*, 12 J. of L. & Econ. 1 (1969).

[69] See supra note 3.

[70] See Chapter 2, pp. 48–50.

[71] The following brief historical review is taken from Ernest Gellhorn and William E. Kovacic, *Antitrust Law and Economics in a Nutshell* 13–14 (St. Paul, MN: West Publishing, 4th edn 1994).

[72] *U.S. v. Addyston Pipe & Steel Co.*, 85 Fed. 271 (6th Cir. 1898), aff'd 175 U.S. 211 (1899).

[73] See for example, Friedrich A. Hayek, *Individualism and Economic Order* 112–13 (Chicago: University of Chicago Press 1948). See also the sources above mentioned in Chapter 2, note 135.

[74] See von Mises in *Human Action,* supra note 4 at 311–12.

[75] Hayek seems to have been aware of this problem, in noting that law's recognition of the principle of private property does not necessarily solve all the problems because much depends on the precise definition of the right of property as applied to different things. In this context he specifically mentions the shortcomings of patent law that might have led to the destruction of competition in certain areas. See Friedrich A. Hayek, *The Road to Serfdom* 43 (Chicago: Chicago University Press, 1944, 50th Anniversary Edition, 1994).

[76] An interesting linguistic note is in order here. Part of the human action presumption of the Austrian competition concept is that entrepreneurs keep improving and differentiating their products as part of their profit-seeking pattern which is the driving force of the competitive struggle and the market (see, for example, von Mises, *Human Action,* supra note 4 at 294–300). It is worth noting that the English word 'improve' originally meant 'for profit' – see, for example, Merriam–Webster online dictionary available at http://www.m-w.com. This supports the view that human action is motivated by profit-seeking speculation.

[77] In other words, the private property institution is embraced as a necessary defining institution for the market that cannot be created endogenously by the market itself. See, for example: Israel M. Kirzner, 'The Limits of the Market – The Real and the Imagined', in Kirzner, *The Driving Force of the Market*, supra note 20 at 77, 83–4 (the text originally published in *Marktwirtschaft und Rechtsordnung* (Nomos, W. Moeschel, M.E. Streit and U. Witt eds 1994); and Hayek, supra note 73 at 110–11.

[78] Any lay consumer is well aware of this reality which is reflected through the known fact that industries are constantly trying to collect commercially useful information about their consumers (for example, the questionnaires that come with most electrical appliances and encourage the consumer to fill in abundant personal information such as income, interests, preferences and so on).

[79] Apart from those who conscientiously fill in the questionnaires mentioned in note 78.

[80] See, for example: Hayek, supra note 73 at 115–16 suggesting that antitrust legislation has contributed to the decline of competition; and von Mises, supra note 9 on the anti-interventionist agenda of competition.

[81] See, for example: Walter Block, *Total Repeal of Antitrust Legislation: A Critique of Bork, Brozen, and Posner,* 8 (1) Rev. of Austrian Econ. 35 (1995); Armentano, supra note 9; Dominick T. Armentano, *Antitrust Policy: The Case for Repeal* (Washington, DC: Cato Institute 1986); and Dominick T. Armentano, *The Myths of Antitrust* (New Rochelle, NY: Arlington House 1972). See also Donald J. Boudreaux and Thomas J. DiLorenzo, *The Protectionist Roots of Antitrust*, 6 (1) Rev. of Austrian Econ. 81 (1993) where the authors not only adopt Armentano's view, but also claim that the goal of antitrust laws has always been protectionist rather than promotion of competition.

[82] See id.

[83] See, for example, Hayek, *Competition as a Discovery Procedure*, supra note 7 at 190 (at 196 in the Littlechild source book).

[84] See, for example, von Mises, *Human action*, supra note 4 at 682–4.

[85] See Scherer and Ross, supra note 26 at 11–12.

[86] The reason why the traditional Austrian scholars themselves did not specifically address this distinction may be attributed to the fact that they worked in Europe in the first half of the twentieth century, a time when antitrust was practically unheard of there. However, modern Austrian scholars are well aware of this distinction, see, for example, O'Driscoll and Rizzo, supra note 11 at 142. Furthermore, traditional Austrian scholars who emigrated to the U.S. have embraced similar views, see Hayek, supra note 75 at 44–5. It should be noted that some scholars would disagree with this view. Most notable in this respect is the work of Dominick T. Armentano, which calls for a repeal of antitrust laws as a form of excessive governmental intervention, see the various Armentano publications, supra notes 9 and 81.

[87] This fact was demonstrated earlier in Chapter 1, where some of the economic models were shown to have little to do with reality.

[88] Hayek himself has expressed views that are consistent with this argument. He acknowledged that there are empirical conditions in which competition falters or in his words 'cannot be effective'. Such cases, he admits, call for state activity, 'since an effective competitive system needs an intelligently designed and continuously adjusted legal framework as much as any other'. See Hayek, supra note 75 at 44–5. This view reflects a variation on earlier Austrian thought, which can be partially attributed to the influence of U.S. scholarship as this book was

written after Hayek emigrated to the U.S. Nevertheless Hayek's dedication to the basic Austrian anti-unterventionist premise remains evident throughout the book.

[89] See Michael E. DeBow, *Markets, Government Intervention, and the Role of Information: An 'Austrian School' Perspective, with an Application to Merger Regulation*, 14 Geo. Mason U. L. Rev. 31 (1991), which applies Austrian economic thinking to merger issues while assuming the existence of antitrust policy as a given, without any calls to its repeal.

[90] See supra note 3.

[91] See, for example, *Eastman Kodak Co. v. Image Technical Services Inc.*, 112 S. Ct. 2072, 119 L. Ed. 2d 265 (1992). For a broader review of the post-Chicago school, see the collection of articles in *Symposium: Post-Chicago Economics*, 63 Antitrust L. J. 445-695 (1995). On the interesting links between Austrian and post-Marshallian economics, see: Nicolai J. Foss, 'Austrian and Post-Marshallian Economics: The Bridging Work of George Richardson' in *Economic Organization, Capabilities and Co-ordination* 138 (Nicolai J. Foss and Brian J. Loasby eds, London: Routledge 1998).

4. Application of the Dynamic Model on Refusal to License Intellectual Property (Magill)

In his travels around the galaxy, the little prince visited a number of planets. One day he arrived at a planet inhabited by a businessman and the following conversation took place:

> '... Twenty-six and five make thirty-one. Phew! Then that makes five-hundred-and-one million, six-hundred-twenty-two thousand, seven-hundred-thirty-one.'
> 'Five hundred million what?' asked the little prince.
> 'Millions of those little objects' he said, 'which one sometimes sees in the sky.'
> 'Flies?'
> 'Oh, no. Little glittering objects.'
> 'Bees?'
> 'Oh, no. Little golden objects that set lazy men to idle dreaming. As for me, I am concerned with matters of consequence. There is no time for idle dreaming in my life.'
> 'Ah! You mean the stars?'
> 'Yes, that's it. The stars.'
> 'And what do you do with five-hundred millions of stars?'
>
> ....
>
> 'What do I do with them?'
> 'Yes.'
> 'Nothing. I own them.'
> 'You own the stars?'
> 'Yes.'
> 'But I have already seen a king who —'
> 'Kings do not own, they reign over. It is a very different matter.'
> 'And what good does it do you to own the stars?'
> 'It does me the good of making me rich.'
> 'And what good does it do you to be rich?'
> 'It makes it possible for me to buy more stars, if any are discovered.'
>
> ....
>
> 'How is it possible for one to own the stars?'
> 'To whom do they belong?' the businessman retorted, peevishly.
> 'I don't know. To nobody.'
> 'Then they belong to me, because I was the first person to think of it.'
> 'Is that all that is necessary?'

> 'Certainly. When you find a diamond that belongs to nobody, it is yours. When you discover an island that belongs to nobody, it is yours. When you get an idea before any one else, you take out a patent on it: it is yours. So with me: I own the stars, because nobody else before me ever thought of owning them.'
> 'Yes, that is true,' said the little prince. 'And what do you do with them?'
> 'I administer them,' replied the businessman. 'I count them and recount them. It is difficult. But I am a man who is naturally interested in matters of consequence.'
> The little prince was still not satisfied.
> 'If I owned a silk scarf,' he said, 'I could put it around my neck and take it away with me. If I owned a flower, I could pluck that flower and take it away with me. But you cannot pluck the stars from heaven …'
> 'No. But I can put them in the bank.'
> 'Whatever does that mean?'
> 'That means that I write the number of my stars on a little paper. And then I put this paper in a drawer and lock it with a key.'
> 'And that is all?'
> 'That is enough,' said the businessman.
> 'It is entertaining,' thought the little prince. 'It is rather poetic. But it is of no great consequence.'
> On matters of consequence, the little prince had ideas which were very different from those of the grown-ups.
> 'I myself own a flower,' He continued his conversation with the businessman, 'which I water every day. I own three volcanoes, which I clean out every week (for I also clean out the one that is extinct; one never knows). It is of some use to my volcanoes, and it is of some use to my flower, that I own them. But you are of no use to the stars …'
> The businessman opened his mouth, but he found nothing to say in answer. And the little prince went away.
> 'The grown-ups are certainly altogether extraordinary,' he said simply, talking to himself as he continued on his journey.
>
> (Antoine de Saint Exupéry, *The Little Prince*, ch. 13, pp. 52–7, New York: Harcourt Brace & Company, New York, 1943, reprinted 1971, Trans. Katherine Woods).

4.1 INTRODUCTION

The above dialogue from Antoine de Saint Exupéry's celebrated novel demonstrates some of the confusion often created by property ownership that, unlike traditional property rights, are not based upon tangible possession.[1] The little prince's skepticism towards ownership of stars seems to originate from an instrumental theory of property that rests on a 'public good' justification for the private property institution.[2] More specifically, the notion expressed in the quote relates to prosperity. The implied argument is that assignment of property rights to individuals creates incentives for productive use and development of resources, by securing the benefits of these activities for the owners.[3] Legal scholarship has further developed this argument into the suggestion that a property regime facilitates an efficient division of labor and allocation of resources, by establishing the starting point for voluntary exchange. Thus, it is claimed, wasteful depletion of resources is prevented, by ensuring that the person entitled to exploit them will also bear the costs of their overuse.[4] The little prince expresses doubt as to whether this balancing mechanism of property as enhancing the public good still holds true where actual possession of the property by the owner is not possible. It seems to him that there is no justification for a property right in such a context where the owner is neither able to ameliorate the property nor enjoy it himself (that is, where both the public and private benefits of property are missing).

Patents and copyrights confer property rights over intangible subject matter. Ownership of IP is different from the case of star ownership that was discussed between the little prince and the businessman, in a number of respects. Patentees and copyright owners are able to work on their inventions or compositions and improve them. They are also able to extract direct benefits from their property, for example, by utilizing their innovative invention in their production line. And finally, arguably the public benefits from the IP institution because it is said to enhance innovation. Yet the little prince's observation as to the problematic nature of ownership over stars captures an extreme example of a problem often encountered, only to a lesser extent, where ownership of IP is involved. The problem is a suboptimal working of the property right, namely, its deployment only to a limited extent, which does not maximize the public good.[5] It is such suboptimal use which may pull the ground from under a concept of owning stars, or may justify imposing a compulsory license where a refusal to deal in an IPR is sufficiently harmful.

Real-life cases prove that in maximizing their personal utility and benefit, IPR owners often underutilize their IP. In other words, they often employ their IP in a suboptimal manner that obtrusively harms the public interest. This chapter addresses one of these behavior patterns: cases where refusal to license IPRs carries significant harm to the public good, measured from an antitrust perspective, namely, where the public interest is defined as the existence of a free-flowing competitive process.

As noted earlier, the working assumption of this study, which is written from an antitrust perspective, is that patents and copyrights are a desirable legal institution. The little prince lived only in Saint Exupéry's imagination and was thus free to express theoretical ideas. However, today's realities of deep IP law roots, and the enormous strength of the entities interested in IP's preservation and expansion, render it practically impossible to second-guess the justification for given IPRs. Therefore the following analysis, in conformity with contemporary legal practice,[6] refrains from calling into question the justification for any given IPRs. It is assumed that this has already been done within the IP legal frame. Once a patent or copyright has been granted, the assumption in the following text is that it is a valid one. Accordingly, the only examined aspect will be whether IPRs are *used* in a legitimate manner, as far as the well-being of the competitive process is concerned, rather than whether they were justly granted.

The general notion that under utilization of IPRs is problematic, and in some cases sufficiently conflicting with the public good so as to merit legal intervention with the patentee's conduct, is not new nor is it unique to antitrust law. The patent law instrument of (paid) compulsory licenses, which has been recognized by many nations, has employed such rationale for many years now.[7] Traditionally, the primary conduct pattern that merited a compulsory license intervention was absolute failure by the patentee to work its patented invention. The rationale behind this principle was that the patent law contributes to the public good by promoting innovation, and thus patent suppression prevents the public from enjoying the fruits of such protected innovation.[8] The language adopted in a number of international IP treaties suggests that 'absolute failure to work' is not the only abusive conduct pattern that may justify imposition of compulsory licenses. Rather, the widely accepted notion is that governments maintain the discretion to limit IP protection where its exercise compromises the public good.[9] Having said that, it seems clear that intervention in 'refusal to license' contexts raises more difficult questions than intervention in absolute 'failure to work' cases. This is because in the latter it is easier to prove harm to the public good from not being able to enjoy the fruits of the invention, while in the former a more complicated set of interest balancing is involved, since the patentee *is* working the invention, and the question becomes whether the resulting circumstances sufficiently harm the public interest.

Compulsory licensing of patents within a refusal to license context has already received a fair amount of consideration.[10] This chapter focuses on the less-explored path of refusal to license *copyrighted* subject matter. Where traditional copyright subject matter is concerned, namely copyright in artistic and literary works, it was historically thought that no major public good problems would arise. This rationale stems from the relatively narrow scope of copyright protection, as compared to patent protection. Since copyright protects only expressions, rather than ideas, it was assumed that competitors could legitimately work their way around a copyright by extending the expression with sufficient added original content. Thus, it was suggested that copyright in traditional subject matter would rarely raise any antitrust concerns, let alone justify instituting compulsory licenses in copyright.[11] However, as copyright protection has expanded to protect technological products (such as software and databases), in addition to more traditional literary works, antitrust practice is witnessing a change to the traditional setting, namely, it is no longer uncommon for copyright to successfully create a bottleneck in an industry.[12] Indeed, as we shall see later on, under certain 'essential facilities' circumstances, copyright may block others from entering the market. It is these circumstances that present us with the task of finding coherent analytical criteria that identify when 'refusal to license' circumstances display underusage that sufficiently harms the public good so as to merit antitrust intervention.

This chapter will harness the dynamic competition model for the task. It will apply the model to a case of refusal to license a copyright, thus demonstrating how the theoretical model can be used to help define the borderline between legitimate conduct and abusive antitrust behavior. Section 4.2 looks into the distinction between existence of an IPR and its exercise. This issue is crucial so as not to conflict with the working assumption that granted IPRs are valid. Obligatory licensing measures serve as the most common remedy for abusive refusals to license. Therefore it is important to show why, under some extreme circumstances, antitrust law's imposition of positive duty on a corporation to license its copyright does not conflict with the working assumption. Section 4.3 harnesses the general dynamic model suggested in Chapter 3 for analysis of a specific refusal to license copyrighted subject matter example, namely the Magill case. It demonstrates how the application of a dynamic analysis can guide the analysis of the main question mentioned above, that is, evaluating whether conduct is indeed subcompetitive to a degree which justifies antitrust intervention. This theoretical application consciously takes place within the context of European Community (EC) antitrust jurisprudence because, as demonstrated in the Magill decision, this jurisprudence often seems more prone to accepting antitrust intervention in refusal to license contexts than its counterpart across the Atlantic.[13] However, despite their differences, there are significant theoretical similarities between the European and U.S. federal antitrust regimes,[14] and the antitrust remedy of compulsory licensing at reasonable royalties has also been applied by the latter.[15] Therefore many of the arguments promoted below are valid *mutatis mutandis* within the context of American antitrust jurisprudence. Accordingly, references in this chapter refer to sources of both systems. Finally, a concluding section follows.

4.2 PRELIMINARY NOTIONS

4.2.1 Refusal to Deal versus Refusal to License

The context of 'refusal to deal' calls for some preliminary observations. First, note the distinction between the intellectual property right itself (IPR), and the product to which the IPR pertains (product). The relationship between the two may take on a number of forms. One possible form takes place where the product is the direct subject matter of the IPR, for example: copyrighted source code such as Microsoft Corporation's Microsoft Word,[16] or a product whose physical mechanism is patented. A second possible scenario is one in which the proprietary IP is utilized as input in the manufacturing process of the product, but is not later physically present in the final product itself. This can be the case in the example of a process patent utilized in the production of a product. Finally, a third possible scenario is one in which an IPR is utilized as a tactical business instrument that is not directly related to the suspect entity's manufacturing process. This is the case, for example, where the suspect entity suppresses its IPR, thus effectively preventing it from being used in the marketplace either by itself or by others.

The distinction between these three scenario types results in a potential difference between what is generally known as refusal to supply or refusal to deal and the more specific case of refusal to license an IPR. Generally, when referring to refusal to supply or deal, the case law depicts a scenario in which the suspect entity is already engaged in selling the type of good or service that is being sought by the refused complainant as an integral part of its main business.[17] However, this is not necessarily the case, and perhaps more often so where the sale or licensing of IPRs is concerned. This is because proprietary IP is often not part of the commercial widget, for example, where IPRs are used as strategic or business instruments as in the third scenario type described above. Therefore, it should be borne in mind that refusal to license an IPR is often significantly different from refusal to sell the actual product whose sales form the business of the suspected market enterprise. Therefore in many cases, the relevance of general antitrust jurisprudence on 'refusal to deal' to the IPR scenario, is questionable. However, in specific cases of the first type, namely where the IPR is directly implemented into the product itself, the boundaries between the 'refusal to deal' and 'refusal to license IPR' categories may disappear. In these cases, where the suspect's main business activity is licensing his/her inventions, the suspected refusal to license should then be examined under the category of discriminatory treatment, since the licensing or sales of IPRs is already taking place as part of the main business activity.

4.2.2 The Distinction between Existence of an IPR and Its Exercise

As noted above, the working assumption of this study, which is similar to that of EC jurisprudence on this aspect,[18] is that existence of a copyright shall not be questioned. Hence, it is only the *exercise* of an IPR rather than its existence that may be evaluated to examine whether it is abusive in an antitrust context. It is in this context that we must consider the argument that a mere refusal to license goes back to the basic existence of the IPR. An IPR is in effect annulled where the owner's discretion to keep it from the use of others is replaced by a paid compulsory license imposed by an antitrust authority. The notion behind this argument is that the exclusive legal monopoly, namely the discretion whether to license an IPR at all or whom to license it to, lies at the very heart of every IPR; therefore, refusal to license forms part of the subject matter of an exclusive IPR.[19] If that argument is to be taken at face value, then it serves as a basis for arguing that refusal to license IPRs is never a conduct pattern that may be questioned by antitrust law, since refusal to license is synonymous with the very existence of an IPR.

However, it seems that such a refusal, although more 'negative' in its character than other more 'positive' forms of abuse such as abusive licensing practices, is still a form of exercise of a valid and living IPR. Therefore an effective IPR still exists even where a compulsory license is imposed as a remedy, where the refusal to license is found abusive. There are a number of reasons for this assertion.

First, note that IP treaties have generally recognized that the property conferred by IPRs is not an absolute one. These treaties recognize that under certain circumstances IPRs must be balanced against the public good, resulting in a limitation or compromise of their protection scope, such as by way of compulsory licenses.[20] Therefore, since their inception it has been recognized that IPRs may have to be subjected to certain limitations (including compulsory licenses) to ensure that the public good is not harmed by their utilization. These limitations have been accepted as part of the IP regime. It is surprising, then, that an argument is being made that a compulsory license equals an annulment of an IPR, where the public good balanced against it is based on antitrust policy concerns. The question is clearly one of degree. It is plausible to argue that a refusal to license should not merit a compulsory license. But, if the claim was never made that a traditional compulsory license based on mere 'failure to work' annuls IPRs altogether, then it is hard to see on what basis it is made in this potentially criminal context.

A second reason why a compulsory license, as a remedy for a refusal to license, should not be considered as cancellation of the IPR altogether is that an imposed compulsory license has to be paid for — it is not imposed gratis. The fact that there is a consideration set for the compulsory license, namely that the licensee must pay the IPR owner for the license, demonstrates that the IPR still exists. If the IPR were repealed altogether then there would be no payment set for permission to utilize the no-longer protected information.[21] Clearly, this argument is susceptible to the counterargument that the fee for a compulsory license is compensation for the loss of the right, just like the compensation paid for the seizure of real property. However, the crucial difference between the two is that an IP owner can still make use of the IP where a compulsory license is imposed upon him/her, while the landowner can no longer make use of his/her appropriated land.

Third, note that the U.S. IP misuse doctrine that was discussed earlier in this study[22] prevents the patentee from winning an infringement suit where he/she is found to have misused his/her IPR. Hence, the remedy in cases of an IPR misuse is in effect a compulsory license freely available to everyone (because the patentee cannot enforce his/her patents) – clearly a harsher result than that of a paid compulsory license. Antitrust violation is one of the grounds that may lead to a finding of an IPR misuse and result in such a free and open compulsory license. Hence, it would be paradoxical to argue that a paid compulsory license as a remedy for an abusive refusal to license is never justified because it repeals the IPR altogether, while at the same time the harsher sanction of a patent misuse finding and its result of a free compulsory license may often still be used against the same enterprise.

Fourth, note that even without a finding of misuse, there has already been an antitrust case that ended with a consent decree which prevented the IPR owner from enforcing his/her right[23] (a remedy which is identical to the free open compulsory license of a misuse finding). This case shows that antitrust enforcement agencies have already utilized even harsher methods than paid compulsory licenses in order to remedy significantly abusive conduct patterns. In comparison, paid compulsory licenses do not raise any IPR existence questions that are more complex than those raised in the Dell case.

For the reasons stated above it is difficult to find convincing qualitative arguments as to why compulsory licensing, as a remedy for a refusal to license, repeals the existence of existing IPRs.[24] This should not come as a surprise, since it is part of a broader truth. Ownership over real property is no more absolute than ownership of intellectual property. Its use of the property may be subject to appurtenant easements (to the benefit of an adjoining parcel to which it occupies the only access path), zoning, nuisance and even laws of eminent domain. Yet these are accepted today as necessary limitations of traditional property rights. Indeed, the businessman's general statement to the little prince in this respect seems to apply in this context – ownership is different from complete control, thus owning an IPR is a different matter from 'reigning over' it. A compulsory license should not be viewed as substantively different from non-discrimination laws, which may compel landlords to lease properties without discrimination.[25] In both cases the intervening (non-discrimination or antitrust) law limits the property right to some extent, and in neither does it touch upon the basic existence of that right.

It is understandable that IP professionals may be suspicious of balancing IP against the public good, an exercise that is carried out by para-IP institutions such as antitrust policy makers. Indeed, such an application is less likely to favor IP in the balancing process, and may even favor antitrust. In any event, the question seems to boil down to a quantitative debate: whether or not there are circumstances in which refusal to license indeed justifies antitrust intervention by way of compulsory license (and what these circumstances may be). As a result, the theoretical road seems clear for an antitrust evaluation of refusal to license IPRs, as a form of IPR exercise, which if found abusive may legitimately be remedied by way of a paid compulsory license.

4.3 REFUSAL TO LICENSE: THE MAGILL CASE

This section utilizes the dynamic competition model that was developed in the previous chapter[26] as the basis of antitrust evaluation of one specific case of refusal to license a copyright. The chosen case is an actual refusal to license case that went to trial in front of the European antitrust courts – the Magill case.[27] This case is probably the most significant European antitrust–IP case decision of the 1990s, and surely the most significant refusal to license case of that decade, as can be evidenced by the extensive amount of related literature published around it[28] and its potential international impact.[29] Therefore it seems a worthy choice of a case for this 'refusal to deal' chapter, which offers a slightly different analysis from the court's analysis of it. The following discussion is divided into six parts. Section 4.3.1 briefly reviews the factual circumstances of the case. Section 4.3.2 describes the legal structure of the Magill decisions. The review will be restricted to the decision elements that are interesting in our context, namely those that look into whether there was indeed an abuse of a dominant position to an extent that merits an antitrust intervention.[30] Section 4.3.3, which forms that heart of this chapter, goes on to apply a dynamic analysis of the Magill fact pattern, one which utilizes the Austrian economics-based antitrust model proposed in the previous chapter. As we shall see, the dynamic analysis eventually reaches the same practical conclusion as the one adopted by the Magill court, that the refusal to license in the case was abusive enough to merit antitrust intervention by way of compulsory license. However, it arrives at this conclusion through a different line of reasoning. Section 4.3.4 fits the suggested dynamic analysis into the positivistic framework of EC competition law as set forth in Article 82 of the EC Treaty. Section 4.3.5 compares the Magill notion of 'economic dependence' of market entities upon the abusive dominant players with the Austrian notion of the dominant abuser enjoying 'insulation from the competitive threats'. It reconciles the two different notions, observing that there is probably no conflict between them. Finally, Section 4.3.6 highlights certain advantages of the dynamic analysis in refusal to license contexts that are demonstrated through its application to the Magill circumstances.

4.3.1 Magill Case: Findings of Fact

The Magill case evolved in three rounds: a 1988 European Commission decision[31] (Commission Decision), three parallel decisions by the European Court of First Instances[32] (CFI-RTE, CFI-BBC and CFI-ITP), and finally a decision on an appeal by the European Court of Justice[33] (ECJ Decision). The fact pattern described below relies on these sources. The case involved advance television and radio program listings (TPLs) in Ireland and Northern Ireland. TPLs were lists of forthcoming television programs that specified the title, channel, date, and time of broadcast. TPLs were produced by television broadcasting organizations as part of their program scheduling, in a drafting process which started off with a general draft that became increasingly detailed and precise until a final weekly schedule was completed approximately two weeks before transmission.[34] In other words, TPLs were byproducts of the program scheduling process.[35] From an IP aspect, TPLs enjoyed national copyright protection in Ireland and Northern Ireland.

At the germane time period there were three national broadcasting entities in Ireland and Northern Ireland: the BBC (broadcasting BBC1 and BBC2), RTE (broadcasting RTE1 and RTE2), and IBA (the Independent Broadcasting Authority that franchised ITV and Channel 4) (hereinafter: Broadcasting Organizations). These Broadcasting Organizations were statutory authorities that operated under a governmental license. They enjoyed statutory monopoly or duopoly position by law. RTE enjoyed a statutory monopoly for the provision of national radio and television broadcasting services in Ireland. Similarly, the BBC and the IBA enjoyed a statutory duopoly for the provision of national television broadcasting services in the United Kingdom (including Northern Ireland).[36]

Besides the national channels, at the time of the Commission decision, a limited number of viewers in the United Kingdom were able to receive additional television channels by cable operators, while such service was not available in Northern Ireland.[37] By the time of the CFI decision many television viewers in Great Britain and Ireland were already able to receive cable television channels. However, Northern Ireland residents still could not enjoy these channels.[38]

Apart from their broadcasting activities, the Broadcasting Organizations were also engaged in the production and sales of weekly television program publications, which provided their readers with advance TPL information. RTE acted directly in the TV guide market. The BBC and the IBA did so vicariously: the former through its wholly owned subsidiary BBC Enterprises,[39] and the latter through ITP (Independent Television Publications Ltd.) whose shareholders were the same contractors franchised by the IBA to supply independent television programs, namely ITV and Channel 4.[40] At the time of the European Commission's decision in the case, the three weekly TV guides published by RTE, the BBC and ITP were the only ones marketed in Ireland and Northern Ireland. Each of the three guides was specialized (or exclusive) in the sense that it provided program information only for the two respective channels offered by its related organization. One weekly TV guide, *TV Times*, was published by ITP and listed TPLs for ITV and Channel 4 TV channels. The second TV guide on the market, *Radio Times*, was published by BBC enterprises and provided TPL information for the two BBC television channels. Finally, the third guide, *RTE Guide*, was published by RTE and offered TPLs for programs in the two RTE TV channels.[41] Thus, viewers who wished to obtain advance weekly information on program listings of all the national channels, needed to buy three different TV guides. Thus, in effect, the Broadcasting Organizations, which were by law the only three such organizations in Ireland and Northern Ireland at the time, were effectively also the only market players offering TV guides in that geographical market.

TPLs were a necessary input for putting together and publishing TV guides, because TV guides by their very nature provide the same type of information as contained in television program listings, namely, the details of forthcoming TV programs.[42] The three Broadcasting Organizations seemed keenly aware of this importance since they adopted a strict policy for the licensing of their TPLs. Under their respective licensing schemes, which were virtually identical to one another,[43] TPLs were made available to newspapers and magazines free of charge, under the condition that their reproduction would only be made on a daily (rather than weekly) basis, and on a two-day basis on weekends and holidays. Publication of 'highlights' of the week was also allowed under the license terms. However, the conditions of the TPL licensing did not allow for their use on a weekly format. The licensing policy was strictly enforced by the Broadcasting Organizations,[44] who ensured compliance with it by taking up legal proceedings, where necessary, against publications that failed to comply with them. It should be noted that, at the same time, broadcasting and services were also being offered in the same geographic area by cable and satellite companies. The cable and satellite companies did not impose any limitations on the publication of their program listings which were also distributed free of charge.[45]

Magill TV Guide Ltd. (Magill) was an Irish company established for the purpose of publishing a weekly magazine containing information on TV programs in Ireland and Northern Ireland.[46] Magill planned to penetrate the weekly TV guide market by offering a *comprehensive* weekly paper, namely, a magazine containing the weekly listings for all the TV channels that could be received in Ireland and Northern Ireland at that time. Thus, Magill's TV guide product offered a new feature missing from any of the three existing TV guides described earlier, since it included information about all six TV channel programs in one guide, as opposed to the existing guides that covered only two channels each. In May 1986, Magill began to publish its comprehensive weekly TV guide. In response, the Broadcasting Organizations immediately filed a copyright infringement suit in an Irish court, claiming that Magill's conduct infringed their copyright in their respective TPLs. Soon thereafter, in June 1986, the Irish Court issued an interim injunction restraining Magill from publishing its comprehensive weekly program listings. The final decision of the Irish High Court upheld the injunction, finding the TPLs to be original literary work protected by copyright, and finding Magill's TV guide to have breached that copyright by reproducing a substantial part of RTE's copyright material.[47] The result was that Magill had to cease its TV guide publishing activities soon after their initiation, since the activities were found by the Irish Court to infringe ITP's copyright in its TPLs.

4.3.2 Magill Case: Findings of Law

European Commission decision

In April 1986, in anticipation of the above chain of events, Magill lodged a complaint with the European Commission under Article 3 of Regulation 17,[48] seeking a finding that the BBC, RTE and ITP abused their dominant position by refusing to grant Magill licenses for utilizing their TPLs, in violation of Section 86 of the EC Treaty.[49] In December 1988, the Commission adopted its decision in the case, accepting Magill's allegations.[50] The Commission Decision follows the methodical four-element test developed by EC jurisprudence for establishing a violation of abuse of a dominant position according to EC Treaty Article 82 namely: defining a relevant product and geographic market; establishing whether the suspected undertaking holds a (static) dominant position in this relevant market; evaluating whether the suspect has committed an abuse of the dominant position according to Article 82; and finally, examining whether the suspicious conduct affects trade between the EC member states.[51]

In following the EC jurisprudence model, the first element of the Commission Decision looked at the relevant product and geographic market. It defined the relevant product market as 'advance weekly listings of ITP, the BBC and RTE, and also the TV guides in which those listings are published'. The relevant geographic market was held to be the area within which the programs at hand could be received. The weekly listings of the three Broadcasting Organizations were considered separately as three distinct markets since they concerned different programs and thus were not seen as interchangeable.[52] The second element of the Commission's evaluation was dominance. Here, the Commission did not apply the traditional economic market power test.[53] Instead, it found that the Broadcasting Organizations possessed a 'factual monopoly' over weekly TPLs, since the listings were a byproduct of the program scheduling process that was inherently known only to them as program planners.[54] This was found to create economic dependence of all other market players who wished to obtain TPLs on the Broadcasting Organizations. Such a position of economic dependence was seen as characteristic of the existence of a dominant position. The copyright protection was found to strengthen this factual monopoly into a legal one that prevented competition from third parties. Hence, the Commission found ITP, the BBC and RTE to enjoy a monopoly over their respective weekly listings.[55] The language of the decision suggests that the rationale behind the finding of dominance relies on viewing the broadcasting activity and its byproduct of TPLs as an essential facility for competition in the TV guide market. After establishing dominance, the third element of the Commission's analysis examined whether the conduct could be considered an 'abuse' under (then) Article 86 of the EC Treaty. The analysis found an abuse because the licensing policy prevented publishers (other than the Broadcasting Organizations) from producing weekly TV guides for consumers. This constituted an abuse under (then) Article 86 (b) of the Treaty, according to which an abuse is committed where an undertaking of a dominant position limits production, markets or technical development to the prejudice of consumers.[56]

Specifically, the decision found two elements of abuse. First, it found substantial potential demand for comprehensive TV guides. Therefore it viewed employment of this dominant position to prevent the introduction of a new product to the market, namely a comprehensive weekly TV guide, as an abuse of Article 86.[57] Second, it found abuse, since by virtue of the offending policy regarding information on its programs, the Broadcasting Organizations retained for themselves the derivative market for weekly guides for those programs.[58] In other words, the Commission found that the Broadcasting Organizations leveraged their market power in broadcasting services market into the ancillary market for weekly TV guides. Finally, the fourth element of the analysis found the abuse to have an effect on trade between member states.[59] In the operative part of its decision, the Commission ordered the three Broadcasting Organizations to put an end to the infringement by supplying each other and third parties upon request (on a non-discriminatory basis) with their individual advance TPLs, and permitting reproduction of those listings by such parties.[60]

CFI Decisions

The Broadcasting Organizations sought to void the Commission Decision in an appeal to the European Court of First Instance (CFI), which upheld the decision in three similar opinions.[61] The opinions seem to have proceeded along a traditional analysis,[62] namely: relevant product and geographic market definition, market power of the suspect, whether the conduct amounted to an abuse, and whether it affected trade between member states.[63] The CFI Decisions upheld the Commission's relevant market definition[64] and its finding of dominance on behalf of the Broadcasting Organizations.[65] The court also upheld the finding of abuse. It verified the Commission's view that by reserving the exclusive right to publish its weekly TPLs, the Broadcasting Organizations prevented the emergence of a new product (a comprehensive weekly TV magazine) likely to compete with their own magazine. This utilization of the copyright in the TPL, produced as part of the broadcasting activity for securing a monopoly in the derivative market of weekly TV guides, was found to abuse Article 86 since it excluded all competition in the market while extending beyond what was necessary to fulfill the essential function of the copyright as permitted in Community law.[66]

The court addressed the more general question of when exercise of a national copyright may constitute an abuse under EC law. It noted EC jurisprudence, which determines that, in the absence of Community standardization or harmonization of national laws, it is for national legislatures of member states to lay down the conditions and procedures relating to copyright protection and, in particular, to determine what products are to enjoy such protection.[67] Article 30 (formerly Article 36 at the time of the Magill decisions) of the European Treaty regulates this relationship between national IPRs and general Community law (which includes antitrust), which is aimed at ensuring free movement of goods between member states.

Community member states may derogate from rules relating to the free movement of goods on grounds of the protection of industrial or commercial property. However, that derogation is subject to the conditions set out in the second sentence of Article 30. Under that provision, restrictions on free movement arising out of protection of IP 'shall not ... constitute a means of arbitrary discrimination or a disguised restriction on trade between Member States'. Thus the court emphasizes that the requirement of free movement of goods must be reconciled with IPRs, in a manner that protects the legitimate exercise of the former. The European Court has interpreted this to mean that the exercise of national IPRs must be restricted as far as is necessary for reconciliation.[68] More specifically, it upheld that where an IPR is exercised in such ways and circumstances as to pursue an aim manifestly contrary to the objectives of Article 86, it is no longer exercised in a manner that corresponds to its essential function, within the meaning of Article 30 of the Treaty, which is to protect the moral rights in the work and ensure a reward for the creative effort while respecting the aims of Article 86. Therefore, in such cases, the primacy of Community competition law prevails over such use of national IP law.[69]

ECJ decision

Two of the Broadcasting Organizations (ITP and RTE) appealed the CFI Decisions to the European Court of Justice, on the ground that the decisions misconstrued the concept of 'abuse of a dominant position' as contained in Article 86 of the EC Treaty.[70] In its decision, the ECJ affirmed the CFI analysis and finding of abuse of a dominant position.

With respect to the 'dominance' element, the court started off with a perplexing assertion that the 'mere ownership of an IPR *cannot* confer a such a [dominant] position' (italics added).[71] The court then found that under the circumstances the Broadcasting Organizations enjoyed a de facto monopoly over the information used to compile TPLs. This de facto monopoly over TPLs, reasoned the ECJ, put them in a position to prevent effective competition on the market for weekly TV guides.[72]

With respect to the 'abuse' element, the ECJ admitted that the exclusive right of reproduction forms part of the author's rights, so that refusal to grant a license, even by a dominant undertaking, cannot in itself constitute abuse of a dominant position.[73] However, the court affirmed that an exercise of an exclusive right by the proprietor may, under exceptional circumstances, amount to abusive conduct if it is combined with some other additional element of abusive conduct, such as excessive prices, arbitrary refusal to supply, or failing to supply spare parts which are needed, in order to force consumers to buy new products to replace the old ones.[74] The ECJ noted the following elements as legitimate considerations by the CFI in finding that such exceptional circumstances existed in the case: the fact that the refusal to license prevented the appearance of a new product on the market, for which there was potential consumer demand;[75] that there was no substitute available;[76] that there was no business justification for the refusal to deal;[77] and that the defendants' conduct reserved for themselves the secondary market of weekly TV guides.[78]

4.3.3 Magill Case: Dynamic Analysis

The dynamic antitrust analysis model developed in Chapter 3 of this study[79] offers an alternative economic approach to traditional antitrust analysis. A very brief recap of the model is in order. The model is based on the Austrian economics competition notion, and focuses on evaluation of the competitive process as a whole through various criteria (of which little attention, if any, is paid to static market share of the suspect player or to market structure). The evaluation results of these different criteria assist in diagnosing the state of the competitive process in a market area.[80] A diagnosis of a flawed competitive process (also called 'process monopoly') may then be attributed either to objective market circumstances or to abusive conduct by a market enterprise (of course it may be a result of some combination thereof – however, the assumption is that in each case one of these two categories is recognizably dominant). In practical terms, the dynamic analysis comprises two steps: first, establishing whether the competitive process in the relevant market area has been significantly curtailed to a level of process monopoly; and second, establishing a causal connection between the conduct of the suspected market entity and the process monopoly observed in the first stage.

Analysis of the Magill fact pattern of refusal to license copyrighted materials through the dynamic paradigm is carried out below in the manner just described. The first part of the analysis evaluates whether the Magill circumstances demonstrated a process monopoly. The second part looks into whether the refusal to license was the cause responsible for the significant impediment of the competitive process observed in the first stage. In an IPR context, it is important to stress that the conduct itself must be the cause of the problem, rather than the IP right. Barriers to market entry, which are one of the primary indications of a stifling of the competitive process (both under the traditional and the dynamic models) often boil down to property rights.[81] It is, however, important to establish specifically that a specific property-derivative conduct (refusal to license) created the obstacle to the competitive process, rather than the intellectual property right as a whole (that is, the broad bundle of rights it confers). Otherwise, the analysis may conflict with the aforementioned assumption regarding the inherent validity of granted IPRs.

Was a process monopoly in place?

Rate of innovation The first analysis criterion is the observed rate of innovation in the examined market area, both by way of IP protected innovation and by non-protected market innovation, such as introduction of novel products and new features to existing products, and so on – all of which should be reflected in differentiation in products' features and presentation. With respect to general market innovation, unfortunately the various Magill decisions do not reveal sufficient factual information. We are not told whether any innovation trend could be detected within the three existing weekly TV guide products over the years, or whether new features, layout or graphical presentation were added to the magazines over time. Apart from individual innovation in the products themselves, there is also no information provided on the question of comparative differentiation between the three magazines. We are not told whether they were similar or different in their features or layout. Hence, there is lack of information for reviewing this point. With respect to innovation protected by IPRs, it seems clear from the decisions that the TPLs forming the subject matter of the copyright at hand involved little creative effort, if any. There is no hint of any creativity in the way the TPLs were presented or edited. Again, information is lacking, but it seems plausible to speculate that such a lack of creativity conveyed some sense of an innovative stalemate that is typical of a flailing competitive process.

Although the different Magill decisions do not refer to the above facts that could assist in evaluating the rate of innovation in the TV guide market area, they do offer one significant clue in this respect. The decisions emphasize that the Broadcasting Organizations' conduct enabled them to successfully block the introduction of a *new* product, a comprehensive weekly television guide, into the market.[82] Indeed, Magill's innovative product, as well as similar attempts to offer weekly TPLs, were blocked from reaching the market, by injunctions obtained by the Broadcasting Organizations on the basis of their copyright and licensing policy. This demonstrates how, within the TV guide market area, the innovation process, which forms an integral part of a competitive pattern, was severely stifled. Magill's inability to introduce a new product to the market, a product that it was technically and financially able to introduce (as proven by the fact that it indeed offered it for a while before being blocked by an injunction) proves that the innovation facet of the market process was significantly impaired.

Sensitivity of the suspected firm's behavior to consumer trends and to behavior of the other market players This evaluation aspect is important because it examines the suspect entity's behavior for any clues which may suggest it has become 'insulated from the cold winds of competition', a position which runs contrary to the reality of a healthy competitive process. In such a process, market players aim to please consumers in an effort to win their business. Therefore behavior that ignores obvious consumer demand trends contradicts the basic notions of a competitive process, thus suggesting that such a process does not take place within the examined market area.[83]

With respect to sensitivity to consumer trends, the Magill decisions establish that there was considerable consumer demand in place for a comprehensive weekly TV guide. Such a demand was confirmed by a number of indicators: first, the willingness of many consumers to purchase one or more of the weekly TV guides offered by the three Broadcasting Organizations; second, Magill's choosing to publish a comprehensive guide; third, the brief market experience of Magill, which had offered such guides in May and June 1986; and finally, the market experience in other member states where comprehensive weekly TV guides were available.[84] However, in spite of consumer demand for a comprehensive TV guide, not one of the Broadcasting Organizations heeded these consumer calls. All three of them failed to produce the comprehensive weekly guide that consumers sought. Furthermore, it seems clear that the Broadcasting Organizations were well aware of this demand. Their adoption and enforcement of the licensing scheme described above can only be explained by a motivation to prevent any other entity from entering their turf and offering an alternative and improved product. In any event, the circumstances reflect a situation in which the suspect organizations blatantly ignored consumers' wishes for a comprehensive weekly guide. Such disregard for consumer demand suggests that there was no viable competitive process in place within the market area examined in Magill.

The fact that all three Broadcasting Organizations failed to offer a comprehensive weekly TV guide (the material also reveals no effort on their behalf to do so) also demonstrates that they felt themselves shielded from competition in the TV guide market. The demand for a comprehensive weekly guide dictates that, if such a guide were offered, consumer demand for the existing specialized two-channel weekly guides of RTE, the BBC or ITP would drop significantly, if not disappear. This is because consumers who would purchase a comprehensive guide will not invest additional funds for a specialized guide that provides information already existing in the comprehensive guide. Furthermore, it is hard to imagine viewers who were so religiously loyal to only two TV channels (of RTE, the BBC or the IBA) that they would prefer a specialized guide over a comprehensive one (for a similar price, even such 'specialized' viewers would probably prefer more TPLs for their money). However, their failure to offer weekly guides proves that the Broadcasting Organizations did not fear a competing weekly product such as Magill, which shows that they managed to insulate themselves from the competitive threat of a comprehensive weekly guide.[85]

Availability of alternatives for the suspects' products Dynamic thinking implies that consumer demand will be met since entrepreneurs are constantly trying to discover what it is that consumers want. Therefore a robust competitive market area is likely to offer consumers a number of alternatives, reflecting competing entrepreneurial efforts to cater to consumer taste. In the Magill case, the decisions establish that the three available weekly TV guides, namely those published by the Broadcasting Organizations, were complementary, since each provided TPLs for different television channels.[86] Hence, these exclusive weekly TV guides did not directly compete among themselves, nor were they alternatives. Furthermore, they were the only weekly guides for these channels, because all other available listings for them, whether in daily newspapers, periodical newspapers, magazines (in the case or RTE) or on the television teletext information services (of the BBC, ITV and Channel 4) were provided only on a daily (and in some cases two-day) basis.[87] Hence, to obtain weekly TPLs consumers had no alternative other than the exclusive weekly TV guides offered by the Broadcasting Organizations.

This lack of alternatives reflected a pattern in which consumers' function as the engine of the competitive discovery process is somewhat curtailed, because they were unable to express their preferences (for lack of alternatives). Therefore (as explained in Chapter 3) this lack of availability of alternatives for the suspected firm's product may be indicative of a questionable vigor of the competitive process. It should be recalled that the conclusiveness of a lack of alternatives as an indication for a process monopoly should be examined carefully.[88]

Note that the European Court of Justice acknowledged these circumstances where 'there was … no actual or potential substitute for a weekly television guide offering information on the programs for the week ahead'[89] as evidence when concluding that the conduct at stake was abusive.[90] It therefore seems that the court's analysis of this issue differs from the one suggested here. The latter is twofold – lack of alternatives is one of the indicators for a process monopoly, and the second element traces the causal relation between such market observation and the suspected conduct. On the other hand, the court's analysis bundles these two stages together, by taking the lack of alternatives as evidence of abusive conduct on behalf of the suspected organizations.

Existence of barriers to entry into the market area The dynamic and traditional models both recognize the importance of freedom of market entry to the competitive process. Where a significant entry barrier to a market area is in place, a healthy competitive process cannot develop. This link is double-edged, namely, the existence of a barrier to entry is also a distinctive indication for the existence of a process monopoly, since it stifles the competitive process. As noted earlier, in the Magill case the Broadcasting Organizations enjoyed statutory monopoly and duopoly positions in Ireland and the United Kingdom, respectively.[91] Hence, the organizations were ensured by statute an unchallenged position in the national broadcasting market. TPLs were a byproduct of the national broadcasting activity, and could only be produced by the broadcasting service itself (since it was the broadcasting service that planned its program schedule). Furthermore, TPLs were necessary input for publication of TV guides. Therefore, in effect the Broadcasting Organizations enjoyed inherent exclusive control over an essential production resource, namely over TPLs for nationally broadcast (their own) programs. The fact that TPLs were a necessary input for the publication of TV guides, and that they enjoyed copyright protection, enabled the structure and enforcement of the Broadcasting Organizations' TPLs' licensing policy, which allowed use of TPLs only on a daily publication basis. This policy ensured that no other market player would be able to compete with the Broadcasting Organizations in the market area of weekly television guides for nationally broadcast programs. Therefore these circumstances reflect the existence of a barrier to entry into this market area.

The existence of such a barrier to entry is further supported by the fact that, although there was a recognized consumer demand for a comprehensive weekly TV guide,[92] no such guide existed in the market (although there was no technology problem). The most likely reason for such a market phenomenon is the existence of a barrier to entry, since otherwise potential entrepreneurs (such as Magill) would have been lured by the potential profit from offering such a guide. This barrier to entry significantly interferes with the competitive process, since the process-oriented approach presumes an ongoing ability of competitors to join a market area and challenge existing market entities as essential for a healthy competitive process.

Degree of uncertainty in the market area The dynamic competition notion entails a certain degree of uncertainty because it assumes information to be neither perfect nor free and because market players cannot predict the next competitive moves taken by existing competitors or potential new entrants (theoretically they do not even know the latter's identity).[93] Similarly, uncertainty is also an indicator of the vigor of the competitive process, since the process is viewed as an iterative discovery process in which enterprises perennially search for what it is that consumers want, and how to get it to them in the most profitable manner. Therefore some uncertainty is necessary to create a habitat for this discovery process. The degree to which a suspect market player is able to insulate him/herself from the detriment of uncertainty is thus relevant for identifying a process monopoly. Where the circumstances suggest that a market entity has successfully created for itself what seems to be a certain position and market picture, one should take this as a possible indication, which, where taken with other indications, may suggest that the competitive process is damaged.[94]

The Magill case suggests that the Broadcasting Organizations may have enjoyed a high level of certainty, to an extent that may reflect a hindered market process. The key is, again, the usage of IPRs (copyrights) as an instrument for overcoming the market's inherent uncertainty disadvantage. Weekly TPLs were a necessary and main input required for producing weekly TV guides. The combination of the copyright protection with the identical licensing scheme adopted by the three organizations, effectively divided the market for such guides among them. The scheme ensured each of the organizations exclusive publication rights of its weekly TPLs, which were indispensable for producing weekly TV guides. As a result the organizations were able to prevent access of any potential market players into the weekly TV guide market area.

Up to this point, the analysis seems identical to the one just offered under the 'barriers to entry' caption. The difference is in the subjective element. The Broadcasting Organizations were to a certain extent 'on top' of the market process. They conducted their business on a level above the one in which the market process itself ran its course, since they were the only ones in direct control of this licensing scheme. Each of them *knew* that, as long as it maintained this licensing policy, no other entity could compete with it in the weekly TV guide market. Furthermore, each of them was inherently the only one to know the exact policy, and to what extent it would choose to enforce it. In addition, the uncertainty in the market was further reduced by the UK and Irish statutes that ensured the organizations a monopoly and duopoly status in their national markets. Thus, they were ensured (at least for the foreseeable future) a unique position as sole providers of national TV and radio broadcasts, and hence of TPLs for their national TV channels (this is the 'de facto' monopoly that the CFI decisions refer to). The combined effect of the copyright and statutory broadcasting monopoly was that everybody in the market knew that there was only one source for TPLs. There was no 'window of opportunity' for entrepreneurs to discover new sources, to independently develop a competing version of TPLs, or to develop any new product that involved weekly TPLs. The result was an assured and quiet market life for the Broadcasting Organizations that contrasts with the typical characteristics of a vigorous competitive process.

Certainly, this analysis does not suggest that a copyright or monopoly-granting statute inherently (or often) reduces uncertainty levels to an extent that suggests a broad-process monopoly market phenomenon. Nor is it suggested that this is the case whenever there is only one known source that is vital for a product input. It seems that a unique cumulative effect of the Magill set of circumstances had brought about this result, namely, the statutory monopolies, the substantive 'thinness' of the copyright that protected very little creative efforts with a broad protection scope which rendered it virtually impossible to work around it without infringement, and the conduct of the Broadcasting Organizations which adopted a harsh and uniform licensing policy. Attention is drawn again to the significant subjective element in the case – it was not only the 'objective' circumstances of a copyright or a monopoly granted by statute but also the specific line of action taken by the suspect organizations. Furthermore, the fact that the licensing policy was identical (perhaps coordinated) for the three organizations exacerbated the situation from a competition point of view. This is because the combined effect was probably higher than the effect of only one broadcasting organization adopting such a licensing policy. For example, if only one of the organizations had adopted the said licensing policy, Magill or another publisher could have perhaps offered a broader guide than a two-channel one, one that listed TPLs for the four channels of the two organizations that did not adopt the policy. Such a broad (although not comprehensive) guide might have persuaded viewers to prefer such a four-channel guide to the specialized two-channel ones. Thus, market forces could have 'broken down' the resistance of the third organization, which would prefer to license its TPLs for a fee rather than face very small sales of its specialized guide.

Volatility of the market area population over time Common sense dictates that within a healthy competitive process any significant consumer demand draws in entrepreneurial market entrants who hope to cash in on it. These entrepreneurs then compete against one another in a struggle that acts as a 'natural market selection' mechanism. Some of these entrepreneurs may succeed while others may fail. It is also possible, in a constantly growing market area, that there is a profitable niche for all of these market entrants. In any event, overall, this pattern is likely to result in volatility in the market area composition over time as new entrants attempt to penetrate the market area. Conversely, very little volatility in the population of the market players occupying a market area over many years may raise doubts as to the well-being of the market process in that area.

The Magill materials do not directly address the issue of historical market demographics in the TPL market area. However, they do reveal that even before the Magill case, the three Broadcasting Organizations had strictly enforced their licensing policy by taking successful legal action against any publication exceeding the permitted licensing terms.[95] Such strict enforcement would have immediately eliminated any other publisher attempting to produce a weekly TV guide (as was the case in Magill). Therefore it seems likely that the three Broadcasting Organizations were consistently over the years the only market entities active in the market area of weekly TPL publications. While this in itself cannot be taken as proof of a process monopoly,[96] it does add up and support the other indicators noted earlier in Magill case that the competitive process was significantly damaged.

Degree of price volatility in the market area The degree of price volatility in the market area both in terms of products' real prices (excluding inflation of course) and in terms of relative prices of different players' products may serve as an indicator as to the vigor of the competitive process. Unfortunately, the Magill materials do not provide any information on this (with respect to relative prices it seems that no information existed since the three specialized TV guides were complementary and thus did not compete with one another). The lack of factual information therefore prevents an evaluation of this indicator in the Magill case.

Fluctuating volatility of suspect firms' static market shares Recall that in the proposed dynamic analysis, minimal volatility of the suspect firms' static market shares over time, namely an observation that a company has held a solid dominant position for several years or more, may also be utilized as a prima facie indicator for a shuffling of the competitive process rather than a clear indication of a process monopoly. However, this indicator is irrelevant in the Magill case, where each of the Broadcasting Organizations was found to possess a 100 percent market share for weekly TPL publications of its own programs. Thus their static market shares were constant.[97] It would also have been useful to know whether any significant decreases were observed in the sales of any of the specialized weekly TV guides during the years they were published. Such decreases could have suggested the existence of an effective competitive struggle beneath the façade of a constant 100 percent market share. However, none of these facts is revealed in the Magill decisions, and therefore this notion cannot be explored further.

Coordination among entities in the same market area In a classical Schumpeterian competitive environment, the different entrepreneurs compete against each other, each to his/her own. Thus, the competitive struggle takes the form of an individual contest, in which each entrepreneur seeks to maximize his/her own profits. Thus none of market players enjoy a protected activity turf. Any indication of coordination among market players in the same market area should attract some attention in this respect, namely, to the extent that it may create such a protected commercial turf for market entities. Except in the unique case of adoption of industry standards in network industries, coordination among non-affiliated players in the same market area may reflect some stifling of the competitive process. This is because in theory market players constantly compete against one another on all fronts, whereas coordination among competitors conflicts with this notion. Furthermore, such coordination may suggest that the suspected entity did not initially feel itself insulated from 'the cold winds of competition' and hence chose coordination with its competitors as a means of mitigating these competitive drafts. In other words, it may allude to a rather healthy competitive reality prior to the coordination. In any event, to the extent that it can be shown that a seemingly concerted conduct pattern (regardless of whether coordination can indeed be proven) clearly compromises the competitive struggle – such a pattern should raise a red flag as to the vigor of the competitive process. The argument is admittedly a cautious one, namely, a coordinated pattern in itself is not suspicious, but rather the ostensible coordinated pattern must be expressly counterintuitive to a healthy competitive process. In other words, the coordinated conduct must in some way stand against the rationale of a competitive process. One possible example of such a case is where the coordinated behavior categorically runs against the interests of consumers[98] to the point where consumers discern it but are unable to express their discontent through market choices.

This notion of the coordination aspect relates to the previous elements mentioned above. It relates to the 'sensitivity of the suspect's behavior to competitors' demand and to consumers' in the example just given, adding an additional problematic dimension to it – the insulation from competitive pressures extended to the coordinating entities rather than to one player. It also relates to the 'alternatives' notion, in cases where the coordinated conduct directly results in denial of alternative products from consumers.

It should be reiterated here that this study focuses on the analysis of conduct patterns under the unilateral provisions. Therefore the coordination discussed here is not raised with respect to an EC Treaty Article 81 (equivalent of a Sherman Act §1) analysis (note, however, that EC competition law also includes collective dominance as abusive conduct as part of Article 82).[99] However, while antitrust analysts may prefer neat fact patterns that are either horizontal-concerted or unilateral-dominance-abusing, that is not always the case in reality. In reality, EC Treaty Article 82 and Sherman Act §2 cases may also display coordinated conducts that may fall short of a horizontal violation but may still serve as an indication of a slowing of the competitive process.[100] The argument is that certain market behavior of competitors (or would-be competitors) that seems coordinated may serve as an *indication* of the fact that the competitive process is not vigorously running its course.

In Magill, the Broadcasting Organizations applied a strikingly uniform licensing policy with respect to their TPLs and cooperated in bringing legal action against entities that they deemed to infringe the licensing policy.[101] The adopted uniform licensing policy effectively divided the weekly TV guide market between the three Broadcasting Organizations, in such a way that consumers interested in comprehensive weekly TPL information had no choice but to buy all three specialized guides separately. Consumers could not express their discontent by turning to alternative weekly guides since one did not exist on the market. Indeed, this was because the joint policy also prevented third parties from entering this market area. This seemingly coordinated policy meant that there was no leeway for a competitive dynamics to run its course. For example, if only one or two of the Broadcasting Organizations had adopted the said licensing policy, there would still have been room for entrepreneurs to offer a weekly guide for the cable, satellite and two channels of one national broadcaster (the one that did not adopt the licensing policy). The success of such a guide, perhaps at the expense of the two existing specialized guides, could have pushed the two remaining organizations to change their policies (for example, perhaps licensing their weekly TPLs for a fee would have been more profitable than continued publication of their specialized guides). These are all theoretical speculations of what could have happened. The main point is that the seemingly coordinated licensing policy among the Broadcasting Organizations protected a whole market area from the competitive tides. The result was obvious damage to the competitive process, since the ostensible cooperation effectively isolated the weekly TPL market area from it.

Note that the fact that the Magill decisions did not characterize the Broadcasting Organizations as competitors in the weekly TPL publication market does not weaken the analysis. First, there seemed to have been indirect competitive forces in place between organizations.[102] Second, and perhaps more importantly, the organizations would have been *potential* competitors in this market area had it not been for the conduct that effectively divided the market area among them.

Was the suspects' conduct the cause of the process monopoly?

The second part of the dynamic antitrust analysis evaluates whether a causal connection can be established between the stifling of the competitive process, observed in the first part, and the suspicious conduct. Without an evident causal relation between the two, there can be no basis for a finding of an antitrust violation. This is true both from a legal viewpoint, and from an Austrian economics viewpoint, which already views antitrust as a *mala per se* market intervention that should be used only when it is utterly necessary. The intuitive way to establish the causal relation is by showing how the suspected conduct brought about the process-monopoly findings observed in the first part of the analysis. Besides direct causal evidence, another way to establish this causal relation indirectly is by deductive negativity, proving that the initial objective circumstances of the market area accorded with the 'untold assumptions of the Austrian model'.[103] Where that is the case, the natural culprit to be blamed for the stifling of the process becomes the suspicious conduct – since a robust competitive process presumably develops naturally in any market area whose circumstances accord with the basic assumptions of the Austrian model.

The assumed Austrian market assumptions (the deductive–indirect proof method The assumptions are as follows:

- *Lack of governmental market intervention* It seems that in Magill there was no direct market intervention in the TPL market area by way of price or other regulation (no direct information is provided in the decisions). However, there was direct governmental intervention in the national broadcasting market area through statutes that conferred monopoly and duopoly status on the Broadcasting Organizations. Without going into the justifications for the statutes, such intervention would be anathema to Austrian economists, since it interferes with endogenous market processes.[104] The crucial question is: to what extent did the monopoly-conferring statutes interfere with the necessary habitat for the growth of a competitive process? The interference seems significant. Clearly the statutes provided their nominated national Broadcasting Organizations with a de facto monopoly over TPLs, since the latter were a byproduct of the organizations' broadcasting activity, and the only way in which TPLs could be produced. Such a de facto monopoly is 'unnatural' in the sense that it resulted from artificial market entry barrier erected by the monopoly-conferring statutes.
- *Availability of entrepreneurial opportunities* In terms of entrepreneurial motives to join the market, there is little doubt that such motives existed in the Magill case. This is evident simply from the fact that Magill chose to join the weekly TPL publication market, and that other entities attempted to do the same.[105] This proves that Magill and these other enterprises all deemed the weekly TPL publication market area to be sufficiently profitable and promising to make joining it worthwhile. The fact that Magill joined the market for two short weeks also shows that there were not any exceedingly large initial investments associated with joining the market that rendered such joining not worthwhile.

The second element of entrepreneurial opportunities relates to objective obstacles to entrepreneurial market entry. In this sense, Magill demonstrates a unique combination of objective circumstances that may seem to threaten entrepreneurial opportunities in the weekly TPL publications market.[106] The combination included the statutorily-created de facto monopoly over TPLs, along with the copyright that prohibited their free reproduction and the fact that TPLs were an essential input for publication of weekly TV guides. This objective combination applied to the TPL market as a whole (that is, both daily and weekly TPLs), and resulted in exclusive control of the Broadcasting Organizations over production and dissemination of TPLs.[107] However, it seems that this combination in itself was insufficient to fatally stifle competition in TPL publications. This is demonstrated by the fact that a variety of sources, namely newspapers, magazines and a television teletext service, offered *daily* TPLs to their readers and viewers. In other words, consumers did enjoy a variety of alternatives for obtaining daily TPL publications despite the combination of those three objective restrictive market circumstances. It was only in the *weekly* TPL publications that process monopoly was observed, and the subjective licensing policy of the Broadcasting Organizations applied restrictions only to this segment. This close correlation between the two, along with the lack of process monopoly in daily TPL publications where the objective restrictive circumstances applied *mutatis mutandis*, goes to prove that the process monopoly in weekly TPL publications was a result of the *subjective* licensing policy adopted by the Broadcasting Organizations, and not a result of objective market circumstances.

- *Uncertainty notions* The essential question is whether the restrictive combination of the three objective market circumstances significantly eliminated the assumed uncertainty notions to a level that hindered the organic development of a competitive discovery process. This combination of circumstances included a de facto monopoly in TPLs, copyright protection over them, and TPLs being an essential facility for publishing weekly TV guides. There are a number of considerations that suggest that despite the restrictive effect of the objective circumstances' combination, a sufficient amount of uncertainty would have been maintained to allow for a competitive discovery process, had it not been for the licensing policy adopted by the Broadcasting Organizations. First, the decisions show that there was at least one obvious measure by which products in the relevant market area could improve, namely by introduction of *comprehensive* weekly TV guides. This shows that there were still unexplored opportunities in the way such guides were compiled that were not blocked by the objective circumstances described. Second, the objective circumstances still leave a level of uncertainty, since the different market players seeking to publish weekly TV guides may each try to obtain a better licensing deal on TPLs *vis-à-vis* the others. However, the uniform licensing policy of the Broadcasting Organizations eliminated this leeway. For publication of daily TPLs it set the market price at zero (for the three organizations). For publication of weekly TPLs it categorically eliminated the possibility of purchasing such a license. Third, and perhaps most importantly, the fact that Magill and others attempted to enter the weekly TPL publications market area proves that, in their mind, there was sufficient uncertainty left in that area to allow for profitable competitive exploitation. They all thought they could bring something to the weekly TPL publication market that would successfully compete with the three existing guides. It is this subjective perception that is the determinative factor in this respect, since uncertainty is all about what existing or potential market players do know and, more importantly, what they do not know.

Positive causal relation The argument for a positive casual relation between the licensing conduct and the Broadcasting Organizations' licensing policy has already been developed in the Magill decisions described, where it does not differ from dynamic analysis thinking. Therefore it will only be briefly recounted here. The decisions established that the fact that no comprehensive weekly television guide was available in the market was a *result* of the licensing policy of the Broadcasting Organizations.[108] Thus, the decisions show a correlation between the licensing conduct and a variety of competition-stifling indicators mentioned above: barrier to entry, the lack of alternative TV guides, the sluggish rate of innovation and lack of sensitivity to consumer demand (since there was consumer demand for a comprehensive weekly guide).

The Magill courts' strong belief in this causal relation is also expressed through their choice of remedy, namely licensing of the TPLs on a non-discriminatory basis for all interested parties, and for uses that include weekly publications. The remedy does not address the monopoly and duopoly status of the Broadcasting Organizations,[109] nor does it allude to the validity of the copyright.[110] It is narrowly tailored to address only the Broadcasting Organizations' licensing policy. This shows that the decisions recognized a clear causal thread between the licensing policy utilized and the observed damage to the competitive process.

Summary

The first part of the dynamic analysis revealed that many of the indicators suggest that the competitive process was stifled in the Magill fact pattern. Especially convincing are the findings related to the indicators of barrier to entry, lack of sensitivity to consumer demand, lack of alternatives for consumers, stifled innovation and seemingly coordinated conduct among market entities. The above analysis also suggested, in less convincing terms, that the circumstances displayed diminished uncertainty notions, and lack of volatility of market area population over time. Thus, the result of the first part of the analysis is an unmistakable portrayal of a process monopoly.

The second part of the analysis established a correlation between the licensing policy and the process monopoly observed in the first part. However, while it seems clear that the licensing policy brought about the process monopoly, the second part of the analysis drew attention to the objective market circumstances in Magill. It must be conceded that the unique objective market circumstances of Magill created an initially non-level playing field that made it all the more difficult for a competitive process to flourish. These circumstances included the statutory monopoly of the national Broadcasting Organizations, the copyright protection over TPLs and the fact that those copyrighted TPLs were essential for publishing TV guides. As a result, there was a clear head start advantage for the Broadcasting Organizations in the market area of weekly TPLs. Furthermore, the copyright provided the organizations with a legitimate legal instrument for directing the manner in which competition in the market would run, if at all. Therefore, the objective market circumstances should definitely share some of the responsibility for the failure of the competitive process. Nevertheless, it was the uniform licensing policy adopted by the organizations that, on top of the already-restrictive circumstances, went the extra mile to make competition in that market area an impossibility. In other words, the suspected conduct itself was a *sine qua non* of the observed competitive market failure.

4.3.4 Fitting the Dynamic Analysis into the Framework of EC Law

It is important to clarify how the theoretical dynamic analysis fits into a positivistic legal framework in this case which is an EC competition law one. The rationale behind this analysis is that where a company's conduct is successful in creating a process monopoly, one may safely deduce that such a company enjoys a 'dominant position' (in EC antitrust terms) or possesses 'monopoly power' (in U.S. antitrust terms). The assumption is that a non-dominant company acting on its own will never be sufficiently powerful to stop, or significantly stifle, the mighty wheels of the organic competitive process. Furthermore, antitrust laws are seen as aiming to ensure a free-flowing competitive process (a process that is harmonious with the tenets of IP law). Therefore, an application of the accumulative twofold dynamic analysis on a case's circumstances which demonstrates a positive result in both elements (that is, stifled process due to the suspected conduct) should be seen as an indication that 'an abuse by an undertaking of a dominant position' has taken place. In other words, the dynamic analysis replaces the traditional Article 82 analysis elements of defining a distinct relevant market, establishing that the suspected player holds a dominant market share thereof, and finding the conduct abusive.[111]

In order to establish an antitrust violation, one still needs to establish an adherence to the remaining requirements of the relevant antitrust statute. Under EC jurisprudence this means establishing that within EC Treaty jurisprudence the suspect entity is indeed an 'undertaking', that the abuse took place 'within the common market or in a substantial part of it' and that it had an effect on 'trade between Member States'. Note that since subsections (a)–(d) of Article 82 enumerate four types of abusive conduct patterns, rather than provide an exhaustive list of such scenarios,[112] then there is no legal requirement for the suspected conduct to fit exactly into one of the behavior patterns mentioned in Article 82. Under U.S. antitrust jurisprudence, the remaining statutory elements required for establishing a Sherman Act §2 violation require proof that the monopolizing activity takes place with respect to 'any part of the trade or commerce among the several States, or with foreign nations'. These additional elements are not reviewed in this study since they are outside the realm of the proposed dynamic analysis.

Admittedly, application of the proposed dynamic analysis is limited to cases where the abusive (or monopolizing) conduct was successfully completed to the extent that it already produced the unlawful result that antitrust statutes seek to prevent. Therefore the proposed analysis cannot be applied in EC Article 82 cases where the abuse of the dominant position has not actually had an appreciable effect on trade.[113] For the same reasons the proposed analysis cannot be utilized to evaluate §2 Sherman Act 'attempt to monopolize' cases. Perhaps this limitation carries some benefits with it. The major task in EC Treaty Article 82 or Sherman Act §2 cases lies in distinguishing legitimate competitive conduct from proscribed abusive or monopolizing conduct. This is a difficult task to begin with, and it becomes even more so where the suspected conduct was not completed, in the sense that it was yet to inflict significant effects on the competition process at the time of the fact-finding. Therefore applying a test as broad and untested as the dynamic analysis may be imprudent in the sense that its results may demonstrate a high margin of error.

4.3.5 Economic Dependence versus Insulation from Competition

In finding an abuse of a dominant position the Magill decisions find third parties wishing to enter the market to be in a state of economic dependence on the Broadcasting Organizations (which were thus in a position to hinder the emergence of any effective competition). This position of economic dependence is characteristic of the existence of a dominant position.[114] In other words, the court implies that the abuse of the dominant position there has rendered the non-dominant market players (or potential market players) dependent upon the conduct of the dominant players, or that the latter is indicative of the former. This notion is different from the perspective of dynamic analysis developed in the previous chapter. Recall that the dynamic approach focused on the independence of a successful abusive entity from the market process. It searched for indications that the dominant market player has successfully managed to 'insulate itself from the cold winds of competition'[115] as suggesting failure of the competitive process. The question is whether these two different notions can be reconciled, if at all.

Initially, this perspective of the Magill decisions seems very different from that of the dynamic analysis. This is mainly because the Magill perspective focuses on the position of the non-suspicious market players *vis-à-vis* the suspected abusers, while the dynamic perspective rather focuses on the position of the suspicious dominant player *vis-à-vis* the rest of the market (both competitors and consumers).

However, note that the two notions do not necessarily contradict each other, but rather may feasibly reflect two aspects of the same situation. There is something paradoxical about the competitive process. On the one hand, it is in nature a perennial process of struggle between different market actors. In this struggle every market player is acting alone, independently seeking to maximize profits and market holdings. However, this individual struggle inherently creates some level of interdependency among the market players, since they continually react to changes introduced by rival players in order to survive. For example, where a certain PC maker introduces a product with enhanced memory, its rivals are likely to soon follow, in order to maintain their competitive edge in the market area. This individual-yet-interdependent market reality forms the core of the competitive process. By definition the process itself streams spontaneously without any of the market players placing themselves above it by controlling or directing it. Both the terminology used in the Magill decisions and the dynamic terminology reflect a situation in which this competitive formula failed. The Magill notion of market entities becoming dependent on the Broadcasting Organizations reveals a context in which the organizations achieved a position 'above the process', because they were able to determine who could enter the market. The dynamic terminology reflects failure because the interdependence notion does not exist where market players demonstrate obliviousness to competitors' actions and consumer demand. A third possible competitive failure is that of the individual element of the competitive process – such failure is demonstrated in concerted conduct cases (EC Treaty Article 81 or Sherman Act §1 cases). Thus, the Magill and the unilateral dynamic notions are consistent with each other, both reflecting different facets of a competitive process failure.

4.3.6 Advantages of Dynamic Analysis in Refusal to License Contexts

The above application of the dynamic analysis to Magill reveals some of its advantages, as well as some of its drawbacks, both of which are discussed herein.

An arbitrary definition of a relevant product market is unnecessary

EC Treaty Article 82 cases (similarly to Sherman Act §2 'monopolizing' cases) stand or fall on the basic element known as relevant market definition. Metaphorically, they depend on whether the suspected big fish is playing out its strategy in a small pond (relevant market) or in a big pond. It is only where the pond is sufficiently small in comparison to the suspected fish that it may be characterized as 'dominant'. In the absence of such established 'dominance' Article 82 does not apply to a conduct. As a result of this requirement, it seems that the European Commission and courts often define the relevant product market narrowly, seeking to overcome the 'dominance' obstacle and enter into the realm of Article 82.[116]

This trend is also demonstrated in the Magill case. Both the Commission and the courts considered the weekly TPLs of each of the Broadcasting Organizations as a separate market in itself,[117] which resulted in a finding of a 100 percent market by each of the organizations. Such a narrow product market definition may seem artificially forced. Take the example of the Magill market definition, which seems puzzling from a number of respects. First, the argument that the TV guides of the three organizations categorically did not compete one with another implicitly assumes that the broadcast programs themselves did not compete among themselves. This assumption is puzzling. For example, was there really a marked difference, in consumers' eyes, between the news editions of the different channels or their sports coverage? It seems plausible that there was at least some level of substitutability between the offered news and sports broadcasts, and hence the different TPLs. Thus it seems highly probable that some viewers with a focused interest in news or sport subjects may well have found it sufficient to regularly purchase only one or two of the available guides.

Second, common sense indicates that viewers formed their TV viewing preferences based on their experience with the quality of the broadcasts themselves rather than on television program listings. This means that demand for the three TPLs themselves was to a significant degree derived from the popularity of the different channels among viewers. As there are only 24 hours in a day, and since most people also engage in activities other than watching TV, this has to mean that some level of substitutability existed between the different TV channels, and hence the three TV guides to the extent that consumers purchased them for the TPLs and not for other features.

Third (and alternatively to the previous notion), note that the TV guides (as opposed to the listings) could have competed through aspects not directly related to the TPLs. For example, they could have offered exclusive interviews with leading media figures (as is often the case in U.S. TV guides). In fact, competitive thinking suggests that this is exactly what they would do in order to gain an edge in the TV guide market.

In short, the fact that the Broadcasting Organizations could not compete on the listings level (each could offer only their own TPLs) does not mean that they could not (or did not) compete in weekly TV guides.[118] There is clearly a difference between TPLs and TV guides. This casts serious doubt on the soundness of the relevant market definition adopted by the Magill authorities, and its assertion of 100 percent unchallenged market share for each of the Broadcasting Organizations.[119] On the other hand, as the Commission was probably aware, despite the clear damage to the competitive process in that market area, without adoption of such a problematic market definition it would have been difficult, if not impossible, to apply Article 82 because of lack of a proof of 'dominance'. The dynamic analysis obviates this dilemma of having to choose between employment of a narrow counterintuitive market and product definition and inability to apply antitrust rules to a competition-stifling conduct. Thus, its employment may assist in achieving a more intuitive and less arbitrary analysis.

Refusal to license need not relate to a secondary market

The courts' analysis in Magill highlighted the fact that there were two markets involved in the case: a first market for broadcasting and a secondary derivative market of TPLs (which were used to produce weekly guides). It was the Broadcasting Organizations' effort to expand their statutory monopoly over broadcasting into the secondary market of TV guide publications that was deemed the gist of the abuse. The court explained that the conduct was found abusive because the copyright in the TPLs, which were produced as part the broadcasting activity, was used to secure a monopoly in the derivative market of television guides.[120] Such analysis accords with other European jurisprudence (and U.S. essential facilities jurisprudence), which found an antitrust violation where the refused access to the essential facility stifled innovation in a *secondary* downstream market distinguishable from the first main market.[121] In other words, it seems that under current jurisprudence a refusal to deal may only be frowned upon by antitrust enforcers to the extent that it can be proven to stifle competition in a secondary market that is distinguishable from the primary market for which the IPR was originally granted. Therefore, such a first and secondary market finding may be necessary for application of antitrust rules to problematic refusal to license scenarios. The result could be either a senseless attempt to stretch product market definitions in order to reach such a first and secondary market distinction, or failure of antitrust policy to address certain injuries that stem from refusal to license IPRs.

The requirement of distinction between a first and a secondary market loses its relevance in dynamic analysis contexts. This is because an Austrian analysis makes no use of a strict product market definition in the first place, preferring instead to speak of 'market area'. Therefore, where there are no distinct markets to speak of, there is no call to speak of a main and a secondary market. Thus the requirement that the refusal to license will be with respect to a secondary market that is distinct from the one for which the IPR was granted, cannot hold under a dynamic analysis. As a result, the dynamic analysis can apply a more open, or less confined approach to refusal to license scenarios. Besides its practical advantage of allowing for a less strict application of antitrust rules, eliminating the first/secondary market analysis requirement also seems to make substantive sense. The requirement itself implies that a significant stifling of the competitive process will be exempt from antitrust treatment to the extent that the stifling occurs in the primary market for which the IPR was granted. In other words, it claims that IPRs may legitimately cause a process monopoly in a primary market. Given the close synonymy between competition and innovation,[122] this stands in conflict with the basic justification behind IPRs as an innovation-enhancing institution. In other words, where IPRs are allowed to stifle competition and innovation there is no justification for them in the first place. Note also that the first/secondary market distinction requirement assumes that IPRs are originally granted for the purpose of providing a legal monopoly in some specific recognizable product market. Such an assumption is perhaps workable where the relevant IPR is a patent, since patents are granted for specific useful inventions. However, this notion seems utterly unworkable with respect to copyright, since its protection extends to forms of expression, and those can be used in the context of numerous product markets. For these reasons, the rationale behind the first/secondary market distinction requirement for application of antitrust policy in refusal to license scenarios seems questionable, especially where copyright licensing is at stake.[123]

Evaluation of intent or objective justification for the refusal is unnecessary

Unlike §2 of the Sherman Act, which requires the finding of a subjective element that establishes 'willful acquisition or maintenance of [monopoly] power',[124] intent is not an element in the largely objective language of Article

82, and therefore initially seems less important in cases brought thereunder.[125] However, under existing jurisprudence the unique nature of antitrust–IP interface cases seems to reintroduce the intent element of the analysis through the back door. In Magill, the Commission found the conduct to be abusive to the extent that its use fell outside the scope of the specific subject matter of that intellectual property right.[126] The Magill court examined this issue through interpretation of the provisions of Article 30 of the EC Treaty.[127] Accordingly it found that the only legitimate restrictions on freedom of competition, free movement of goods, or freedom to provide services were those which were inherent in the protection of the actual substance of the IPR. By this, the court meant that derogation from the freedom of competition was only justified for the purpose of safeguarding rights that constituted the specific subject matter of such property.[128]

Thus, the European jurisprudence formula for drawing the competition–IP borderline in a refusal to license context involves three steps. First, one must identify or define the specific subject matter of the IP at hand. Then, one must determine whether the suspicious conduct is objectively justified for the purpose of safeguarding rights that reside in this subject matter. And finally, one must evaluate whether there was objective justification for the refusal to license in the main activity.[129] While semantically, this test seems not to include a subjective intent element this may be simply because of its 'negative' layout. The second and third elements of the test deal precisely with the portrayal of the borderline between the objectively justified conduct, which is deemed legitimate, and subjectively tainted conduct, deemed illicit on antitrust grounds. Therefore in effect the test does implicate the subjective elements of the conduct.

Application of this test is a daunting task. Defining the specific subject matter of an IPR is not easy, but at least it is rather theoretical. However, determining whether an activity is objectively justified for safeguarding the subject matter and evaluating whether an objective business justification exists for a refusal to license are both very dependent upon the subjective views of the analyst. Furthermore, in practice it is difficult to determine the state of mind that governed the refusal. Apart from the practical difficulty, there is also an inherent theoretical difficulty in determining whether the conduct is objectively justified or not. This is because every wish to protect one's IPRs is also inherently a wish to exclude others, therefore a subjective will to disadvantage and exclude competitors is inherent in any market action. This difficulty has led U.S. courts and scholars to reject an analysis requiring evaluation of the subjective element behind refusals to license.[130]

The proposed dynamic analysis resolves the difficulty described above because it obviates the need to evaluate whether the conduct exceeds the specific subject matter of the IPR. This is because the proposed analysis assumes that IPR-related conduct which results in a process monopoly will, by definition, exceed the specific subject matter of IP – since process monopoly defeats innovation, and innovation is the original mandate for IP.[131] This simplifies the analysis, replacing the troublesome three-stage test with a shorter two-step one. Where the first part reflects a process monopoly and the second part recognizes the suspicious conduct as its cause, the assumption is that the conduct, by definition, exceeds the subject matter of a given IPR, and that there can be no legitimate justification for such conduct. In other words, under the dynamic analysis any conduct inflicting grave injury on the competitive process should be proscribed by antitrust laws.

A cautionary note

Despite the advantages listed above, it should be admitted that the dynamic analysis does not provide a magic solution to antitrust–IP cases. Its suggested paradigm shift replaces the focus from defining the relevant market and establishing a static dominant position to evaluating the vitality of the competitive process in a market area and the causal relation between a flawed process and suspicious conduct. Thus, one obvious criticism may be that it simply trades the difficult issue of defining the relevant product market and establishing static market share for the no less difficult tasks of evaluating the competitive process and its causes. Furthermore, it may be argued that the suggested approach may seed unwanted uncertainty in the marketplace because of its broad general formula that is different from current jurisprudence. These are weighty arguments.

4.4 CONCLUSION

Magill is a debated case. While some commentators have praised it as a welcomed progress in the area,[132] others have rejected it. The critical literature rests on a number of arguments. First, it has been suggested that the Magill decision demonstrates an excessively obtrusive implementation of antitrust policy, one that goes too far and effectively strives against the tenets of IP protection. It is said that such an erroneous balance may mark the beginning of a slippery slope of undermining legal rights where antitrust becomes a concern.[133] Further, some have also expressed fears that such a decision may lead to widespread compulsory licensing of IP which may in turn result in a chill-out effect on R&D.[134] A second criticism regards Magill as a formalistically erroneous decision. This criticism views Magill as wrongly decided as the exercise of an IPR within the specific subject matter of the right should not be subject to EC Treaty Article 82, and the decision whether to license or not is regarded as part of this specific subject matter.[135]

A theoretical analysis such as the dynamic one can only shed a little light on the possible empirical results of the Magill decisions.[136] It can, however, and it does support the theoretical validity of the decision. The application of the dynamic analysis to the fact pattern of Magill has resulted in a similar finding of abuse of a dominant position. It found that the Magill circumstances demonstrated a clear case of a dynamic market failure directly resulting from the defendants' illicit conduct. The dynamic analysis also revealed that a combination of objective market circumstances had considerably contributed to the observed restriction of the competitive process. Nevertheless, it was demonstrated that the refusal to license activity was directly responsible for the competitive failure. Furthermore, arriving at the same conclusion as the Magill court by way of the dynamic model redresses some of the claims that its result does injustice to IP. This is because the dynamic competition concept is practically synonymous with innovation, and innovation is nowadays the main justification for the IP institution. Therefore such analysis is less susceptible to claims that it fails to sufficiently consider the goals of the IP institution. In other words, the dynamic analysis provides the necessary customized approach for antitrust in IP land.

The dynamic analysis paves the way for the necessary broader review of refusal to license antitrust cases. Our modern day businesspeople, just like the businessman from *The Little Prince*, see themselves as 'people of consequence'. Thus they repeat the self-serving mantra that IP equals innovation, and warn of an overly-active antitrust policy where IPRs are involved that is likely to destroy innovation in our markets as well as their organic competitive evolution.[137] While there are sound rationales behind the IP institution, the analysis suggested here has shown that refusal to license, despite its 'negative' character may under certain circumstances inflict significant harm on the competitive process in a market area.[138] Furthermore, the circumstances evidencing such injurious effects may be on the rise in light of the general expansion of IP into new fields and its strengthening over the past decade.[139] Therefore, just like the little prince we should ponder over the extreme pro-IP views that are often pronounced by businesspeople, since their practical results may at times prove harmful to the public good to the extent that they may destroy the competitive process in certain market areas.

NOTES

[1] Note how the little prince only manages to guess correctly on his third guess, with the first two wrong guesses (bees and flies) representing more traditional tangible chattels. This is another allusion to the fact that ownership over intangible property is somewhat counterintuitive. On

the close link between property and possession, see Carol M. Rose, *Possession as the Origin of Property*, 52 U. Chi. L. Rev. 73 (1985).

[2] The little prince refers to property in general, rather than to intellectual property. For an interesting development of the notion that the common public good justification for IP applies equally to tangible property, see I. Trotter Hardy, *Not So Different: Tangible, Intangible, Digital, and Analog Works and Their Comparison for Copyright Purposes*, 26 Dayton L. Rev. 211 (2001).

[3] For a similar argument developed in legal literature, see: for example, Jeremy Bentham, *The Theory of Legislation* chs VII–VIII (C.K. Ogden ed., 1931); and Richard A. Posner, *Economic Analysis of Law* 32 (Boston, MA: Little, Brown & Co. 4th edn 1992).

[4] See: Garrett Hardin, *The Tragedy of the Commons*, 162 Science 1243 (1968); and Posner, id. at 32–4.

[5] Clearly there is a question of degree involved here. An IP can be used in a manner that fails to maximize public utility, in a manner that fails to benefit the public at all, or even to an extent which actively harms the public good. The following analysis attempts to focus on the last, because this will minimize the margin of error which stems from the difficulty (perhaps impossibility) of measuring optimal levels of IP deployment from a public good point of view.

[6] See §2.2 of the U.S. Department of Justice and Federal Trade Commission's *Antitrust Guidelines for the Licensing of Intellectual Property* stating that to the extent that an IPR does confer market power, such market power in itself is not an offense. In other words, 'passive' as opposed to conduct-related effects of a given IPR are considered legitimate. The guidelines are available at http://www.usdoj.gov/atr/public/guidelines/ipguide.htm (January 10, 2003).

[7] See, for example, the language of the Paris Convention of the Protection of Industrial Property: 'Each country of the Union shall have the right to take legislative measures providing for the grant of compulsory licenses to prevent the abuses which might result from the exercise of the exclusive rights conferred by the patent, for example, failure to work'. Paris Convention for the Protection of Industrial Property, opened for signature, July 14, 1967, Art. 5(A)(2), 828 U.N.T.S. 321; Art. 31 of the WTO–TRIPS (World Trade Organization's Agreement on the Trade-related Aspects of Intellectual Property Rights) also acknowledges that under certain circumstances compulsory licenses may be justified. It is interesting to note that there was significant U.S. discussion of a compulsory license system in the late 1950s. See F.M. Scherer, *Industrial Market Structure and Economic Performance* 456–7 (Chicago: Rand-McNally, 2nd edn 1980) (this review does not appear in the more recent edition).

[8] Note that part of the historic reasoning behind compulsory patent licensing is a different protectionistic one, namely, the will to reserve power to force domestic manufacture over importation. See Phillip Areeda and Louis Kaplow, *Antitrust Analysis – Problems, Text, Cases* (New York: Aspen Law & Business, 5th edn 1997) §280 (d) note 63.

[9] See: Paris Convention Art. 5(A)(2) supra note 7; and WTO–TRIPS, supra note 7 Arts 8 and 40, which explicitly recognize that the exercise of IPRs can be limited by reasons of competition policy to restrain anticompetitive practices. The Berne Convention for the Protection of Literary and Artistic Works (concluded in 1886, last revised in Paris in 1971 and amended in September 1978) § 9(2) recognizes the rights of members to maintain limitations and exceptions to exclusive rights. The Berne Convention is available at http://www.biblit.it/leggi/Conv-Berna.pdf (January 10, 2003).

[10] See, for example: Nuno Pires de Carvalho, *The Primary Function of Patents*, 2001 U. Ill. J. L. Tech. & Pol'y 25, 68–73 (2001); Joel M. Cohen and Arthur J. Burke, *An Overview of the Antitrust Analysis of Suppression of Technology*, 66 Antitrust L. J. 421 (1998); and Eugene Crew, *Symposium: Antitrust and the Suppression of Technology in the United States and Europe: Is there a Remedy?*, 66 Antitrust L. J. 415 (1998).

[11] See Ramsey Hanna, (Note) *Misusing Antitrust: The Search for Functional Copyright Misuse Standards*, 46 Stan. L. Rev. 401, 415 (1994); and Dennis S. Karjala, *Copyright Protection of*

Operating Software, Copyright Misuse, and Antitrust, 9 Cornell J. L. & Pub. Pol'y 161, 164–7 (1999).

[12] For convincing reasons as to why this has come about, see Karjala, id. at 164--9.

[13] The U.S. patent laws contain no provision for compulsory licensing. Furthermore, in 1988 the U.S. Congress bolstered patent holders' general right to refuse to license. Congress amended the patent laws to provide that 'No patent owner otherwise entitled to relief for [patent] infringement ... shall be denied relief or deemed guilty of misuse or illegal extension of the patent right be reason of ... refusing to license or use any rights to the patent' (35 U.S.C. 271(d)(4)). This section has been broadly interpreted by some courts who suggested that it may also prohibit antitrust claims based on a refusal to license a patent (see: *In re Indep. Serv. Orgs. Antitrust Litig.*, 989 F. Supp. 1131, 1135 (D. Kan. 1997); and *Data General Corp. v. Grumman Systems Support Corp.*, 36 F.3d 1147, 1187 (1st Cir. 1994). However, note that § 271(d) contains the following proviso: 'unless, in view of the circumstances, the patent owner has market power in the relevant market for the patent or patented product on which the license or sale is conditioned'. The significance of this proviso was recognized by the Federal Circuit in *Schlafly v. Caro-Kann Corp.*, No. 98-1005, 1998 U.S. App. LEXIS 8250, at 20 (Fed. Cir. April 29, 1998). An important exception to U.S. courts' reluctance to condemn unilateral refusal to license is the controversial remand decision *Image Technical Services v. Eastman Kodak Co.*, 125 F.3d 1195 (9th Cir. 1997), cert. denied, 523 U.S. 1094 (1998).

[14] See Diane P. Wood, *The Impossible Dream: Real International Antitrust*, 1992 U. Chi. Legal Forum 277, 290–91 (1992).

[15] See, for example, *U.S. v. Glaxo Group*, 410 U.S. 52 (1973), *U.S. v. National Lead Co.*, 332 U.S. 319 (1947). Note also the 20 May 1996 consent decree in the Dell case under which Dell agreed it could not enforce its previously undisclosed patent rights against computer manufacturers: *Dell Computers*, FTC File No. 931-0097 information is available at http://www.ftc.gov/opa/1996/9606/dell2.htm (January 10, 2003). One possible interpretation of such a consent decree that it is equivalent to a royalty-free compulsory license. For a broad review of U.S. antitrust jurisprudence in this area, see James C. Burling, William F. Lee and Anita K. Krug, *Symposium: The Antitrust Duty to Deal and Intellectual Property Rights*, 24 Iowa J. Corp. L. 527 (1999).

[16] Note that even in this case, arguably the actual 'product' that consumers are paying for is the functionality provided by the source code (for example, word processing services) rather than the source code itself. In fact, the consumer has no access to the source code, but only to the compiled executable product itself. Nevertheless, from a practical point of view the sold product incorporates a copyrighted component.

[17] As, for example, Cases 6 and 7/73 *Instituto Chemioterapico Italiano SpA and Commercial Solvents v. Commission*, ECJ March 6, 1974, 1974 ECR 223 (commonly referred to as Commercial Solvents). See similarly in the seminal American refusal-to-deal case of *U.S. v. Colgate*, 250 U.S. 300 (1919); and *Otter Tail Power Co. v. U.S.*, 410 U.S. 366 (1973).

[18] See, for example: Case 78/70 *Metro v. Deutsche Grammophon*, ECJ July 8, 1971, 1971 ECR 487 paras. 11–12 (copyrighted products); and Case 24/67 *Parke Davis v. Probel*, ECJ February 29, 1968, 1968 ECR 55, 72 (patents).

[19] See, for example, this argument raised in Joined Cases C-241/91 and C-242/92 P. *Radio Telefis Eireann (RTE) and Independent Television Publications Ltd. (ITP) v. Commission*, ECJ April 6, 1995, 1995 ECR I-743 paras 37–8.

[20] See supra note 9.

[21] Note that Article 31(h) of the WTO–TRIPS Agreement, supra note 7, provides some guarantee against total confiscation of patent rights by ensuring compensation for a compulsory license. The article holds that 'Where the law of a Member allows for other use of the subject matter of a patent without the authorization of the right holder, including use by the government or third parties authorized by the government, the following provisions shall be respected: . . .

(h) the right holder shall be paid adequate remuneration in the circumstances of each case, taking into account the economic value of the authorization'.

[22] See Chapter 1, pp. 8–9.

[23] The FTC Dell case, supra note 15.

[24] In fact, it seems as if the businessman in *the Little Prince* was also aware of this notion. See the quote in the preamble of this chapter where he contends that reigning over something is not like owning it. The same rationale supports the finding that the right to decide whether to license or not is not the same as the existence of the IPR in somebody's hands.

[25] An argument can be made here that there is a significant difference between the two because the landlord expressed initial will to lease the property by putting it out on the market, while a patentee usually does not express such will in the first place. While this may be true, there are many factors that complicate the thinking here to both sides. To name two: on the one hand, patents often affect many people whose life depends on them (for example, in the pharmaceutical industry), while a single housing unit does not. There are sometimes no close substitutes to a patented product, probably more so than in housing examples. On the other hand a patent's lifetime is limited and hence time is more of the essence, while a house will still stand there when the tenant moves out, which he/she will at some point. Furthermore, secrecy can often be a crucial aspect of IP that is affected by compulsory licensing, while there is no such aspect related to housing.

[26] Chapter 3, Section 3.3.2.

[27] For the complete cites, see notes 31–3, below.

[28] Among the commentary, see for example: Darren Fitzgerald: *Magill Revisited (Tiercé Ladbroke SA v. The Commission)*, 20 Eur. Intell. Prop. Rev. 154 (1998); John Temple Lang, *European Community Antitrust Law: Innovation Markets and High Technology Industries*, 20 Fordham Int'l L. J. 717; John Temple Lang, *Defining Legitimate Competition: Companies' Duties to Supply Competitors and Access to Essential Facilities* (Hawk ed.), 1994 Fordham Corporate Law Institute 245, 303–8 (1995); Tom Skinner, *Magill: Consumer Interests Prevail*, 6 Europ. Bus. L. Rev. 90 (1995); H.H. Paul Lugard, *ECJ Upholds Magill: It Sounds Nice in Theory, But How Does it Work In Practice?*, Eur. Business L. Rev. 231 (1995); Rosa Greaves, *Magill Est Arrivé... RTE and ITP v. Commission of the European Communities*, [1995] 4 Eur. Competition L. Rev. 244 (1995); Thomas C. Vinje, *The Final Word on Magill: The Judgment of the ECJ*, Eur. Intell. Prop. Rev. 297 (1995); Thomas C. Vinje, *Harmonising Intellectual Property Laws in the European Union: Past, Present and Future*, 17 Eur. Intell. Prop. Rev. 361, 374–6 (1995); Peter Crowther, *Compulsory Licensing of Intellectual Property Rights*, 20 Eur. L. Rev. 521 (1995); Noel Travers, *Magill: Expropriation or a Fine Balancing Act?*, Irish Competition L. Reports 2-1 (1995); Nigel Jones, *Euro-Defences: Magill Distinguished*, 20 Eur. Intell. Prop. Rev. 352 (1998); Gerard van der Wal, *Article 86 EC: The Limits of Compulsory Licensing*, 4 Eur. Competition L. Rev. 230 (1994); Marleen van Kerckhove, *The Advocate General Delivers his Opinion on Magill*, [1994] 2 Eur. Competition L. Rev. 276 (1994); Clifford G. Miller, *Magill: Time to Abandon the 'Specific Subject-matter' Concept*, 16 Eur. Intell. Prop. Rev. 415 (1994); Tom Skinner, *The Oral Hearing of the Magill Case*, [1994] 2 Eur. Competition L. Rev. 103 (1994); Charles B. Cohler and Hilary E. Pearson, *Software Interfaces, Intellectual Property and Competition Policy*, 16 Eur. Intell. Prop. L. Rev. 434, 436–8 (1994); Aidan Robertson, (Note), *Compulsory Copyright Licensing under EC Law?*, 108 L. Q. Rev. 39 (1992); James Flynn, *Intellectual Property and Anti-trust: EC Attitudes*, 14 Eur. Intell. Prop. Rev. 49, 52–4 (1992); Ian S. Forrester, *Software Licensing in the Light of Current EC Competition Law Considerations*, [1992] 5 Eur. Competition L. Rev.; Jonathan Smith, *Television Guides: The European Court Doesn't Know 'There's So Much In It'*, [1992] 3 Eur. Competition L. Rev. 135 (1992). Additional commentary has been written in European languages other than English and is not quoted here.

[29] See, for example, Abraham I. van Melle, *Refusals to License Intellectual Property Rights: The Impact of RTE v. European Commission (Magill) on Australian and New Zealand Competition Law*, 25 Australian Bus. L. Rev. 4 (1997).

[30] Note that the available information on the circumstances of the case is limited to the factual details that the different Magill decisions chose to highlight. This is unfortunate, since additional factual details that are more interesting from a dynamic analysis point of view may have been overlooked by these existing materials.

[31] EC Commission Decision 89/205/EEC, December 21, 1988 relating to a proceeding under Article 86 of the EEC Treaty (IV/31.851, *Magill TV Guide/ITP, BBC and RTE*), OJ 1989 No. L 78, p. 43 (hereinafter: Commission Decision).

[32] Judgment of the Court of First Instance (Second Chamber), July 10, 1991, Case T-69/89 *Radio Telefis Eireann (RTE) v. Commission*, 1991 ECR II-485, 1991-4 CMLR 586, reproduced in 24 IIC 83 (1993) (hereinafter: CFI-RTE]; Judgment of the Court of First Instance (Second Chamber) of July 10, 1991, Case T-70/89 *British Broadcasting Corporation and BBC Enterprises v. Commission*, 1991 ECR II-535, 1991-4 CMLR 669 (hereinafter: CFI-BBC); Judgment of the Court of First Instance (Second Chamber), July 10, 1991, Case T-76/89 *Independent Television Publications (ITP) Ltd. v. Commission* [1991] ECR II-575, 1991-4 CMLR 745, 1991-2 CCH 174 (hereinafter: CFI-ITP).

[33] Joined Cases C-241/91 and C-242/92 P. *Radio Telefis Eireann (RTE) and Independent Television Publications Ltd. (ITP) v. Commission*, April 6, 1995, 1995 ECR I-743 (hereinafter: ECJ Decision).

[34] CFI-ITP, supra note 32 at para. 2.

[35] Commission Decision, supra note 31 at para. II-A-22.

[36] Commission Decision, supra note 31 at para. I-B-6.

[37] Commission Decision, supra note 31 at para. I-F-13.

[38] CFI-ITP, supra note 32 at para. 2.

[39] Commission Decision, supra note 31 at para. I-A-3.

[40] Commission Decision, supra note 31 at para. I-A-2.

[41] For ease of reference, and since there was essential identity between BBC and BBC Enterprises and between ITP and the IBA's franchisers, the following text will address these three enterprises involved in publishing weekly TV guides simply as RTE, BBC (which will refer to both BBC and BBC Enterprises) and ITP (which will also refer to IBA's policy).

[42] See CFI-ITP, supra note 32 at para. 48, noting that third parties were unable to publish comprehensive weekly guides unless they have at their disposal all the weekly TPLs; ECJ Decision, supra note 33 at para. 53 which called the information on program scheduling 'the indispensable raw material for compiling a weekly television guide'.

[43] The Commission decision describes the licensing practices of all three organizations together, noting that there were only 'minor variations in their individual policies', see para. I-F-14 of the Commission Decision, supra note 31.

[44] See Commission Decision, supra note 31 at para. I-F-14; CFI-RTE, supra note 32 at para. 9.

[45] See Commission Decision, supra note 31 at para. I-F-14 (the last lines in this long paragraph).

[46] See CFI-RTE, supra note 32 at para. 10.

[47] *RTE et al. v. Magill et al.* [1990] ILRM 534, 541–2 and 557 (Judgment of July 26, 1989). Although these details are actually legal findings of the Irish Court, they are detailed here as part of the facts sections since all the antitrust decisions that followed (and the basic methodology of this study) accept the finding of valid copyright protection as a given fact that is not to be second-guessed.

[48] Article 3 of Regulation 17 of the Council, February 6, 1962, First regulation implementing (then) Articles 85 and 86 of the Treaty. The EC Treaty has since been re-edited, and Articles 85 and 86 are now numbered 81 and 82, respectively. The text here will make use of both numbering systems.

[49] The principal European competition rules were adopted as Articles 85 and 86 of the Treaty of Rome and entered into force in 1958. These provisions have remained unchanged since.

Article 15 of the Treaty of Amsterdam amending the Treaty on European Union, the Treaties establishing the European Communities and certain related acts (1997 OJ C 340/1), which entered into force in 1999, provided for a renumbering of the EC Treaty (but left the provisions themselves unchanged). Thus, EC Treaty articles numbered 85 and 86 at the time of the Magill decisions are now numbered 81 and 82, respectively. For reasons of convenience the following text will refer to both the new and the old numbering system (old numbering will be referred to in brackets in some places). Note that the Magill decisions utilized the former numbering system. The EC competition provisions are available at:

http://europa.eu.int/comm/competition/antitrust/legislation (January 10, 2003).

[50] See supra note 31.

[51] As we shall see below, the more interesting notions for the purpose of this study are the first two, because that is where the difference exists between the traditional analysis and the dynamic analysis suggested in this study.

[52] Commission Decision, supra note 31 at paras II-A 20 & 21.

[53] Criticism on this choice was voiced by IPOs (intellectual property owners) who later intervened in the stage of the appeal to the European Court of Justice. See ECJ Decision, supra note 33 at paras 44–5.

[54] Commission Decision, supra note 31 at para. II-A-22.

[55] Id.

[56] Commission Decision, supra note 31 at para. II-A-23.

[57] Id.

[58] Id.

[59] Commission Decision, supra note 31 at para. II-A-24.

[60] Commission Decision, supra note 31 at the penultimate paragraph (captioned ‘Article 2’).

[61] Supra note 32.

[62] Note that at some places the decisions speak of the defendant’s conduct as modifying the ‘structure of competition on the market’ (for example, para. 77 of the CFI-RTE judgment, supra note 32). This language, which relates to competition structure rather than market structure, may initially seem like a hybrid between the traditional market-structure antitrust approach, and the competitive-process approach suggested in this study. However, this language is used in the context of whether the conduct affects trade between member states, rather than within the general context of ‘competition’.

[63] See, for example, CFI-RTE, supra note 32 at para. 60.

[64] CFI-ITP paras 47–8; CFI-BBC paras 48–50; CFI-RTE paras 61–2 (full cites, see in supra note 32).

[65] CFI-ITP para. 49, CFI-BBC para. 51, CFI-RTE para. 63 (full cites, see in supra note 32).

[66] CFI-ITP paras 58–60; CFI-BBC paras 60–62; CFI-RTE paras 73–75 (full cites, see in supra note 32).

[67] CFI-ITP, supra note 32 at paras. 50–51 and the case law cited there: Case 238/87 *AB Volvo v. Erik Veng (UK) Ltd.* [1988] ECR 6211, 1989–4 CMLR 122, CCH 14,498, October 5, 1988 para. 7; Case 144/81 *Keurkoop v. Nancy Kean Gifts* [1982] ECR 2853, September 14, 1982 para. 18.

[68] See CFI-BBC, supra note 32 at para. 54 and the case law cited there.

[69] CFI-ITP para. 56; CFI-BBC para. 58; CFI-RTE para. 71 (full cites, see in supra note 32).

[70] The appeal relied on additional grounds. RTE claimed that the CFI misconstrued the concept of effects on trade between member states and wrongly refused to take into consideration the Berne Convention. ITP claimed that the CFI misconstrued Article 3 of Regulation 17, and infringed Article 190 of the Treaty (see paras 21–2 of the ECJ Decision, supra note 33). However, these grounds are less interesting for our comparative context, since the dynamic analysis that follows does not touch upon them. Therefore, they are not reviewed here.

[71] ECJ Decision, supra note 33, at para. 46. The assertion is not supported or explained in the decision. It also seems to conflict with common sense – possession of a dominant position (or 'market power') is not in itself an offense, and it is hard to see why a lucky commercial patent can never win a dominant position for its brilliant commercial patentee. It seems likely that the court meant to express the modern notion that IPRs do not *necessarily* confer a dominant position (or 'market power' in U.S. antitrust terms), namely, that there is no presumption that IPRs confer a dominant position (see discussion in Chapter 1 of this study, notes 20–22 and accompanying text). Another plausible explanation is that the court spoke of 'mere ownership of an IPR' as a case where the IPR is not utilized in any way but merely formally owned (although arguably, suppression of an IPR can assist an enterprise in maintaining market power where it employs a second-best technology on its production lines).

[72] ECJ Decision, supra note 33 at para. 47. In this analysis the ECJ made reference to para. 30 of Case 322/81 *Michelin v. Commission*, ECJ November 9, 1983, 1983 ECR 3461; 1985-1 CMLR 282. The Michelin case interpreted Article 82 of the EC Treaty as prohibiting 'any abuse of a position of economic strength enjoyed by an undertaking which enables it to hinder the maintenance of effective competition on the relevant market by allowing it to behave to an appreciable extent independently of its competitors and customers and ultimately of consumers'.

[73] The court cites previous European case law in support of this notion (*Volvo v. Veng*, supra note 67).

[74] ECJ Decision, supra note 33 at paras 50–52.

[75] ECJ Decision, supra note 33 at para. 54.

[76] ECJ Decision, supra note 33, at para. 52.

[77] ECJ Decision, supra note 33 at para. 55.

[78] ECJ Decision, supra note 33 at para 56.

[79] Chapter 3, Section 3.3.2.

[80] Note the usage of the term 'relevant market area' rather than 'relevant market' since the working assumption in the dynamic analysis is that market environments cannot be neatly broken down into distinct well-defined markets. Hence, any attempt to define a distinct 'relevant market' as in the traditional model is an impractical one. See Chapter 3, supra note 16.

[81] See Harold Demsetz, *Barriers to Entry*, 72 Am. Econ. Rev. 47 (1982).

[82] Commission Decision, supra note 32 at para. II-A-23; CFI-RTE, supra note 33 at para. 73; ECJ Decision, supra note 33 at para. 54.

[83] It is interesting to note that these same notions are recognized by EC competition case law. In *Hoffman-La Roche* the European Court of Justice defined dominant position as: 'a position of economic strength enjoyed by an undertaking which enables it to prevent competition ... by *affording it the power to behave to an appreciable extent independently of its competitors, its customers, and ultimately of the consumers*. Such a position ... enables the undertaking ... to act largely in disregard of [competition]' (italics added) (Case 85/76 *Hoffmann-La Roche & Co. AG v. Commission*, February 13, 1979, 1979 ECR 461, 520 paras 38–9). See also Case 322/81 *Michelin v. Commission*, supra note 72 at 3461, 3503, para. 30.

[84] Commission Decision, supra note 31 at para. II-A-20. The second indicator is mentioned in the Commission Decision para. II-A-23 6th subdivision.

[85] Note that the fact that preventing weekly guides from entering the market was in the best business interest of the Broadcasting Organizations is irrelevant here. The relevant notion is that their behavior ignores the competitive threat from a weekly guide. Such insulation cannot exist where a competitive process runs its course.

[86] Commission Decision, supra note 31 at para. II-A-20, second subdivision.

[87] Commission Decision, supra note 31 at para. I-F-14.

[88] See Chapter 3, p. 95.

[89] ECJ Decision, supra note 33 at para. 52, which cites the CFI decision.

[90] Id.

[91] See supra note 36. RTE also enjoyed a monopoly over national radio broadcasts.

[92] Commission Decision, supra note 31 at last part of para. II-A-20.

[93] Recall that the uncertainty referred to in this context focuses more on full information about the current market (prices, possibilities, consumer demand, potential new market niches) than on predicting the future (see Chapter 3, Section 3.3.2.

[94] Admittedly, this indicator is probably more subjective than the others discussed here. This is because the suspected entity will always claim (and often will also subjectively believe) that it is in a more uncertain market position than estimated by third parties such as antitrust agents (let alone its potential competitors). Furthermore, 'uncertainty' is not only a subjective term, but it is also probably more difficult to recognize or measure than notions such as 'barrier to entry' or volatility in market shares.

[95] Commission Decision, supra note 31 towards the end of para. I-F-14.

[96] See Chapter 3, pp. 92–3.

[97] It should be noted that this market share finding by the Magill decisions is somewhat puzzling and not entirely convincing. In effect the decisions define three separate markets, each for TPLs of one national Broadcasting Organization. The result is a finding of a 100 percent static market share for each of the Broadcasting Organizations' TPL publications, and hence seemingly there is no direct competition between the three weekly TV guides that offered listings for different channels. However, such clear independence between sales of the three publications seems unlikely. Note that there must have been competition among the six national TV channels themselves, as well as with the cable and satellite channels mentioned in the fact-findings section. This competition among the different broadcasting channels must have inherently affected the various TPL listings because demand for TPL publications was a direct derivative of how popular the channels were with viewers. Thus, indirect competitive forces were clearly present. Note that cross-effects were also possible – for example, a cheap or free weekly TPL publication could have encouraged viewing of specific channels, whose TPLs were thus made more available. In short, there may be considerable doubts as to the accuracy of the finding that the three TV guides were complementary and thus independent of one another. For more on this issue, see Section 4.3.5, below.

[98] Note that caution is called for in this respect. 'Consumers' do not comprise one entity. They usually display different demands and tastes. Therefore it is often the case that enterprises' conduct is good for some consumers and bad for others. It is stressed that the conduct should be *categorically* against the interest of consumers.

[99] See Article 82, which reads 'Any abuse by one or more undertakings'. See also Commission Decision 89/93/EEC *Industria Vetraria Alfonso Cobelli v. Societa Italiana Vetro spa et al.* [1990] 4 CMLR 535 which found such an abuse. Note that in its complaint Magill alleged the existence of a tacit agreement between the three Broadcasting Organizations as a breach of Article 81 (see CFI-RTE, supra note 32 at para. 54, CFI-BBC, supra note 32 at para. 39 and CFI-ITP, supra note 32 at para. 36). However the court did not pursue this claim.

[100] Furthermore it is also possible for the same practice to infringe upon both Articles 81 and 82. See *Hoffman La-Roche,* supra note 83 at para. 116; Case T-51/89 *Tetra Pak v. Commission,* July 10 1990, 1990 ECR II-309 para. 21.

[101] For example, the action in the Magill case was a joint one, see supra note 47.

[102] See supra note 97.

[103] These assumptions were initial circumstances deemed necessary for the development of the Austrian competition process. See discussion in Chapter 3, Section 3.2 (pp. 81–90 and 97).

[104] On the solid anti-interventionist market postulate of Austrian economics, see Chapter 3, note 9 and accompanying text, and notes 81–2 and accompanying text.

[105] This fact is alluded to in the decisions, which reveal that in the past the Broadcasting Organizations have taken legal action against entities attempting to publish weekly TPLs. See supra note 44 and accompanying text.

[106] The circumstances are 'objective' in the sense that they were present in the market regardless of the suspects' business behavior (the term 'behavior' here excludes of course any conduct related to obtaining the copyright, which is presumed legitimate throughout this study).

[107] The Magill decisions also note the restrictive effect of this objective combination. They call it an effect created 'by force of circumstance' (see ECJ Decision, supra note 33 at para. 47).

[108] CFI-RTE, supra note 32 at §2 of the decision: 'At the material time, no comprehensive guide was available on the market ... *owing to* the policy of the organizations to which the [Commission] decision was addressed regarding the dissemination of information on the programmes of the six channels' (italics added). The complete line of argument was reviewed earlier, see Section 4.3.2, above.

[109] The following constitutional law context should be noted. In general, the EC Treaty does not contain any express supremacy clause rendering Community law superior to national law in the event of conflict. However, EC competition case law has consistently held that where Community law and national law conflict, the former takes precedence (see Case 14/68 *Walt Wilhelm v. Bundeskartellamt* 1969 ECR 1, 13; Case C-67/91 *Spanish Banks: Dirección General de Defensa de la Competencia v. Asociación Española de Banca Privada (AEB)*, 1992 ECR I-4785, para. 12). Therefore the Commission could theoretically strike down the national laws which granted monopoly and duopoly status to the Broadcasting Organizations, to the extent that it found the national laws to sufficiently conflict with the EC Treaty and its goals.

The more specific interface between EC competition law and national copyright laws is more complex. Determination of conditions and procedures for granting IPR protection is a matter for national rules which is untouched by the EC Treaty (see ECJ Decision, supra note 33 at para. 2). The interface between Community and State law in this context is governed by EC Treaty Articles 295 (ex Art. 222) and 30 (ex Art. 36). Article 295 provides that the treaty shall not prejudice member states' rules governing the system of property ownership which include industrial property rights. Article 30 provides for the possibility of derogating from the rules relating to the free movement of goods on grounds of the protection of industrial or commercial property. However, that derogation is explicitly made subject to certain reservations set out in the second sentence of Article 36. Under these reservations, restrictions on free movement arising out of the protection of intellectual property 'shall not ... constitute a means of arbitrary discrimination or a disguised restriction on trade between Member States'. Without going further into this specific issue, it seems probable that the Commission was not empowered to issue a remedy which affects the validity of the copyrights that were recognized by the Irish law. Therefore the argument can be made that the opinions did not address the issue of the validity of the copyright not because it was not responsible for stifling innovation, but rather because of lack of EC jurisdiction over this issue which is pre-empted by national copyright laws. Even if that is the case, the opinions could still have hinted that the copyright itself was responsible for hindering competition, but they did not do so.

[110] See discussion on existence versus exercise of an IPR, Section 4.2.2, above.

[111] The parallel elements under Federal U.S. antitrust jurisprudence of §2 Sherman Act, are 'The possession of monopoly power in the relevant market' and establish 'the willful acquisition or maintenance of [monopoly] power as distinguished from growth or development as a consequence of a superior product, business acumen, or historical accident' (see *U.S. v. Grinnell Corp.*, 384 U.S. 563, 570–71 (1966)). Although the two jurisdictions differ and utilize a different terminology, significant similarities seem to exist between the EC 'dominant position' term and the American 'monopoly power' concept, and even more in the 'relevant market' term utilized by both jurisdictions. A comparative review of these issues exceeds the purpose of this study. However, this resemblance should be borne in mind as a reminder of the fact that despite the difference between the two systems, the thinking and reasoning in EC antitrust law in

general, and the Magill case in particular may not be entirely removed from American antitrust thinking.

[112] See the language of Article 82: 'Such abuse may, *in particular*, consist in:' (italics added). See also Case 6-72 *Europemballage Corp. and Continental Can v. Commission*, February 21, 1973, [1973] ECR 215, 244–5, paras 23–6 which held that the concept of 'abuse' according to Article 82 is a broad one and comprises any type of conduct that runs counter to the principle of Article 3 (g) of the EC Treaty (Article 3(g) calls for maintenance of effective competition in the Common Market).

[113] Article 82 does not require proof that the abusive conduct has actually had an appreciable effect on trade between member states but only that it is capable of having such an effect. See *Michelin v. Commission*, supra note 71 at paras 102–4; Case 226/84 *British Leyland v. Commission* November 11, 1986, 1986 ECR 3263, 3302 para. 20; Cases T-24-26 and 28/93 *Compagnie Maritime Belge de Transport v. Commission* October 8, 1996, 1996 ECR II-1201 para. 149.

[114] See Commission Decision, supra note 31 at para. II-A-22; CFI-RTE, supra note 32 at para. 63; CFI-ITP, supra note 32 at para. 49. The ECJ Decision prefers to use a different terminology, perhaps in light of the IPO arguments against it (see ECJ Decision, supra note 33 at para. 46–7).

[115] See discussion in Chapter 3, Section 3.3.1.

[116] For an exhaustive review of the narrow definition of product markets in European antitrust jurisprudence, see Lennart Ritter, W. David Braun and Francis Rawlinson, *European Competition Law: A Practitioner's Guide* 332–4 (The Hague: Kluwer Law International, 2nd edn 2000).

[117] See supra note 86 and note 97 with its accompanying text.

[118] For a criticism similar to this one, in the sense that it argues that the court's analysis failed to consider its distinction between TPLs and TV guides, see Smith, supra note 28 at 137.

[119] Recall that the adopted definition of the relevant market was 'advance weekly listings of ITP, the BBC and RTE, and also the TV guides in which those listings are published', see Section 4.3.2, above.

[120] See CFI-RTE, supra note 32 at the second half of para. 73.

[121] *Alaska Airlines v. United Airlines*, 948 F.2d 536, 544 (9th Cir. 1991) (a facility considered 'essential' only if its control carries the power to eliminate competition in the *downstream* market); *Volvo v. Veng* supra note 67; Case 53/87 *Consorzio Italiano (CICRA) v. Renault*, 1988 ECR 6039 (both cases involved car manufacturing as a main market and a secondary market of spare parts for cars).

[122] See Chapter 2, Section 2.3.1.

[123] Note that a recent European Commission decision echoed this same view. In COMP/D3/38.044 *NDC Health/IMS Health,* Commission Decision 2002/165/EC: Commission, OJ L59, February 28, 2002, pp. 18–49, the Commission found an abuse and ordered a compulsory license in refusal to license case where the refusal to deal involved the one primary market discussed there. In other words, direct competitors of IMS sought a compulsory license in order to compete against it on the same market. The case is currently on appeal, and it would be be interesting to see how it develops. Similar notions can also be found in U.S. jurisprudence in *Aspen Highlands Skiing Corp. v. Aspen Skiing Corp.*, 738 F2d 1509, 1518 (10th Cir. 1984), aff'd 472 U.S 585 (1985). The case involved refusal to deal which related to a direct competitor in the same market (the Court of Appeals noted it was not convinced that the touchstone of bottleneck cases is vertical integration). However, there were three distinct facts in the Aspen case which may account for these notions. First, there was no IP involved, thus it was a refusal to deal case rather than a case of refusal to license IP. Second, the essential facilities doctrine was employed as the basis of the analysis. And finally, the defendant made a sudden change after many years in which it did deal with its rivals (see p. 603 of the decision).

[124] *U.S. v. Grinnell,* supra note 111 at 570–71; see also *Aspen Skiing Co. v. Aspen Highlands Skiing Corp.,* 472 U.S. 585, 602 (stating that subjective intent is relevant for determining

whether the conduct may properly be characterized as exclusionary); *United States v. United States Gypsum Co.*, 438 U.S. 422, 435 (1978) where the Supreme Court held that proof of the defendant's state of mind or intent is an essential element of a criminal antitrust offense; and *U.S. v. Andreas*, 216 F.3d 645 (7th Cir. 2000) (stating that the defendant's subjective intent is a required element of criminal antitrust violation).

[125] See the text of Article 82; *Hoffman-La Roche,* supra note 83 at para. 91. See also John Temple Lang, *Defining Legitimate Competition: Companies' Duties to Supply Competitors and Access to Essential Facilities*, 18 Fordham Int'l L. J. 437, 522 (1994) ('Abuse under Article 86 is normally objective and intent is irrelevant.').

[126] Commission Decision, supra note 31 towards the end of para. II-A-23.

[127] See supra note 109 for the constitutional context of Article 30 of the EC Treaty.

[128] See CFI-ITP, supra note 32 at para. 54. The court based its view on the Court of Justice decision in *Deutsche Grammophon v. Metro,* supra note 18 at para. 11, which held that, although Article 30 permitted prohibitions or restrictions on the free movement of products which were justified for the purpose of protecting industrial and commercial property, the article only admitted derogations from that freedom to the extent to which they were justified for the purpose of safeguarding rights which constituted the specific subject matter of such property.

[129] See CFI-RTE, supra note 32 at para. 73; CFI-IPR, supra note 32 at para. 58. See also *Volvo v. Veng,* supra note 67 at para. 9 which characterized arbitrary refusal to supply parts protected by design as abusive. Note that the test is not much different in U.S. antitrust jurisprudence. The U.S. 9th Circuit has held that if the defendant merely intended to refuse to license in order to protect its IPRs, then its refusal was legitimate; however, if it intended to create a service market monopoly then its refusal was unlawful. See *Kodak,* supra note 13 at 1219–20.

[130] See: *In re Indep. Serv. Orgs. Antitrust Litig.*, supra note 13; David McGowan, *Networks and Intention in Antitrust and Intellectual Property*, 24 J. Corp. L. 485, 511–18 (1999); and Phillip E. Areeda and Herbert Hovenkamp, *Antitrust Law: An Analysis of Antitrust Principles and Their Application* 704.1, at 231 (New York: Aspen Law & Business, 2nd edn 2000).

[131] For a fuller development of these notions see Chapter 2, Section 2.3.1.

[132] Vinje, *The Final Word on Magill*, supra note 28; D. Ridyard, *Essential Facilities and the Obligation to Supply Competitors under UK and EC Competition Law*, 8 Eur. Competition L. Rev. 439, 445 et seq. (1996).

[133] See Miller, supra note 28.

[134] See Crowther, supra note 28; Aidan Robertson, *The Existence and Exercise of Copyright: Can It Bear the Abuse?,* 111 L. Q. Rev. 588 (1995); Daniel Alexander and James Mellor, *Current Developments: EC Law,* 44 I. C. L. Q. 712, 714 et seq. (1995).

[135] See, for example, van der Wal, supra note 28 at 233. Van der Wal believes the Magill decision to be erroneous because it goes beyond preceding European case law in finding conduct within the IPR subject matter to be abusive.

[136] In this context, we should mention some of the empirical work that has been conducted in this area. F.M. Scherer has analyzed the extent to which the granting of compulsory licenses affected R&D expenditures by firms and, particularly, whether such licenses diminished or destroyed the incentives to undertake R&D by patent holders. His statistical findings showed no negative effect on R&D in companies subject to compulsory licenses but, on the contrary, a significant rise in such companies' R&D relative to companies of comparable size not subject to such licenses. See F.M. Scherer, 'Comments', in *Competition Policy and Intellectual Property Rights in the Knowledge-Based Economy* 107–8 (Robert D. Anderson and Nancy T. Gallini eds., Calgary: University of Calgary Press, 1998).

[137] See, for example the position of IPO (Intellectual Property Owners Co.), which intervened in the Magill ECJ appeal in support of the broadcasting organizations, and stated that 'copyright is by nature beneficial for competition'.

[138] In fact even some pro-IP forums have admitted that sometimes a lack of licensing may represent greater anticompetitive harm than a restrictive license. See, for example, OECD,

---

Competition Policy and Intellectual Property Rights (Roundtable Discussion, 1998) at the bottom of p. 8 and the second bullet point of p. 10, available at http://www.oecd.org/daf/ccp (January 10, 2003). But compare with Dana W. Hayter, *When a License is Worse than a Refusal: A Comparative Competitive Effects Standard to Judge Restrictions in Intellectual Property Licenses*, 11 Berkeley Tech. L. J. 281 (1996).

[139] Such trends can generally be observed since the 1994 adoption of the WTO–TRIPS agreement (supra note 7). The agreement has set a global minimum standard of IP protection that has obliged many countries around the world to adopt massive changes in their IP systems. Other IP expansive developments of the last decade include the trend of expanding patent protection to software (in the U.S. see *Diamond v. Diehr*, 450 U.S. 175 (1981). Similar legislative initiatives are underway by the EC and the European Patent Office, and many patents for software have already been granted by the EPO); the overturning of the traditional 'business methods exception' which paved the way for granting patents to business methods (see *State Street Bank v. Signature Financial Group*, 149 F.3d 1368 (Fedn Cir. 1998); and the granting of certain broad patents to e-commerce inventions (for example, the debated Amazon.com patent over '1-click' purchasing technology). Note again the analogy to *The Little Prince* quote that opened this chapter, where the businessman's wealth and strategy allow him to acquire any and all new stars that are discovered.

5. Application of the Dynamic Model in Network Industries (the Dell Case)

5.1 INTRODUCTION

This chapter applies the dynamic analysis model that was developed earlier in Chapter 3 within the context of network industries. The chapter is organized as follows. Section 5.2 provides a brief introduction to network industries, their definition and the common market phenomena they tend to display. It highlights the standardization phenomenon that seems to play an important role in this area. Section 5.3 presents three main themes in existing antitrust discourse on network industries: the debate about whether antitrust policy should apply, the role of static market power, and the argument of lock-in effects within these industries. Section 5.4 develops a dynamic antitrust evaluation of industry standards, which seem to play a decisive role in network industries. The analysis is made in comparison with existing legal argument, and demonstrates where and how the dynamic antitrust model is different from the existing model. Sections 5.5 and 5.6 set up an application of the Austrian model, and the general notions raised in the three previous sections to the actual fact pattern of the 1996 Dell case. Section 5.5 presents the Dell case's circumstances and the legal structure of the Federal Trade Commission's majority and dissenting opinions in the matter. Section 5.6 applies the dynamic model analysis to this same fact pattern, which leads to a conclusion that is different from that reached by the FTC's majority's view. Section 5.7 concludes.

5.2 INTRODUCING NETWORK INDUSTRIES, THEIR COMPETITIVE PATTERNS AND STANDARDS

In today's marketplace, there are a growing number of market areas where some sort of uniform industry standard is deemed highly beneficial to the prosperity of market activity. The main market areas in which industry standards are now playing a growing role are 'new-economy' market areas such as telecommunications, electronic commerce, and computer hardware and software (for brevity these areas will be addressed hereinafter interchangeably as 'high-tech market areas', 'new-economy industries', or 'network industries').

Virtually all of these new-economy industries are characterized by what is known by economists as 'network effects'. By definition, in markets characterized by network effects, 'the utility that a user derives from consumption of the good increases with the number of other agents consuming the [same] good'.[1] An individual consumer's demand to use (and hence his/her benefit from) a telephone network provides a classic example of a network effect. Consumer demand for a telephone increases with the number of other users on the network whom he/she can either call or receive calls from.[2]

The literature draws a distinction between actual network effects, virtual network effects and positive feedback effects (consumer-side economies of scale).[3] Actual network effects occur where the main benefit from a product lies in facilitating interactions between a consumer and others who own the same product (for example, a telephone or a fax machine). Virtual network effects occur where the pertinent product provides consumers with some inherent independent benefit that increases with the number of additional users of identical or interoperable goods (for example, a computer operating system that provides a single user with benefits regardless of whether other users own the same software. However, the value of an operating system to a consumer increases as the number of additional purchasers of the same system increases, because the consumer may only be able to exchange data and documents with those who use the same system that he/she does, or one that is interoperable with it). Finally, positive feedback effects occur in goods that increase in value as consumption increases even where the goods are not themselves connections to a network and do not interoperate[4] with 'compatible' goods. In other words, positive feedback effects occur where mass production of a certain product increases the value of another product, or 'economies of scale' in the same product. This chapter will focus on network effects of the second type, namely, virtual network effects (both in the three general sections and in the case study section involving a hardware case that displayed virtual network effects).

The main market phenomenon observed in market areas that feature network effects is that their market process tends to voluntarily converge towards a single dominant standard. This result comes about in a snowball effect that stems from the network effects. Most consumers are quite aware of the network effects that increase their utility from a product the more other consumers utilize the same product. Therefore consumers in new-economy market areas have an interest in purchasing the product of the type that will eventually prove most popular with other consumers, because such a choice will maximize their utility from their product. The other side of this same phenomenon is that consumers will want to avoid becoming 'stranded' with any products that will eventually prove less popular and will only be purchased by the minority of consumers in that market area. The common result of this set of considerations is known as the 'orphan effect',[5] whereby consumers are fearful of paying the high costs of being among the last to switch from a less-popular product type, and therefore rush to buy any new products which they expect to be the ones used by the majority of consumers.[6] In a way this behavior pattern is a self-fulfiling prophecy because the more consumers expect a certain product or product standard to become the most widely used one, the more consumer demand for it grows. On the other hand once some consumers come to see a certain product as incompatible with the current (or soon to be) industry standard, their decreased demand to it might draw the attention of more consumers to the fact that the product's technology is about to die out – which creates an opposite self-feeding process.

Apart from the consumer side of the story, the tendency of high-tech markets to converge towards a dominant standard also has significant effects upon the behavior of producers. Producers are threatened by lost-standard-race scenarios in which enormous R&D efforts (and sometimes expensive production lines) may rapidly become worthless as the market tips to converge around a different product standard that is incompatible with the one they use in their production lines. It seems probable that, overall, producers have much more to lose here than consumers, since significant portions of their business and past investments that depend upon consumers may collapse as soon as consumers perceive their specific product as destined to lose a standard struggle. Consumers, on the other hand, face only the risk of making certain wrong choices in purchasing specific products that will lose the standard struggle, but their overall livelihood is only rarely dependent upon these specific choices. However, this specific notion is nowhere to be seen in the literature, which tends to portray both consumers and producers in the same situation as having an equal interest and benefit from industry standards. The argument is usually made generally and broadly, that 'if *everyone* used interoperable systems, commerce in these industries would be cheaper and easier than in a world without a dominant standard'[7] (italics added).

Industry standards are created in one of three ways. First, the government can accommodate the choice of a particular standard. Second, the different industry players can cooperate within the framework of a standard-setting organization to select consensual industry standards upon which they will base their products. Finally, as noted earlier, in high-tech market areas where no one positively selects a specific standard, the market process tends to create its own standard by voluntarily 'tipping' towards one particular product or product type (which will become the de facto industry standard) at the expense of competing products.[8]

Apart from the network effects, it should also be noted that innovation plays a key role in the market process of new-economy industries, and is often described as their defining characteristic.[9] In Professor Carl Shapiro's words: 'Innovation is King'[10] in these industries, in which 'competition is typically Schumpeterian in character, with a fierce struggle to be the next temporary monopolist'.[11] Performance in these markets is significantly dependent upon innovation. The significance of innovation as the main engine of the market process in these industries creates a striking similarity between their observed behavior and the theoretical Austrian competition notion developed in the previous chapters, since both portray innovation as a crucial element of the competitive process.[12] This similarity suggests that the Austrian economic competition model developed in the study may provide an especially appealing instrument for antitrust analysis of high-tech industries, as common sense dictates that industries significantly driven by Schumpeterian innovation will best benefit from antitrust analysis which focuses on this very same tenet.[13]

The close link between new-economy industries and innovation also renders them significantly intertwined with IPRs. This is because IPRs are the practical legal means for protecting innovative inventions and original works, and thus often serve as indicators of an innovative context. New-economy corporations' basic strategy commonly involves attempts to acquire IPRs (either through self-development or by acquisition) which they can use both to improve and differentiate their products and thus also as a lever for their commercial success. As a result, the new economy has become nearly synonymous with IPRs,[14] rendering them especially suitable for evaluation within the context of this study, which focuses on the antitrust–IP interface.

5.3 EXISTING ANTITRUST JURISPRUDENCE ON NETWORK INDUSTRIES

As high-tech market areas seem to play an ever-growing part in the economy, antitrust theory has developed specific jurisprudence for analysis of competition issues in these industries. The following sections highlight some of the main trends in current antitrust debate over these issues, and evaluate them in light of the dynamic model promoted in this study.

5.3.1 Applicability of Antitrust Policy

There is currently an ongoing debate among academics and practitioners over the extent to which traditional §2 monopolization doctrines are appropriate for analysis of competition in dynamic technological markets that are characterized by network effects.[15] There seems to be a consensus that once a product or standard achieves wide acceptance, it becomes more or less entrenched as the standard struggle dies out. As a result, it is often said that competition in new-economy industries is 'for the field' rather than 'within the field' since the winner of the standard struggle 'takes all' in that market.[16] However, antitrust scholars differ as to what to make of this network industry market pattern from an antitrust perspective.

On one end of the spectrum lies the school of thought that views this difficulty of reversing standard as a call for special vigilance on the part of antitrust agencies, to prevent the manipulation of competition through the use of entrenched standards.[17] This view has also been expressed by the federal antitrust authorities who have characterized high-tech industries as being particularly prone to competitive failure and thus as deserving an especially close degree of antitrust scrutiny.[18]

On the other end of the spectrum are those who argue that the rapid innovation that characterizes new-economy market areas more than compensates for the phenomenon of standard market tipping, because it continually alters the competitive playing field. Therefore, they claim that there is no place for a more vigilant antitrust scrutiny in network industries.[19] Some have even gone further to proclaim that these industries should not be subject to any antitrust evaluation, since their inherent innovative nature ensures the natural occurrence of a healthy competitive process.[20] Another argument why antitrust should not be applied in network industries derives from the fear that antitrust enforcement may have a chilling effect on standardization (we shall see more on that in the sections below on the Dell Case). This line of argument deems standardization as both inevitable and beneficial, therefore it claims that antitrust authorities should adopt a hands-off approach to standard-setting in order not to interfere with standardization activities.[21]

The position taken by this study falls somewhere along the continuum between these two views.[22] The broad argument that antitrust policy should stay away from evaluation of certain market areas has already been rejected in detail back in Chapter 3,[23] as has been the traditional static antitrust analysis of unilateral scenarios. It is suggested that antitrust analysis of network industries would be most accurate if the dynamic economic model that was developed in this study were applied.

5.3.2 Static Market Power

Apart from the general debate on whether antitrust policy should apply to new economy industries, and setting aside the argument that they should not, network effects also complicate the antitrust analysis of static market power. On the one hand an argument has been made that the increasing returns afforded by network effects render a corporation that enjoys monopoly power even more injurious to other competitors and to consumers.[24] On the other hand, the counterargument asserts that in the presence of network effects, the role of static market power as the main basis for antitrust monopolization evaluations should be played down. This is because in network industries very large static market shares are allegedly common, since corporations' monopoly positions often result largely or entirely from network effects. In these cases a suspected firm's monopoly power is legitimate since it simply reflects aggressive (and successful) competition in an industry area that is prone to standardization, and thus tends to converge around a dominant product or standard.[25] Note that from the Austrian model's viewpoint, this debate bears little relevance, since that model attributes little importance to static market power as an indicator of the soundness of the competitive process.

5.3.3 Lock-in Arguments

An important theme in the literature on network effects highlights the recurring pattern of customers' lock-in to a particular network and the possibility of technological path dependence that derives from it.[26] Network externalities often confer unique benefits upon the first firm in a market to gain a significant early lead in market penetration (or the first firm that is expected to gain this lead – which is in effect almost synonymous with the former). Such an early lead (or expectation thereof) can have a decisive and constricting effect on market process because it triggers the tipping pattern. Consumers are attracted to the goods that are likely to offer the largest network benefit, and the first firm that is expected to win the tipping struggle soon after indeed takes all. The main consequence is that consumers can become 'locked in' to a particular network because switching later on from the market leader to any non-interoperable rival will be avoided because of its loss in network benefit.[27] In other words, in network industries 'history matters',[28] since consumers may be unwilling to join alternative networks that may be cheaper or superior because of choices that they have made in the past. This creates an inherent advantage for the older installed network, thus posing significant barriers to new competition in these markets.[29]

The literature does not present this 'lock-in' feature in absolute terms as setting a non-penetrable entry barrier. Rather, this market pattern is commonly portrayed as having a merely raising effect on the entry barrier into the market scene. This is because, in order to enter the market, a firm whose product differs from the standard must offer a sufficiently attractive product so that consumers find it worthwhile to incur switching costs.[30] This appeal can be created either by means of prices or by means of product quality. In other words, the new product can either try to offer a cost advantage that can compensate consumers for the costs of switching away from the dominant standard, or it can claim to be sufficiently technologically superior in comparison with the existing standard so as to compensate for it. However, it must be borne in mind that the firm (or firms) producing the leading standard products are probably well aware of this state of affairs. Therefore, in order to avoid being in such a catch-up position, the incumbents have the incentive to gear strategies towards maintaining their lead, either by continual innovation aimed at staying ahead of potential rivals who might 'leapfrog' over their incumbent lead position, or by maintaining a low price level. On the face of it, this pattern seems highly competitive and pro-consumer – low prices and innovative products are generally considered good news that keep antitrust enforcers at bay. The problem is, however, that it is difficult, perhaps even impossible, to ascertain whether a failure to observe any successful new entrants to the market area is indeed a result of the legitimate competitive edge preserved by the incumbents or the result of the standard barrier to entry.

Note, for example, the case of personal computer operating systems (OS). Linux is an 'open source' OS[31] that consumers can obtain gratis. Microsoft's recent version of Windows OS sells today for about \$100–\$300 (depending on the version).[32] Nevertheless, despite this striking price difference only a small fraction of private consumers use a Linux OS. The vast majority of consumers prefer to buy Windows rather than the free Linux OS. To some extent this preference may be attributed to other considerations, such as the claim that Windows is a technologically supreme product or that the Linux OS is not really free because the consumer must pay for the costs of its support and maintenance.[33] In other words, there is some leeway for the argument that consumers prefer Windows as part of a legitimate competitive pattern under which the Microsoft product is both technologically superior and price competitive. However, note that the lock-in effect of the Windows standard may be higher than is evident from this version of the story. For example, many computer users who are not information technology professionals invested significant amounts of time and energy in learning about and becoming familiar with Windows OS. Clearly these users will have a strong preference for continuing to work with an OS they know instead of investing more time and effort in learning to work with another system. Furthermore, the potential prospect of incompatibility problems may be a decisive consideration against using Linux. OS users do not work in a vacuum; they need to be able to exchange files and documents with other users. Switching to a non-Windows OS certainly raises concerns as to such compatibility prospects. Finally, note that by now the thousands of computer applications on the market have been developed exclusively for the Windows platform, and cannot ride on other platforms. Therefore potential Linux users must also take into consideration that the variety of applications they will be able to use may be rather limited (this phenomenon is known as 'the applications barrier to entry').[34] This dynamic may also discourage the innovative efforts of rivals to the dominant network because rivals know that even a technologically successful innovation will be hard to sell.

To sum up this point, network effects seem to entail significant lock-in effects that hinder the competitive process. While it is true that standard owners in new-economy industries often display a competitive behavior with regard to innovation, it may still be difficult to tell whether these lock-in effects allow for any real competitive process, or rather, whether the behavior of the incumbents is but the last nail in the coffin of a curtailing competitive process.

5.3.4 Summary

This section has demonstrated some of the difficulties involved in antitrust evaluation of new-economy industries. Antitrust enforcement authorities have come to recognize the significant complexity of fully evaluating the competitive effects of standards. Courts have expressed similar reflections in admitting that the effects of market standardization on new-economy industries are very difficult to evaluate.[35] Consequently, scrutiny of high-tech industry cases seems to have been set at a cautious 'rule of reason' level which examines whether the standards are 'reasonably necessary' to achieve legitimate (pro-competitive) ends and, if so, whether the benefits of the standard outweigh its costs.[36]

5.4 DYNAMIC EVALUATION OF THE EFFECTS OF STANDARDS ON THE COMPETITIVE PROCESS

Current literature has identified both potential pro- and anticompetitive effects of industry standards. This section addresses these considerations and evaluates them from the perspective of the dynamic model suggested in this study. Note that the terms 'standards' and 'standardization' are used to denote standards that were set by an industry organization's standard-setting process (as opposed to standards that were set by governmental agencies or by the voluntary tipping of the market process). As we shall see, many of the arguments that are presented in the literature as pro-competitive are not necessarily viewed as such from an Austrian economic point of view.

5.4.1 Arguments on Pro-competitive Aspects of Standards

Facilitating consumer comparison

It has been suggested that standardization is pro-competitive because it facilitates consumer comparison between competing products. This argument has two variations. First, the broader argument that standardization eliminates a significant factor of product differentiation between competing products, thus facilitating price competition between rival producers – a benefit for consumers.[37] And second, the more specific argument that standards facilitate consumers' product comparison by eliminating the burden of acquiring information on the merits of two competing standards.[38]

This line of argument seems to bear little relevance within the context of the Austrian competition model suggested in this study. Note that the argument originates from the price-theory focus and tendency of much of the traditional antitrust scholarship. It rests upon the notion that where all other things are equal, consumers prefer the cheapest product, and assumes that products based on the same standard are sufficiently significantly 'equal'. However, product differentiation is one of the inherent tenets of the dynamic model,[39] which assumes competing products to be inherently different (and thus differentiation serves as an indicator to the soundness of the competitive process). Under the dynamic model, in real life 'all other things' are never equal; in other words, the 'all things are equal' assumption never materializes. Therefore the underlying assumption implicit in this argument, that competing products based on the same standard are equal, is problematic from the Austrian model's point of view, under which a vigorous competitive process results in a differentiated product scene.

Furthermore, note that this argument is also consistent with the static notion of perfect competition that includes perfect information, since it implicitly assumes uncertainty (lack of full information) to be undesirable. This notion is at odds with the model developed in this study, under which uncertainty (on both the producer and the consumer sides) is one of the engines of the market's discovery process. Uncertainty is one of the untold market assumptions under which the Austrian competitive model gains true relevance. Eliminating uncertainty defeats one of the basic tenets of the Austrian competition model. Therefore this line of argument is surely not regarded as pro-competitive from the Austrian viewpoint, but on the contrary alludes to concepts that may seem anticompetitive.

Standardization prevents inefficient duplication of investments.
Another argument advanced as a pro-competitive aspect of standards is that they prevent inefficient duplication of investments in comparable, yet incompatible innovation.[40] The Austrian model is not concerned with the static model's notion of allocative efficiency. Furthermore, not only is the model not especially concerned with efficiency, its concept of a competitive struggle is perhaps even implicitly wasteful. This is because it speaks of an evolutionary market struggle in which, naturally, some market actors lose after having invested in efforts to penetrate the market. Therefore the exact argument here is not very interesting from an Austrian point of view.

Note, however, that on a broader level, this argument connects well to one of the Austrian model's market assumptions. As can be recalled, the relevance of the model relies on two types of basic notions: a dynamic time notion and an uncertainty notion.[41] Treatment of the dynamic notions was divided into two categories that focused on the importance of entrepreneurial opportunities. It warned of circumstances in which entrepreneurs' motives to join the market are weakened, or where market entry is blocked. It seems plausible that the greater the initial probability of losing in the market struggle, the weaker the motives of entrepreneurs to join the market. Therefore, where investors expect a significant probability that their added value and innovation will not give them the upper hand in the market because of compatibility problems, their motives to join a market area may be significantly weakened. This, in turn, weakens one of the two objective market assumptions that are necessary for the prosperity of a healthy competitive market process. Hence, eliminating inefficient duplication of investments may indeed be pro-competitive from an Austrian point of view, whereby it helps ensure that entrepreneurs' motives to join markets and keep the competitive process going are not undermined.

It should be noted, however, that this argument derives its strength directly from the extent to which market players in new-economy industries are risk-averse. The more they are risk-averse, the greater effect the risk of incompatibility (or loss in the market struggle) is likely to have on their willingness to join a market area. The same is true vice versa: the risk of incompatibility and loss in the market struggle is likely to have a less significant effect on market players who are less risk-averse. In reality it seems that players in high-tech market areas are often quite willing to take risks.[42] Furthermore, although new-economy markets as a whole are known for their high-risk nature, there is little to suggest that they have suffered from diminished market entry in recent years, which supports the assertion that market players in these industries are not especially risk-averse. Therefore the direct effect of elimination of duplicate investments upon the market process may be rather limited.

Standardization maximizes welfare

An additional pro-competitive effect of standardization is attributed to the welfare-maximizing effect of interoperability that results from network externalities. Welfare is said to be maximized because both consumers and producers prefer the industry to subscribe to a single standard. Consumers prefer standards because it ensures that they do not find themselves on the losing end of a standard struggle (a scenario which forces them to incur the costs of switching to a product based on the winning standard). Furthermore, standards are thought to promote interoperability, thus consumers are guaranteed that any joining consumer joins their own network and this increases their own utility from the product. Suppliers are said to prefer standards because the previous notion renders consumers willing to spend more money on products in that market area; this, together with the decreasing average costs in these industries generates more profit to suppliers.[43]

Even within traditional antitrust thinking it is not easy to see how this argument relates directly to competition. Recall that the traditional static competition model focused on maximizing allocative efficiency as the main goal of competition policy, and not on enhancing welfare.[44] Furthermore, the notion that standardization is pro-competitive because it makes producers richer, may in fact stand in contrast with certain views on antitrust goals, which viewed antitrust as aimed at transferring wealth from corporation to consumers.[45] In any event, from the point of view of the dynamic model promoted in this study, the above argument, which is based on welfare maximization, seems to carry little weight. This is because the Austrian model focuses on ensuring a healthy competitive process as its end. It does not concern itself directly with welfare considerations, but rather presumes that a free-flowing competitive process is the optimal market pattern that maximizes welfare.

Note, however, that the first element in the above argument seems reminiscent of certain Austrian notions. The claim that standardization is beneficial because it is what consumers want is reminiscent of the Austrian model, in which producers perennially try to cater to consumer taste. One may argue that if consumers prefer standards and standards are indeed a common phenomenon, then it is a sign that the competitive process is working well since consumers are receiving what they want. It is suggested, though, that these notions be taken with a pinch of salt: first, because standards are also, and perhaps even more so, representative of what producers want, therefore their prevalence may, to a considerable extent, actually be a result of producers' rather than consumers' interest; and second, because a broad argument that consumers as a whole prefer this or that is bound to be inaccurate. Consumers are inherently different in their needs and preferences, they are often interested in certain product features or in the freedom to make consumer choices and not only in saving money (while producers are generally similar in the broad sense that they strive to make as much money as possible). Therefore the claim that 'consumers want standards' is probably too broad to hold water.

Standards promote innovation

Another pro-competitive contribution of standardization is said to have come from its promotion of innovation. The argument is that in the absence of standards, producers would have to balance their wish to make money via an improvement in existing technologies against the potential loss of having invested in a 'losing' technology. Since standardization provides firms with certain assurances against finding themselves at the losing end of an uncontrolled standard struggle, the rationale is that standardization thus renders firms more likely to invest in innovation, because it minimizes the counter-considerations to such investment.[46] In other words, standardization is said to promote innovation because it renders investment in innovation more lucrative than under a scenario of a raging market struggle.

This argument touches on one of the main principles of the Austrian model, which views innovation as a vital element (and in fact an engine) of a robust competitive market process. To the extent that standardization indeed promotes innovation under the above rationale, it will be deemed essentially pro-competitive by the model suggested in this study. Note, however, that while standards seem to promote innovation they also, at the same time, limit it to a certain extent because once an industry standard is set, producers are relieved of the need to compete through innovations to the standard. This is because once the standard is *set* (note the static quality of the verb 'set'), it creates in effect a tacit agreement between all the industry players to adhere to it. Producers will not deviate from the standard or utilize any improvements to it to the extent that this may affect the compatibility of their product with the set standard. This is because of the negative effects of dropping out of the networked system (consumers will rarely buy into a product they recognize as incompatible with the industry standard). While it is true that standards are replaced as technology advances, the combined effect of strong consumer-side network effects of an existing standard and the time-consuming standard-setting process imposes constraints upon innovation in the context of standards themselves. As a result, the innovation-enhancing standards effect is probably limited to the non-standardized segments of the product. The relative significance (from the consumers' point of view) of the standardized versus the non-standardized portions of a product may vary from product to product. The more significant the non-standardized segment, the stronger is the 'standardization promotes innovation' argument, and vice versa.

Standards broaden consumer choice

It is said that the existence of a single accepted industry standard allows consumers to 'mix and match' components by different manufacturers because the standardization ensures their interoperability.[47] This argument has been said to be pro-competitive because it further stimulates firms' investment in innovation.[48] It plays a central role in the dynamic model suggested in this study, perhaps a bigger role than in existing literature. Note, however, that it does so from a slightly different angle. The dynamic model's core views the competitive process as a discovery process in which producers pick up signals from consumers' behavior that help them understand what consumers want. Therefore, under the model consumer choice is a vital element of a healthy competitive process, and anything that broadens consumer choice facilitates and contributes to the competitive market process.

Note that this consideration actually presupposes the existence of a reasonable competitive process in the different components' market areas, as this effect may be forfeited otherwise. This is because, where certain market players feel immune from competitive threats, they can successfully tie in the sale of certain components to the sale of the component over which they have dominance and feel immune from competition. Thus producers can effectively eliminate the theoretic consumers' 'mix and match' options that are said to be accommodated by standardization. An example is the case of the Netscape Navigator and Microsoft's Internet Explorer web browsers. Both browsers run a similar Windows standard and are compatible with the Windows OS. However, once Microsoft began to bundle its Internet Explorer into its Windows OS, it seems likely that consumers lost any incentive to go to the trouble of downloading (let alone paying for) the alternative Netscape web browser component. This example demonstrates how the 'mix and match' pro-competitive argument relies on the assumption that 'mixing and matching' is indeed a viable consumer choice in the market area to begin with. However, this assumption is not always a true one to make.

5.4.2 Arguments on Anticompetitive Effects of Standards

Single standard inhibits innovation

It has been suggested that a single standard may produce less innovation than will a variety of single and joint efforts employing alternative approaches.[49] As an argument that touches on innovation, it is also anticompetitive from the Austrian point of view. This argument seems to take a different line from the one discussed above under 'Standards promote innovation'. The argument is not that innovation is effectively blocked with respect to the standardized elements of products. Rather, it suggests that standards impoverish the multiplicity of technical approaches that naturally develops in high-tech markets. This multiplicity is assumed to promote innovation through its diffusion of ideas and its cross-pollination effect in the market of ideas, which sets the base for innovative progress.[50]

Although this argument seems appealing, its overall empirical effect may be debatable. As noted earlier, new-economy market areas that display network effects tend to voluntarily 'tip' towards a single standard even in the absence of centrally-set standards. Despite this observed tendency to converge around a single standard, many of these market areas were not stagnant, but rather seem to have enjoyed a high rate of innovation in recent years. Some have suggested that this high rate should be attributed to the strong innovative drive that characterizes these industries, which easily works its way around standards and dominance of certain market areas.[51] Without going into these arguments here, suffice it to say that the impressive innovative activity observed in new-economy market areas may call into question the extent to which a single standard inhibits innovation.

Consumers deprived of non-compatible products

It has been suggested that standards are anticompetitive in the sense that they deprive consumers of incompatible technological choices (and the innovation that builds upon them).[52] This argument holds an appeal for the dynamic model developed here, because under this model consumer choice is one of the basic engines of the market process as it sends producers signals that reflect consumer preferences. If consumers are deprived of making choices that fall outside the standardized zone, then, to a certain extent their consumer voices are stifled from fully expressing their preferences. This is because in effect they cannot express a preference for product features that are present only in products that are incompatible with the standard. This in turn may curtail the competitive process because it prevents consumers from expressing preferences for products that they would have preferred had they been compatible with the standard.

Clearly, this argument is a tricky one. One can say that in making their educated choices, consumers weigh up a variety of considerations. Consequently, where incompatibility with the standard is a crucial factor in rejecting a product, then it is clearly a consumer choice to reject incompatible products and nobody is depriving them of any choice – on the contrary, they chose to reject these products. This counterargument may seem convincing. However, it is important to remain focused on the reason why consumers reject incompatible technologies. Where network effects are strong then consumers will reject any incompatible technology, even where such products offer a more advanced technology or unique features which consumers find desirable. In this sense, consumer choices will be made for them on the higher standard-setting level because consumers will reject incompatible products. This is why standards narrow consumer choices – because they effectively manipulate consumers into making only choices that fall within the standard-compatible borders.

In this context, an important caveat to bear in mind is that this effect of narrowing consumer choices to standardized technologies may be unavoidable. As noted earlier, new-economy markets often tend to voluntarily converge or 'tip' around single technologies. Therefore in these markets even in the absence of centrally-set standards, the tipping effect will effectively lead consumers to avoid technologies that are about to lose (or have lost) the organic standard struggle. As a result, these technologies will die out.

Reduction of product differentiation curtails competition

It has been suggested that since standards reduce product differentiation, they thus eliminate one important aspect of competition.[53] The importance of this argument from the dynamic model's perspective has already been discussed above in Section 5.4.1 under 'Facilitating consumer comparison'.

Standard-setting smoothes innovative leaps and fluctuations in market share

Another anticompetitive effect of standards has been the implication that standard-setting allows corporations to manipulate the rate of innovation and maintain market shares in markets that would otherwise be characterized by fast innovation and rapidly fluctuating market shares.[54]

This argument is surely interesting from the dynamic model's perspective, since it deals with elements that are also important in the model. Indeed, the suggestion that standards smooth innovative leaps is convincing. The network effects discussed earlier create a certain stability of standards, under which industry players adhere to existing standards and those are only updated or changed once every few years. Such a smoothing effect clearly works against the tenets of the Austrian competition model, which is based on a raging innovation process that Joseph Schumpeter has characterized as a 'perennial gale of creative destruction'.[55] Schumpeter spoke of 'creative destruction' to express the idea that the pursuit of market power is a creative and dynamic force that 'incessantly revolutionizes the economic structure from within, incessantly destroying the old one, incessantly creating a new one'.[56]

The problem is that standards may prevent some of this destruction. The spontaneously robust competitive process is stripped of one of its basic elements whereby the technology behind all products in a certain market area is dictated by a set standard that is only changed (if at all) every few years. This is probably why corporate market players support standards so much, namely, because they eliminate or significantly minimize the devastating risk that a new technology will be introduced tomorrow and the market will tip towards it. The process of creative *destruction* is restrained by standards exactly because standards create the opposite situation – a stable protocol that a market area will adhere to for a couple of years. Once a standard is set, everybody in the market area (including potential entrants) knows (and no-less-importantly expects) that this standard will rule that market area for a while. Suppliers can rest assured knowing that a new and different technology cannot emerge and supplant the set standard, which is stabilized by the network effects. This gives producers a certain 'quiet life' quality that is unthinkable in Austrian competition terms.

Note, however, that standards do not necessarily predict less fluctuation in market shares between the existing market shares. A standard only predicts an unchallengeable market position that is immune from competitive forces to the extent that it is a proprietary standard over which a market player holds IPRs. Where a producer holds a patent over a set standard, he/she effectively enjoys immunity from competitive forces because it can eliminate any competition by bringing a patent infringement suit against competitors who utilize his/her proprietary standard. This issue will be further developed below when we discuss the circumstances of the Dell case.

The standard-setting process sets the ground for abusive cooperation

The process of standard-setting is in effect a type of coordination in industry behavior. Therefore, the standard-setting forum may provide a convenient forum for additional abusive cooperation.[57] This idea is simple, and is based on Adam Smith's ancient notion that when competitors of the same trade meet, their meeting is often utilized for coordination of market behavior that ultimately hurts consumers. Standard-setting meetings may thus prove fertile ground for illegitimate coordination between competitors. These notions are not purely theoretical, there is already specific case law whose findings have hinted that under certain circumstances, collective action of competitors in a standard-setting organization might itself violate the antitrust laws[58]. Note that this tendency may be made worse because standard-setting procedures require a discussion of know-how and production methods which are issues that under normal trade circumstances are not shared by competitors.

These notions are also significant under the dynamic model. In fact under the dynamic model many forms of cooperation that may be deemed legitimate under the traditional legal analysis, may be considered questionable. Within a standard-setting process producers are actually agreeing on an important tenet upon which their products will be based. They create a consensual 'common denominator' between their competing products, and in effect agree not to differ or compete between them on the specifications of this consensual component. Such a set 'common denominator' stands in complete contrast to the Austrian notions of 'dog-eat-dog' competitive struggle, whereby producers act individually to better their positions in the market. To a certain extent, competitors setting a standard no longer have to struggle against one another to guess how to design the standardized matter to better fit what consumers want. They agree 'on behalf of the consumers' how the standardized component will be designed. These notions of cooperation among competitors, even by way of standard-setting, seem to contradict the spirit of the dynamic competition model, under which competitors struggle individually against one another in an effort to cater to consumer preferences. These comments relate to standard-setting cooperation that is considered *legitimate*, but the fact that standard-setting forums themselves may lay the groundwork for flagrantly anticompetitive cooperation (such as price-fixing and so on) is also of concern from the Austrian perspective.

Note that there are two different arguments here. One is that the mere notion of cooperation between competitors (even by way of standard-setting consortia) contradicts the basic notion of the dynamic model. Another is that standard-setting forums may nurture 'classic' anticompetitive cooperation between competitors, and this is also of concern from the dynamic point of view.

5.4.3 Summary

To sum up this section, it seems that industries that rely on many set standards are likely to suffer from a variety of phenomena that run counter to the dynamic competition process developed in this study. They may be likely to display less product differentiation, a slower and more controlled rate of innovation and less consumer choice. The conclusion of these issues does not point in a clear-cut anticompetitive direction; the considerations work in both directions, as some of them suggest certain pro-competitive aspects of standardization, such as the claim that by reducing producers' risks standards may increase producer's investment in innovation. Indeed, as has also been noted by courts, the competitive story in this context may be especially difficult to read where innovation is concerned.[59] Overall, the above analysis suggests that standardization generally involves a number of phenomena that interfere with the Austrian competitive process model. These phenomena demonstrate that standards are not necessarily pro-competitive. In this, they are consistent with the literature that admits to conflicting pro- and anticompetitive aspects of standardization.[60] It seems clear that equating standards with competition cannot belong in the Austrian model. This point is revisited in Section 5.6, below.

5.5 FROM THEORY TO PRACTICE: THE DELL CASE

Now that different aspects of the interplay between standards and the dynamic competition model have been reviewed, it is time to see how these various considerations arise in a real case. The Dell case, which was considered rather revolutionary when the Federal Trade Commission brought it in the mid-1990s, provides an excellent circumstantial framework for reviewing these issues. Therefore this section will review the factual and legal structure of the Dell decision, and section 5.6 will review it from the dynamic model's perspective.

5.5.1 The Dell Case Facts

The Dell case involved an alleged abuse of the standard-setting process by Dell as a patent holder. Compared with the case's controversial legal analysis and outcome, the facts were relatively uncontroversial and straightforward. The key public documents that recount these facts are the proposed Consent Agreement with Analysis document published by the FTC in November 1995[61] (Proposed Decision), and the Final Decision and Consent Order on the matter adopted by agency six months later after receiving public comments on its proposal document (Final Decision).[62] It should, however, be noted that the facts described in these documents were only partially uncontested. Dell admitted to all the facts set out in the draft complaint as part of the consent agreement it signed with the FTC.[63] However, Dell did not admit to any additional facts detailed in the explanatory statement that was issued along with it (since the statement was not part of the consent agreement).[64] The following outline draws upon these documents.

Dell Computer Corporation was a computer systems company that provided various computer products and services. According to the complaint, in February 1992 Dell became a member of the Video Electronics Standards Association (VESA), a non-profit standards-setting association comprising all the major U.S. computer hardware and software manufacturers. At about the same time VESA began the process of setting a standard for a computer bus design, later known as the 'VL Bus', through its *ad hoc* Local Bus Committee.[65]

By June 1992, VESA's Local Bus Committee, which included members of Dell Corporation, completed the development of the VL bus design standard as an improvement upon the then-existing bus technology that was designed to meet the faster transmission needs of video-intensive software.[66] During July and August of that year, Dell voted twice in the committee's two-round voting process on the standard in favor of approving the VL bus as an official industry standard. As part of the approval process, a Dell representative certified in writing before each vote that to the best of his knowledge, the proposal 'did not infringe on any trademark, copyright, or patents that Dell possessed'. Such certification was required as part of VESA's policy, because of its preference for adopting standards that did not include proprietary technology. Soon afterwards, following approval by all of VESA's voting members, the VL bus standard was adopted by VESA. The standard described a uniform interface, architecture, timing, electrical and physical specification which allowed users to interchange VL bus-based products from various manufacturers.[67] The focus then was on bus *designs* rather than bus manufacturing.

Approximately one year prior to the approval of the VL bus standard, in July 1991, Dell had received a certain U.S. patent ('481 patent), which, according to Dell, granted it 'exclusive rights to the mechanical slot configuration used on the motherboard to receive the VL bus card'. However at no time, before, during or soon after the relevant standard-setting process, did Dell disclose to VESA's Local Bus Committee the existence of the '481 patent.[68]

As will be set out in the following sections, the questions of Dell's knowledge and intention came to play a key role in the legal analysis of the case. The FTC complaint describing the facts did not allege that Dell's representative to VESA had any knowledge of the '481 patent or its potential infringement by the VL bus design at the time he cast his vote ballot (this issue was not addressed in the complaint). However, the language of the order prescribing the remedy may imply that the FTC did, in fact, consider Dell's conduct to be intentional. This is because, in addition to restricting enforcement of the specific '481 patent, the order generally prohibited Dell, for a period of 10 years, from enforcing any patents relating to standards where, in response to a written inquiry from the standard-setting organization, Dell '*intentionally* failed to disclose such [conflicting] patent rights while such industry standard was under consideration' (italics added).[69] Therefore the wording of the order alludes to the fact that Dell's failure to disclose its patent was consciously conducted.

After VESA's standardized VL bus design became successful and was installed in more than 1.4 million computers sold in the eight months following the standard's adoption, Dell began to inform certain VESA members who manufactured computers that utilized the VL bus design that their 'implementation of the VL bus was a violation of Dell's exclusive rights'. Dell then demanded that these companies meet with Dell representatives to 'determine ... the manner in which Dell's exclusive rights will be recognized'. Dell then followed up its initial demands by meeting with several companies, and did not renounce the alleged claim regarding infringement of its rights.

5.5.2 Dell: Legal Setting of the Complaint

Statement of the majority

The FTC voted 4–1 to accept the proposed consent agreement with Dell. The legal structure of the Dell Majority Statement is quite short and perhaps not entirely clear. The Final Decision document contains, in addition to the complaint and the remedial order, a brief explanatory statement on behalf of the majority that helps shed some light on the Commission's legal interpretation of the above facts. The statement promulgates the view that once VESA's VL bus standard had become widely accepted, the standard effectively conferred market power upon Dell as the patent holder. It postulates that this market power would not have been created had VESA known of the Dell patent, in which case it would have opted for the adoption of an alternative non-proprietary standard. Furthermore, it observes that the said market power would have translated into increased computer prices for consumers, as Dell would have been able to impose a royalty on each VL bus installed in 486-generation computers.[70] The statement also alludes to a lock-in argument, noting that at that stage computer manufacturers could not have readily shifted to a new standard (that is, an alternative to the VL bus standard), because the market had already overwhelmingly adopted the VL bus standard.[71]

The complaint This determines that by engaging in the acts or practices described above,

> 'Dell has unreasonably restrained competition in the following ways, among others:

(a) Industry acceptance of the VL-bus design standard was hindered because some computer manufacturers delayed their use of the design standard until the patent issue was clarified.
(b) Systems utilizing the VL-bus design standard were avoided due to concerns that patent issues would affect the VL-bus' success as an industry design standard.
(c) The uncertainty concerning the acceptance of the VL-bus design standard raised the costs of implementing the VL-bus design as well as the costs of developing competing bus designs.
(d) Willingness to participate in industry standard-setting efforts has been chilled.'[72]

For these reasons, the FTC found Dell's alleged practices to be to the prejudice and injury of the public, and to constitute unfair methods of competition or affect commerce in violation of Section 5 of the Federal Trade Commission Act.

The explanatory statement admits the legal and economic theories underlying the order to be 'somewhat novel'.[73] Consequently, the statement stresses that the scope of the decision is limited to its specific fact pattern, in which there was evidence that VESA would have implemented a different non-proprietary design had it been informed of the patent conflict during the standard-adoption process, and where Dell failed to act in good faith to identify and disclose patent conflicts.[74] Therefore the effective scope of the decision seems limited to cases where there is reason to believe that the failure to disclose the patent was not inadvertent.[75] Furthermore, the statement clarified that the decision did not take a stance on broader issues such as whether non-proprietary industries standards were more desirable than proprietary ones, or whether there existed a general duty to search for patents when a firm engages in a standard-setting process.[76]

The Remedy The FTC estimated that the practices described above were to continue in the absence of relief. Therefore it issued an order which prohibited Dell from enforcing its '481 patent against any firm that uses it for implementation of the VESA VL bus design for the life of the patent.[77] Furthermore, the order prohibited Dell for a period of 10 years from enforcing or threatening to enforce patent rights by asserting that an implementation of an industry standard infringes them, if, in response to a written inquiry from the standard-setting organization to a Dell representative, Dell intentionally failed to disclose such patent rights while the proposed standard was under consideration.[78]

Dissenting statement of Commissioner Mary Azcuenga
The detailed dissenting statement of Commissioner Azcuenga extends over more than half of the Final Decision.[79] The dissent rests upon two main pillars. The first argues that the fact pattern alleged in the Dell complaint does not establish a violation of Section 5 of the FTC Act under any then-existing theories of law. The second maintains that basing the Dell decision on a novel theory of law is inappropriate.[80]

Existing legal theories The statement begins by recalling the traditional antitrust analysis formula for monopolization cases. It maintains that application of the traditional formula on the Dell case facts renders a finding of liability dependent on two necessary elements: that Dell *intentionally* led VESA into adopting the VL bus standard that was covered by its patent; and that as a result of adoption of that standard Dell obtained market power beyond that lawfully conferred by the patent.[81] The dissenting statement's reading of the FTC Complaint and Majority Statement finds no allegation that Dell intentionally or knowingly misled VESA, or any convincing finding to the effect that Dell obtained market power as a result of its misstatement.[82] Therefore the dissenting opinion takes the view that, according to the existing jurisprudence, the complaint utterly failed to establish a violation under Section 5 of the FTC Act.[83] Furthermore, the dissenting opinion deduces from the majority statement's second count of competitive damage (the one that described a scenario in which 'systems utilizing the VL-bus design standard were avoided'), that a Dell monopoly was in fact impossible because computer producers could readily switch to alternative bus designs that did not incorporate Dell's technology.[84]

Novel legal theories In light of the above, the dissenting opinion characterizes the statement of the majority as novel and unprecedented whereby it based its finding of an FTC Act Section 5 violation upon constructive knowledge by Dell (namely, that Dell must have known of the patent, because obviously some of the Dell people knew about it), rather than clear knowledge and intention to mislead. Commissioner Azcuenga's statement regards the adoption of such a novel 'strict liability'[85] standard as unwise because of its unclear competitive implications.[86] It identifies a chilling effect on the standard-setting process as the main damage that such a legal standard may inflict. Such an effect would come about because corporations would be placing their IPRs at risk simply by participating in the standard-setting process. It is argued that this, in turn, may lead to corporate reluctance to participate in standard-setting altogether, or difficulties in collecting the votes required for the adoption of new standards (as firms may opt to avoid potential antitrust exposure or IPR curtailment by simply not voting).[87]

The dissenting statement expresses serious doubts as to whether the four points that particularize the anticompetitive effects of Dell's conduct in the majority statement indeed reflected anti-competitive harm. It argues that the list of anticompetitive effects in the majority statement, three of which relate to the speed and breadth of industry acceptance of the standard, do not necessarily translate into clear harm to consumers or competition (such as higher prices of computers for consumers or restricted output of computers in any relevant geographic market).[88] Furthermore, it finds the fourth anticompetitive effect mentioned by the majority, namely, the chilling effect on corporate willingness to participate in industry standard-setting efforts, especially odd. This is because the dissenting view expected the Dell remedial order to induce the same chilling effect on standard-setting processes, since corporations may want to avoid potential antitrust liability and endangerment to their IPR by refraining from voting in standard-setting proceedings altogether.[89]

The remedy The dissenting opinion disagrees with the majority's choice of remedy, which it characterizes as 'unnecessarily harsh'. It notes that the majority's case resembles a patent estoppel case. Therefore it draws an analogy with the private legal remedy of patent estoppel, whose three elements are misleading communication by a knowledgeable patentee, reliance by another party on the communication, and material prejudice to the other party if the patent holder is allowed to proceed. It holds the FTC's failure to allege expectation by VESA members as an element of the offense, or to allege anticompetitive effects, as crucial in two respects. First, it maintains this failure as undermining the basis of the majority's structure itself. Second, it asserts that a proper remedy should include some proof of expectation, namely, proof that other VESA members relied on Dell's misstatements, and acted upon them to an extent that now renders them specifically susceptible to Dell's patent claim. Finally, the dissenting statement points out that, as a practical matter, the FTC order could do little to correct any uncertainty and delay that might have occurred three years earlier, since in the time that had elapsed, companies had already decided what bus design to select.[90]

5.6 THE DELL CASE: A DYNAMIC ANALYSIS

5.6.1 A Review of the FTC Dell Decision

The Dell decision is structured in a manner that is very different from the Austrian competition model. This section will briefly review these marked differences, and then go on to develop an Austrian analysis of the Dell fact pattern. The purpose here is not to develop a complete critique of the decision, but rather to highlight the methodical differences between the actual decision (including the dissenting opinion) and the Austrian model, and then suggest what the alternative analysis would look like under the Austrian model.

The majority decision

The majority view focuses on three arguments, only the third of which is truly relevant from the dynamic model's perspective. Its first argument relates to the fact that once the VL bus standard became widely accepted it conferred static market power upon Dell as the patent holder, which would not have been conferred had VESA known of the Dell patent. However, since static market power plays little role in the Austrian model, this pillar is not very important from the dynamic model's perspective. The second element is the Commission's observation that Dell's market power would have translated into increased consumer prices; this is not particularly relevant to the dynamic model, either, which, contrary to the traditional model, does not pay special attention to product prices, but rather focuses on the competitive process as a whole. The third argument was a lock-in argument that noted that, at that stage, computer manufacturers could not have shifted to any alternative since the market had already adopted the VL bus standard. As we shall see in detail below, this argument is crucial from the dynamic point of view. This is because the dynamic model is based on consumer choice as the engine of the competitive process. A lock-in on the supply side essentially harms this process, because producers become restrained in their ability to cater to consumer preferences to the extent that their production options are limited to the rooted standard.

The majority decision identifies four specific harms to competition as a result of the above mechanisms and as setting the basis for the intervening order. Three of these specific harms are probably not very convincing from an Austrian point of view. The first was that industry acceptance of the VL bus design standard was hindered. As explained in detail above in Section 5.4, it is far from clear whether the acceptance of standards is pro-competitive from a dynamic point of view. Therefore hindrance of the process of adopting a standard would not necessarily be seen as anticompetitive from the dynamic viewpoint. For the very same reason, the second and fourth harms named in the decision would not be very convincing from this model's perspective. The second harm listed is that systems utilizing the VL bus design standard were avoided, and the fourth speaks of a chilling effect on industry standard-setting efforts. This is because, on the practical level, the market success of products utilizing the standard and hence of the standard itself, is not necessarily to be taken as pro-competitive from an Austrian point of view. Similarly, on the more abstract level, the success of standard-setting efforts is not seen as necessarily pro-competitive.

The third harm listed in the Dell decision is uncertainty concerning the acceptance of the VL bus design standard, which raises the costs of implementing that design or developing competing bus designs. As explained throughout this study, the uncertainty element in itself is not considered anticompetitive in the Austrian model. On the contrary, uncertainty is considered an inherent part of the competitive process, which is characterized as a discovery process. However, as noted earlier,[91] the point of elevated costs definitely touches on one of the Austrian market assumptions because very high costs of implementation may well diminish entrepreneurial incentives to join the market process. Therefore such high costs may conflict with the basic objective circumstances upon which the competitive process develops.

The dissenting opinion

The dissenting opinion, which tends to cling to the traditional mode of antitrust analysis, also seems rather remote from the dynamic model's thinking. Its first part criticizes the majority view for failing to demonstrate the elements of Dell's intention to mislead VESA as well as Dell's acquisition of static market power beyond that conferred by a patent. As noted earlier, both static market power and subjective intention play little role in the dynamic antitrust model,[92] and therefore this line of argument bears little relevance from this perspective.

At the same time, note that the dissenting opinion's reservations as to the majority's argument that slowing down the adoption of the industry standard inherently brings about anticompetitive effects, correspond well with the dynamic analysis suggested here. This is because the dynamic analysis similarly fails to identify clear anti-competitive harm in a slowed process of standard acceptance. While it seems credible that standards promote the growth of certain industries (by speeding their development), it was demonstrated earlier that standards are not necessarily pro-competitive, and that in fact there may be some trade-off between standardization and a healthy competitive process.

5.6.2 Dynamic Analysis of the Dell Fact Pattern

Let us, then, develop a full analysis of the Dell fact pattern according to the dynamic antitrust model suggested in this study. Note that the following analysis must unfortunately be limited to the facts revealed in the FTC documents. Consequently, facts that are interesting from the dynamic model's perspective but were not deemed relevant by the FTC are missing from the analysis. As we shall see, this restricts the analysis significantly. Nevertheless, there are still interesting conclusions to be drawn from the application that follows.

As can be recalled from Chapter 3, the model calls for a two-stage analysis. The first part of the analysis involves an assessment of the level of robustness of the competitive process in the specific market area. The vitality of the process is assessed through a variety of dynamic indicators. These indicators include the observed rate of innovation; sensitivity of the suspect corporation's behavior to consumer and competitors actions; volatility of the market area population, market share of the suspect firm and degree of price volatility; the availability of alternatives; the lack of barriers to market entry; and some minimal degree of uncertainty remaining in the market area. To the extent that the first part of the analysis suggests that the competitive process is hindered, a second part then evaluates the initial circumstances in the market area, namely, to what extent the market area circumstances correspond with the untold assumptions of the dynamic model. The more the initial circumstances correspond with the model's initial objective assumptions, the stronger the causal connection that may be established between the suspicious conduct and the process monopoly observed in the first part.

Also recall that the dynamic model does not concern itself with the subjective intention of the suspected players. Therefore the debate over the required intention element that occupies much of the dissenting opinion (and is tacitly alluded to in the majority opinion) is not relevant in the analysis that follows.

Stage I: evaluating the state of the competitive process:

The observed rate of innovation This is one important indicator of the vitality of the competitive process (both IP-protected innovation and non-protected market innovation, such as the introduction of novel products, adding of new features to existing products, new product imaging and so on). The Dell documents do not reveal many facts in this respect. However, it is interesting to take a glimpse into the history of the evolution of computer hardware buses.[93]

To recap briefly: a computer bus is a data pathway that connects one part of the computer to another. A bus is like a network of roads that carry truckloads of data back and forth. The capacity of each truckload of data moved along that data road is measured in bits. One end of the bus connects to the processor and memory; the other end connects to slots. Those slots take internal expansion cards, such as sound cards, internal modems, drive controllers and so on.

In the beginning of the personal computer (PC) era, around 1982, IBM created the ISA (or Industry Standard Architecture) XT bus. It was the bus architecture that moved 8-bit chunks. Then in 1984 came a bus known as the PC/AT bus, which was an improved version of the ISA bus and shuttled 16-bit chunks of data back and forth. In 1987 IBM presented the market with its proprietary MCA bus, which offered both 16-bit and 32-bit versions. The MCA bus did not gain wide popularity, though, perhaps because it was not backwardly compatible with the then-existing ISA cards, or because it was a proprietary standard and IBM (at least initially) charged a relatively high fee for its use.

The next innovation introduced in late 1988 was EISA (or Extended Industry Standard Architecture) bus. EISA was a 32-bit bus initiative that also allowed for more than one central processing unit (CPU) to share the bus. It was non-proprietary, and was developed by the 'Gang of Nine' (nine non-IBM manufacturers of IBM-compatible PCs, led by Compaq) when a 32-bit PC bus standard was needed and IBM demanded a high royalty fee for the use of its MCA bus. At around the same time, Apple came out with its NuBus, which it built into its machines from the Macintosh II through to the Performa.

The VESA Local Bus or VL Bus was pioneered by the Video Electronics Standard Association. The original VL bus v1.0 that was adopted in 1992 (and which stood at the center of the Dell case) was a 32-bit pathway. In 1994 VESA adopted an improvement to the original VL bus, VL bus v2.0, which was a 64-bit standard. The VL bus was used mainly on 486-66 computers and in the low-end Pentiums up to the 75 MHz Pentium.

The common bus in today's computers (both PC systems and Apple machines) is the PCI bus (Peripheral Component Interconnect) invented by Intel in 1993. The architecture is innovative because it can be found in PC systems as well as in Apple machines, and it is available in both 32- and 64-bit versions. It should also be noted that through many of these innovations, the ISA standard has endured. ISA expansion slots (or more accurately the PC/AT version of ISA) can still be found in today's computers alongside the PCI slots. EISA buses are used today mostly in high-end PCs such as file servers. However, most new systems use AGP (Accelerated Graphics Port) for video cards, so use of ISA is currently declining.

This very brief historical review of the bus industry, which is absent from the Commission documents, seems to suggest that the introduction of the VL bus did not significantly hinder the rate of innovation in the bus industry. This may be inferred from the fact that an improved PCI bus architecture was introduced after the adoption of the VL bus standard by VESA, and has become the prevalent bus used in today's computers. Furthermore, the fact that a second version of the VL Bus design was introduced in 1994 suggests that innovation continued. This information was already available in 1995 when the FTC reviewed these issues.

The only caveat to bear in mind in this respect is the questionable effect that the Dell FTC case may have had on the historical development reviewed above. One may argue that, had the FTC not intervened, the design of the VL bus would have prevailed over that of the PCI, and as a proprietary design would have hindered further innovation. It is impossible to assess these hypotheses. We see in the historical account that when IBM charged a high price for its proprietary MCA bus, the market responded by introducing the non-proprietary EISA standard. However, the possibility of such innovation is limited to the availability of alternative solutions (within a reasonable time and investment frame) that would not breach the patent. Since patents provide a very broad scope of protection, they may prove an obstacle to such sequential innovation.

The sensitivity of the suspected firm's behavior to consumer trends and behavior of the other market area players Here too, the Dell documents do not provide specific details. The only relevant detail available in this respect is the one noted above that in 1994, two years after the adoption of the 32-bit VL bus standard, VESA adopted a second faster 64-bit version of the standard. The adoption of the faster standard (presumably with Dell's consent and enthusiasm) suggests that Dell was mindful of consumer needs for a faster bus design.

The volatility of the market area population over time Due to the lack of data in the Dell documents over these issues, it is difficult to assess how this indicator behaved under the circumstances of the Dell case.

The fluctuating volatility of the suspect firm's static market shares over time In other words, market data that reflect both upward and downward changes of its static market share. The Dell documents do not reveal relevant data in this respect, therefore this factor cannot be evaluated here. Perhaps this is not too serious, since, as noted in Chapter 3,[94] this factor should only be considered positively, that is, as an indication of a dynamic competition process, yet the lack of such market share volatility should *not* be considered as conclusive indication of a process monopoly.

The degree of price volatility in the market area This concerns the volatility of both real relative prices of different players' products. There is no relevant information in the Dell documents on these issues, partly because although Dell sent letters to various producers suggesting that they meet to reconcile the patent issues, it seems that the FTC intervened before Dell actually put a price tag on a license for the VL bus design. There is also no information available on the cost of the PCI bus design.

The availability of alternatives to the suspect firm's products This may be indicative as to the vigor of the competitive process. When the VL bus 32-bit design standard was adopted in 1992, it was not the only 32-bit bus design on the market. IBM's MCA bus design and the non-proprietary EISA had already been available on the market for at least four years (which is a long time in computer market areas). Furthermore, a year later in 1993 and still long before the FTC inquiry, the PCI 32-bit standard appeared on the market.

It is important to note that these bus designs differed in many ways, and not only in their data path widths (measured in bits). Computer bus designs are defined by many precise specifications (such as peak throughput measured in Mbytes/s, bus speed measured in MHz, compatibility, direct memory access channels and so on). This is not the place to go into a detailed technical evaluation of the differences among the bus design standards. The broad point to bear in mind is that the different buses were not 100 percent interchangeable in every context. In fact, the Dell documents themselves hint that the VL bus design enjoyed some unique speed advantages. Nevertheless, it is probably safe to say that, at the time of the FTC inquiry, the market area offered at least three alternative 32-bit bus designs in addition to the VL bus. Therefore as far as this indicator is concerned, the Dell circumstances do not reflect failure of the competitive process in that market area.

The degree of uncertainty in the market area The degree to which a suspect market player is able to insulate itself from the detriment of uncertainty is relevant for identifying a process monopoly. Therefore the important question in this respect is whether Dell's behavior, which relied on its '481 patent claims, provided it with a significant degree of certainty in the bus design market area, so much so that Dell had become immune from the uncertainty that is inherent in a healthy competitive process. This question is not an easy one to answer under the Dell circumstances. It is clear that, to the extent that Dell's '481 patent indeed covered the VL bus design, this patent gave Dell a stranglehold over the production of the VL design buses. This would have meant that VL buses could only be produced or used through a license from Dell, and Dell was free to set the license price as it pleased or to decide whether to grant a license at all. Dell's correspondence demonstrated its keen interest in implementing this potential stranglehold.

Note that the VL bus design was preceded by another proprietary bus design standard – IBM's MCA bus. However, there is a marked distinction between the two. While the MCA design was internally developed by IBM, the VL bus design was adopted by VESA, which was a standard-setting industry organization. Therefore, while MCA was simply promoted by IBM, the VL bus received a certain 'seal of approval' from an association whose members were all the important industry players in that market area. An approval by VESA, which included written declarations by all market players including Dell that they would claim no IPRs over the VL bus standard, carried important implications. It sent a clear message to the whole industry that the VL design was not proprietary. This signal was important because, in planning their future, computer hardware makers relied on a design that they thought would be non-proprietary – in other words, free. The moment Dell revealed its patent in its threatening correspondence the rules of the market game changed. Were Dell's patent claims allowed in this context, Dell would have acquired a secure stranglehold over the implementation of the VL bus design.

In light of the above, it seems evident that Dell's reliance on the '481 patent eliminated any competitive uncertainty relating to the VL bus. The question remains, however, as to how significant Dell's stranglehold over the VL bus design was, and how this affected the resulting certainty within that market area as a whole at the time. In other words – how significant was this decrease in uncertainty? There may be no clear answer for these questions. However, from the manner in which the facts are portrayed in the Dell documents, it seems that the influence was quite significant. The documents reveal that at the time the Commission was examining the case, the VL bus design had already been implemented in the 486 computers. In the mid-1990s, 486 computers were the dominant PC (as opposed to Macintosh) computer sold on the market. Therefore Dell's patent would have allowed it to control a hardware component that was then in effect an essential component in most of the PCs sold on the market.

Nevertheless, it is important to consider the above facts with a grain of salt. From a historical perspective (now that it is some ten years since the Dell case events took place and six since the FTC Decision), we know that in the long run the VL bus design was not very successful and was surpassed by the PCI bus design that is used in most of today's computers. This should serve as a reminder that the computer hardware industry's rate of innovation is high, which creates a level of uncertainty that is inherent in this industry. This intrinsically uncertain character may forewarn us that, in this industry, scenarios that might otherwise have been considered paralysing, in the sense of eliminating uncertainty from the market, are perhaps not a significant process monopoly indicator because computer hardware components evolve rapidly.

The existence of barriers to entry into the market area Another important indicator of a process monopoly is where a barrier to market entry that is created by subjective corporate behavior may shield the current market players from the competitive threats of potential competitors (that is, create a process monopoly). Under the Dell circumstances, it is not entirely clear whether at the time of the FTC inquiry, to the extent that the '481 patent would have been fully recognized as asserted in Dell's correspondence, this would have created a significant barrier to entry into the computer manufacturing business. The majority decision seems convinced that the patent would have indeed created such a significant barrier to entry because it claims that at that time computer manufacturers were locked into the VL design and could not have switched to an alternative one. Unfortunately, the documents do not reveal more details in this respect. There is a lot of technical and practical information that would have been useful for evaluating this argument but is missing from the Dell documents. Was there indeed an alternative bus design (such as MCA, EISA or PCI) that computer manufacturers could have switched to within an immediate timeframe? Was that alternative design equally compatible with the 486 computers and their peripherals? In the absence of additional sources, all that is left is the FTC claim that manufacturers were locked into the VL design. To the extent that this claim was accurate, it seems to reflect a classic barrier to entry.

Summary The above review does not provide a clear-cut result as to the state of the competitive process in the market area examined in the Dell decision. The equation is a complicated one. Some of the factors clearly suggest that the competitive process was vigorous: the rate of innovation seemed to have been reasonable; there were at least three alternative 32-bit bus designs available on the market; and the computer hardware industry seemed to have retained some minimal level of competition. Other factors suggest that the competitive process may have been hindered: the claim that the patent created a barrier to entry; and the fact that the patent removed a significant degree of uncertainty from the market area. In addition to these two types of considerations, there is also certain practical information that is missing and therefore could not be evaluated, for example: the extent to which alternative bus designs became interchangeable with the VL bus; the fluctuating volatility of market shares; the price volatility of buses and the extent of practical differentiation between the different bus designs on the market at the time.

Therefore, in sum, from the above analysis it is not clear that the Dell circumstances indeed reflected a real failure of the competitive process. Accordingly, an antitrust approach that is based on the Austrian model would probably have refrained from antitrust intervention under these specific circumstances. In other words, the result of the Austrian analysis is similar to that of Commissioner Azcuenga's dissenting opinion, finding no basis for antitrust policy to intervene, but using a different line of reasoning. It should be stressed that this result is limited to the information upon which the analysis was structured. The missing information may have perhaps tipped the balance in the other direction or strengthened the same finding, but this information was unfortunately not available here.

It is essential to note that the competitive scene may have seemed very different had the VL bus design succeeded in becoming the overly dominant design in the PC industry over a long period (in computer industry terms). Such a scenario would have translated into a much more significant stranglehold of the proprietary and patent-protected VL design, which would probably have had greater anticompetitive effects from a dynamic perspective.

A brief look at Stage II: the initial market circumstances

The first stage of the analysis concludes with no convincing evidence of the failure of the competitive process in the computer bus market area. Therefore there is no actual need to continue into the second leg of the analysis, which evaluates the initial market circumstances, in order to verify whether an observed competitive failure was caused by a suspected line of conduct. Nevertheless, since this is a theoretical study, it is still an interesting exercise to make some observations in this respect, since the initial circumstances provide the subjective context within which the competitive process itself takes place, and therefore closely affects its character. The notions briefly touched upon below are the elements that the second evaluation phase would have looked into had the competitive process in the Dell case been clearly found to be flawed. They are briefly noted since the purpose of this chapter is to demonstrate how the dynamic model is to be applied to actual network industry scenarios.

Dynamic notions Generally, the computer hardware industry is considered a dynamic one. It is common knowledge that within the industry, products and new technologies evolve so fast that products are constantly being reinvented.[95] Therefore the computer bus industry, as part of the computer hardware industry, may also enjoy this halo of dynamic reputation.

Nevertheless, there can be no sweeping assumption that the initial competitive environment in all the computer hardware market areas is a dynamic one. Therefore each specific market area must be individually evaluated. Some of the additional factual information that would have been useful for a more accurate evaluation of the initial Dell circumstances includes the following questions. Was the profit margin from the sales of computer buses sufficiently lucrative to justify the R&D costs for a new bus design? Were bus designs sufficiently distinct and differentiated so that potential competitors had a feasible incentive to join that market area? Was there a realistic chance for new unfamiliar players to offer a bus design that would catch on? (For example, the procedures at the standard-setting organization were probably heavily influenced by the major market players, who usually have representatives sitting on the important committees.[96]) Was it feasible to create alternative bus designs that would have been no less compatible with the existing hardware components than the VL bus hardware? (The compatibility issue directly implicates the initial competitive environment since it locks consumers into purchasing only compatible products options.) How broad was the effective protection conferred by the claims of patents related to the various bus designs? The important notion is whether the patents were broad enough so that the threat of infringement suits deterred potential players from joining this market area. How powerful were the network effects in that market area? Namely, did consumers extract more utility from a system utilizing a VL bus the more other consumers utilized the same bus design?

In general, findings of low profit margins from computer bus sales, of little possibility of creating alternative differentiated bus designs either technically or because of broad patent protection on existing designs, and of strong network effects would all suggest that the initial market circumstances represented a difficult environment for the development of the competitive process. Therefore where the flow competitive process is found to be hindered by the first evaluation stage, this would have suggested that the competitive failure was the result of objective difficult opening conditions of the market area, rather than conduct that is suspected as being abusive.

Uncertainty notions Recall that uncertainty has both producer and consumer sides. Producers do not know exactly what consumers' preferences are, or how much consumers are willing to pay for a certain product. By the same token, consumers lack full information on the different features of competing products.[97] The general considerations for evaluation of the uncertainty notion in new-economy industries seem to point in opposite directions. On the one hand, the rapid innovation rate and dynamic notions commonly observed in these industries entail an inherent degree of uncertainty, because where changes are frequently observed it means that not all market players will have full information of all the changes; furthermore they will translate these changes into different market conclusions (some of which will prove correct and some not). Therefore high-tech can generally be said to display some level of uncertainty. On the other hand, standards often seem to increase certainty in markets on a number of levels.

The certainty-enhancing mechanism works on a number of levels. First, because once standards are adopted the industry and consumers rely on them, expecting them to remain unchanged for at least a couple of years (furthermore, producers have little incentive to deviate from a standard, unless they are convinced that they can suggest a competing technology that is so much better than the standard that it will overcome the network effects that reinforced the incumbent standard). Second, note that standards alleviate producer's uncertainty notions, not because they tell producers what consumers want but because they render consumer preferences less significant in the process. Once all the industry players (as in the Dell case) meet to set a standard, they no longer care what consumers think about this standard. They practically force this standard upon consumers and thus no longer need to worry about what consumers want. Thus, the uncertainty related to guessing consumer preferences is diminished as consumer preferences become less relevant than in a classic competitive process. Finally, consumer-side uncertainty is reduced because, as alluded to earlier in this chapter,[98] standards often reduce consumer uncertainty related to product features since this obviates their need to compare the standardized component between competing products.

Note that standards are not always part of the objective initial-circumstances picture. In the Dell case, for example, the VL standard was adopted in a process that involved Dell's suspicious misleading conduct. In other words, the standard in that case was the fruit of the suspicious conduct, and not an objective initial circumstance. Therefore their effects should probably not be evaluated within this phase of the analysis, but rather only within the first phase, and the relevant questions for examining whether the initial circumstances significantly eliminated the uncertainty notions should probably relate to the circumstances prior to the adoption of the VL standard.

5.7 CONCLUSION

This chapter attempted to examine various awkward questions related to antitrust analysis in network industries, from the unique perspective of the dynamic model that was developed earlier in this study. The evaluation offered was twofold: first, a general dynamic evaluation of the antitrust issues in these industries compared with the existing analysis; and second, a specific application of the dynamic notions to the circumstances of the Dell case. The conclusion of this application is the same as the one reached by the dissenting opinion in that case but from a different perspective.

Network industries in general and standard-ridden scenarios in particular seem like an antitrust scholar's nightmare. Their analysis exposes a plethora of considerations, some of which seem clearly pro-competitive, some of which seem clearly anticompetitive, and with the rest there may not even be a consensus as to their exact effect on the competitive process; it depends on the perspective of the antitrust scholar being asked. This renders the antitrust evaluation of network industry contexts a notably complex task.[99]

Note that with respect to the model developed in this study, this complexity may specifically encumber the second stage of the proposed analysis, namely the one that concerns itself with the initial circumstances of the market. This stage attempts to discern whether an observed competitive failure derives from a specific conduct, or should rather be attributed to the organic opening circumstances in that industry. However, the complex features of network industries may make it difficult to determine the extent to which the organic market circumstances indeed sustain the development of a competitive process. This, in turn, complicates the evaluation (and establishment) of a causal connection between an observed market failure and specific suspected conduct, since the clarity of such a causal connection directly depends on the clarity of the organic circumstances being sufficiently fertile to sustain a healthy market process. Perhaps this difficulty may also account for some of the debate around today's controversial IT industry antitrust cases (for example, the Microsoft case), whereby the different parties differ on whether an alleged competitive failure (process monopoly) is the result of specific conduct or rather an organic market development that is not the result of any specific conduct. Such debate may reflect this very same complexity of establishing a causal relation between specific conduct and an observed competitive failure where the initial circumstances are unclear.

On a final note, the results of the practical application of the dynamic model to the Dell case may suggest that the model is not necessarily a pro-intervention vigilant antitrust one. This is because the conclusion of the dynamic analysis actually concurred with the dissenting opinion, as both found an antitrust intervention unnecessary under the circumstances. This warning about applying antitrust policy in the absence of a clear causal connection between an observed competition failure and the suspected conduct may reassure the information industry players. Such industry players often oppose traditional antitrust policy, which they accuse of ignorance about their trade and a tendency towards unjustified market intervention.[100] Therefore they may be more tolerant towards an antitrust analysis that is admittedly a tentative one. In this respect, not only may the industry people be reassured, but also the Austrian economics scholars, since this cautious notion fits well with their traditionally anti-interventionist agenda.[101]

NOTES

[1] Michael L. Katz and Carl Shapiro, *Network Externalities, Competition, and Compatibility*, 75 Am. Econ. Rev. 424, 424 (1985). Literature on network effects is vast and growing, and it is not the purpose here to review it all, but rather to provide a basic introduction to the analysis in the sections that follow. For an excellent exhaustive review on network effects and their legal implications, see Mark A. Lemley and David McGowan, *Legal Implications of Network Economic Effects*, 86 Calif. L. Rev. 479, 488–99 (1998). See also Bruce R. Snapp, Network Industries and Antitrust: A Cautionary Note, in *Cutting Edge Issues in Network Industries* 1 (American Bar Association, Antitrust Law Section, May 1996). For an overview from a European perspective, see John Temple Lang, *European Community Antitrust Law: Innovation Markets And High Technology Industries* (NY: Fordham Corporate Law Institute 1996), also available at http://europa.eu.int/comm/competition/index_en.html (January 10, 2003). For economic literature, see the Internet site for the Economics of Networks at http://www.stern.nyu.edu/networks/site.html (January 10, 2003).

[2] This example is from Howard A. Shelanski and J. Gregory Sidak, *Antitrust Divestiture in Network Industries*, 68 U. Chi. L. Rev. 1, 8 (2001).

[3] See Lemley and McGowan, supra note 1 at 488–94.

[4] Interoperability (also referred to as 'compatibility') is the ability to exchange information and mutually to use the information which has been exchanged (see the preamble of the European Council Directive 91/250/EEC, May 14, 1991, on the legal protection of computer programs, OJ L 122 p. 42 (May 17, 1991). On compatibility as an antitrust issue, see Lemley and McGowan, supra note 1 at 517 et seq.

[5] See Douglas D. Leeds, *Raising the Standard: Antitrust Scrutiny of Standard-setting Consortia in High Technology Industries*, 7 Fordham I. P., Media & Ent. L. J. 641, 653 (1997).

[6] On the intricate effects of consumer expectation in these contexts see also: David Balto and Robert Pitofsky, *Antitrust and High-tech Industries: The New Challenge*, 43 Antitrust Bull. 583, 588–90 (1998); and Daniel L Rubinfeld, *Antitrust Enforcement in Dynamic Network Industries*, 43 Antitrust Bull. 859, 865–6 (1998).

[7] Mark A. Lemley, *Symposium: Standardizing Government Standard-setting Policy for Electronic Commerce*, 14 Berkeley Tech. L. J. 745, 747 (1999). See also Nicholas Economides, United States v. Microsoft: A Failure of Antitrust in the New Economy, 32 U. West. L.A. L. Rev. 3, 12 (2001) (on why standardization is often beneficial even at the price of having a monopoly).

[8] See Katz and Shapiro, supra note 1, for a full discussion of the 'tipping' phenomenon.

[9] See, for example: Daniel L. Rubinfeld, Deputy Assistant Attorney General, Antitrust Division, U.S. Dept. of Justice, *Competition, Innovation, and Antitrust Enforcement in Dynamic Network Industries*, 17–18 Address before the Software Publishers Association 1998 Spring Symposium (March 24, 1998), San Jose, California, available at http://www.usdoj.gov/atr/public/speeches/1611.htm (January 10, 2003); and Federal Trade Commission Staff, *Anticipating the 21st Century: Competition Policy and the New High-tech, Global Marketplace* 11–24 (May 1996), available at http://www.ftc.gov/opp/global.htm (January 10, 2003).

[10] Carl Shapiro, Deputy Assistant Attorney General, Antitrust Division, U.S. Dept. of Justice, 'Antitrust In Network Industries', Section III A (Address before the American Law Institute and American Bar Association, January 25, 1996) available at http://www.usdoj.gov/atr/public/speeches/shapir.mar.htm (January 10, 2003); Carl Shapiro, *Competition Policy in The Information Economy* (1999) section II A, available at http://www.berkeley.edu/~shapiro (January 10, 2003).

[11] See Shapiro, *Competition Policy in the Information Economy,* id.

[12] Note that the U.S. Department of Justice Antitrust Division has echoed a similar view in Shapiro's 'Antitrust in Network Industries' Address, supra note 10: 'This is Schumpeterian "creative destruction" at work to deliver ever-better products to consumers. The single most important goal of antitrust in network industries is to insure that competition from new products and new technologies is not stifled'.

[13] For a development of a similar formal economic expression of the notion that a dynamic model is the correct model applying to innovative industries, see James Bessen and Eric Maskin, '*Sequential Innovation, Patents and Imitation*' (Cambridge, MA: Massachusetts Institute of Technology, Working Paper, 1997) at 12 et seq, available at http://www.researchoninnovation.org/patent.pdf (January 10, 2003). Note that the dynamic model developed there takes a different spin from the one developed in this study – it focuses on sequential innovation, and is mathematically based.

[14] For empirical support for these notions, see David S. Evans and Richard Schmalensee, 'Some Economic Aspects of Antitrust Analysis in Dynamically Competitive Industries', Working Paper No. 8268, National Bureau of Economic Research 4–7 (May 2001), available at http://www.nber.org/papers/w8268.pdf (January 10, 2003).

[15] See, for example: Steven C. Salop and R. Craig Romaine, *Preserving Monopoly: Economic Analysis, Legal Standards, and Microsoft*, 7 Geo. Mason U. L. Rev. 617, 654–5, 663–4 (1999); Ronald A. Cass and Keith N. Hylton, *Preserving Competition: Economic Analysis, Legal Standards and Microsoft*, 8 Geo. Mason U. L. Rev. 1, 36–9 (1999); and Shelanski and Sidak, supra note 2 at 6–7.

[16] See: Harold Demsetz, *Why Regulate Utilities*?, 11 J. L. & Econ. 55, 57 & n.7 (1968); David Friedman, *Standards as Intellectual Property: An Economic Approach*, 19 U. Dayton L. Rev. 1109, 1121 (1994); Nicholas Economides and Frederick Flyer, 'Compatibility and Market Structure for Network Goods', Discussion Paper EC-98-02, Stern School of Business, New York University (1998), available at http://www.stern.nyu.edu/networkds/98-02.pdf (January 10, 2003). For an original economic review of these issues see Eduardo Engel, Ronald Fischer and Alexander Galetovic, 'Competition in or for the Field: Which is Better?', NBER Working Paper No. w8869 (April 2002) available at http://papers.nber.org/papers/W8869 (January 10, 2003).

[17] See, for example, Joel Klein and Preeta Bansal, *International Antitrust Enforcement in the Computer Industry*, 41 Vill. L. Rev. 173, 178 (1996).

[18] See: Joel Klein, Statement Before the Antitrust, Business Rights and Competition Subcommittee, Committee on the Judiciary, United States Senate, March 22, 2000; Robert Pitofsky, 'Antitrust Analysis in High Tech Industries: A 19th Century Discipline Addresses 21st Century Problems', Prepared Remarks for the American Bar Association Section of Antitrust Law's Antitrust Issues in High Tech Industries Workshop, February 25–26 1999; and Rubinfeld, supra note 9.

[19] See, for example, Shelanski and Sidak, supra note 2 at 11–12 (the argument developed in reliance on Schumpeterian notions of competition through innovation). Another argument made in this regard is that very high static market shares in these industries are often naturally occurring and not the result of foul play, which is quoted as another reason for antitrust to adopt a hands-off policy in these areas (see, for example, Economides, supra note 7 at 11.

[20] Robert J. Barro, *Why the Antitrust Cops Should Lay Off High Tech*, Business Week, August 17, 1998, at 20. See also the testimony of Marshall Phelps of IBM at the FTC Hearings on

Global and Innovation-based Competition, November 30, 1995 where he noted that 'one could assert that the industry has a built-in remedial force. Occasionally, some companies might acquire inappropriate power. But the inexorable march of technology generally has made their grip transitory'. Note that this argument is similar to the extreme Austrian view cited earlier in this study, see Chapter 2, p. 65 and Chapter 3, page 106 (especially endnote 81).

[21] Mark A. Lemley, *Antitrust and the Internet Standardization Problem*, 28 Conn. L. Rev. 1041, 1042–3 (1996) (developing this argument in the context of the Internet).

[22] For another example of a middle-road approach, see A. Douglas Melamed, *Does Regulation Promote Efficiency in Network Industries? Network Industries and Antitrust*, 23 Harv. J. L. & Pub. Pol'y 147 (1999).

[23] See Chapter 3, Section 3.4.2.

[24] See Rubinfeld, supra note 6, section II.A (discussing the relatively greater capacity of a monopolist in high-tech industries to negatively affect economic performance through anticompetitive conduct).

[25] See Lemley, supra note 21 at 1068 ('In this case the monopolist may have some legitimate claim that its monopoly has been "thrust upon it" and is therefore not illegal under the rule of *United States v. Aluminum Co. of America* [148 F.2d 416, 429 (2d Cir. 1945)]').

[26] See: Shelanski and Sidak, supra note 2 at 8; Paul Klemperer, *Competition When Consumers Have Switching Costs: An Overview*, 62 Rev. Econ. Stat. 515 (1995); Joseph Farrell, *Standardization and Intellectual Property*, 30 Jurimetrics J. 35, 43 (1989); and Michael Katz and Carl Shapiro, *Systems Competition and Network Effects*, 8 J. Econ. Persp. 93, 103–4 (1994).

[27] One good example of this phenomenon was observed by Judge Jackson in the *Microsoft* case, see *U.S. v. Microsoft Corporation*, 98 CIV 1232 (TPJ), Findings of Fact, November 5, 1999 para. 30.

[28] This term was coined by Professor Economides, see Nicholas Economides, *The Economics of Networks*, 16 Int'l J. of Indus. Org. 673, 5 (1996).

[29] See, for example: Lemley, supra note 21; and Sean P. Gates, *Standards, Innovation, and Antitrust: Integrating Innovation Concerns into the Analysis of Collaborative Standard Setting*, 47 Emory L. J. 583, 595 (1998). Most of the literature seems to agree that this effect is an anticompetitive one. For a unique opposite notion suggesting that this effect benefits consumers, see Richard B. McKenzie and Dwight R. Lee, *How Digital Economics Revises Antitrust Thinking*, 46 Antitrust Bull. 253 (2001), under the section entitled 'The benefits of switching costs and lock-ins' (footnote 41 and accompanying text).

[30] See Evans and Schmalensee, supra note 14 at 10.

[31] The term 'open source software' describes software over which no one company has proprietary control.

[32] For example, a new product versus an upgrade product, or a home edition of a product as opposed to its professional edition.

[33] For a detailed account of these considerations, see, for example, Stephen Shankland, 'Linux hits Microsoft Where it Hurts' (January 28, 1999), available at http://news.com.com/2100-1001-220845.html (May 22, 2003). Note that there are many different distributions of Linux available, and indeed they are not all free. Consumers often pay to get a Linux OS in a nice box with documents and support (for example, RedHat Linux which is the lead distribution sells for about $30–$40).

[34] For more on this notion of 'applications barrier to entry' see testimonies of the government's two economic experts in the Microsoft case: *U.S. v. Microsoft Corporation*, Franklin M. Fisher, Direct Testimony filed October 14, 1998 ¶14 available at http://www.usdoj.gov/atr/cases/f2000/2057.pdf (January 10, 2003); *U.S. v. Microsoft Corporation*, Frederick R. Warren-Boulton, Direct Testimony filed November 18 1998 ¶¶ 53–4, available at http://www.usdoj.gov/atr/cases/f2000/2079.htm#footbody_27 (January 10, 2003).

[35] *Addamax Corp. v. Open Software Foundation, Inc.*, 888 F. Supp. 274, 282 (D. Mass. 1995); 1995 U.S. Dist. LEXIS 7805; 1995-1 Trade Cas. (CCH) P 71,036. Section V-A-1 ('it is clear that the effects of market standardization on the computer industry are extraordinarily difficult to gauge').

[36] James Anton and Dennis Yao, *Standard Setting Consortia Antitrust and High Technology Industries*, 64 Antitrust L. J. 247, 251 (1995) (citing *U.S. v. Reality Multi-List*, 29 F.2d 1351, 1375 (5th Cir. 1980)).

[37] Leeds, supra note 5 at 644, citing Jack E. Brown, *Technology Joint Ventures to Set Standards of Define Interfaces*, 61 Antitrust L. J. 921, 922–3 (1993); Gates, supra note 29 at 598.

[38] See Leeds, supra note 5 at 644.

[39] See Chapter 3, in the preliminary part of Section 3.3.2.

[40] See Leeds, supra note 5 at 644. For another perspective on how standards can promote efficiency, see Brown, supra note 37 at 924.

[41] See Chapter 3, Section 3.2.

[42] For support of this view, see the testimony of William Baxter at the Federal Trade Commission's Hearings on Global and Innovation-based Competition (November 30, 1995). Professor Baxter expressed his belief that 'people who make decisions in these highly experimental technology, cutting edge industries, tend to behave as risk preferrers' (the transcript of the hearings is available through the FTC web site at http://www.ftc.gov/opp/gic.htm (May 9, 2002).

[43] Leeds, supra note 5 at 646–8.

[44] See Chapter 1, note 38 and surrounding text pages.

[45] These notions were developed by Professor Lande; see: Robert H. Lande, *Chicago's False Foundation: Wealth Transfers (Not Just Efficiency) Should Guide Antitrust*, 58 Antitrust L. J. 631 (1989); Robert H. Lande, *The Rise and (Coming) Fall of Efficiency as the Ruler of Antitrust*, 33 Antitrust Bull. 429 (1988); and Robert H. Lande, *Wealth Transfers as the Original and Primary Concern of Antitrust: The Efficiency Interpretation Challenged*, Hastings L. J. 65 (1982).

[46] Leeds, supra note 5 at 648. On the innovation-inducing effect of standards, see also: David McGowan, *Innovation, Uncertainty, and Stability in Antitrust Law*, 16 Berkeley Tech. L. J. 729 (2001); and Joseph Farrell and Michael L. Katz, *The Effects of Antitrust and Intellectual Property Law on Compatibility and Innovation*, 43 Antitrust Bull. 609 (1998).

[47] See Leeds, supra note 5 at 648.

[48] Id.

[49] See: Leeds, supra note 5 at 649, quoting the U.S. Dept. of Justice *Antitrust Guide Concerning Research Joint Ventures* 11–12 (1980); Gates, supra note 29 at 605–6; and Lemley and McGowan, supra note 1 at 517–18. For more on injury to innovation as an antitrust injury, see McGowan, supra note 46 at 765–9.

[50] Similar notions have been mentioned earlier in this study, see Chapter 1, p. 13.

[51] See supra note 20.

[52] Leeds, supra note 5 at 649.

[53] See Leeds, supra note 5 at 649–50. It should be noted that economic analysis that focuses on efficiency may take an opposite view and characterize product differentiation as undesirable to the extent that the variety created is inefficient. See, for example, Albert N. Link, *Market Structure and Voluntary Product Standards*, 15 Applied Econ. 393 (1983).

[54] See: Leeds, supra note 5 at 650–51; and William J. Curran III, *Mystery or Magic? The Intriguing Interface of Antitrust Law and Today's Information Technologies*, 43 Antitrust Bull. 775, 781–2 (1998), where in section III Curran discusses a practical example of such a scenario – the ASME case.

[55] Joseph A. Schumpeter, *Capitalism, Socialism, and Democracy* 81–6 (New York and London: Harper & Row 1942).

[56] Schumpeter, id. at 83.

[57] See Adam Smith's famous quote: 'people of the same trade seldom meet together, even for merriment and diversion, but the conversation ends in conspiracy against the public, or in some contrivance to raise prices', Adam Smith, *An Inquiry into the Nature and Causes of the Wealth of Nations* 145 (R.H. Campbell and A.S. Skinner eds, Oxford: Oxford University Press 1976). On collaborative standard-setting activity that invokes Section 1 of the Sherman Act, see: Gates, supra note 29 at 600; and Lemley, supra note 21 at 1079–83.

[58] See: *Addamax v. Open Software Foundation, Inc.*, 888 F. Supp. 274, 281, 284 (D. Mass. 1995); *Addamax Corp. v. Open Software Foundation, Inc.*, 964 F. Supp. 549 (D. Mass. 1997); *Addamax Corp. v. Open Software Foundation, Inc..*, 152 F.3d 48 (1st Cir. 1998); *Allied Tube & Conduit Co. v. Indian Head, Inc.*, 486 U.S. 492, 500 (1988); *American Society of Mechanical Engineers, Inc. v. Hydrolevel Corp.*, 456 U.S. 556, 570–71 (1982); and *American Society of Sanitary Engineering* 106 F.T.C. 324 (1985).

[59] See *Berkey Photo, Inc. v. Eastman Kodak Co.*, 603 F.2d 263, at 286–7 (2d Cir. 1979), cert. denied 444 U.S. 1093 (1980) where the court admitted that antitrust policy is incapable of determining whether newly-introduced standards indeed improve technology and are hence pro-competitive, or are rather anticompetitive in the sense that they inhibit rival innovation.

[60] See, for example: Curran, supra note 54; Lemley and McGowan, supra note 1; and Shane Greenstein, *Markets, Standards, and the Information Infrastructure*, IEEE Micro, December 1993.

[61] *Dell Computer Corp.*; Consent Agreement with Analysis to Aid Public Comment (November 22, 1995) 60 FR 57870, 1995 WL 688383 (F.R.) (hereinafter: Proposed Decision).

[62] *In the matter of Dell Computer Corporation, Consent and Order* (May 20, 1996) (hereinafter: Final Decision), 121 F.T.C. 616 (1996), 1996 WL 350997 (F.T.C.). A summary of the Final Decision is available at http://www.ftc.gov/opa/1996/9606/dell2.htm (January 10, 2003).

[63] See Final Decision, id. at the preamble, second para.

[64] The discrepancies between the two documents are highlighted in the dissenting opinion, see Final Decision, supra note 62, Dissenting Statement of Commissioner Mary L. Azcuenga in Dell Computer Corporation, Section VI, which also expresses considerable reservations as to the validity of some of these additional facts.

[65] A computer bus is a pathway that carries data from one part of a computer to another. A local bus is a high-speed data bus that connects directly, or almost directly, to the computer's central processing unit (CPU), and allows for exchange of information between the CPU and the computer's peripheral devices, such as a hard disk drive, a video display terminal, or a modem. A local bus is used for data that requires especially fast transfer speeds, such as video data. Thus, the purpose of the standard was to standardize the hardware interface of peripherals to a high-speed bus (see: Proposed Decision, supra note 61, first para. of the complaint; and Final Decision, supra note 62, paras four and five of the complaint available at http://www.vesa.org/dload/summary/sumvlbus.htm (January 10, 2003). See also under 'bus' and 'local bus' at the online encyclopedia of computer technology available at http://www.pcwebopedia.com (January 10, 2003).

[66] See: Proposed Decision, supra note 61, paras 2 and 3 of the complaint; and Final Decision, supra note 62, paras 6 and 7.

[67] Available at http://www.vesa.org/dload/summary/sumvlbus.htm (January 10, 2003).

[68] See: Proposed Decision, supra note 61, para. 2; and Final Decision, supra note 62, para. 6.

[69] Final Decision, supra note 62, Order, Section IV.

[70] Final Decision, supra note 62, Statement of the Federal Trade Commission, footnote 2.

[71] Id. at footnote 3.

[72] Final Decision, supra note 62, Complaint, para. 9.

[73] Final Decision, supra note 62, Statement of the Federal Trade Commission, end of para. 9.

[74] Id., para. 4.

[75] Id., para. 8.

[76] Id., paras 6 and 7.

[77] Final Decision, supra note 62, Order, Sections II and III.

[78] Id., Section IV.

[79] The dissenting statement extends over 12 of the Final Decision's 19 pages (thus is preamble, complaint, statement of the majority, and order fit altogether into seven pages).

[80] See Final Decision, supra note 62, Dissenting Statement of Commissioner Mary L. Azcuenga in Dell Computer Corporation, para. 2 of the preamble.

[81] Id., Section II, para. 1.

[82] The dissenting statement did acknowledge the majority statement claim mentioned earlier, according to which once the VL bus standard became widely accepted it effectively conferred market power upon Dell as the patentee. However, it dismisses the soundness and significance of this claim since the majority statement failed to identify the relevant market in which the asserted market power was conferred. Furthermore, it points out a lack of causal connection as the majority opinion did not allege that Dell did anything to acquire the said market power (see Final Decision, supra note 62, Dissenting Statement of Commissioner Mary L. Azcuenga in Dell Computer Corporation, Section III, para. 2).

[83] Id., Section II, para. 2.

[84] Id., Section III, para. 1.

[85] Commissioner Azcuenga's statement interprets the majority statement as imposing strict liability. From reading the majority statement and complaint, it remains unclear whether this reading is indeed accurate.

[86] See Proposed Decision, supra note 61, Dissenting Statement of Commissioner Mary L. Azcuenga in Dell Computer Corporation, para. 1.

[87] See id., para. 4.

[88] See the Final Decision, supra note 62, Dissenting Statement of Commissioner Mary L. Azcuenga in Dell Computer Corporation, Section III, para. 1.

[89] See Final Decision, supra note 62, Dissenting Statement of Commissioner Mary L. Azcuenga in Dell Computer Corporation, Section III, para. 3.

[90] See Final Decision, supra note 62, Dissenting Statement of Commissioner Mary L. Azcuenga in Dell Computer Corporation, Section IV.

[91] Section 5.4.1, second Subsection, above.

[92] Chapter 3, pp. 94–7.

[93] The following review is based on a number of web-based resources on the history of computer hardware that are available at http://www.cyberwalker.net/columns/sep97/090497.html; http://wombat.doc.ic.ac.uk/foldoc/foldoc.cgi?EISA; http://www.ora.com/reference/dictionary/ (January 10, 2003). For a more detailed and concise overview of the different computer buses see under the search term 'bus' that is available at http://www.ora.com/reference/dictionary/tsearch.cgi (January 10, 2003).

[94] See Chapter 3, p. 93.

[95] See Shelanski and Sidak, supra note 2 at 11–12 (discussing Schumpeterian competition, which proceeds 'sequentially over time rather than simultaneously across a market'). A good demonstration of the fast pace of development in this industry is found in Moore's Law. Moore's Law is an observation made in 1965 by Gordon Moore, co-founder of Intel, that the number of transistors per square inch on integrated circuits had doubled every year since the integrated circuit was invented. Moore predicted that this trend would continue for the

foreseeable future. In subsequent years, the pace slowed down a bit, but data density has doubled approximately every 18 months, and this is the current definition of the law Moore himself has blessed. Most experts, including Moore himself, expect the law to hold for at least another two decades. On Moore's Law, see any dictionary of computer and Internet technology, for example, http://www.webopedia.com/ (May 23, 2002).

[96] See Lemley and McGowan, supra note 1 at 518.

[97] See Chapter 3, Section 3.2.2.

[98] In this chapter, pp. 172–3.

[99] See: Gates, supra note 29 at 609–12; and Lemley and McGowan, supra note 1 at 498–9.

[100] James F. Rill seems to have captured the gist of these sentiments in speaking of the 'protectionist elements of the trade-driven academics … enforcers and policymakers' (see James F. Rill, Testimony at FTC Hearings on Global and Innovation-based Competition, November 12, 1995, available at http://www.ftc.gov/opp/global.htm (January 10, 2003).

[101] See Chapter 3, p. 104.

Postscript

This study looked into the troubled twilight zone in which competition and intellectual property rights are at odds with each other. The theoretical, let alone the practical, solution to scenarios of antitrust-IPR clashes has always been a challenging one. As this problematic realm is now entering its second century, not only does it not seem to draw closer to any theoretical rapprochement than before, but on the practical side its scope actually seems to be growing as both doctrines are gaining ground in today's markets. On the one hand, antitrust enforcement is spreading around the globe as more and more countries adopt antitrust rules, and international antitrust harmonization initiatives gather pace (for example, the International Competition Network and the OECD Global Forum on Competition). On the other hand, the importance of intellectual property rights is also on the rise. IPRs seem to play an ever-increasing role in today's high-technology industries, and to demonstrate a process of spreading around the globe through international treaties such as the WTO–TRIPS agreement as well as the growth of industries that are rich in IPRs.

In light of the complexity and magnitude of these issues, they are not likely to be resolved in one study, and probably not even in many studies. This study merely highlighted and expanded on a number of specific areas within this realm. First, it reviewed the theoretical origins of this conflict. Second, it developed a notion of antitrust as a property institution, which may embrace interesting implications on these issues. And finally, the main exercise of this study has been to promote a dynamic antitrust model as an analytical instrument for resolving unilateral antitrust–IP conflict scenarios. The suggested analysis model was based on the notions of the Austrian school of economics. It was suggested that such a dynamic analysis is better tailored for the considerations that arise in these contexts than the traditional antitrust analysis, which relied on positive correlation between static market share and market power. Its advantages over the traditional model in evaluating IP–antitrust conflict cases, as were fully demonstrated throughout the book, seem promising indeed.

The last two chapters of the study, which applied the suggested model to actual cases, have implied that the suggested dynamic analysis model is more than a mere theoretical notion. It can in fact be used as a practical evaluation tool for difficult antitrust–IP cases. It is hoped that readers of the book recognize the benefits of the suggested model, from both its theoretical as well as its practical angle, as a viable and pragmatic instrument. Furthermore, it is hoped that this study will earn the correct notions of the Austrian school of economics some of the overdue consideration they truly deserve.

Bibliography

LITERATURE AND DOCUMENTS

Ackerman, Susan Rose, *Inalienability and the Theory of Property Rights*, 85 Colum. L. Rev. 931 (1985).

Adams, Walter and Brock, James, *The Bigness Complex* (New York: Pantheon Books 1986).

Addanki, Sumanth, 'Should Antitrust Enforcers Rely on Potential Competition Analysis or the Concept of Innovation Markets?', Testimony at the Federal Trade Commission Hearings on Global and Innovation-based Competition (October 25, 1995), available at http://www.ftc.gov (January 10, 2003).

Aghion, Philippe and Howitt, Peter, 'A Schumpeterian Perspective on Growth and Innovation', in *Advances in Economics and Econometrics: Theory and Applications* (David Kreps and Ken Wallis eds, Cambridge: Cambridge University Press 1997).

Alchian, Armen A. and Kessel, Reuben A., 'Competition, Monopoly, and the Pursuit of Money', in *Aspects of Labor Economics* 157 (Princeton, NJ: Princeton University Press 1962).

Alexander, Daniel and Mellor, James, *Current Developments: EC Law*, 44 I. C. L. Q. 712 (1995).

Alexander, Gregory, *Commodity and Propriety: Competing Visions of Property in American Legal Thought 1776–1970* (Chicago, IL: University of Chicago Press 1997).

Anton, James and Yao, Dennis, *Standard Setting Consortia Antitrust and High Technology Industries*, 64 Antitrust L. J. 247 (1995).

Areeda, Phillip E. and Hovenkamp, Herbert, *Antitrust Law: An Analysis of Antitrust Principles and Their Application* (New York: Aspen Law & Business, 2nd edn 2000).

Areeda, Phillip and Kaplow, Louis, *Antitrust Analysis – Problems, Text, Cases* (New York: Aspen Law & Business, 5th ed. 1997).

Armentano, Dominick T., *The Myths of Antitrust* (New Rochelle, NY: Arlington House 1972).

Armentano, Dominick T., *Antitrust Policy: The Case for Repeal* (Washington, DC: Cato Institute 1986).

Armentano, Dominick T., *Antitrust and Monopoly: Anatomy of a Policy Failure* (San Francisco, CA: The Independent Institute, 2nd edn 1990).

Arrow, Kenneth J., 'Economic Welfare and the Allocation of Resources for Invention', in *The Rate and Direction of Inventive Activity: Economic and Social Factors* (Princeton: NBER, Princeton University Press 609, 614–15 (1962).

Arrow, Kenneth J., 'Economic Welfare and the Allocation of Resources for Innovation', in *Essays in the Theory of Risk-bearing* 144 (NY: North-Holland, 3rd edn 1976).

Arthur, Thomas C., *The Costly Quest for Perfect Competition: Kodak and Nonstructural Market Power,* 69 N.Y.U. L. Rev. 1 (1994).

Austin, John, *Lectures on Jurisprudence* (Robert Campbell ed., London: J. Murray 1911).

Bain, Joe S., *Barriers to New Competition* (Cambridge, MA: Harvard University Press 1956).

Bain, Joe S., *Industrial Organization* (New York: John Wiley, 2nd edn 1968).

Baker, Jonathan B., *Promoting Innovation Competition Through the Aspen/Kodak Rule*, 7 Geo. Mason U. L. Rev. 495 (1999).

Baldwin, William L. and Scott, John T., *Market Structure and Technological Change* (Chur, Switzerland: Harwood Academic 1987).

Balto, David and Pitofsky, Robert, *Antitrust and High-tech Industries: The New Challenge*, 43 Antitrust Bull. 583 (1998).

Barro, Robert J., 'Why the Antitrust Cops Should Lay Off High Tech', *Business Week*, August 17, 1998.

Baumol, William J., *Entrepreneurship in Economic Theory*, 58 Am. Econ. Rev. 66 (1968).

Baumol, William J. and Ordover, Janusz A., 'Antitrust: Source of Dynamic and Static Inefficiencies?', in *Antitrust Innovation and Competitiveness* (Thomas M. Jorde and David J. Teece eds, New York: Oxford University Press 1992).

Baxter, William, Testimony at the Federal Trade Commission's Hearings on Global and Innovation-based Competition (November 30, 1995), available at http://www.ftc.gov/opp/gic.htm (January 10, 2003).

Becker, Gary S., *The Economics of Discrimination* (Chicago, IL: Chicago University Press 1957).

Becker, Lawrence C., *Deserving to Own Intellectual Property*, 68 Chi.-Kent L. Rev. 609 (1993).

Bentham, Jeremy, *Of Laws in General* (H. Hart ed., London: Athlone Press 1970).

Besen, Stanley M. and Raskind, Leo J., *An Introduction to the Law and Economics of Intellectual Property,* 5 (1) J. Econ. Persp. 3 (1991).

Bessen, James and Maskin, Eric, '*Sequential Innovation, Patents and Imitation*' (Cambridge, MA: Massachusetts Institute of Technology, Working Paper, 1997), available online at http://www.researchoninnovation.org/patent.pdf (January 10, 2003).

Blackstone, William, *Commentaries on the Laws of England* (1765, Chicago, IL: University of Chicago Press, with an Introduction by Stanley N. Katz 1979).

Blake, Harlan M. and Jones, William K., *Toward a Three-Dimensional Antitrust Policy*, 65 Colum. L. Rev, 422 (1965).

Block, Walter, *Total Repeal of Antitrust Legislation: A Critique of Bork, Brozen, and Posner,* 8 (1) Rev. of Austrian Econ. 35 (1995).

Boettke, Peter J. (ed.), *The Elgar Companion to Austrian Economics* (Aldershot, UK and Brookfield, USA: Edward Elgar 1994).

Boettke, Peter J., 'What is Wrong with Neoclassical Economics (and What is Still Wrong with Austrian Economics?)', in *Beyond Neoclassical Economics: Heterodox Approaches to Economic Theory* 22 (Fred E. Foldvary ed., Cheltenham, UK and Brookfield, USA: Edward Elgar 1996).

Bork, Robert H., *Legislative Intent and the Policy of the Sherman Act*, 9 J. L. and Econ. 7 (1966).

Bork, Robert H., in E. William Barnett et al., *Panel Discussion: Merger Enforcement and Practice,* 50 Antitrust L. J. 233 (1981).

Bork, Robert H., *The Antitrust Paradox: A Policy at War with Itself* (New York: Free Press 1993 – a reprint of the 1978 edition with a new introduction and epilogue).

Bork, Robert H., 'Judicial Precedent and the New Economics', in *Antitrust Policy in Transition: The Convergence of Law and Economics* 16 (Chicago, IL: American Bar Association 1984).

Bouckaert, Boudewijn, *What is Law?,* 13 Harv. J. of L. and Pub. Pol'y 775 (1990).

Boudreaux, Donald J. and DiLorenzo, Thomas J., *The Protectionist Roots of Antitrust*, 6 (1) Rev. of Austrian Econ. 81 (1993).

Bowman, Ward S. Jr., *Patent and Antitrust Law: A Legal and Economic Appraisal* (Chicago, IL: University of Chicago Press 1973).

Brandeis, Louis D., *Other People's Money* (Washington, DC: National Home Library Foundation 1933).

Brennan, Timothy J., *Mistaken Elasticities and Misleading Rules* (Landes and Posner on Market Power: Four Responses), 95 Harv. L. Rev. 1849 (1982).

Brennan, Timothy J., *Copyright, Property, and the Right to Deny*, 68 Chi.-Kent L. Rev. 675 (1993).

Brown, Jack E., *Technology Joint Ventures to Set Standards of Define Interfaces*, 61 Antitrust L. J. 921 (1993).

Burke, Terry, Genn-Bash, Angela and Haines, Brian, *Competition in Theory and Practice* (Kent: Croom Helm 1988).

Burling, James C., Lee, William F. and Krug, Anita K., *Symposium: The Antitrust Duty to Deal and Intellectual Property Rights*, 24 Iowa J. Corp. L. 527 (1999).

Calabresi, Guido and Melamed, A. Douglas, *Property Rules, Liability Rules, and Inalienability: One View of the Cathedral*, 85 Harv. L. Rev. 1089 (1972).

Calamari, John D. and Perillo, Joseph M., *The Law of Contracts* (St. Paul, MN: Hornbook Series, 4th edn 1998).

Calandrillo, Steve P., *An Economic Analysis of Property Rights in Information: Justifications and Problems of Exclusive Rights, Incentives to Generate Information, and the Alternative of a Government-run Reward System*, 9 Fordham Intell. Prop. Media and Ent. L. J. 301 (1998).

Caldwell, Bruce J. and Boehm, Stephan, *Austrian Economics: Tensions and New Directions* (Boston/Dordrecht/London: Kluwer Academic 1992).

Calvani, Terry, *Rectangles and Triangles: A Response to Mr. Lande,* 58 Antitrust L. J. 657 (1989).

Carter, Stephen L., *Does It Matter Whether Intellectual Property is Property?*, 68 Chi.-Kent L. Rev. 715 (1993).

Carvalho, Nuno Pires de, *The Primary Function of Patents*, 1 U. Ill. J. L. Tech. and Pol'y 25 (2001).

Cass, Ronald A. and Hylton, Keith N., *Preserving Competition: Economic Analysis, Legal Standards and Microsoft*, 8 Geo. Mason U. L. Rev. 1 (1999).

Chamberlin, Edward H., *The Theory of Monopolistic Competition: A Reorientation of the Theory of Value* (Cambridge, MA: Harvard University Press 1933).

Christman, John, *The Myth of Property* (New York: Oxford University Press 1994).

Coase, Ronald H., *The Problem of Social Cost*, 3 J. of Law and Econ. 1 (1960).

Cohen, Joel M. and Burke, Arthur J., *An Overview of the Antitrust Analysis of Suppression of Technology*, 66 Antitrust L. J. 421 (1998).

Cohen, Wesley M., Nelson, Richard R. and Walsh, John, 'Protecting Their Intellectual Assets: Appropriability Conditions and Why U.S. Manufacturing Firms Patent (or Not)', NBER Working Paper No. w7552 (February 2000) available at http://papersdev.nber.org/papers/W7552 (January 10, 2003).

Cohler, Charles B. and Pearson, Hilary E., *Software Interfaces, Intellectual Property and Competition Policy*, 16 Eur. Intell. Prop. L. Rev. 434 (1994).
Coleman, Jules L., *Markets Morals and the Law* (Cambridge: Cambridge University Press 1988).
Comanor, William S., *Vertical Territorial and Customer Restrictions: White Motor and Its Aftermath*, 81 Harv. L. Rev. 1419 (1968).
Cordato, Roy, *Subjective Value, Time Passage, and the Economics of Harmful Effects*, 12 Hamline L. Rev. 229 (1989).
Cornes, Richard and Sandler, Todd, *The Theory of Externalities, Public Good, and Club Goods* (New York: Cambridge University Press, 2nd edn 1996).
Cowen, Tyler, *Law as a Public Good*, 8 Econ. & Phil. 249 (1992).
Crespi , Gregory Scott, *Exploring the Complicationist Gambit: An Austrian Approach to the Economic Analysis of Law*, 73 Notre Dame L. Rev. 315 (1998).
Crew, Eugene, *Symposium: Antitrust and the Suppression of Technology in the United States and Europe: Is there a Remedy?*, 66 Antitrust L. J. 415 (1998).
Croskery, Patrick, *Institutional Utilitarianism and Intellectual Property*, 68 Chi.-Kent L. Rev. 631 (1993).
Crowther, Peter, *Compulsory Licensing of Intellectual Property Rights*, 20 Europ. L. Rev. 521 (1995).
Curran, William J. III, *Mystery or Magic? The Intriguing Interface of Antitrust Law and Today's Information Technologies*, 43 Antitrust Bull. 775 (1998).
Czarnetzky, John M., *Time, Uncertainty, and the Law of Corporate Reorganization*, 67 Fordham L. Rev. 2939 (1999).
Dam, Kenneth W., *The Economic Underpinnings of Patent Law*, 23 J. Legal Stud. 247 (1994).
Dasgupta, Partha S. and David, Paul A., *Resource Allocation and the Institutions of Science* (Stanford, CA: Stanford University 1991).
DeBow, Michael E., *Markets, Government Intervention, and the Role of Information: An 'Austrian School' Perspective, with an Application to Merger Regulation*, 14 Geo. Mason U. L. Rev. 31 (1991).
De Jasay, Anthony, *Social Contract, Free Ride: A Study of the Public Goods Problem* (Oxford: Clarendon Press 1989).
Demsetz, Harold, *Toward a Theory of Property Rights*, 57 Am. Econ. Rev. Pap. & Proc. 347 (1967).
Demsetz, Harold, *Why Regulate Utilities?*, 11 J. of L. & Econ. 55 (1968).
Demsetz, Harold, *Information and Efficiency: Another Viewpoint*, 12 J. of L. & Econ. 1 (1969).
Demsetz, Harold, *Barriers to Entry*, 72 Am. Econ. Rev. 47 (1982).

Denison, Edward F., *Accounting for U.S. Economic Growth: 1929–69* (Washington, DC: Brookings Institution 1974).
Dewey, Donald, *Monopoly in Economics and Law* (Chicago, IL: Rand McNally 1959).
Dewey, Donald, *The Economic Theory of Antitrust: Science or Religion?*, 50 Va. L. Rev. 413 (1964).
Dewey, Donald, *Antitrust and Economic Theory: An Uneasy Friendship* (Book Review), 87 Yale L. J. 1516 (1978).
Dewey, Donald, *What Price Theory Can – and Cannot – Do for Antitrust*, 3 Contemp. Pol'y Issues 3 (1984–85).
Dewey, Donald, *The Antitrust Experiment in America* (New York: Columbia University Press 1990).
Dirlam, Joel B. and Kahn, Alfred E., *Fair Competition – The Law and Economics of Antitrust Policy* (Ithaca, NY: Cornell University Press 1954).
Dixon, Paul R. and Mueller, Charles E., *Antitrust Law: The Magna Carta of the Free Enterprise System*, 27 Antitrust L. & Econ. Rev. 25 (1996).
Dixon, Paul R. and Mueller, Charles E., *Competition: The Moral Justification for Capitalism*, 27 Antitrust L. & Econ. Rev. 11 (1996).
Dolan, Edwin, *The Foundations of Modern Austrian Economics* (Kansas City: Sheed & Ward 1976).
Drahos, Peter, *A Philosophy of Intellectual Property* (Aldershot, UK: Dartmouth 1996).
Dyson, Esther, speech at the Federal Trade Commission hearings held in fall 1995 (November 29, 1995) available at http://www.ftc.gov.
Easterbrook, Frank H., *Intellectual Property is Still Property*, 13 Harv. J. L. & Pub. Pol'y 108 (1990).
Eatwell, John, Milgate, Murray and Newman, Peter, *A Dictionary of Economics* (London: Macmillan 1987).
Economides, Nicholas, *The Economics of Networks*, 16 Int'l J. of Indus. Org. 673 (1996).
Economides, Nicholas and Flyer, Frederick, 'Compatibility and Market Structure for Network Goods', Discussion Paper EC-98-02, Stern School of Business, N.Y.U. (1998) available at http://www.stern.nyu.edu/networkds/98-02.pdf.
Economides,Nicholas, *United States v. Microsoft: A Failure of Antitrust in the New Economy*, 32 U. West. L.A. L. Rev. 3 (2001).
Edgeworth, Francis Y., *Papers Relating to Political Economy* (London: Macmillan 1925).
Ekelund, Robert B., Jr. and Saurman, David S., *Advertising and the Market Process: A Modern Economic View* (San Francisco, CA: Pacific Research Institute for Public Policy 1988).

Elzinga, Kenneth G. and Breit, William, *The Antitrust Penalties: A Study in Law and Economics* (New Haven, CT: Yale University Press 1976).

Elzinga, Kenneth G., 'Unmasking Monopoly: Four Types of Economic Evidence', in *Economics and Antitrust Policy* (Robert J. Larner and James W. Meehan Jr. eds, Westport, CT: Quorum Books 1989).

Engel, Eduardo, Fischer, Ronald and Galetovic, Alexander, 'Competition in or for the Field: Which is Better?', NBER Working Paper No.w8869 (April 2002) available at http://papers.nber.org/papers/W8869 (January 10, 2003).

Epstein, Michael A., *Epstein on Intellectual Property* (New York: Aspen Law & Business, 4th edn 1994).

Epstein, Richard A., *Takings: Private Property and the Power of Eminent Domain* (Cambridge, MA: Harvard University Press 1985).

Epstein, Richard A., *Why Restrain Alienation?*, 85 Colum. L. Rev. 970 (1985).

Evans, David S. and Schmalensee, Richard, 'Some Economic Aspects of Antitrust Analysis in Dynamically Competitive Industries', Working Paper No. 8268, National Bureau of Economic Research (May 2001), available at http://www.nber.org/papers/w8268.pdf (January 10, 2003).

Farnsworth, E. Allan, *Contracts* (Boston, MA: Little, Brown & Company, 2nd edn 1990).

Farrell, Joseph, *Standardization and Intellectual Property*, 30 Jurimetrics J. 35 (1989).

Farrell, Joseph and Katz, Michael L., *The Effects of Antitrust and Intellectual Property Law on Compatibility and Innovation*, 43 Antitrust Bull. 609 (1998).

Federal Trade Commission Staff, *Anticipating the 21st Century: Competition Policy in the New High-tech Global Marketplace* (May 1996), available at http://www.ftc.gov/opp/global.htm (January 10, 2003).

Festa, Lawrence T. III, Comment, Eastman Kodak Co. v. Image Technical Services, Inc.*: The Decline and Fall of the Chicago Empire?*, 68 Notre Dame L. Rev. 619 (1993).

Fischer, Stanley, Dornbusch, Rudiger and Schmalensee, Richard, *Introduction to Microeconomics* (New York: McGraw-Hill, 2nd edn 1988).

Fisher, Franklin M., McGowan, John J. and Greenwood, Joen E., *Folded, Spindled and Mutilated: Economic Analysis and U.S. v. I.B.M.* (Boston, MA: Charles River Associates 1983).

Fisher, Franklin M., Direct Testimony in *U.S. v. Microsoft Corporation* filed October 14, 1998 available at http://www.usdoj.gov/atr/cases/f2000/2057.pdf (January 10, 2003).

Fitzgerald, Darren, *Magill Revisited (Tiercé Ladbroke SA v. The Commission)*, 20 Eur. Intell. Prop. Rev. 154 (1998).

Flynn, James, *Intellectual Property and Anti-trust: EC Attitudes*, 14 Eur. Intell. Prop. Rev. 49 (1992).

Forrester, Ian S., *Software Licensing in the Light of Current EC Competition Law Considerations*, 13 Eur. Competition L. Rev. 5 (1992).

Foss, Nicolai J., 'Austrian and Post-Marshallian Economics: The Bridging Work of George Richardson', in *Economic Organization, Capabilities and Co-ordination* 138 (Nicolai J. Foss and Brian J. Loasby eds, London: Routledge 1998).

Fox, Eleanor M. and Sullivan, Lawrence A., *Antitrust Retrospective and Prospective: Where Are We Coming From? Where Are We Going?*, 62 N.Y.U. L. Rev. 936 (1987).

Franklin, Benjamin, 'Poor Richard's Almanac', in *The Sayings of Poor Richard: The prefaces, proverbs, and poems of Benjamin Franklin* (Paul Leicester Ford ed, New York: Burt Franklin Reprints 1975, reprint of the 1890 edn).

Freeman, Chris and Soete, Luc, *The Economics of Industrial Innovation* (Cambridge, MA: MIT Press 3rd edn 1997).

Friedman, David, *Standards as Intellectual Property: An Economic Approach*, 19 U. Dayton L. Rev. 1109 (1994).

Friedman, Milton, 'The Methodology of Positive Economics', in *Essays in Positive Economics* (Chicago, IL: University of Chicago Press 1953).

Friedman, Milton, *Capitalism and Freedom* (Chicago, IL: University of Chicago Press 1962).

Frischmann, Brett and Moylan, Dan, *The Evolving Common Law Doctrine of Copyright Misuse: A Unified Theory and Its Application to Software*, 15 Berkeley Tech. L. J. 865 (2000).

Fuller, Lon L., 'Means and Ends', in The Principles of Social Order: Selected Essays of Lon L. Fuller 48 (Kenneth I. Winston ed., Durham, NC: Duke University Press 1981).

Gallaway, Lowell, *Some Austrian Perspectives on Unintended Consequences,* 10 (2) Rev. of Austrian Econ. (1997), available at http://mises.org (January 10, 2003).

Gates, Sean P., *Standards, Innovation, and Antitrust: Integrating Innovation Concerns into the Analysis of Collaborative Standard Setting*, 47 Emory L. J. 583 (1998).

Gellhorn, Ernest and Kovacic, William E., *Antitrust Law and Economics in a Nutshell* (St. Paul, MN: West Publishing 4th edn, 1994).

Gilbert, Richard J. and Sunshine, Steven C., *Incorporating Dynamic Efficiency Concerns in Merger Analysis: The Use of Innovation Markets*, 63 Antitrust L. J. 569 (1995).

Gloria-Palermo, Sandye, *The Evolution of Austrian Economics: From Menger to Lachmann* (New York: Routledge 1999).

Gordon, Robert J., 'Technology and Economic Performance in the American Economy', NBER Working Paper No. w8771 (February 2002) available at http://papers.nber.org/papers/w8771 (January 10, 2003).

Gordon, Wendy J., *A Property Right in Self Expression: Equality and Individualism in the Natural Law of Intellectual Property*, 102 Yale L. J. 1533 (1993).

Gould, David M. and Gruben, William C., *The Role of Intellectual Property Rights in Economic Growth*, 48 J. of Dev. Econ. 323 (1996).

Greaves, Rosa, *Magill Est Arrivé ... RTE and* ITP v. Commission of the European Communities, 16 Eur. Competition L. Rev. 244 (1995).

Greenstein, Shane, *Markets, Standards, and the Information Infrastructure*, IEEE Micro, December 1993.

Grey, Thomas C., 'The Disintegration of Property', *in* NOMOS XXII: *Property* (J. Roland Pennock & John W. Chapman eds, 1987).

Grunzweig, Paul S., *Prohibiting the Presumption of Market Power for Intellectual Property Rights: The Intellectual Property Antitrust Protection Act of 1989*, 16 J. Corp. L. 103 (1990).

Gutterman, Allan S., *Innovation and Competition Policy* (London: Kluwer Law International 1997).

Hahn, Robert W. and Hester, Gordon L., *Marketable Permits: Lessons for Theory and Practice*, 16 Ecology L. Q. (1989).

Hanna, Ramsey, (Note) *Misusing Antitrust: The Search for Functional Copyright Misuse Standards*, 46 Stan. L. Rev. 401 (1994).

Hardin, Garrett, *The Tragedy of the Commons*, 162 Science 1243 (1968).

Hardy, I. Trotter, *Not So Different: Tangible, Intangible, Digital, and Analog Works and Their Comparison for Copyright Purposes*, 26 Dayton L. Rev. 211 (2001).

Harris, D.J., *On the Classical Theory of Competition*, 12 Cambridge J. of Econ. 139 (1988).

Hart, David M., *Antitrust and Technological Innovation*, Issues in Science and Technology 9 (Winter 1998) available at http://www.nap.edu/issues/15.2/hart.htm.

Hart, H.L.A., *The Concept of Law* (Oxford: Clarendon Press 1961).

Hayek, Friedrich A., *The Road to Serfdom* (Chicago, IL: Chicago University Press 1944, 50th Anniversary Edition 1994).

Hayek, Friedrich A., 'The Meaning of Competition', in *Individualism and Economic Order* (Chicago, IL: University of Chicago Press 1948).

Hayek, Friedrich A., *Individualism and Economic Order* (Chicago, IL: Chicago University Press, 1948).

Hayek, Friedrich A., *Law Legislation and Liberty* (Chicago, IL: University of Chicago Press 1973).

Hayek, Friedrich A., 'Competition as a Discovery Procedure', in *New Studies in Philosophy, Politics, Economics and the History of Ideas* (London: Routledge, Chicago, IL: University of Chicago Press 1978).

Hayek, Friedrich A., *New Studies in Philosophy, Politics, Economics, and the History of Ideas* (Chicago, IL: University of Chicago Press 1978).

Hayter, Dana W., *When a License is Worse than a Refusal: A Comparative Competitive Effects Standard to Judge Restrictions in Intellectual Property Licenses*, 11 Berkeley Tech. L. J. 281 (1996).

Heertje, Arnold and Perlman, Mark (eds), *Evolving Technology and Market Structure – Studies in Schumpeterian Economics* (Ann Arbor, MI: University of Michigan Press 1990).

Hegel, Georg Wilhelm Friedrich, *Philosophy of Right* (T.M. Knox trans., Oxford: Clarendon Press, 1952 1st edn, 1967 reprint) (1821).

Hicks, Sir John R., *The Theory of Monopoly* 3 Econometrica 1 (1935).

Hicks, John R., *Value and Capital* (Oxford: Clarendon Press 1939).

Hicks, John R. and Weber, Wilhelm (eds), *Carl Menger and the Austrian School of Economics* (Oxford: Clarendon 1973).

Hochman, Harold M. and Rodgers, James D., *Pareto Optimal Redistribution*, 59 Am. Econ. Rev. 542 (1969).

Hohfeld, Wesley N., *Some Fundamental Legal Conceptions as Applied in Judicial Reasoning,* 23 Yale L. J. 16 (1913) (also published as a book: Hohfeld, Wesley Newcomb, *Fundamental Legal Conceptions as Applied in Judicial Reasoning and Other Essays* (New Haven, CT: Yale University Press 1920)).

Holmes, Oliver W., *Privilege, Malice, and Intent*, 8 Harv. L. Rev. 1, 6 (1894).

Holocombe, Randall G., *A Theory of the Theory of Public Goods*, 10 (1) Rev. of Austrian Econ. 1 (1997).

Hoppe, Hans-Hermann, *The Economics and Ethics of Private Property* (Boston/Dordrecht/London: Kluwer Academic 1993).

Howitt, Peter, 'On Some Problems in Measuring Knowledge-based Growth', in *The Implications of Knowledge-based Growth for Micro-economic Policies* (Peter Howitt ed., Calgary: University of Calgary Press 1996).

Jackson, John H., *The Jurisprudence of GATT and the WTO* (Cambridge: Cambridge University Press 2000).

Jacobs, Michael S., *An Essay on the Normative Foundations of Antitrust Economics*, 74 N. C. L. Rev. 219 (1995).

Jolls, Christine, Sunstein, Cass R. and Thaler, Richard H., 'A Behavioral Approach to Law and Economics', in *Behavioral Law and Economics* (Cass R. Sunstein ed., Cambridge: Cambridge University Press 2000).

Jones , John Phillip, *When Ads Work: New Proof That Advertising Triggers Sales* (New York: Lexington Books 1994).

Jones, Nigel, *Euro-Defences: Magill Distinguished*, 20 Eur. Intell. Prop. Rev. 352 (1998).

Jorde, Thomas M. and Teece, David J. (eds), *Antitrust Innovation and Competitiveness* (New York: Oxford University Press 1992).

Jorde, Thomas M. and Teece, David J., 'Innovation, Cooperation, and Antitrust', in *Antitrust, Innovation, and Competitiveness* (Thomas M. Jorde and David J. Teece eds, New York: Oxford University Press 1992).

Kamien, Morton I. and Schwartz, Nancy L., *Market Structure and Innovation: A Survey*, 13 J. of Econ. Literature 16 (1975).

Kaplow, Louis, *The Accuracy of Traditional Market Power Analysis and a Direct Adjustment Alternative* (Landes and Posner on Market Power: Four Responses), 95 Harv. L. Rev. 1817 (1982).

Kaplow, Louis, *The Patent–Antitrust Intersection: A Reappraisal*, 97 Harv. L. Rev. 1813 (1984).

Kaplow, Louis, *Extension of Monopoly Power Through Leverage*, 85 Colum. L. Rev. 515 (1985).

Karjala, Dennis S., *Copyright Protection of Operating Software, Copyright Misuse, and Antitrust*, 9 Cornell J. L. and Pub. Pol'y 161 (1999).

Katz, Michael L. and Shapiro, Carl, *Network Externalities, Competition, and Compatibility*, 75 Am. Econ. Rev. 424 (1985).

Katz, Michael and Shapiro, Carl, *Systems Competition and Network Effects*, 8 J. Econ. Persp. 93 (1994).

Katz, Ronald S., Arnold Hart, Janet and Safer, Adam J., 'Intellectual Property v. Antitrust: A False Dilemma', in *Antitrust/Intellectual Property Claims in High Technology Markets: Litigating and Advising* (ALI-ABA Course, April 22–23, 1999).

Kaufer, Erich, *The Economics of the Patent System* (Chur, Switzerland: Harwood Academic 1988).

Kennedy, Duncan, *A Symposium of Critical Legal Study: The Role of Law in Economic Thought: Essays on the Fetishism of Commodities*, 34 Am. U. L. Rev. 939 (1985).

Keyte, James A., *Market Definition and Differentiated Products: The Need for a Workable Standard*, 63 Antitrust L. J. 697 (1995).

Kirzner, Israel M., *Competition and Entrepreneurship* (Chicago, IL: University of Chicago Press 1973).

Kirzner, Israel M., 'Uncertainty, Discovery, and Human Action: A Study of the Entrepreneurial Profile in the Misesian System', in *Method, Process and Austrian Economics: Essays in Honor of Ludwig von Mises* (Israel M. Kirzner ed., Lexington, MA: Lexington Books 1982).

Kirzner, Israel M., 'Prices, the Communication of Knowledge, and the Discovery Process', in *The Political Economy of Freedom: Essays in Honour of F.A. Hayek* (Kurt R. Leube and Albert H. Zlabinger eds, Munich and Vienna: Philosophia Verlag 1984).

Kirzner, Israel M., *Discovery and the Capitalist Process* (Chicago, IL: University of Chicago Press 1985)

Kirzner, Israel M., 'Roundaboutness, Opportunity and Austrian Economics', in *The Unfinished Agenda: Essays on the Political Economy of Government Policy in Honour of Arthur Seldon* 93 (Martin J. Anderson ed., London: Institute of Economic Affairs 1986).

Kirzner, Israel M., *Discovery, Capitalism and Distributive Justice* (Oxford: Basil Blackwell 1989).

Kirzner, Israel M., *The Meaning of the Market Process: Essays in the Development of Modern Austrian Economics* (London: Routledge 1992).

Kirzner, Israel M., 'The Limits of the Market – The Real and the Imagined', in *The Driving Force of the Market – Essays in Austrian Economics* 77 (London and New York: Routledge, 2000) (originally published in *Marktwirtschaft und Rechtsordnung* (Nomos, W. Moeschel, M.E. Streit and U. Witt eds 1994)).

Kirzner, Israel M., *Entrepreneurial Discovery and the Competitive Market Process: An Austrian Approach*, 35 J. of Econ. Literature 60 (1997).

Kirzner, Israel M., 'The Driving Force of the Market: The Idea of "Competition" in Contemporary Economic Theory and in the Austrian Theory of the Market Process', in *Why Economists Disagree* (David L. Prychitko ed., Albany, NY: State University of New York Press 1998).

Kirzner, Israel M., *The Driving Force of the Market – Essays in Austrian Economics* (Routledge: London and New York 2000).

Kirzner, Israel M., *Ludwig Von Mises: The Man and his Economics* (Wilmington, DE: ISI Books 2001).

Kitch, Edmund W., *The Nature and Function of the Patent System*, 20 J. L. & Econ. 265 (1977).

Kitch, Edmund W., *Patents: Monopolies or Property Rights?*, 8 Res. in L. & Econ. 31 (1986).

Kitch, Edmund W., 'Chicago School of Law and Economics' in *The New Palgrave Dictionary of Economics and the Law* (Peter Newman ed., New York: Stockton Press 1998).

Klein, Joel I. and Bansal, Preeta, *International Antitrust Enforcement in the Computer Industry*, 41 Vill. L. Rev. 173 (1996).

Klein, Joel I., *A. Cross-licensing and Antitrust Law,B.* U.S. v. G.E. *in the U.S. District of Montana*, 483 PLI/P 339 (1997).

Klein, Joel I., Statement Before the Antitrust, Business Rights and Competition Subcommittee Committee on the Judiciary, United States Senate, March 22, 2000.

Klein, Lawrence R., *The Keynesian Revolution* (New York: Macmillan, 2nd edn 1966).

Klemperer, Paul, *Competition When Consumers Have Switching Costs: An Overview*, 62 Rev. Econ. Stat. 515 (1995).

Knable Gotts, Ilene and Fogt, Howard W. Jr., *Clinton Administration Expresses More Than Intellectual Curiosity in Antitrust Issues Raised by Intellectual Property Licensing*, 22 AIPLA Q. J. 1 (1994).

Knowles, Dudley, *Hegel on Property and Personality*, 33 Philosophical Q. 45 (1983).

Kramer, Victor H., *The Supreme Court and Tying Arrangements: Antitrust as History*, 69 Minn. L. Rev. 1013 (1985).

Krattenmaker, Thomas G. and Salop, Steven C., *Anticompetitive Exclusion: Raising Rivals' Costs to Achieve Power Over Price*, 96 Yale L. J. 209 (1986).

Kronman, Anthony, *Paternalism and the Law of Contracts*, 92 Yale L. J. 763 (1983).

Lande, Robert H., *Wealth Transfers as the Original and Primary Concern of Antitrust: The Efficiency Interpretation Challenged*, 34 Hastings L. J. 65 (1982).

Lande, Robert H., *The Rise and (Coming) Fall of Efficiency as the Ruler of Antitrust*, 33 Antitrust Bull. 429 (1988).

Lande, Robert H., *Chicago's False Foundation: Wealth Transfers (Not Just Efficiency) Should Guide Antitrust*, 58 Antitrust L. J. 631 (1989).

Landes, William M. and Posner, Richard A., *Market Power in Antitrust Cases*, 94 Harv. L. Rev. 937 (1981).

Landes, William M., and Posner, Richard A., *An Economic Analysis of Copyright Law,* 18 J. Legal Stud. 325 (1989).

Laudien, Dieter, 'Patents and Competition', in *Intellectual Property Rights and Global Competition* (Horst Alback and Stephanie Rosenkranz eds, Berlin: Edition Sigma 1995).

Leeds, Douglas D., *Raising the Standard: Antitrust Scrutiny of Standard-setting Consortia in High Technology Industries*, 7 Fordham I. P., Media & Ent. L. J. 641 (1997).

Lemley, Mark A., *Antitrust and the Internet Standardization Problem*, 28 Conn. L. Rev. 1041 (1996).

Lemley, Mark A. and McGowan, David, *Legal Implications of Network Economic Effects*, 86 Calif. L. Rev. 479 (1998).

Lemley, Mark A., *Symposium: Standardizing Government Standard-setting Policy for Electronic Commerce*, 14 Berkeley Tech. L. J. 745 (1999).

Leopold, Aldo, *A Sand County Almanac* (New York: Oxford University Press 1966).

Letwin, William L., *The English Common Law Concerning Monopolies*, 21 U. Chi. L. Rev. 355 (1954).

Letwin, William L., *Law and Economic Policy in America – The Evolution of the Sherman Act* (New York: Random House 1965).

Levin, Richard C., Klevorick, Alvin K., Nelson, Richard R. and Winter, Sidney G., *Appropriating the Returns from Industrial Research and Development*, 3 Brookings Papers on Economic Activity 783 (M. Baily and C. Winston eds, Washington, DC: Brookings Institution 1987).

Li, David D. and Wu, Changqi, *Economic Growth and Productivity Around GATT/WTO Accessions: Evidence from the World, 1960–89*, 13th NBER East-Asian Seminar on Economics (Melbourne, Australia, June 20–22, 2002) available at http://www.nber.org/books/ease13/li-wu8-26-02.pdf (January 10, 2003).

Link, Albert N., *Market Structure and Voluntary Product Standards*, 15 Applied Econ. 393 (1983).

Littlechild, Stephen, *Austrian Economics* (Schools of Thought in Economics Series), (Aldershot, UK and Brookfield, US: Edward Elgar 1990).

Locke, John, *Two Treatises of Government* (Peter Laslett ed., Cambridge: Cambridge University Press 1988) (1690).

Lombardy, Russell, *The Myth of Market Power: Why Market Power Should Not Be Presumed When Applying Antitrust Principles to the Analysis of Tying Agreements Involving Intellectual Property*, 8 St. Thomas L. Rev. 449 (1996).

Lugard, H.H. Paul, *ECJ Upholds Magill: It Sounds Nice in Theory, But How Does it Work In Practice?*, 6 Eur. Bus. L. Rev. 231 (1995).

Macpherson, Crawford B., *The Political Theory of Possessive Individualism* (Oxford: Clarendon Press 1969).

Madison, James, '*The Federalist*, No. 43', in *The Federalist Papers* (Isaac Kramnick ed., Harmondsworth: Penguin 1987).

Maiorana, David M., *Privileged Use: Has Judge Boudin Suggested a Viable Means of Copyright Protection for the Non-literal Aspects of Computer Software in* Lotus Development Corp. v. Borland International*?*, 46 Am. U. L. Rev. 149 (1996).

Mair, Douglas and Miller, Anne G. (eds), *A Modern Guide to Economic Thought* (Cheltenham, UK and Northampton, MA, USA: Edward Elgar Publishing 1999).

Marshall, Alfred, *Principles of Economics* (London: Macmillan, 8th edn 1920) (1890).

Mas-Colell, Andreu, Whinston, Michael D. and Green, Jerry R., *Microeconomic Theory* (New York: Oxford University Press 1995).

Mason, Edward S., *Schumpeter on Monopoly and the Large Firm*, 33 Rev. of Econ. & Stat. 139 (1951).

Masten, Scot E., 'A Legal Basis for The Firm', in *The Nature of the Firm: Origins, Evolution, and Development* (Oliver E. Williamson and Sidney G. Winter eds, New York: Oxford University Press 1993).

McGowan, David, *Networks and Intention in Antitrust and Intellectual Property*, 24 J. Corp. L. 485 (1999).

McGowan, David, *Innovation, Uncertainty, and Stability in Antitrust Law*, 16 Berkeley Tech. L. J. 729 (2001).

McKenzie, Richard B. and Lee, Dwight R., *How Digital Economics Revises Antitrust Thinking*, 46 Antitrust Bull. 253 (2001).

McNulty, Paul J., *Economic Theory and the Meaning of Competition*, 82 Q. J. of Econ. 639 (1968).

Meade, James E., *The Theory of Economic Externalities – The Control of Environmental Pollution and Similar Social Costs* (Geneva: Sijthoff-Leiden 1973).

Meehan, James W. Jr. and Larner, Robert J., 'The Structural School, Its Critics, and Its Progeny: An Assessment', in *Economics and Antitrust Policy* (Robert J. Larner and James W. Meehan eds, Westport CT: Quorum Books 1989).

Melamed, A. Douglas, *Does Regulation Promote Efficiency in Network Industries? Network Industries and Antitrust*, 23 Harv. J. L. and Pub. Pol'y 147 (1999).

Menger, Carl, *Principles of Economics* (James Dingwall and Bert F. Hoselitz trans., New York: New York University Press 1981) (1871).

Menger, Carl, *Investigations Into the Method of the Social Sciences with Special Reference to Economics* (Francis J. Nock trans., Lawrence White ed., New York: New York University Press 1985) (1883).

Merges, Robert P., 'Antitrust Review of Patent Acquisitions: Property Rights, Firm Boundaries, and Organization', in *Competition Policy and Intellectual Property Rights in the Knowledge-based Economy* (Robert D. Anderson and Nancy T. Gallini eds, Calgary: University of Calgary Press 1998).

Michelman, Frank I., *Property, Utility and Fairness: Comments on the Ethical Foundations of 'Just Compensation' Law*, 80 Harv. L. Rev. 1165 (1967).

Mill, John Stuart, *On Liberty* (Elizabeth Rapaport ed., Indianapolis, IN: Hacket Pub. Co. 1978) (1859).

Miller, Clifford G., *Magill: Time to Abandon the 'Specific Subject-matter' Concept*, 16 Eur. Intell. Prop. Rev. 415 (1994).

Montgomery, William, *The Presumption of Economic Power for Patented and Copyrighted Products in Tying Arrangements*, 85 Colum. L. Rev. 1140 (1985).

Mowery, David C., *The U.S. National Innovation System: Origins and Prospects for Change*, 21 Res. Pol'y 125 (1992).

Mr. Justice Brandeis, Competition and Smallness: A Dilemma Re-examined (Note), 66 Yale L. J. 69 (1956).

Munzer, Stephen R., *A Theory of Property* (Cambridge: Cambridge University Press 1990).

Nagel, Ernst, *Assumptions in Economic Theory*, 53 Am. Econ. Rev. 211 (1963).

Nannes, John M. (U.S. Dept. of Justice), *Antitrust in an Era of High-Tech Innovation* (October 22, 1998) available at http://www.usdoj.gov/atr (January 10, 2003).

National Bureau of Economic Research, *The Rate and Direction of Inventive Activity: Economic and Social Factors* (Princeton, NJ: Princeton University Press 1962).

Nelson, Richard R. and Winter, Sidney G., *In Search of a More Useful Theory of Innovation*, 5 Res. Pol'y 36 (1977).

O'Driscoll, Gerald P. Jr., *Economics as a Coordination Problem: The Contributions of Friedrich A. Hayek* (Kansas City, KS: Sheed, Andrews & McMeel 1977).

O'Driscoll, Gerald, *Justice, Efficiency, and the Economic Analysis of Law: A Comment on Fried*, 9 J. Legal Stud. 355 (1980).

O'Driscoll, Gerald P. and Rizzo, Mario J., *The Economics of Time and Ignorance* (Oxford: Blackwell 1985, London and New York: Routledge 1996 reissue).

O'Neill, John, *The Market: Ethics, Knowledge and Politics* (London: Routledge 1998).

Oakley, Alan, *The Revival of Modern Austrian Economics* (Cheltenham, UK and Northampton, MA, USA: Edward Elgar 1999).

Organization for Economic Cooperation and Development (OECD), *Competition Policy and Intellectual Property Rights*, (Paris: OECD 1989).

Olson, Mancur and McFarland, David, *The Restoration of Pure Monopoly and the Concept of the Industry,* 76 Q. J. of Econ. 613 (1962).

Olson, Mancur Jr., *Logic of Collective Action* (Cambridge, MA: Harvard University Press, 1965, 2nd edn 1971).

Organization for Economic Development, 'Competition Policy and Intellectual Property Rights' (Roundtable Discussion 1998 available online on the OECD web site at http://www.oecd.org/daf/ccp.

Ottosen, Garry K., *Monopoly Power: How It Is Measured and How it Has Changed* (Salt Lake City, UT: Crossroads Research Institute 1990).

Paepke, C. Owen, *An Economic Interpretation of the Misappropriation Doctrine: Common Law Protection of Investments in Innovation*, 2 High Tech. L. J. 55 (1987).

Patterson, Mark R., *The Market Power Requirement in Antitrust Rule of Reason Cases: A Rhetorical History*, 37 San Diego L. Rev. 1 (2000).

Pelczynski, Z.A., *Hegel's Political Philosophy: Problems and Perspectives* (Z.A. Pelczynski ed., Cambridge: Cambridge University Press 1971).

Peritz, Rudolph J., *The 'Rule of Reason', in Antitrust Law: Property Logic in Restraint of Competition*, 40 Hastings L. J. 285 (1989).

Peritz, Rudolph J.R., *Some Realism About Economic Power in a Time of Sectorial Change*, 66 Antitrust L. J. 247 (1997).

Petzinger, Tom, *The New Pioneers* (New York: Simon & Schuster 1999).

Phelps, Marshall (IBM), Testimony at the FTC Hearings on Global and Innovation-based Competition, November 30, 1995.

Phillips, Jeremy, *Introduction to Intellectual Property Law* (London: Butterworths 1986).

Pigou, Arthur C., *The Economics of Welfare* (London: Macmillan, 4th edn 1946).

Pitofsky, Robert, *The Political Content of Antitrust*, 127 U. Pa. L. Rev. 1051 (1979).

Pitofsky, Robert, 'Antitrust Analysis in High Tech Industries: A 19th Century Discipline Addresses 21st Century Problems', Prepared Remarks for the American Bar Association Section of Antitrust Law's Antitrust Issues in High Tech Industries Workshop, February 25–26, 1999.

Porter, Michael E. (interview), 'Innovation, Rivalry and Competitive Advantage', *Antitrust* 5 (Spring 1991).

Posner, Richard A., *Antitrust Law: An Economic Perspective* (Chicago, IL: Chicago University Press 1976).

Posner, Richard A., *The Chicago School of Antitrust Analysis*, 127 U. Pa. L. Rev. 925 (1979).

Posner, Richard A., *Legal Formalism, Legal Realism, and the Interpretation of Statutes and the Constitution*, 37 Case W. Res. L. Rev. 179 (1987).

Posner, Richard A., *Economic Analysis of Law* (New York: Aspen Law & Business, 5th edn 1998).

Radin, Margaret J., *Property and Personhood*, 34 Stan. L. Rev. 957 (1982).

Radin, Margaret J., *Market-Inalienability*, 100 Harv. L. Rev. 1849 (1987).

Radin, Margaret J., *Reinterpreting Property* (Chicago, IL: University of Chicago Press 1993).

Rapp, Richard T., *The Misapplication of the Innovation Market Approach to Merger Analysis*, 64 Antitrust L. J. 19 (1995).

Rawls, John, *Political Liberalism* (New York: Columbia University Press 1993).

Reichman, J.H., *Legal Hybrids Between the Patent and Copyright Paradigms*, 94 Colum. L. Rev. 2432 (1994).

Reinganum, Jennifer F., 'The Timing of Innovation', in *Handbook of Industrial Organization* (Richard Schmalensee and Robert D. Willig eds, New York: Elsevier Science 1989).

Ridyard, Derek, *Essential Facilities and the Obligation to Supply Competitors under UK and EC Competition Law*, 8 Eur. Competition L. Rev. 439 (1996).

Rill, James F., Testimony at FTC Hearings on Global and Innovation-based Competition, November 12, 1995, available at http://www.ftc.gov/opp/global.htm (January 10, 2003).

Ritter, Lennart, Braun, W. David and Rawlinson, Francis, *European Competition Law: A Practitioner's Guide* (The Hague: Kluwer Law International, 2nd edn 2000).

Rizzo, Mario J. (ed.), *Time, Uncertainty, and Disequilibrium: Exploration of Austrian Themes* (Lexington, MA: D.C. Heath & Co. 1979).

Rizzo, Mario, *A Theory of Economic Loss in the Law of Torts*, 11 J. Legal Stud. 281 (1982).

Rizzo, Mario, *Foreword: Fundamentals of Causation*, 63 Chi.-Kent L. Rev. 397 (1987).

Robertson, Aidan, (Note) *Compulsory Copyright Licensing under EC Law?*, 108 L. Q. Rev. 39 (1992).

Robertson, Aidan, *The Existence and Exercise of Copyright: Can It Bear the Abuse?*, 111 L. Q. Rev. 588 (1995).

Robinson, Joan, *The Economics of Imperfect Competition* (London: Macmillan 1933).

Rose, Carol M., *Possession as the Origin of Property*, 52 U. Chi. L. Rev. 73 (1985).

Ross, Stephen F., *Principles of Antitrust Law* (Westbury, NY: Foundation Press 1993).

Rothbard, Murray N., *Man, Economy and State* (Los Angeles, CA: Nash 1972).

Rothbard, Murray N., 'Praxeology: The Methodology of Austrian Economics', in *The Foundations of Modern Austrian Economics* (Edwin Dolan ed., Kansas City, KS: Sheed & Ward 1976).

Rothbard, Murray N., 'Praxeology, Value Judgments, and Public Policy', in *The Foundations of Modern Austrian Economics* 89 (Edwin Dolan ed., Kansas City, KS: Sheed & Ward 1976).

Rowe, Frederick M., *The Decline of Antitrust and the Delusions of Models: The Faustian Pact of Law and Economics*, 72 Geo. L. J. 1511 (1984).

Rubinfeld, Daniel L. (Deputy Assistant Attorney General, Antitrust Division, U.S. Dept. of Justice), 'Competition, Innovation, and Antitrust

Enforcement in Dynamic Network Industries', Address before the Software Publishers Association 1998 Spring Symposium (March 24, 1998) San Jose, California, available at http://www.usdoj.gov/atr/public/speeches/1611.htm (January 10, 2003).

Rubinfeld, Daniel L., *Antitrust Enforcement in Dynamic Network Industries*, 43 Antitrust Bull. 859 (1998).

Rule, Charles F. and Meyer, David L., *An Antitrust Enforcement Policy to Maximize the Economic Wealth of all Consumers,* 33 Antitrust Bull. 677 (1988).

Saint Exupéry, Antoine de, *The Little Prince* (New York: Harcourt Brace and Company 1943, reprinted 1971, Trans. Katherine Woods).

Sakakibara, Mariko and Branstetter, Lee, 'Do Stronger Patents Induce More Innovation? Evidence from the 1998 Japanese Patent Law Reforms', Working Paper No. 7066, National Bureau of Economic Research, available at http://www.nber.org/papers/w7066.pdf (January 10, 2003).

Salmond, John W., *First Principles of Jurisprudence* (London: Stevens & Haynes 1893).

Salop, Steven C. and Romaine, R. Craig, *Preserving Monopoly: Economic Analysis, Legal Standards, and Microsoft*, 7 Geo. Mason U. L. Rev. 617 (1999).

Samuels, Warren J. (ed.), *The Chicago School of Political Economy* (East Lansing, MI: Michigan State University 1976).

Samuelson, Pamela, Davis, Randall, Kapor, Michell D. and Reichman, J.H., *A Manifesto Concerning the Legal Protection of Computer Programs*, 94 Colum. L. Rev. 2308 (1994).

Samuelson, Paul A., *Foundations of Economic Analysis* (Cambridge, MA: Harvard University Press 1947).

Samuelson, Paul A., *The Pure Theory of Public Expenditure*, 36 Rev. of Econ. & Stat. 387 (1954).

Samuelson, Paul A., *A Diagrammatic Exposition of a Theory of Public Expenditure*, 37 Rev. of Econ. & Stat. 350 (1955).

Sax, Joseph L., *Some Thoughts on the Decline of Private Property*, 58 Wash. L. Rev. 481 (1983).

Scherer, Frederic M., *Industrial Market Structure and Economic Performance* (Chicago, IL: Rand-McNally, 2nd edn 1980).

Scherer, Frederic M. and Ross, David, *Industrial Market Structure and Economic Performance* (Boston, MA: Houghton Mifflin, 3rd edn 1990).

Scherer, Frederic M., 'Comments', in *Competition Policy and Intellectual Property Rights in the Knowledge-based Economy* 107 (Robert D. Anderson and Nancy T. Gallini eds, Calgary: University of Calgary Press 1998).

Schmalensee, Richard, *Another Look at Market Power* (Landes and Posner on Market Power: Four Responses), 95 Harv. L. Rev. 1789 (1982).

Schmidt, Ingo L.O. and Rittaler, Jan B., *A Critical Evaluation of the Chicago School of Antitrust Analysis* (Dordrecht: Kluwer Academic 1989).

Schumpeter , Joseph A., *Capitalism, Socialism and Democracy* (Harper and Row: New York, first edn. 1942 reprinted 1965, London: Unwin University Books).

Schwartz, Alan, *The Myth that Promisees Prefer Supracompensatory Remedies: An Analysis of Contracting for Damage Measures*, 100 Yale L. J. 99 (1990).

Schwartzstein, Linda A., *Austrian Economics and the Current Debate Between Critical Legal Studies and Law and Economics*, 20 Hofstra L. Rev. 1105 (1992).

Schwartzstein, Linda A., *An Austrian Economic View of Legal Process*, 55 Ohio St. L. J. 1049 (1994).

Sened, Itai and Riker, William H., *Common Property and Private Property: The Case of Air Slots*, 8 J. of Theoretical Pol. 527 (1996).

Sened, Itai, *The Political Institution of Private Property* (Cambridge: Cambridge University Press 1997).

Shankland, Stephen, 'Linux hits Microsoft Where it Hurts' (January 28, 1999), available at http://news.com.com/2100-1001-220845.html (January 10, 2003).

Shapiro, Carl (Deputy Assistant Attorney General, Antitrust Division, U.S. Dept. of Justice), 'Antitrust In Network Industries' (Address before the American Law Institute and American Bar Association, January 25, 1996), available at http://www.usdoj.gov/atr/public/speeches/ shapir.mar.htm (Jan. 10, 2003).

Shapiro, Carl, *Competition Policy in the Information Economy* (August 1999) available at http://haas.berkeley.edu/~shapiro (January 10, 2003).

Shelanski, Howard A. and Sidak, J. Gregory, *Antitrust Divestiture in Network Industries*, 68 U. Chi. L. Rev. 1 (2001).

Shepherd, William G., *Market Power and Racial Discrimination in White-collar Employment*, 14 Antitrust Bull. 141 (1969).

Sherwin, Emily, *Two- and Three-dimensional Property Rights*, 29 Ariz. St. L. J. 1075 (1997).

Simons, Henry C., *Economic Policy for a Free Society* (Chicago, IL: Chicago University Press 1948).

Singer, Joseph W., *The Legal Rights Debate in Analytical Jurisprudence from Bentham to Hohfeld*, Wis. L. Rev. 975 (1982).

Singer, Joseph William, *The Reliance Interest in Property*, 40 Stan. L. Rev. 611 (1988).

Skinner, Tom, *The Oral Hearing of the Magill Case*, 15 Eur. Competition L. Rev. 103 (1994).

Skinner, Tom, *Magill: Consumer Interests Prevail*, 6 Eur. Bus. L. Rev. 90 (1995).

Smith, Adam, *An Inquiry into the Nature and Causes of the Wealth of Nations* (R.H. Campbell and A.S. Skinner eds, Oxford: Oxford University Press 1976).

Smith, Jonathan, *Television Guides: The European Court Doesn't Know 'There's So Much In It'*, 13 Eur. Competition L. Rev. 135 (1992).

Snapp, Bruce R., 'Network Industries and Antitrust: A Cautionary Note', in *Cutting Edge Issues in Network Industries* 1 (American Bar Association, Antitrust Law Section, May 1996).

Sobel, Gerald, *The Antitrust Interface with Patents and Innovation: Acquisition of Patents, Improvement Patents and Grant-Backs, Non-Use, Fraud on the Patent Office, Development of the New Products and Joint Research*, 53 Antitrust L. J. 681 (1985).

Solow, Robert M., *Technical Change and the Aggregate Production Function*, 39 Rev. of Econ. and Stat. 312 (1957).

Sowell, Thomas, *Race and Economics* (New York: Longman 1977).

Stevenson, Glenn G., *Common Property Economics: A General Theory and Land Use Applications* (Cambridge: Cambridge University Press 1991).

Stigler, George J., *The Case Against Big Business*, 47 Fortune May 1952, 123.

Stigler, George J., 'Monopolistic Competition in Retrospect' in George J. Stigler, *The Organization of Industry* (Chicago, IL: University of Chicago Press 1968).

Stiglitz, Joseph E., speech at the Federal Trade Commission hearings held in fall 1995 (October 12, 1995) available at http://www.ftc.gov.

Sullivan, E. Thomas, *First Amendment Defenses in Antitrust Litigation*, 46 Mo. L. Rev. 517 (1981).

Sullivan, Lawrence A., *Handbook of the Law of Antitrust* (St. Paul, MN: West Publishing Co. 1977).

Symposium: Antitrust Jurisprudence: The Economic, Political and Social Goals of Antitrust Policy, 125 U. Pa. L. Rev. 1182 (1977).

Symposium: Post-Chicago Economics, 63 Antitrust L. J. 445–695 (1995).

Taylor, Charles, *Hegel and Modern Society* (Cambridge: Cambridge University Press 1979).

Taylor, C.T. and Silberston, Z.A., *The Economic Impact of the Patent System* (Cambridge: Cambridge University Press 1973).

Teece, David J. and Coleman, Mary, *The Meaning of Monopoly: Antitrust Analysis in High-technology Industries*, 43 Antitrust Bull. 801 (1998).

Temple Lang, John, *Defining Legitimate Competition: Companies' Duties to Supply Competitors and Access to Essential Facilities* (Hawk ed.), 1994 Fordham Corporate Law Institute 245 (1995); 18 Fordham Int'l L. J. 437 (1994).

Temple Lang, John, *European Community Antitrust Law: Innovation Markets and High Technology Industries*, 20 Fordham Int'l L. J, 717 (1996), also available at http://europa.eu.int/comm/competition/speeches/text/sp1996_054_en.html (January. 10, 2003).

Thorelli, Hans B., *The Federal Antitrust Policy – Origination of an American Tradition* (Baltimore, MD: Johns Hopkins University Press 1955).

Tirole, Jean, *The Theory of Industrial Organization* (Cambridge, MA: MIT Press 1988).

Tom, Willard K. and Newberg, Joshua A., *Antitrust and Intellectual Property: From Separate Spheres to Unified Field*, 66 Antitrust L. J. 167 (1997).

Trachtenberg, Zev, *The Environment: Private or Common Property?*, 50 Okla. L. Rev. 399 (1997).

Travers, Noel, *Magill: Expropriation or a Fine Balancing Act?*, Irish Competition L. Reports 2-1 (1995).

Tully, James, *A Discourse on Property* (Cambridge: Cambridge University Press 1980).

U.S. Department of Justice, *Antitrust Guide Concerning Research Joint Ventures* (1980).

U.S. Department of Justice and Federal Trade Commission (DOJ–FTC), *Antitrust Guidelines for the Licensing of Intellectual Property* (April 6, 1995), available at http://www.usdoj.gov/atr/public/guidelines/ipguide.htm (January 10, 2003).

U.S. Department of Justice and Federal Trade Commission (DOJ–DTC), *Horizontal Merger Guidelines* (April 2, 1992, Revised April 8, 1997) reprinted in 4 Trade Reg. Rep. (CCH) pp. 13,104, also available at http://www.usdoj.gov/atr (January 10, 2003).

U.S. Department of Justice and Federal Trade Commission (DOJ–FTC), *Joint Hearings on Competition and Intellectual Property Law and Policy in the Knowledge-based Economy*, held during 2002 and available at: http://www.ftc.gov/ (August 2, 2002).

U.S. Department of Justice Antitrust Division, *Opening Markets and Protecting Competition for America's Business and Consumers* (April 7, 1995) available at http://www.usdoj.gov/atr (August 2, 2002).

U.S. Department of Justice Antitrust Division, *Antitrust Enforcement and the Consumer*, available at http://www.usdoj.gov/atr (January 10, 2003).

U.S. Senate Judiciary Committee Hearings: S. Hrg. 105–790, Serial No. J-105-66 on 'Competition, Innovation, and Public Policy in the Digital Age' (November 4, 1997, March 3, 1998 and July 23, 1998).

Van der Wal, Gerard, *Article 86 EC: The Limits of Compulsory Licensing*, 4 Eur. Competition L. Rev. 230 (1994).

Van Kerckhove, Marleen, *The Advocate General Delivers his Opinion on Magill*, 15 Eur. Competition L. Rev. 276 (1994).

Van Melle, Abraham I., *Refusals to License Intellectual Property Rights: the Impact of* RTE v. EC Commission *(Magill) on Australian and New Zealand Competition Law*, 25 Australian Bus. L. Rev. 4 (1997).

Vandevelde, Kenneth, *The New Property of the Nineteenth Century: The Development of the Modern Concept of Property*, 29 Buffalo L. Rev. 325 (1980).

Vaughn, Karen I., *Austrian Economics in America – The Migration of a Tradition* (New York: Cambridge University Press 1994).

Vinje, Thomas C., *Harmonising Intellectual Property Laws in the European Union: Past, Present and Future,* 17 Eur. Intell. Prop. Rev. 361 (1995).

Vinje, Thomas C., *The Final Word on Magill: The Judgment of The ECJ*, 17 Eur. Intell. Prop. Rev. 297 (1995).

Von Mises, Ludwig, *Human Action: A Treatise on Economics* (New Haven, CT: Yale University Press 1949, reprinted 1963. Chicago, IL: Henry Regnery Company, 3rd edn 1966).

Von Mises, Ludwig, *The Ultimate Foundations of Economic Science: An Essay on Method* (Kansas City, KS: Sheed, Andrews & McMeel 1962, reprinted 1978).

Von Mises, Ludwig, *Interventionism: An Economic Analysis* (Bettina Bien Greaves ed., Irvington-on-Hudson, NY: The Foundation for Economic Education, Inc. 1998. The text was written by von Mises in 1940 but was not previously published).

Waldron, Jeremy, *The Right to Private Property* (Oxford and NewYork, NY: Oxford University Press 1988).

Warren-Boulton, Frederick R., Direct Testimony in *U.S. v. Microsoft Corporation* filed November 18, 1998, available at http://www.usdoj.gov/atr/cases/f2000/2079.htm#footbody_27 (January 10, 2003).

Weeks, Edward P., *The Doctrine of Damnum Absque Injuria Considered in its Relation to the Law of Torts* (San Francisco, CA: S. Whitney 1879).

Weinrib, Ernst J., *The Jurisprudence of Legal Formalism*, Harv. J. L. & Pub. Pol'y 583 (1993).

Weinreb, Lloyd, *Copyright for Functional Expression*, 111 Harv. L. Rev. 1149 (1998).

White, Barbara A., *Countervailing Power – Different Rules for Different Markets? Conduct and Context in Antitrust Law and Economics*, 41 Duke L. J. 1045 (1992).

Williamson, Oliver E., *Economics as an Antitrust Defense: The Welfare Tradeoffs*, 58 American Econ. Rev. 18 (1968).

Witt, Ulrich, 'Turning Austrian Economics Into an Evolutionary Theory', in *Austrian Economics: Tensions and New Directions* 215 (Bruce J. Caldwell and Stephan Boehm eds, Boston/Dordrecht/London: Kluwer Academic 1992).

Wonnel, Christopher T., *Contract Law and the Austrian School of Economics*, 54 Fordham L. Rev. 507 (1986).

Wood, Diane P., *The Impossible Dream: Real International Antitrust*, 1992 U. Chi. Legal Forum 277 (1992).

World Intellectual Property Organization (WIPO), *Introduction to Intellectual Property – Theory and Practice*, (Boston, MA: Kluwer Law International 1997).

U.S. CASES AND DECISIONS

Addamax Corp. v. Open Software Foundation, Inc., 888 F. Supp. 274, 282 (D. Mass. 1995); 1995 U.S. Dist. LEXIS 7805; 1995-1 Trade Cas. (CCH) P 71,036.

Addamax Corp. v. Open Software Foundation Inc., 964 F. Supp. 549 (D. Mass. 1997).

Addamax Corp. v. Open Software Foundation Inc., 152 F.3d 48 (1st Cir. 1998).

Alaska Airlines v. United Airlines, 948 F.2d 536 (9th Cir. 1991).

Allied Tube & Conduit Co. v. Indian Head, Inc., 486 U.S. 492 (1988).

American Society of Mechanical Engineers, Inc. v. Hydrolevel Corp., 456 U.S. 556 (1982).

American Society of Sanitary Engineering, 106 F.T.C. 324 (1985).

Andrew Byars v. Bluff City News Company, 609 F.2d 843 (6th Cir. 1979).

Appalachian Coals Inc. v. U.S., 288 U.S. 344 (1932).

Aspen Skiing Co. v. Aspen Highlands Skiing Corp., 738 F2d 1509 (10th Cir. 1984), aff'd 472 U.S. 585 (1985).

Atari Games Corp. v. Nintendo of America, Inc., 897 F.2d 1572 (Fed. Cir. 1990).

Baldwin v. G.A.F. Seelig, Inc., 294 U.S. 511 (1935).

Berkey Photo, Inc. v. Eastman Kodak Co., 603 F.2d 263 (2nd Cir. 1979), cert. denied, 444 U.S. 1093 (1980).

Bleistein v. Donaldson Lithographing Co., 188 U.S. 239, 250 (1903).

Blue Cross & Blue Shield United of Wisconsin v. Marshfield Clinic, 883 F. Supp. 1247 (D. Wis. 1995).
Boston Scientific Corp., F.T.C. File No. 951-0002 (February 24, 1995).
Brooke Group Ltd. v. Brown & Williamson Tobacco Corp., 509 U.S. 209 (1993).
Brown Shoe Co., Inc. v. U.S., 370 U.S. 294 (1962).
Brunswick Corp. v. Pueblo Bowl-O-Mat, Inc., 429 U.S. 477 (1977).
Central Hudson Gas & Elec. Corp. v. Public Service Communication, 447 U.S. 557 (1980).
Data General Corp. v. Grumman Systems Support Corp., 36 F.3d 1147 (1st Cir. 1994).
Dell Computer Corp., Consent Agreement with Analysis to Aid Public Comment (November 22, 1995) 60 FR 57870, 1995 WL 688383 (F.R.).
Dell Computers (consent decree), FTC File No. 931-0097 (1996) available through the FTC web site at http://www.ftc.gov/opa/1996/9606/dell2.htm.
Diamond v. Diehr, 450 U.S. 175 (1981).
Digidyne Corp. v. Data General Corp., 734 F.2d 1336 (9th Cir. 1984) & 473 U.S. 908 (1985).
Dimmit Agri Industries, Inc. v. CPC International, Inc., 679 F.2d 516 (5th Cir. 1982), *cert. denied*, 460 U.S. 1082 (1983).
Eastern Railroad President's Conference v. Noerr Motor Freight, Inc., 365 U.S. 127 (1961).
Eastman Kodak Co. v. Image Technical Services Inc., 112 S. Ct. 2072, 119 L.Ed.2d 265 (1992).
Fashion Originators' Guild of America v. FTC, 312 U.S. 457 (1941).
Great Western Directories, Inc. v. Southwestern Bell Telephone Company, 63 F.3d 1378 (5th Cir. 1995).
Hartford-Empire Co. v. U.S., 323 U.S. 386 (1944).
Hecht v. Pro-Football, Inc., 570 F.2d 982 (D.C. Cir. 1977), cert. denied, 436 U.S. 956 (1978).
Image Technical Services, Inc. v. Eastman Kodak Co., 125 F.3d 1195 (9th Cir. 1997), cert. denied, 523 U.S. 1094 (1998).
In re Indep. Serv. Orgs. Antitrust Litig., 989 F. Supp. 1131 (D. Kan. 1997), 203 F.3d 1322 (Fed. Cir. 2000).
In the Matter of Dell Computer Corporation, Consent and Order (May 20, 1996) 121 F.T.C. 616 (1996), 1996 WL 350997 (F.T.C.).
International Wood Processors v. Power Dry, Inc., 792 F.2d 417 (1986).
Jefferson Parish Hospital Dist. No. 2 v. Hyde, 466 U.S. 2 (1984).
Klor's Inc. v. Broadway-Hale Stores, Inc., 359 U.S. 207 (1959).
Lasercomb America Inc. v. Reynolds, 911 F.2d 970 (4th Cir. 1990).
Lear v. Adkins, 395 U.S. 653 (1969).
Northern Pacific Railway v. U.S., 356 U.S. 1 (1958).

Northern Securities Co. v. U.S., 193 U.S. 197 (1904).
Oregon Steam Navigation Co. v. Windsor, 87 U.S. 74 (1873).
Otter Tail Power Co. v. U.S., 410 U.S. 366 (1973).
Paramount Famous Lasky Corp. v. U.S., 282 U.S. 30 (1930).
Reiter v. Sonotone Corp., 442 U.S. 330 (1979).
Roche Holdings, 113 F.T.C. 1086 (1990).
Sargent-Welch Scientific Co. v. Ventron Corp., 567 F.2d 701 (7th Cir. 1977), cert. denied, 439 U.S. 822 (1978).
Schlafly v. Caro-Kann Corp., No. 98-1005, 1998 U.S. App. LEXIS 8250, (Fed. Cir. April 29, 1998).
SCM Corp. v. Xerox Corp., 645 F.2d 1195 (2nd Cir. 1981).
Sensormatic Electronics Corp., F.T.C. File No. 941-0126 (January 4, 1995).
Standard Oil Co. v. U.S., 221 U.S. 1 (1911).
Standard Oil Co. v. FTC, 340 U.S. 231 (1951).
Standard Oil of California v. U.S., 337 U.S. 293 (1949).
State Street Bank v. Signature Financial Group, 149 F.3d 1368 (Fed. Cir. 1998).
Studiengesellschaft Kohle M.B.H. v. Shell Oil Co., 112 F.3d 1561 (Fed. Cir. 1997).
Trans Sport, Inc. v. Starter Sportswear, Inc., 964 F.2d 186 (2nd Cir. 1992).
Union Carbide Corp. v. Ever-Ready, 531 F.2d 366 (7th Cir. 1976).
Union Leader Corp. v. Newspapers of New England, Inc., 180 F. Supp. 125 (D. Mass. 1959), modified, 284 F.2d 582 (1st Cir. 1960), cert. denied, 365 U.S. 833 (1961).
U.S. v. Trans-Missouri Freight Association, 166 U.S. 290 (1897).
U.S. v. Addyston Pipe & Steel Co., 85 Fed. 271 (6th Cir. 1898), aff'd 175 U.S. 211 (1899).
U.S. v. Terminal Railroad Ass'n, 224 U.S. 383 (1912).
U.S. v. Colgate, 250 U.S. 300 (1919).
U.S. v. Aluminum Co. of America et al., 148 F.2d 416 (2nd Cir. 1945).
U.S. v. National Lead Co., 332 U.S. 319 (1947).
U.S. v. United Shoe Machinery Corp., 110 F. Supp 295 (D. Mass 1953), aff'd per curiam, 347 U.S. 521 (1954).
U.S. v. E.I. du Pont de Nemours & Co., 351 U.S. 377 (1956).
U.S. v. Loew's Inc., 371 U.S. 38 (1962).
U.S. v. Grinnell Corp., 384 U.S. 563 (1966).
U.S. v. Von's Grocery Store Co., 384 U.S. 270 (1966).
U.S. v. Glaxo Group, 410 U.S. 52 (1973).
U.S. v. United States Gypsum Co., 438 U.S. 422 (1978).
U.S. v. Reality Multi-List, 29 F.2d 1351 (5th Cir. 1980).
U.S. Healthcare, Inc. v. Healthsource, Inc., 986 F.2d 589 (1st Cir. 1993).

U.S. v. Microsoft Corporation, 98 CIV 1232 (TPJ), Findings of Fact, November 5, 1999.

U.S. v. Andreas, 216 F.3d 645 (7th Cir. 2000).

Virginia State Board of Pharmacy v. Virginia Citizens Consumer Council, Inc., 425 U.S. 748 (1976).

Wheaton v. Peters, 33 U.S. (8 Pet.) 591 (1834).

Zenith Radio Corp. v. Hazeltine Research, Inc., 395 U.S. 100 (1969).

EUROPEAN AND ENGLISH CASES AND DECISIONS

AB Volvo v. Erik Veng (UK) Ltd., Case 238/87 [1988] ECR 6211; 1989-4 CMLR 122; CCH 14,498.

British Broadcasting Corporation and BBC Enterprises v. Commission, Judgment of the Court of First Instance (Second Chamber) of 10 July 1991, Case T-70/89, 1991 ECR II-535, 1991-4 CMLR 669.

British Leyland v. Commission, Case 226/84, [1986] ECR 3263; 1987-1 CMLR 184; CCH 14,336.

Compagnie Maritime Belge de Transport v. Commission, (CEWAL), Cases T-24-26 and 28/93, [1996] ECR II-1201; 1997-4 CMLR 273; 1997 CCH 74.

Consorzio Italiano (CICRA) v. Renault, Case 53/87, [1988] ECR 6039; 1990-4 CMLR 265; 1990 CCH 267.

Consten & Grundig v. Commission, Cases 56 and 58/64 [1966] ECR 299; [1966] CMLR 418; CCH 8046.

Europemballage Corp. and Continental Can v. Commission, Case 6-72, [1973] ECR 215; 1973 CMLR 199; CCH 8171.

General Motors Continental NV v. Commission, Case 26/75, 1975 ECR 1367; 1976-1 CMLR 95; CCH 8320.

Hoffmann-La Roche & Co. AG v. Commission, Case 85/76, [1979] ECR 461; 1979-3 CMLR 211; CCH 8527.

Independent Television Publications (ITP) Ltd. v. Commission, Judgment of the Court of First Instance (Second Chamber) of 10 July 1991, Case T-76/89 [1991] ECR II-575, 1991-4 CMLR 745, 1991-2 CCH 174.

Industria Vetraria Alfonso Cobelli v. Societa Italiana Vetro spa et al, Commission Decision 89/93/EEC 1990 4 CMLR 535.

Instituto Chemioterapico Italiano SpA and Commercial Solvents v. Commission, Cases 6 & 7/73, [1974] ECR 223; 1974-1 CMLR 309; CCH 9644.

Keurkoop v. Nancy Kean Gifts, Case 144/81 [1982] ECR 2853.

Magill TV Guide/ITP, BBC and RTE, EC Commission Decision 89/205/EEC of 21 December 1988 relating to a proceeding under Article 86 of the EEC Treaty (IV/31.851, Magill TV Guide/ITP, BBC and RTE), OJ 1989 No. L 78, p. 43.

Metro v. Deutsche Grammophon, Case 78/70, [1971] ECR 487; [1971] CMLR 631; CCH 8106.

Michelin v. Commission, Case 322/81, [1983] ECR 3461; 1985-1 CMLR 282; CCH 14,031.

Millar v. Taylor, 4 Burrows 2303, 98 Eng. Rep. 201 (1769).

Mitchel v. Reynolds, 24 Eng. Rep. 347 (K.B.) 1711.

NDC Health/IMS Health, 2002/165/EC: Commission Decision of 3 July 2001 relating to a proceeding pursuant to Article 82 of the EC Treaty (Case COMP/D3/38.044 – NDC Health/IMS Health: Interim measures) (notified under document number C(2001) 1995), OJ L59, February 28, 2002, p. 18. Also available at http://europa.eu.int/comm/competition/antitrust/cases/decisions/38044/en.pdf.

Parke Davis v. Probel, Case 24/67, [1968] ECR 55; [1968] CMLR 47; CCH 8054.

Radio Telefis Eireann (RTE) v. Commission, Judgment of the Court of First Instance (Second Chamber) of 10 July 1991, Case T-69/89, 1991 ECR II-485, 1991-4 CMLR 586.

Radio Telefis Eireann (RTE) and Independent Television Publications Ltd. (ITP) v. Commission, Joined Cases C-241/91P and C-242/92P, 1995 ECR I-743; 1995-4 CMLR 718; 1991-2 CCH 114.

RTE et al. v. Magill et al., [1990] ILRM 534.

Spanish Banks: Dirección General de Defensa de la Competencia v. Asociación Española de Banca Privada (AEB), Case C-67/91, [1992] ECR I-4785.

Tetra Pak v. Commission, Case T-51/89, [1990] ECR II-309; 1991-4 CMLR 334; 1990-2 CCH 409.

United Brands Company and United Brands Continental B.V. v. Commission, Case 27/76, [1978] ECR 207; 1978-1 CMLR 429 and 1978-3 CMLR 83 (correction); CCH 8429.

Walt Wilhelm v. Bundeskartellamt, Case 14/68, [1969] ECR 1; 1969 CMLR 100; CCH 8056.

LEGISLATIVE MATERIAL

Agreement on Trade-related Aspects of Intellectual Property Rights (TRIPS), 33 I.L.M. 81, §8, §31, §40. The TRIPS agreement is annex 1C of the Marrakesh Agreement Establishing the World Trade Organization, signed on April 15, 1994.

Berne Convention for the Protection of Literary and Artistic Works (concluded in 1886, last revised in Paris in 1971, and amended in September 1978) §9.

Clayton Act. 38 Stat. 730 (1914) codified as amended, 15 U.S.C. §§12–27.

Copyright Act, 17 U.S.C.A. §106 (1976).

EC Treaty, §3, §81 & 82 (ex §85 & 86 respectively), §295 (ex §222), §30 (ex §36).

European Council Directive 91/250/EEC of May 14, 1991, on the legal protection of computer programs, OJ L 122 p. 42 (May 17, 1991).

Federal Trade Commission Act, 38 Stat. 717 (1914) codified as amended, 15 U.S.C. §§41–58.

Intellectual Property Antitrust Protection Act of 1988, S. 438, 100th Cong. (1988) (earlier titled 'A Bill to Modify the Application of the Antitrust Laws and to Encourage the Licensing and Other Use of Certain Intellectual Property' S. 438, 100th Cong. (1987)).

Intellectual Property Antitrust Protection Act of 1989, H.R. 469, 101st Cong. (1989).

Intellectual Property Antitrust Protection Act of 1995, H.R. 2674, 104th Cong. (1996).

Paris Convention for the Protection of Industrial Property, opened for signature, July 14, 1967, 828 U.N.T.S. 321, §5.

Patent Act, 35 U.S.C. §154 (*a*), 261, 271 (1994).

Robinson–Patman Act, 15 U.S.C. §15 and 15c, §4 and §4C.

Sherman Act, 26 Stat. 209 (1890), codified as amended, 15 U.S.C. §1–7, §1, §2

Treaty of Amsterdam amending the Treaty on European Union, the Treaties establishing the European Communities and certain related acts (1997 OJ C 340/1).

U.S. Constitution Art. I §8[8].

Index